Baby Names

for New Zealanders

ANNE MATTHEWS

This edition published in 2017 by New Holland Publishers
London • Sydney • Auckland

The Chandlery Unit 704 50 Westminster Bridge Road London SE1 7QY United Kingdom
1/66 Gibbes Street Chatswood NSW 2067 Australia
5/39 Woodside Ave Northcote, Auckland 0627 New Zealand

www.newhollandpublishers.com

First published in 1998 by New Holland Publishers
Copyright © 2017 in text: Anne Matthews
Copyright © 2017 New Holland Publishers

ISBN: 978 1 86966 461 9

Publishing manager: Christine Thomson
New Zealand research: Helen Alcock
Cover design: Lorena Susak
Layout: Thomas Casey
Cover photo: Shutterstock

A catalogue record for this book is available from the National Library of Australia and the
National Library of New Zealand

10 9 8 7 6 5 4 3 2 1

Colour reproduction by Image Centre, Auckland
Printed in China at Everbest Printing Co, on paper sourced from sustainable forests.

Acknowledgements
Many thanks to the following people for their assistance and suggestions: Jill Varley, Ainslie
Cahill, Di Robinson and Paul Andrew (Indonesian names), Judy and Tashi Tenzing and
Pem Pem Tshering (Tibetan and Sherpa names), David Watts (Aboriginal names) and
Sandra Thompson (Maori names).

In memory of my parents, George and Christina, who named me, somewhat optimistically, 'graceful follower of Christ'.

And with special thanks to Geoff – the (occasionally) divinely peaceful one – for his patience, ideas and support.

CONTENTS

PREFACE

I have long been fascinated by names. At primary school in England in the late 1950s, it occurred to me that I had a rather unexciting name: other girls were labelled, far more imaginatively I thought, Donna, Cheryl, Wendy, Lindsey, Nicola and Yvonne. It could have been worse, however: Cynthia, Deirdre, Ernest, Gloria, Samson, Rodney and Priscilla – names that seemed old-fashioned even then.

During the 1960s and early 1970s, however – when most of my earlier contemporaries bore traditional names like David, Christine, Elizabeth, Mary, Richard, Susan, Phillip, Jane and Alan – I came across far more interesting names: males called Barry, Hamish, Scott, Evan and Glenn; and girls labelled Tracey, Jessica, Olivia, Rowena, Jacqueline, Karen and Lucy.

Then I began travelling in Europe and another, unimaginably rich, world of names opened up to me. Where, I wondered, had all of these names come from? What did they mean? How many different appellations could a person come across in a lifetime? My interest in the subject was further fuelled by Dr Basil Cottle, my most venerable English lecturer, who was somewhat of an expert on etymology in general, and the meaning of surnames in particular.

My move to Australia at the end of the 1970s, and a long period of working as an adventure travel guide in Asia, South America, Africa and other parts of the world, brought me into contact with yet more intriguing and downright exotic 'people labels'. I spent many months with people called Sonam and Dechen, Emilio and Rosita, Chen and Lee, Salim and Amira. And back home there were always classic Aussie names like Shane, Kerry, Narelle, Wayne, Leanne and Bradley – titles I had rarely come across in the UK – to wonder at.

As its own title indicates, this book is designed particularly for New Zealanders. Its many thousands of entries include names that range from American to Zimbabwean, and the publication is intended for people of all ethnic backgrounds.

Those of you who are curious about names and their origins will find this book enlightening. It is, however, primarily intended for parents who are searching for a meaningful or attractive name for their child, and I hope this publication proves to be a source of inspiration.

Anne Matthews

INTRODUCTION

I suppose it sounds obvious, but naming began as a means of distinguishing one person from another. Personal names generally came first, followed by surnames (family names). If there were ten Williams, Gastons or Wolfgangs living in a village, it was decidedly less confusing to distinguish them by adding something – a surname – that perhaps defined what they looked like, who their father was, or whether they lived at the top of the hill or down by the river.

In that same area, many decades later, there might have been several William Reads, all bearing the distinguishing family name of the original Read, 'the red-haired one'. Middle names thus came into being, with the various William Reads described as William Henry, William Edmund, William Ralph and so on. Names are essentially 'people labels' and a form of description – someone might be described as 'tall, with dark hair', but that person is more often defined as David Evans, or David John Evans.

There are many factors involved in selecting a 'label', and some of these are discussed below. Christian, given, personal or first names – call them what you like – remain with a person for life, and this is one of the most important decisions that a parent has to make for their child.

Choosing a name for your child

Naming for sound

Does the name sound feminine enough for a girl or masculine enough for a boy? Or does this matter, particularly in the 21st century when unisex names are increasingly common.

The sound of names in combination, especially with the family name, should also be considered. A short first name often complements a long surname: for example, Alice Warburton, rather than Jacqueline Warburton. Conversely, you could combine a long first name with a one-syllable family name: Alexander Dale, rather than Jake Dale.

We all tend to make judgements about a name, based on its sound as well as associations with people we have known. Here are a few examples of my own 'associations'.

Regal, important-sounding names

Boys: Alexander, Charles, David, Edward, George, Henry, Hugo, Jacob, James, Justin, Leo, Louis, Marcus, Max, Nicholas, Oscar, Rex, Samuel, William, Xavier.

Girls: Alexandra, Alexis, Anastasia, Audrey, Charlotte, Claudia, Cleo, Edwina, Elizabeth, Eve, Frances, Imogen, Isabella, Julia, Olivia, Phoebe, Rowena, Stephanie, Victoria, Zara.

Names with attitude

Boys: Angus, Caleb, Chase, Cody, Darcy, Fergus, Hunter, Jack, Jackson, Jake, Jasper, Jed, Jett, Kurt, Leon, Leroy, Nate, Phoenix, Tyson, Zac.

Girls: Amber, Chelsea, Coco, Courtney, Georgia, Jade, Layla, Lola, Lorelei, Mackenzie, Maddison, Maxine, Natasha, Rochelle, Roxanne, Ruby, Samantha, Scarlett, Sienna, Zoë.

Ultra-feminine names for girls

Abbey, Alice, Anna, Aria, Ava, Bella, Chiara, Emily, Emma, Isla, Laura, Lily, Mia, Molly, Natalie, Poppy, Sarah, Sienna, Sophie, Willow.

'Softer' names for boys

Archie, Austin, Bailey, Beau, Blake, Dylan, Eli, Gabriel, Harry, Hugh, Jesse, Joel, Kai, Liam, Luke, Michael, Noah, Oliver, Sam, Toby.

Naming for meaning

Many people choose a name for its meaning, such as 'beautiful', 'strong', 'gentle' or 'good'. Despite their popularity, some names have rather unfortunate meanings – examples are Courtney (the short-nosed one) and Brodie (a ditch) – so it's worth checking.

Naming after places and 'things'

You might like to name your child after something or somewhere that is particularly relevant or close to your heart.

- **Places**: you could consider the name of a favourite town, city, country or other geographical feature. You might have grown up in Nelson or Hamilton, for example, lived in Paris or Scotland, and spent your honeymoon in India or Egypt.

- **Things**: there are, for example, names from the world of astronomy (Cosmo, Phoenix, Galaxy and Stella); animal and bird names (Leon, Marlon, Melissa and Jemima); flower and plant names (Willow, Lily, Ashley and Kauri); names of gemstones (Amber, Jet, Jade, Ruby and Garnet); and 'colour names' that describe hair or skin colouring, such as Blake and Jennifer ('fair'), Tynan and Leila ('dark'), and Flynn and Poppy ('red'). What I call 'noun names' are currently very popular – *see* Naming trends on page xi.

Naming after a person

There may be a particular given name that is passed down through the generations (for example, I know a family where the first daughter is always named Ingrid), or a surname, perhaps the mother's maiden name, could be incorporated as a middle name. Surnames are also now popular as first names – *see* Naming trends on page x.

- **Celebrities**: these might be a favourite actor, sporting star or well-known personality. The past popularity of names like Audrey (Hepburn), Ava (Gardner) (incidentally, both currently very popular), Marilyn (Monroe) and Wayne (John Wayne) can be attributed to the celebrity factor – as can modern names such as Ashlee, Charlize, Khloe, Miley, Reese, Sienna and Stella for girls, and Ashton, Cruz, Harry, Jude, Orlando and William for boys.

- **Children of celebrities**: although celebrities are notorious for giving their kids unusual (and sometimes unfortunate) names, many of these are popular with New Zealand parents. Names such as Mia (Kate Winslet), Ava (Reese Witherspoon), Ryder (Kate Hudson), Jaden (Andre Agassi and Steffi Graf) and Brooklyn (David and Victoria 'Posh Spice' Beckham) have certainly caught on.

- **Historical characters**: this includes names from the Bible and other religious texts, or personalities that you particularly admire – Lincoln (Abraham), Nelson (Mandela), Amelia (Earhart) and Florence (Nightingale) are some examples. You could even choose an early settler's name.

- **Fictitious characters**: taken from Greek, Roman, Sanskrit and Norse mythology, or from novels, plays, films or television programs. Shakespearean names such as Jessica, Olivia and Henry have long been popular, while other examples are Rhett and Scarlett from *Gone with the Wind*, Scout from *To Kill a Mockingbird* and Arwen from *The Lord of the Rings*.

Middle names

You may find it difficult to decide between a classic name such as William or Charlotte; going 'modern' with Kai, Ryder, Harper, Savannah or Willow; or 'ethnic' with something like Luca or Gabriella. In this instance, choosing two names is a good solution. You could give your baby a more conventional first name and an unusual middle name (Bella Swan, Matilda Sunshine and Benjamin Blue – all real examples from birth announcements), or the reverse (Jericho James, Emerson Rosa and Indigo Helen).

Interestingly, many 'old-fashioned' names are making a comeback for this role. Rose has been popular as a middle name for over a decade but Anne, Christine, Helen, Susan and, particularly, Elizabeth and Margaret are on the rise. Andrew, Christopher, Brian, Michael, Phillip, Peter, Robert and Thomas are increasingly popular middle names for boys.

Naming trends

The 21st century has seen some significant trends in baby naming – including the following.

- **Classic names**: traditional, often biblical, names such as Charlotte, Sophia, Olivia, Elizabeth, Hannah, Joshua, Benjamin, William, Samuel and Noah have made a big comeback in recent years.

- **Ethnic names**: names from cultures and languages as varied as Gaelic, Arabic, Hebrew, Spanish and Italian are also popular. Examples include Lachlan, Rafael, Elijah, Xavier, Amelie, Mackenzie, Isabella, Isla, Layla and Samira.

- **Unisex names**: in some cultures, Tibetan, for example, it is common for boys and girls to share names such as Nima or Tashi, and this concept is becoming more popular in Western society. Male/female variations (Francis/Frances and Leslie/Lesley) have been around for a long time, but there are now dozens of genuinely unisex names such as Bailey, Charlie, Riley, Harper, Peyton and Tyson. I have even seen Felix, Pierre, Rex and Rory in birth announcements for girls.

- **Surnames as first names**: both boys and girls now have names such as Cameron, Emerson, Harlow, Maddox, Sloan and Weston. Interestingly, many of these are 'occupation names' like Cooper, Hunter, Mason, Miller and Taylor. Celebrity surnames and brand names are popular too, including Jagger, Ledger, Presley, Aniston, Armani, Hurley and Chanel.

- **'Noun names'**: these have always been around (Hope, Grace, Rose, Basil, Heath) but the current trend, almost certainly established by celebrities, means that names such as Affinity, Blessing, Button, Cedar, Chardonnay, Holiday, Mystique, Reef and Spark are not uncommon. Some of these are attractive and unusual but it can be taken too far – consider Bandit, Danger, Martyr, Trick and Wraith.

- **'Adjective names' and 'verb names'**: these are also popular. Examples include Divine, Golden, Gracious, Loyal, Lucky, Noble, Royal, True, Evoke, Flex, Roam and Shine.

- **Made-up names**: another major trend is to make up names. Famous authors of the past created Vanessa (Jonathan Swift), Dorian (Oscar Wilde), Wendy (J M Barrie) and Lorna (R D Blackmore), but today's parents are perhaps going overboard. A New Zealand couple, for example, received a court order to allow their nine-year-old daughter to change the name she understandably hated – 'Talula Does The Hula From Hawaii'. Other names that have been officially 'blocked' in New Zealand include 4real, Fat Boy, and Fish and Chips for twins (although Benson and Hedges *was* allowed!).

  Made-up names can be created by dropping or adding letters – Mackenzie to Kenzie, Ava to Avanna, Sophia to Sophalia, Max to Maxence and Zac to Zacoda. A popular trend in the USA is to add La, Ta, Tal or Tan to female names, creating concoctions such as Lakeisha and Takeisha (from Keisha) Taleisha (from Aisha) and Taneka. There are also many boys' names with D or De prefixes, including DeMarcus and Dwayne.

  Other examples of adapting an existing name are Nason (from Mason), Jamen and Jaylen (from Jay), Jedward (from Edward), Taden (from Jaden), Taniel (from Daniel), Jayla (from Kayla), Brylie (from Riley) and Jelissa (from Melissa). You could even change the order of the letters, whereby Mary becomes Ryma and Liam becomes Mial. Other examples are Etan and Nevaeh, Nate and Heaven respectively in reverse.

- **Combining names**: there are two major options: from two full names – for example, Amalia-Rose, Marie-Claire, Giancarlo and Kobe-Lee – or from parts of two names. Examples of these are Alexavier (Alexander and Xavier), Jaleb (Jay and Caleb), Sacharias (Sacha and Zacharias), Amelinda (Amelia and Linda), Isabeth (Isabel and Beth), Jaslyn (Jasmine and Lynn) and Sarahanna (Sarah and Hannah).

- **Alternative spellings**: many parents like to distinguish a popular name by spelling it differently, so that Oscar becomes Auskah, Jacob becomes Jaykeb, Jackson to Jaxxon, Olivia to Alivyah, Ruby to Rhubee and Georgia to Jorjah. There is nothing essentially wrong with this, but imagine the inconvenience of your child having to constantly spell out his or her name in the future.

What to avoid

Virtually everyone can recall a few name disasters. Although these can be amusing, it isn't wise to land your child with something along the lines of Crispin Bacon, Ida Down, Harley Davis, Wanda Farr, Ophelia Dickey or Jack Daniel. Although not 'disasters' as such it's also probably best to avoid combinations such as Jane Lane, Harry Barry, David Davidson and William Williams.

Diminutives

The shortening and familiarising of names is almost inevitable, but think carefully and consider your surname in particular. Here are some diminutives of Patricia, Richard, Alexander, Christine, John and Timothy respectively – Pat Lamb, Rick Shaw, Sandy Banks, Chris Cross, Jack Frost and Tim Tam. If you're keen to avoid a diminutive, go for short names like Jack, Mia, Anna, Ryan, Jade, Jai, Lara, Tom and Zac. But some of these can still be familiarised by adding a 'y' or 'o' at the end.

Initials

And, finally, think about the initials formed by given and family names. Initials can create some not particularly desirable 'words' that may well cause embarrassment in the future. Real-life examples are JAP, CIG, GAB, DOB, KAK, FAB, PAW, LOB, BAK, LEAP, IMP and ODD.

Origins of names

Following are brief descriptions of some of the less obvious 'origin of name' categories that are used throughout the book. Note that names of modern English origin are not designated as 'English' in the text.

Aboriginal: not necessarily traditional Indigenous Australian names, but rather Aboriginal words from various parts of the continent.

African: the names in this book are predominantly from Ghana, Nigeria, southern Africa and Zimbabwe.

Ancient Egyptian: names from the language of the Egyptians of antiquity, as opposed to modern-day Arabic.

Aramaic: a Semitic language, related to Hebrew.

Babylonian: the language of the ancient region of Babylon, located in Mesopotamia (present-day Iraq).

Baha'i: a religious faith, founded in Persia in the 19th century. The religion has its own calendar, consisting of nineteen months.

Basque: from the western Pyrenees region of Spain and France.

Breton: Celtic names from Brittany in north-western France.

Catalan: the language of Andorra and Catalonia, a region of north-east Spain.

Celtic: Breton, Cornish and Welsh names from the Celtic (Indo-European) languages of extreme-west Europe. Some Gaelic names are similar and may also be included.

Cornish: Celtic names from Cornwall, the most south-westerly English county.

Flemish: from a form of Dutch, used mainly in northern Belgium.

Gaelic: names that originate from the Gaelic (a form of Celtic) languages of Ireland, the Isle of Man and Scotland. The definitions 'Irish' and 'Scottish' generally indicate Gaelic names that have been Anglicised.

Gypsy: names from the language of Europe's Gypsy people, sometimes known as Romany.

Hindi: essentially Sanskrit names, but these are specifically from northern India.

Israeli/Jewish/Modern Jewish: Hebrew, but generally popular modern names rather than ancient names from the Bible and other sources.

Mayan: the language of the Mayan people of Mexico.

Middle English: from the form of English used from approximately AD 1100–1400.

Native American: names from the many languages of the Indigenous peoples of North America.

Nepali: from the language of Nepal, similar to Hindi.

Old English: names from the form of English (Anglo-Saxon) that was in use prior to AD 1100.

Old French: from the form of French used prior to approximately AD 1400.

Old Norse: from the pre-AD 1400 language of Scandinavia and Iceland.

Persian: names from the ancient language of Persia, now Iran.

Sanskrit: the classical language of India, covering names given to Hindus, Buddhists and other groups of the Indian subcontinent.

Sherpa/Tibetan: from the Sino-Tibetan language. Names that are used in Tibet, Bhutan, Ladakh (India) and by the Sherpa people of Nepal.

Sikh: a religious sect, founded in the 16th-century in north-western India. Their main language, Punjabi, is of Indo-Aryan origin.

Slavic: from the Indo-European languages of Russia, the Czech Republic, Slovakia, Poland, Serbia, Croatia, Bosnia, Bulgaria and other Eastern European countries.

Swahili: from an eastern African language that has its origins in Arabic.

Teutonic: of Germanic origin, including names that are (or were) used in Germany, Holland, Scandinavia and Britain.

Urdu: a language derived from Hindustani (Hindi), used primarily in Pakistan and parts of northern India.

Yiddish: a form of Hebrew that has incorporated German and Slavic words.

Using this book

Here are some pointers for using *Baby Names for New Zealanders*.

- **Meaning**: when known, the name's meaning is included.

- **Ethnic origin and usage**: in many instances, names of a particular ethnic or linguistic origin – for example, Abigail (Hebrew) and Andrew (Greek) – are not necessarily in modern usage in their country of origin (Israel and Greece, respectively, for the above examples).

- **Variations and diminutives**: when a name has variations, these are listed under the definition, starting on a new line. When applicable, diminutives are below the variations. Not all variations and diminutives of a name are listed separately within the A–Z format. With Jordan under Boys, for example, some variations (such as Jordaan, Jorden and Jordon) do not have their own separate entry, and these are therefore included only under Jordan. If you think a particular name might be a variation of another – or a name does not seem to be included – you should scan the page for the closest spelling.

- **Unisex naming**: many names are now being used for both sexes, so if you are interested in such a name, look under both Girls and Boys.

- **Star-sign dates:** various astrological signs are mentioned in the A-Zs, so it may be helpful to know the dates:

Aries	21 March–19 April
Taurus	20 April–20 May
Gemini	21 May–20 June
Cancer	21 June–22 July
Leo	23 July–22 August
Virgo	23 August–22 September
Libra	23 September–22 October
Scorpio	23 October–21 November
Sagittarius	22 November–21 December
Capricorn	22 December–19 January
Aquarius	20 January–18 February
Pisces	19 February–20 March

Note: dates are approximate only as there is a slight annual variation.

MOST POPULAR NEW ZEALAND NAMES 2015

The trends for 2015 include Olivia overtaking Charlotte as the most popular name for girls, while new 'Top-30' entries are Scarlett, Isabelle, Hazel and Jessica. Oliver maintains its place at the top of the boys list, and new 'Top-30s' are Carter, Blake and Henry.

Girls

Olivia	Ruby	Georgia
Charlotte	Grace	Aria
Harper	Emma	Scarlett
Sophie	Chloe	Eva
Emily	Ava	Evelyn
Ella	Lucy	Willow
Isla	Zoe	Isabelle
Mia	Mila	Hazel
Amelia	Sophia	Hannah
Isabella	Lily	Jessica

Boys

Oliver	Noah	Carter
Jack	Thomas	Jackson
William	Max	Elijah
James	Lucas	Leo
Benjamin	George	Lachlan
Mason	Samuel	Joshua
Hunter	Ryan	Blake
Charlie	Alexander	Daniel
Liam	Ethan	Henry
Jacob	Cooper	Isaac

Girls

A

Aaliah/Aaliyah *See* Aliya.

Aamor Breton: a sunbeam.

Aana *See* Anne.

Aashlee/Aashleigh/Aashlie *See* Ashleigh.

Abagael/Abbegael *See* Abigail.

Abbe/Abbey/Abbie/Abby Diminutives of Abigail.

Abelia Hebrew: breath. The feminine form of Abel.
Abela, Abella, Abellia.

Abena *See* Abina.

Abeo Nigerian: happy she was born.

Aberah *See* Avera.

Abia Arabic: great.

Abigail Hebrew: father's joy. *See also* Gail.
Abagael, Abbegael, Abbegail, Abegael, Abegail, Abigael, Abigale, Abigayle.
Diminutives: Abbe, Abbee, Abbey, Abbi, Abbie, Abby, Abey, Abie, Gael, Gail, Gale, Gayle.

Abijah Hebrew: God is my father.
Abija, Abisha.

Abilene A biblical placename and a city in Texas.

Abina Ghanaian: born on a Thursday.
Abena, Abinah.

Abir Arabic: the fragrant one.

Abira *See* Adira.

Abisha *See* Abijah.

Abra Hebrew: the father of many. The feminine form of Abraham.

Acacia Greek: thorny, as in the acacia tree.

Acantha Greek: a legendary nymph.

Accalia Latin: the foster mother of Romulus and Remus, the founders of Rome.

Achilla Greek: the feminine form of Achilles.

Acqua Italian: water.

Ada Teutonic: prosperous and joyful.
Adah, Adda, Aida, Ajda (Turkish).
Diminutives: Addi, Addie, Addy.

Adabelle A 'combination name' meaning joyous and beautiful.
Adabela, Adabell.

Adah Hebrew: adornment. A biblical name.

Adair *See* BOYS.

Adalia Hebrew: God is my refuge.
Adali, Adalie.

Adama Hebrew: of the red earth. The feminine form of Adam.
Adamah, Adamina.

Adan *See* Aidan.

Adana A city in Turkey.

Adar Hebrew: fire.

Adara Arabic: a virgin. Greek: beauty.

1

Adda *See* Ada.

Addi/Addie/Addy *See* Ada and Adelaide.

Addison Old English: the son (or daughter) of Adam.
Addis, Addisyn, Addyson, Adison, Adisyn, Adyson.

Adel/Adela *See* Adèle.

Adelaide Old German: noble and kind. *See also* Adèle.
Adelaida, Adelais, Adelheid (German, Swiss), Adelia, Adelice, Adelicia, Adelina, Adelind, Adeline, Adella (Spanish), Adline, Alina, Aline, Alyna, Edeline (German).
Diminutives: Addi, Addie, Addy, Dell, Della, Heidi.

Adèle French: noble, a saint's name. *See also* Adelaide.
Adel, Adela, Adelene, Adelia, Adeline, Adell, Adella, Adelle.
Diminutives: Dell, Della.

Adelfa/Adelfia *See* Adelpha.

Adelheid German and Swiss form of Adelaide.

Adelia *See* Adelaide.

Adelicia Old English form of Adelaide and Alice.
Adelice.

Adelina/Adelind/Adeline *See* Adelaide.

Adelinda From Adelaide and Linda.

Adella/Adelle *See* Adelaide and Adèle.

Adelpha Greek: sisterly.
Adelfa, Adelfia, Adelphia.

Adena/Adene/Adenia *See* Adina.

Adeola Nigerian: a crown.

Aderyn Welsh: a bird.

Adia Swahili: a gift from God.

Adiah.

Adiba Arabic: cultured.

Adiel Hebrew: an ornament of God.
Adiella.

Adila Arabic: equal, like.
Adilah.

Adima Teutonic: noble, famous.

Adin *See* Adina.

Adina Hebrew: slender and delicate. A biblical name.
Adena, Adene, Adenia, Adin, Adine.
Diminutives: Dena, Dina.

Adira Hebrew: strong.
Abira.

Adison/Adisyn *See* Addison.

Adline *See* Adelaide.

Adolpha Teutonic: a noble she-wolf. The feminine version of Adolf.
Adolfa, Adolfina, Adolphina, Adolphine.

Adoncia Spanish: sweet.

Adonia Greek: a beautiful goddess. The feminine form of Adonis.

Adora Latin: the adored one.
Adorah, Adorée.

Adorabelle A combination of Adora and Belle.

Adorée *See* Adora.

Adorna Latin: adorned with jewels.

Adraine/Adrana/Adrea *See* Adriana.

Adriana Latin: a dark woman from the sea. The feminine form of Adrian and generally an Italian name.
Adraine, Adrana, Adrea, Adria, Adriane (German), Adrianna, Adrianne, Adrienne (French), Hadria.

Adrienne French form of Adriana.

Advent Latin: the arrival. Suitable for a child born during Advent, starting on the last Sunday in November and leading up to Christmas.
Adventa, Adventia, Adventina, Aventia, Aventina.

Aegea Greek: of the Aegean.

Aemilia *See* Amelia.

Aerona Welsh: a berry.
Aeronah.

Affinity Middle English: a natural liking or attraction.
Affinité.

Affrica Celtic: pleasant. Also from the name of the continent.
Afric, Africa, Africah, Afrika, Afrikah.

Afra *See* Aphra.

Afraima Arabic/Hebrew: fruitful.

Afrika/Afrikah *See* Affrica.

Agapé Greek: love.

Agata *See* Agatha.

Agate French: a precious stone.

Agatha Greek: good, honourable. St Agatha was a 3rd-century Sicilian martyr.
Agata (Italian, Polish), Agathe (French, German), Agathy, Agda (Swedish), Agueda (Spanish).
Diminutives: Ag, Aggie, Aggy.

Agda Swedish form of Agatha.

Agenda A list or program.
Agendah, Ajenda, Ajendah.

Aglaia Greek: splendid beauty. The goddess of harmony.

Agnes Greek: pure, chaste. The name of a saint of the Middle Ages. *See also* Annice.
Agnese (Italian), Agnessa (Russian),
Agneta (Danish), Agnethe (German, Scandinavian), Agneza, Agnies (French), Agnola (Italian), Agyness, Aigneis (Irish), Akenehi (Maori), Akinehi (Maori), Anaïs, Anezka (Czech), Annis, Annys (Greek), Ines, Inez, Nesta (Welsh), Ynes (Spanish), Ynez (Spanish).
Diminutives: Aggie, Ina, Nessa, Nessi, Nessie, Neysa, Neza.

Agnola Italian form of Agnes.

Agueda Spanish form of Agatha.

Agyness *See* Agnes.

Ahna/Ahnna *See* Anne.

Ahorangi Maori: an enlightened teacher.

Ahurewa Maori: a shrine or sacred place.

Ahuva Hebrew: beloved.
Ahava, Ahuda.

Aida *See* Ada.

Aidan Irish Gaelic: the little fiery one. *See also* Edana, and Aidan in BOYS.
Adan, Eidan.

Aideen *See* Etain.

Aigneis Irish form of Agnes.

Aihe Maori: a dolphin, or driftwood.

Aiko Japanese: the beloved.

Aila/Ailah *See* Ayla.

Aileen/Ailene *See* Eileen.

Aili A popular Finnish name. *See also* Eileen.
Ailee, Ailie.

Ailis Irish Gaelic form of Alice.
Ailise, Ailish, Alish, Aylish, Eilish.

Ailsa Scottish: after a rocky inlet known as Ailsa Craig.

Aimée French: beloved. A form of

Amy.

Aindrea *See* Andrea.

Aine Irish Gaelic: brightness, radiance. The queen of the fairies in Celtic mythology.
Aina, Aithne, Eithne, Ena, Ethene.

Aingeal Irish Gaelic form of Angela.

Aino A figure from Finnish mythology.

Ainsley Old English/Scottish: a wood or clearing. Also a boy's name.
Ainslea, Ainslee, Ainsleigh, Ainslie, Ainsly, Anslea.

Airini Maori form of Irene.

Airlia Greek: ethereal.
Airley, Airlie, Airly.

Aisha Arabic: life. The name of Mohammed's third and favourite wife.
Ayesha, Ayisha.

Aisleen *See* Eileen.

Aisling/Aislinn *See* Ashling.

Aithne *See* Aine.

Aiva/Aivah *See* Ava.

Aiveen An Irish Gaelic name of uncertain meaning.

Ajda *See* Ada.

Ajenda/Ajendah *See* Agenda.

Ajla Slavic form of Ayla.

Aka Hawaiian: a shadow.

Akako Japanese: red.

Akamai Hawaiian: the clever one.

Akana A mountain in Papua New Guinea.

Akela Hawaiian: noble or wise. *See also* Akila.
Akelah.

Akenehi/Akinehi Maori forms of Agnes.

Akiko Japanese: a shining light.

Akila Arabic: wise. Nigerian: a heroine.
Akela, Akelah, Akilah.

Akina Japanese: a spring flower.

Aku Ghanaian: born on a Wednesday.

Alabama A state of the USA.

Alaia Basque: joyful.
Alaya, Aleya.

Alain/Alaina *See* Alana.

Alaine *See* Alana and Elaine.

Alamea Hawaiian: precious.
Alameah.

Alameda Spanish: a poplar tree.

Alana Hawaiian: awakening. Irish Gaelic: the beautiful child. The feminine form of Alan.
Alain, Alaina, Alaine, Alanah, Alanda, Alanis, Alanna, Alannah, Alanya, Alarna, Alayna, Alayne, Aleina, Aliene, Alina, Allaine, Allana, Allanah, Allene, Allyn.
Diminutives: Lana, Lane, Lanna.

Alani Hawaiian: an orange tree.

Alanis/Alanya *See* Alana.

Alaqua Native American: a sweet gum tree.

Alarice Teutonic: the ruler of all. The feminine form of Alaric.
Alarica, Alarise.

Alarna *See* Alana.

Alaska A state of the USA.
Alaskah.

Alastrina Greek: the protector of mankind. The feminine form of Alastair.

Alatea Spanish from Greek: truth.

Alauda Gaelic: a lark.

Alaula Hawaiian: the dawn.

Alaya *See* Alaia.

Alayne *See* Alana.

Alberta Teutonic: noble and illustrious. The feminine form of Albert, and the name of a Canadian province.
Alberte, Albertina, Albertine, Albrette, Alverta, Elberta, Elbertina (Spanish), Elbertine (French).
Diminutives: Ali, Allie, Berta, Berte, Bertie.

Albina Latin: fair or white.
Alba (Italian), Albine, Albinia, Alvina, Aubina, Aubine.
Diminutive: Bina.

Albrette *See* Alberta.

Alchemy Middle English: one with magical powers.
Alcamie, Alchamy, Alchemie, Alchemye, Alkamie, Alkamye.

Alcina Greek: strong-minded. A sorceress in Greek mythology.
Alzina.

Alda Teutonic: wise and rich.

Aldabella From Alda and Bella, Italian for beautiful.

Aldara Greek: a winged gift.

Aldonza Spanish: sweet.

Aldora Old English: of noble rank.

Aldrey Old English: from the alder tree.
Aldree, Aldrie, Aldry,

Alecia *See* Alicia.

Aleda *See* Alida.

Aleece *See* Alice.

Aleen/Alene *See* Eileen.

Aleesha/Aleisha *See* Alicia.

Aleeza *See* Aliza.

Aleina *See* Alana.

Alejandra/Aleksandra/Aleksia *See* Alexandra.

Aleka Greek form of Alexandra.

Aleks *See* Alex.

Aleksija Slavic form of Alexis.

Alena Czech/German: a diminutive of Magdalena (*see* Madeline). Also the Lithuanian form of Helen.
Diminutive: Alenka (Slavic).

Alesana/Alesanna *See* Alexanna.

Alese/Aleshia/Alesia *See* Alice and Alicia.

Alessandra/Alessandria Italian forms of Alexandra.

Alesson/Alessyn *See* Alison.

Aleta/Aletta/Alette *See* Alida.

Aletha *See* Alice, Alida and Althea.

Alethea Greek: truthful. *See also* Alice.
Aletea, Alethia, Aletia, Alithea.
Diminutive: Thea.

Alex A short form of Alexandra.
Aleks, Alix, Allex, Allix, Alyks, Alyx.
Diminutives: Lex, Lexie.

Alexa *See* Alexis.

Alexandra Greek: the defender, or helper of mankind; the feminine form of Alexander. *See also* Alex, Alexis, Sandra, Sasha and Zena.
Alejandra (Spanish), Aleka (Greek), Aleksandra (Russian), Aleksia (Danish, Norwegian), Alessandra (Italian), Alessandria, Alexanderina, Alexandria, Alexandrina, Alexandrine (French), Alexdra (Russian), Alexena, Alexia, Alexina (Scottish),

Alexsia, Alisandra, Alissandra, Alixandra, Alixia, Allixandra, Allixia, Alyksandra, Alyxandra.
Diminutives: Alex, Ali, Alix, Alla (Russian), Allex, Allie, Allix, Alyks, Alyx, Lex, Lexa, Lexie, Lexine, Lexy, Sacha, Sandi, Sandie, Sandra, Sandy, Sascha, Sasha, Xandra, Zandra, Zena (Scottish), Zina.

Alexanna A combination of Alex and Anna (grace).
Alesana, Alesanna, Alexana, Alexzana, Alexzanna, Alezana, Alezanna.

Alexdra A Russian form of Alexandra.

Alexia/Alexina *See* Alexandra and Alexis.

Alexis A form of Alexandra.
Aleksija (Slavic), Alexa, Alexia, Alexina, Alexine.

Aleya *See* Alaia.

Alezana/Alezanna *See* Alexanna.

Alfa *See* Alpha.

Alfonsa Teutonic: noble and ready. Feminine form of Alphonse.
Alfonsine, Alonsa, Alonza, Alphonsa, Alphonsina, Alphonsine.

Alfreda Teutonic: a wise counsellor; the feminine form of Alfred.
Elfreda, Elfreida, Elfrida, Elfrieda, Elfriede (German), Elva.
Diminutives: Alfie, Allie, Freda, Frida, Frieda.

Algerine A woman from Algeria.

Ali/Allie Diminutives of Alberta, Alexandra, Alice and Alison.

Alia/Aliah *See* Aliya.

Alice Greek: the wise counsellor, or the truthful one. Teutonic: noble. The name became popular through

Lewis Carroll's *Alice in Wonderland* books. *See also* Ailis, Alicia and Alison.
Adelice, Adelicia, Ailis (Irish Gaelic), Aleece, Alese, Aletha, Alethea, Alicea, Alicia, Alician, Aliciedik (Breton), Alicien, Alicja (Polish), Aliki (Greek), Alis, Alisa (Italian), Alisha, Aliss, Alissa, Alisse, Alithia, Alletta (Dutch), Allys, Allysa, Alodia (Breton), Alyce, Alys, Alyse, Alyssa, Alysse, Areta (Maori), Aylce (Irish), Aylice (Irish).
Diminutives: Ali, Allie, Ally, Elli, Ellie, Elly, Elsie, Elsa, Ilsa.

Alicen/Aliceson *See* Alison.

Alicia A popular form of Alice.
Alecia, Aleesa, Aleesha, Aleisha, Aleisia, Alesha, Aleshia, Alesia, Alicea, Alicja, Alisha, Alisia, Allecia, Allisha, Allissa, Allysha, Alysa, Alysia, Alyssa, Elecia, Eleesha, Elicia, Elisha, Ellecia, Ellicia, Ellisha, Elysa, Elyse, Elyshia.

Alida Latin: the little winged one.
Aleda, Aleta, Aletha, Aletta (Italian, Spanish), Alette (French), Alita, Alouetta, Alyda, Elida, Elita.
Diminutives: Leda, Lita.

Aliene *See* Alana.

Aliikai Hawaiian: the queen of the sea.

Alika Hawaiian: truthful. Nigerian: very beautiful.

Aliki Greek form of Alice.

Alima Arabic: skilled in dancing and music.

Alina/Aline *See* Adelaide, Alana and Eileen.

Alis/Alisa/Alisha/Alisia/Alithia *See*

Alice and Alicia.

Alisandra/Alissandra *See* Alexandra.

Alish *See* Ailis.

Alison Originally a diminutive of Alice.
Alesson, Alessyn, Alicen, Aliceson, Alisson, Allison, Allson, Allsun (Irish), Allyson, Alson, Alsoun, Alyson, Alysoun, Arihana (Maori). *Diminutives*: Ali, Alie, Allee, Allie, Ally, Aly, Lissie, Lisy.

Aliss/Alissa *See* Alice and Alyssa.

Alivia/Alivya/Alivyah *See* Olivia.

Alix/Alixandra/Alixia *See* Alex and Alexandra.

Aliya Arabic: sublime, exalted. Hebrew: to ascend.
Aalia, Aaliah Aaliya, Aaliyah, Alia, Aliah, Aliyah, Alya, Alyaa.

Aliza Jewish: joy.
Aleeza, Alizah, Alize (French), Alizée (French), Alizeh.

Alkamie/Alkamye *See* Alchemy.

Alla *See* Alexandra.

Allanah/Allene *See* Alana.

Allecia/Allisha *See* Alicia.

Allegra Italian/Spanish: joyous.
Alegra, Alegria, Allegria.

Allex *See* Alexs.

Allie *See* Alexandra and Alice.

Allison *See* Alison.

Allivia *See* Olivia.

Allix/Allixandra/Allixia *See* Alex and Alexandra.

Alloula/Allula *See* Alula.

Allson/Allsun/Ally/Allyson *See* Alison.

Allure Middle English: one who attracts or charms.
Alure.

Allyn *See* Alana.

Allys/Allysa *See* Alice.

Allysha/Alysa *See* Alicia.

Alma Celtic: good. Latin: of the soul. Turkish: an apple.
Almah.

Almada A city in Portugal.

Almasi Swahili: a diamond.
Almas, Almaz, Almazi.

Almeda *See* Almedha and Almeta.

Almedha Welsh: shapely.
Almeda, Almida.

Almeta Latin: ambitious.
Almeda.

Almida *See* Almedha.

Almira Arabic: truth without question.

Almond Middle English: a 'plant name'.

Alodia Breton form of Alice.

Alodie Old English: wealthy, prosperous.
Elodia, Elodie.

Aloha Hawaiian: greetings.
Aloa.

Alohi Hawaiian: brilliant.

Aloisa/Aloise *See* Aloysia and Louise.

Aloma The name of an American actress (Aloma Wright).
Alomah.

Alona Hebrew: from the oak tree.
Allona.

Alonsa/Alonza *See* Alfonsa.

Alouetta *See* Alida.

Aloysia The feminine form of Aloysius. *See also* Louise.

Aloisa, Aloise, Aloisia, Aloyza (Polish).

Alpha Greek: the first. First letter of the Greek alphabet.
Alfa.

Alphonsa/Alphonsina/Alphonsine *See* Alfonsa.

Alson/Alsoun *See* Alison.

Alta Latin: tall.

Altair From the Arabic word for a bright star.

Althea Greek: the healer.
Aletha, Althee, Altheta, Althia.
Diminutive: Thea.

Altheda Greek: flower-like.

Aludra Greek: a virgin.

Alula Latin: a star in Ursa Major.
Alloula, Allula, Aloula.

Aluma Hebrew: a girl.

Alure *See* Allure.

Alva Latin: the white or blonde one.
Also a diminutive of Alvina.

Alverta *See* Alberta.

Alvina Teutonic: a beloved and noble friend; the feminine form of Alvin.
See also Albina and Elvina.
Alva, Alvine, Alvinia.

Alvira *See* Elvira.

Alvita Latin: vivacious, full of life.

Alwin Welsh: beloved by all.
Alwyn.

Alya/Alyaa *See* Aliya.

Alyce *See* Alice.

Alyda *See* Alida.

Alyks/Alyksandra/Alyx/Alyxandra *See* Alex and Alexandra.

Alyna *See* Adelaide.

Alys/Alyse *See* Alice.

Alysia Greek: possessive. *See also* Alicia.

Alyson/Alysoun *See* Alison.

Alyssa Greek: a herb with yellow or white flowers. Also a form of Alicia.
Alissa, Alysse, Alyssia, Alyssum.

Alzena Arabic: a woman.

Alzina *See* Alcina.

Alzubra Arabic: a star.

Ama Ghanaian: born on Saturday.
Sanskrit: a mother.

Amabel Latin: lovable, the sweet one.
See also Mabel.
Amabella, Amabell, Amabelle.

Amada A Spanish form of Amy.

Amadea Latin: beloved of God.

Amadika Zimbabwean: the beloved one.

Amadora Italian: the gift of love.
Amadore.

Amala Arabic: hope. *See also* Amelia.
Amal.

Amalea/Amali/Amalia/Amalie/ Amalita *See* Amelia.

Amalinda *See* Amelinda.

Amana Hebrew: faithful or loyal.

Amanda Latin: worthy of being loved.
Amandah, Amandine (French).
Diminutives: Manda, Mandie, Mandy.

Amandine French form of Amanda.

Amani Arabic: an aspiration or desire.
Amany.

Amara Greek: unfading or eternal beauty.

Amaranth Greek: an unfading flower.

Amaranta (Spanish), Amarantha.

Amaris Hebrew: God has promised.
Amari.

Amarli *See* Amelia.

Amaryllis Greek: a shepherdess. A
'flower name'.
Amarill, Amarillis, Amaryll.

Amata Italian and Spanish form of
Amy. *See also* Amice.

Amaya Japanese: night rain.

Amazonia Greek: warlike. Also after
the Amazon River.

Amba/Ambah *See* Amber and
Ambika.

Ambar Sanskrit: of the sky. *See also*
Amber.

Ambara Arabic: the perfumed one.
Ambarah, Ambarin, Ambarina,
Ambarine.

Amber Arabic: a gemstone. This
name became popular in the 1940s,
after the publication of the novel
Forever Amber. See also Ember.
Amba, Ambah, Ambar (Hindi),
Amberr, Ambeur, Ambr (Welsh),
Ambra (Italian), Ambre (French),
Ambur, Amipa (Tongan), Emba
(Swahili), Embah, Ember, Inbar
(Hebrew).

Amberley A modern made-up name.
Also a South Island town.
Amberlee, Amberleigh, Amberly.

Ambika Hindi: a mother.
Amba.

Ambr/Ambra/Ambre *See* Amber.

Ambriel The angel of the month of
May.
Ambriele, Ambriell, Ambrielle.

Ambrosine Greek: the divine

immortal one. The feminine form of
Ambrose.
Ambrosia, Ambrosina.

Amee *See* Amy.

Ameena *See* Amina.

Ameerah *See* Amira.

Amelia Teutonic: industrious,
striving. *See also* Emily.
Aemilia, Amala, Amalea, Amali,
Amalia (Scandinavian), Amalie
(German), Amalina (Italian,
Spanish), Amalita (Spanish), Amarli,
Amarlie, Amealia, Amela, Amelea,
Amelee, Amélie (French), Amelina,
Ameline, Amelita, Amellia, Amellie,
Amielia, Amilee, Amilia, Amilie,
Amillie, Amily, Amiria (Maori),
Amylee, Amylia, Amylie, Emblyn
(Cornish).
Diminutives: Amy, Mell, Melli,
Mellie, Melly, Milli, Millie, Milly.

Amelinda An attractive 'combination
name'.
Amalinda, Amelinde.

Amena Celtic: pure.
Amene, Amina.

America Italian: a country, named
in honour of the explorer Amerigo
Vespucci.
Americah, Amerika, Amerikah.

Amethyst Greek: a semi-precious
stone.
Amethyste.

Ami/Amia/Amie/Amii *See* Amy.

Amice Latin: friendship. *See also*
Amity.
Amata, Amecia, Amicia.

Amielia/Amilee/Amilia *See* Amelia.

Amina Arabic: honest, faithful. *See
also* Amena.

Ameena, Aminah.

Aminta Greek: the protector.
Amintha, Aminthe.

Amipa Tongan form of Amber.

Amira Arabic: a princess. Hebrew:
speech.
Ameera, Ameerah, Amirah.

Amiria Maori form of Amelia.

Amity Latin: friendship. *See also*
Amice.
Amita (Hebrew).

Amorita Latin: the little beloved one.
Amoretta, Amorette (French).

Amour French: love.
Amore.

Amrita Sanskrit: immortal.

Amy Old French: beloved. Also a
diminutive of Amelia.
Aimee, Aimée (French), Amada
(Spanish), Amata (Italian, Spanish),
Amee, Ami, Amia, Amie, Amiee,
Amii, Aymee, Aymi, Aymie.

Amylee/Amylia/Amylie *See* Amelia.

An Chinese: peace. Vietnamese:
safety.

Ana *See* Anastasia and Anne.

Anabel/Anabella/Anabelle *See*
Annabel.

Anael The angel of the air.

Anahera *See* Anihera.

Anaïs *See* Agnes.

Anala Hindi: fire.

Analise *See* Anneliese.

Anan Arabic: of the clouds.

Ananda Sanskrit: joyful.

Anani Hawaiian: an orange tree.

Anastasia Russian from Greek: she
who will rise again. The name of a

4th-century saint.
Anastacia, Anastase, Anastasie
(French), Anastasija (Slavic),
Anastasiya (Russian), Anastassia,
Anastazia (Slavic), Anastazie (Czech),
Anastazja (Polish), Anstice.
Diminutives: Ana, Nastasia (Russian),
Nastya (Russian), Stacee, Stacey,
Stacia, Stacie, Stacy, Stasya (Russian).

Anata Babylonian: the goddess of the
earth.

Anatola Greek: from the east. The
feminine form of Anatole.
Anatholia, Anatolia.

Anca/Ancika *See* Anne.

Ancela *See* Angela.

Ancelin Old French: a spear
attendant. The feminine form of
Lancelot.
Ancelot.

Anchoret *See* Angharad.

Ancilla Latin: a handmaiden.

Andea A woman of the Andes.
Andeana, Andia, Andiana.

Andela *See* Angela.

Andie *See* Andrea.

Andorra A small principality in
Europe, located between France and
Spain.
Andora, Andorah, Andorrah.

Andra/Andre *See* Andrea.

Andras Norwegian: breath.

Andrea Greek: strong. The feminine
form of Andrew or Andreas.
Aindrea, Andra, Andre, Andreana,
Andreanna, Andrée (French),
Andreea, Andria, Andriana, Andrina,
Andrine.
Diminutives: Andie, Andy.

Andromeda Greek: a ruler of men. A heroine of Greek legend, who was rescued from a sea monster by Perseus. Also the name of a constellation.

Andy *See* Andrea.

Ane/Aneta/Anette *See* Anne.

Aneira Welsh: golden. The feminine form of Aneurin.

Aneko Japanese: older sister.

Anela Hawaiian form of Angela.

Anemone Greek: a wind flower. A mythological nymph who turned into a flower.

Anezka Czech form of Agnes.

Angarua Polynesian: a legendary figure.

Angel *See* Angela.

Angela Greek: a heavenly messenger, an angel. *See also* Angelica. Aingeal (Irish), Ancela (Polish), Andela (Czech), Anela (Hawaiian), Ange (French), Angel, Angèle (French), Angelina (Italian), Angeline, Angiola (Italian), Aniela (Italian, Polish), Anjela (Bohemian), Anjelina.
Diminutives: Ange, Angelita (Spanish), Angi, Angie, Anji, Anjie.

Angelica Latin: the angelic one. A form of Angela and also a 'plant name'. Angelika (Swedish), Angeliki (Greek), Angelique (French), Anjelica.

Angelina/Angeline/Angelita *See* Angela.

Angelique French form of Angelica.

Angharad Welsh: much loved. Anchoret.

Angiola Italian form of Angela.

Angwen/Angwenne *See* Anwen.

Anh Vietnamese: a flower.

Ani/Anica *See* Anne.

Anice *See* Annice.

Aniela Italian and Polish form of Angela.

Anihera Maori: an angel. Anahera.

Anika/Aniko *See* Anne.

Anila Sanskrit: of the wind. The feminine form of Anil.

Anisha Sanskrit: lordly.

Aniston The surname of a famous American actress (Jennifer Aniston). Anniston, Anston.

Anita *See* Anne.
Diminutive: Nita.

Anitra A name created by Norwegian playwright Henrik Ibsen for his play *Peer Gynt*.

Aniwaniwa Maori: a rainbow.

Anjali Sanskrit: an offering, homage. Anjalee, Anjouli, Anjuli.

Anjela/Anjelina/Anji *See* Angela.

Anjelica *See* Angelica.

Anka Turkish: a phoenix. *See also* Anne.

Ann/Anna *See* Anne.

Annabel A combination of Anna (grace) and Belle (beautiful). Anabel (Spanish), Anabela, Anabelah, Anabella, Anabelle, Annabell, Annabella, Annabellah, Annabelle, Annabellina.
Diminutives: Bella, Belle.

Annali *See* Anne.

Annaliese/Annalisa/Anna-Lise *See* Anneliese.

Annamaria A 'combination name'. Anna Maria, Annemarie, Anne Marie.

Annata Italian form of Anne.

Anne From the Hebrew name Hannah, meaning grace, or favoured by God. *See also* Annabel, Annamaria, Anneliese, Hannah and Nancy.
Aana, Ahna, Ahnna, Ana (Slavic, Spanish), 'Ana (Samoan, Tongan) Anca (Bohemian), Ancika (Bohemian), Ane (Lithuanian, Maori), Aneta (Serbian), Anette, Ani (Maori), Anica (Spanish), Anika, Aniko (Hungarian), Anita (Spanish), Anka (Serbian), Anke (German), Ann, Anna, Annah, Annali (Swiss), Annata (Italian), Anneka (Dutch), Anneke (Dutch), Annella (Scottish), Annelle, Annerl (Bavarian), Annetta (French), Annette, Annica (Italian), Annika (Swedish), Annita, Annot (Scandinavian), Annuschka (Russian), Anouska (Swedish), Antje (Dutch), Anu (Finnish), Anusia (Greek, Polish), Anya (Hebrew), Anysia, Hanna, Hannah, Ona (Lithuanian), Panna (Hungarian).
Diminutives: Anney, Anni, Annie, Anninka (Russian), Anny, Ans (Dutch), Anya (Russian), Nan, Nana, Nanci, Nancy, Nanette (French), Nanine, Nanna, Nanon (French), Nina (Russian), Ninette, Ninon (French), Nita (Spanish), Vanka (Russian), Vanni (Italian).

Anneka/Anneke Dutch forms of Anne.

Anneliese German/Scandinavian: from Anne and Liese (*see* Elizabeth). Analise, Anlise, Annaliese, Annalisa, Anna-Lise, Anna-Lisse, Anneliis,
Annelisa, Annelise.
Diminutive: Anneli.

Annetta/Annette *See* Anne.

Anni/Annie *See* Anne.

Annica Italian form of Anne.

Annice Old English form of Agnes. Anice, Annis, Annys, Annyse.

Annika/Anninka *See* Anne.

Annis *See* Agnes and Annice.

Annissa Arabic: charming, gracious.

Anniston *See* Aniston.

Ann-Margret A 'combination name'.

Annot *See* Anne.

Annunziata Italian: the bearer of news. Annunciata.

Annys *See* Agnes and Annice.

Anona Latin: of the harvest. Annona.

Anoush Armenian: sweet. Anousha.

Anouska/Anouskh *See* Anne and Anushka.

Ans Dutch diminutive of Anna.

Anselma Teutonic: a divine helmet. The feminine form of Anselm. Anselme (French).
Diminutives: Selma, Zelma.

Anslea *See* Ainsley.

Anstice *See* Anastasia.

Anston *See* Aniston.

Anteia Greek: a mythological figure.

Anthea Greek: flower-like. Anthia.
Diminutives: Thea, Thia.

Anthonia *See* Antonia.

Antigone Greek: a name from mythology, implying strength of character.

Antje Dutch form of Anne.

Antoinetta/Antoinette *See* Antonia.

Antonia Latin: praiseworthy. The feminine form of Anthony.
Anthonia, Antoinetta, Antoinette (French), Antonea, Antonella (Italian), Antonetta (Slavic), Antoni, Antonica (Italian), Antonie (German), Antonietta (Italian), Antonina, Antonine, Antonya (Lithuanian).
Diminutives: Netta, Nettie, Netty, Nina (Russian), Toinette (French), Toni, Tonia, Tonie, Tonya.

Anu Finnish form of Anna and Anne.

Anushka Sanskrit: a term of endearment.
Anouska, Anoukh, Anusha, Anuska.

Anusia Greek and Polish form of Anne.

Anwen Celtic: very beautiful.
Angwen, Angwenn, Angwenne, Anwenn, Anwenne, Anwyn, Anwynn, Annwynne.

Anya/Anysia *See* Anne.

Anzu Japanese: an apricot.

Aoife Irish Gaelic: life.

Aolani Hawaiian: a heavenly cloud.

Apakura Polynesian: a legendary figure.

Apara Nigerian: one who comes and goes.

Aperira Maori form of April.

Aphra Hebrew: dust. A saint's name.
Afra, Aphrah, Ayfara.

Aphrodite Greek: the goddess of beauty, love and fertility.

Apolline Greek: the sun, sunlight.

Apollene.

Apollonia Greek: belonging to Apollo. The name of a saint.

Aponi Native American: a butterfly.

Apple An unusual name, made famous by actress Gwyneth Paltrow's daughter.

April Latin: the first month in the Roman calendar. *See also* Avril.
Aperira (Maori), Aprila, Aprile, Aprilette, Aprili, Aprilie, Apryl, Apryle, Avril (French), Ebrel (Cornish), Ebril (Welsh).

Aqua A 'gemstone' and 'colour' name.

Aquaria Latin: after the zodiac sign and constellation of Aquarius.

Ara Greek: an altar, or the goddess of destruction.
Arah.

Arabella Latin: a beautiful altar.
Arabel, Arabela (Spanish), Arabelle.
Diminutives: Bel, Bella, Belle.

Arabia A region of the Middle East.
Arabiah.

Arachne Greek: a mythological maiden who was turned into a spider.

Arael The angel of the birds.

Araminta Greek: a beautiful fragrant flower.
Armamanta, Aramintha.

Arancia Italian: orange.

Aranka Hungarian: golden.

Arantxa Spanish: possibly a variation of Arancia.
Arancha.

Arataki Maori: to lead or guide.

Araxia Armenian: from the river.
Araxie.

Arcadia Greek: after Arcady, a mountainous region of Greece.

Archer Old English: a bowman.

Arda Hebrew: bronze. *See also* Ardath and Ardelle.

Ardath Hebrew: a field of flowers. Arda.

Ardelle Latin: warm and enthusiastic. Arda, Ardeen, Ardelia, Ardelis, Ardella, Ardene, Ardine, Ardis.

Arden Old English: the valley of the eagles.

Ardene/Ardine/Ardis *See* Ardelle.

Arduina A hunter-goddess in Celtic mythology. Arduenna, Arduenne, Arduinna.

Arella *See* Ariella.

Arena Latin: a sandy place.

Aresca *See* Ariesca.

Areta Greek: virtuous, one of untarnished reputation. Also a Maori form of Alice. Aretah, Arete, Aretha, Aretta, Arette (French), Arita, Aritah.

Aretha *See* Areta.

Arezou Persian: wishful.

Argenta Latin: silvery.

Aria Latin: a beautiful melody. Ariah, Arija, Arijah, Arya, Aryah.

Ariadne Greek: the holy one. The daughter of King Minos of Crete in mythology. Ariadna, Ariana, Ariane.

Arianrhod Welsh: silvery. The Celtic goddess of the moon. Arianrod.

Arianwen Welsh: like silver. Arian, Arianwenn, Arianwenne, Arianwyn, Arianwynn, Arianwynne.

Ariel *See* Ariella.

Ariella Hebrew: God's lioness. Arella, Ariel, Ariela, Ariell, Ariella, Arielle.

Ariesca A feminine form of Ares/ Aries, the Greek god of war (the equivalent of Mars) and a zodiac sign and constellation. Aresca, Arie, Arien, Ariene, Aries.

Arihana Maori form of Alison.

Arija/Arijah *See* Aria.

Arilda German: a hearth maiden.

Arista Greek: the best. Aristea.

Arita/Aritah *See* Areta.

Ariza Hebrew: a cedar tree.

Arkina Armenian: priceless. Arkeena, Arkinah. *Diminutive*: Arkie.

Arlene A modern name of uncertain origin. Arleen, Arlena, Arline, Arlyne.

Arlette Teutonic: an eagle. Arletta.

Arline/Arlyne *See* Arlene.

Armada Spanish: the armed one.

Armanda Feminine form of Armand. *See* Herman.

Armani After the Italian fashion designer, Giorgio Armani. Armanee, Armanie, Armany.

Armelle French Celtic: a princess.

Armilla Latin: a bracelet.

Armina Teutonic: a warrior maid, a feminine form of Herman. *See also* Erma. Armine, Arminia, Arminie.

Armistice From Latin: a truce.
Armystice.

Armorel Gaelic: one who lives by the sea.
Armorell, Armorelle.

Armynel French: a woman of the army. A feminine form of Armand.

Arnalda Teutonic: strong as an eagle. A feminine form of Arnold.
Arna, Arnette, Arnolda.

Arnica A medicinal plant.
Arnika (German), Arnijka.

Arnice Modern invention; a feminine form of Arnold.

Aroha Maori/Polynesian: love.

Arona Hebrew: exalted. The feminine form of Aaron.
Aronah.

Arorangi Maori: heavenwards.

Arquette The surname of a well-known family of American actors.
Arquet, Arquett.

Artemis Greek: perfect. The Greek goddess of the moon and hunting.
Artemas, Artemisa, Artemise, Artemisia.

Arthura A female form of Arthur, a Celtic name meaning as strong as a bear, or strong as a rock.
Artha (Welsh), Arthah, Arthurah, Arthure, Arthuria, Arthuriah, Arthurina, Arthurine, Artura, Arturah, Arture, Arturia, Arturina, Arturine.

Arti Indonesian. A popular girl's name.

Artis Icelandic: thunder, or a follower of Thor.

Aruna Sanskrit: the dawn.

Arundel *See* BOYS.

Arundhati Sanskrit: the morning star.

Arusha Sanskrit: red.

Arva Greek: an eagle.

Arwen Welsh: a muse. In *The Lord of the Rings* Arwen is taken to mean a noble maiden.
Arwenn, Arwenne, Arwyn, Arwynn, Arwynne.

Arya/Aryah *See* Aria.

Asa Japanese: the morning.

Asahi Japanese: the morning sun.

Asella After St Asella, who was described as 'a flower of the Lord'.

Asera Arabic/Hebrew: the queen of the sea.

Asha Sanskrit: hope.
Ashia.

Ashanti A group of people in Ghana.

Asher Hebrew: the fortunate one. More commonly a boy's name.
Ascher.

Ashira Hebrew: wealthy.

Ashleigh Old English: an ash-tree meadow or wood.
Aashlee, Aashleigh, Aashli, Aashlie, Ashlea, Ashlee, Ashlei, Ashley, Ashli, Ashlie, Ashly, Ashlygh.
Diminutives: Ash, Ashe.

Ashling Irish Gaelic: a vision or dream.
Aisling, Aislinn, Ashlen, Ashlin, Ashlinn, Ashlinne, Ashlyn, Ashlynn, Ashlynne.

Ashly/Ashlygh *See* Ashleigh.

Ashlyn/Ashlynn/Ashlynne *See* Ashling.

Asia Latin: the name of a continent.

15

Asiah.

Asisa Hebrew: ripe.

Asmara An Ethiopian city.

Aspasia Greek: welcome.

Aspen Old English: the aspen tree, a type of poplar.
Aspenn, Aspenne, Aspin, Aspyn.

Assunta Italian: from the Assumption of the Virgin Mary.

Asta Greek/Old Norse: a star. Also a short form of Astrid.
Astah, Astra, Astrah.

Astaire Greek: a star. The surname of a famous actor and dancer (Fred Astaire).
Astair, Asther (Scandinavian).

Aster Greek: a 'flower name'. *See also* Astral.
Astor, Astera, Asteria.

Astra *See* Asta and Astral.

Astral Latin: a star.
Aster, Astra, Astro.

Astrea Greek: innocence. The Greek goddess of justice, who became a constellation.

Astrid Old Norse: divine strength.
Astred, Astride, Astrud.
Diminutive: Asta.

Asucena/Asuzena *See* Azucena.

Ataahua Maori: beautiful.

Atalanta Greek: a swift runner in classical mythology.
Atlanta.

Atalia *See* Athalia.

Ata Marama Maori: moonlight.

Atanua Polynesian: a goddess of the dawn.

Atarah Hebrew: a crown. A name

from the Old Testment. Also a boy's name.
Atara.

Atarangi Maori: the morning sky.

Atarapa Polynesian: of the dawn.

Atarau Maori: moonlight or a moonbeam.

Athalia Hebrew: God is exalted.
Atalia, Athalea, Athali, Athalie (French), Athelie.

Athanasia Greek: immortal.

Athea The name of an Irish village.
Athia.

Athela Old English: noble.

Athena Greek: a wise woman. After Athene, the Greek goddess of wisdom.
Athenaios (Greek), Athenais (French), Athene, Athène (French), Athenee, Athina, Athine.

Atika Indonesian: pure or clear.

Atin Indonesian: a common girl's name.

Atira Hebrew: a prayer.

Atiya Arabic: a gift.

Aubina/Aubine *See* Albina.

Aubrey Teutonic: the golden-haired ruler of the elves. Generally a boy's name.
Aubra, Aubrah, Aubree, Aubrie, Aubry.

Audra *See* Audrey.

Audrey Old English: strong and noble, regal. *See also* Odrey.
Audey, Audra, Audray, Audree, Audrée (French), Audrette, Audri, Audrie, Audrienne, Audrina, Audry, Audrye, Awdree, Awdrey, Awdrie, Awdry.

Diminutives: Aud, Audie, Dee.

August A 'month name'. Also a form of Augusta.

Augusta Latin: majestic, or revered. The feminine form of Augustus. August, Auguste (French, German), Augusteen (Irish), Augustina, Augustine, Augustyna, Austine, Awsta (Welsh). *Diminutives*: Gussie, Gusta, Tina.

Aura Greek: of the air. Latin: a gentle breeze. Aure (French), Aurea, Auria, Aurian.

Aurea *See* Aura and Aurelia.

Aurelia Latin: golden. Aurea, Aurel, Aurela, Aurélie (French), Aureol, Aureole, Auriel, Auriol, Auriole, Aurnia (Irish), Oralee, Oralia, Oralie, Orelia, Oriel, Orla (Irish Gaelic).

Auria/Aurian *See* Aura.

Auristela Chilean: a golden star.

Aurnia *See* Aurelia.

Aurora Latin: daybreak. The goddess of the dawn; also an astronomical term. Aurore (French).

Austine *See* Augusta.

Autumn Like Summer, a popular 'season name', particularly in the USA. Autum.

Ava Greek: an eagle. Aiva, Aivah, Avah, Ayva, Ayvah.

Avalon *See* BOYS.

Avani Sanskrit: of the good earth.

Avanna A combination of Ava and Anna. Avana, Avanah, Avannah.

Avara Sanskrit: the youngest.

Avel Hebrew: breath.

Aveline Old French: from a placename. *See also* Evelyn. Avelaine.

Avena Latin: from the oat field. Avene.

Aventia/Aventina *See* Advent.

Aveolela Samoan: like the rays of the sun.

Avera Hebrew: a transgressor. Aberah.

Averil Old English: the slayer of the boar. Averell, Averill, Averyl, Avyril, Everild, Everilda.

Avery Old English: the ruler of the elves. Also a boy's name. Averey, Averi, Averie.

Aveza *See* Avice.

Avice French: warlike. Aveza, Avicia, Avis, Avisa.

Avis Latin: a bird. Also a variation of Avice.

Aviva Jewish: of the springtime. Avivah.

Avoca Irish: a sweet valley.

Avril The French form of April. Avrile, Avrilette, Avryl, Avrylette.

Avyril *See* Averil.

Awatea Maori: daylight.

Awdree/Awdrey/Awdrie *See* Audrey.

Awhina Maori: to embrace.

Awsta The Welsh form of Augusta.

Awusi Ghanaian: born on a Sunday.

Axelle Teutonic: the father of peace. The feminine form of Axel.

Ayala Modern Hebrew: a deer.

Ayame Japanese: like an iris (the flower).

Ayanna African: a beautiful flower.
Ayana, Ayanah, Ayann, Ayannah.

Ayesha/Ayisha *See* Aisha.

Ayfara *See* Aphra.

Ayla Hebrew: an oak tree. Turkish: moonlight.
Aila, Ailah, Ajla (Slavic), Aylah.

Aylce/Aylice *See* Alice.

Ayleen/Aylene *See* Eileen.

Aylin Turkish: the halo of the moon.

Aylish *See* Ailis.

Aylwen Welsh: a fair brow.

Aymee/Aymi/Aymie *See* Amy.

Ayoka Nigerian: one who brings joy.

Aysel Turkish: like moonlight.

Ayva/Ayvah *See* Ava.

Azalea Latin: dry earth. Teutonic: noble cheer. A 'flower name'.
Azalia, Azaliea, Azelia.

Azami Japanese: a thistle flower.

Azaria Hebrew: helped by God.
Azariah, Azeria, Zaria.

Azelias Hebrew: helped by God.

Aziza Arabic: the cherished one.
Azize.

Azora The daughter of the Aztec king Montezuma.

Azra Arabic: virginal.

Azucena Spanish from Arabic: a lily.
Asucena, Asusena, Asuzena, Azusena, Azuzena.

Azura Old French: from the Persian for blue sky.
Azure, Azuria, Azzura, Azzure.

B

Babara Hungarian form of Barbara.

Babette *See* Barbara.

Bai Chinese: pure or white.

Baibre/Bairbre Irish Gaelic forms of Barbara.

Bailey Old French: a bailiff or administrative official. Also a boy's name.
Bailea, Bailee, Baileigh, Bailen, Bailie, Baillee, Bailley, Baillie, Bailly, Baily, Baylee, Baylen, Bayley, Bayly.

Baku The capital of the republic of Azerbaijan, on the Caspian Sea.

Bala Sanskrit: a young girl.

Bali An Indonesian island.

Bambalina Italian: a little girl.
Bambi.

Baptista Latin: the baptised one.
Baptiste (French), Batista (Italian), Bautista (Spanish).

Barbara From Latin: the foreigner or stranger.
Babara (Hungarian), Babette, Babita, Baibre (Irish Gaelic), Bairbre (Irish Gaelic), Barabal (Scottish Gaelic), Barba (Spanish), Barbary, Barbe (French), Bärbel, Barbera, Barbetta, Barbette, Barbica (Slavic), Barbora (Czech), Barbra, Barbro (Swedish), Varvara (Russian).
Diminutives: Babs, Barb, Barbi, Barbie, Basia (Polish), Biba.

Bärbel German form of Barbara.

Barbica *See* Barbara.

Bardot The surname of a legendary

French actress (Brigitte Bardot).
Bardeau, Bardeaux, Bardo, Bardoe,
Bardow, Bardowe.

Barika Swahili: successful.

Barney *See* BOYS.

Basia Polish diminutive of Barbara.

Basilia Greek: queenly, regal. The
feminine form of Basil.
Basile, Basilla.

Basimah Arabic: the smiling one.
Basima, Basma.

Bathilde Teutonic: the commanding
maiden of war.
Bathilda, Batilda, Batilde.

Bathsheba Hebrew: the daughter of
the oath, or the seventh daughter.
The wife of King David in the Bible.
Batsheva (Jewish).

Batyah Modern Hebrew: the daughter
of God.
Batya.

Baylee/Bayley/Bayly *See* Bailey.

Bearnas *See* Berenice.

Beata Latin: blessed. *See also* Beatrice.

Beatrice Latin: the blessed one.
Beatrix was a 4th-century saint.
Beata, Beatrisa, Beatrix (German),
Beatriz (Spanish), Beitris (Scottish
Gaelic), Betrys (Welsh), Bicetta
(Italian), Peata (Maori).
Diminutives: Bea, Bee, Bice, Trix,
Trixi, Trixie, Trixy.

Beau French: beautiful.
Beaux, Bo.

Beauty One who is a delight to
behold.
Beauté (French).

Bec *See* Bic. Also a diminutive of
Rebecca.

Becca/Becci/Beckie/Becky
Diminutives of Rebecca.

Beda Old English: a warrior maiden.

Bedelia Old English: strength.

Begonia A 'flower name'.

Behira Hebrew: the brilliant one.

Beila Yiddish form of Belle.

Beitris Scottish form of Beatrice.

Bek/Bekki Diminutives of Rebecca.

Bel/Bela *See* Belle and Isabel.

Belda French: a beautiful lady.

Belina French: a goddess.
Beline.

Belinda Italian: beautiful.
Belindah, Bellinda, Bellynda,
Belynda, Bilinda, Billinda, Billynda.
Diminutives: Bella, Belle, Linda,
Lindy.

Belita Spanish: the beautiful one.

Belize Spanish: a Central American
country.

Bella/Bellana *See* Belinda, Belle and
Isabel.

Belle French: beautiful. Also a
diminutive of Annabel, Arabella,
Belinda, Isabel and Isabella.
Beila (Yiddish), Bel, Bela, Belah,
Bell, Bella, Bellah, Bellana, Bellina,
Bello (Italian), Bellino (Italian),
Bellva, Bellve, Belva, Belvia.

Bellona Latin: after the Roman
goddess of war.
Belloma.

Bellva/Bellve *See* Belle.

Bellynda/Belynda *See* Belinda.

Beltane Celtic: an ancient festival,
held on 1 May, which celebrated the
beginning of summer. Suitable for a

Taurus child.

Belva/Belvia *See* Belle.

Bena Hebrew: the wise one.

Benazir Arabic: unique.
Benazeer.

Benedicta Latin: blessed. The feminine form of Benedict.
Benedetta (Italian), Benedikta (Dutch, German), Benedikte (Danish), Benicia (Spanish), Benita (Italian), Benite (Spanish), Benoite (French).

Benicia Spanish form of Benedicta.

Benilda Latin: benign; of good intentions.

Benita/Benite/Benoite *See* Benedicta.

Berdine Teutonic: a glorious maiden.

Berenice Greek: the bringer of victory. *See also* Veronica.
Bearnas (Scottish Gaelic), Bernice, Bernyce, Berrice.
Diminutives: Berni, Bernie, Berny, Berri, Berrie, Berry.

Beril/Berle *See* Beryl.

Berit Scandinavian form of Bridget.

Berlewen Cornish: Venus, the morning star.

Berlina Either a variation of Beryl, or after the German city of Berlin.

Bernadette French from Teutonic: as brave as a bear. The feminine form of Bernard.
Berna, Bernadene, Bernadina, Bernadine, Bernarda, Bernardetta (Italian), Bernardette, Berneen (Irish), Bernetta, Bernita.
Diminutives: Bern, Bernie, Berrie, Berry.

Bernia Old English: a maiden of battle.

Bernice/Bernyce *See* Berenice.

Bernina A peak in the Swiss Alps.

Bernita *See* Bernadette.

Berrice *See* Berenice.

Berry Old English: a fruit or berry. Also a diminutive of Berenice and Bernadette.
Berri, Berrie.

Berta/Berte *See* Alberta, Bertha and Gilberta.

Bertha Teutonic: bright and shining. *See also* Roberta.
Berta (German, Polish), Berte, Berthe (French), Bertia, Bertina, Bertine.
Diminutives: Bertie, Berty.

Berthilda Old English: a shining warrior maid.
Berthilde, Bertilda, Bertilde, Bertilla.

Bertia/Bertina/Bertine *See* Bertha.

Berwyn Welsh: fair-haired, or a bright friend.
Berwin, Berwinn, Berwinne, Berwynn, Berwynne.

Beryan Cornish: the name of a saint.

Beryl Greek: a precious green jewel.
Beril, Berle, Beryle.

Bess/Bessie/Bessy *See* Elizabeth.

Beth A diminutive of Elizabeth and names beginning with Beth.

Bethan Welsh diminutive of Elizabeth.
Diminutive: Beth.

Bethany Hebrew: a house of poverty. A placename from the New Testament.
Bethanie, Bethannie, Bethanny, Betheny, Bethenny.
Diminutive: Beth.

POPULAR MAORI NAMES

Girls

Ahorangi	Ata Marama	Hinengaro	Kura
Ahurewa	Atarangi	Hokaka	Mahia
Aihe	Awatea	Hoki	Mahuika
Airini	Awhina	Humarie	Makareta
Amiria	Erihapeti	Hurihia	Maku
Anahera	Haeata	Iriaka	Mana
Anihera	Hahana	Iwi	Manawa
Aniwaniwa	Hana	Kahu	Marama
Arataki	Harikoa	Kaku	Marika
Areta	Hauku	Karewa	Ngaio
Aroha	Hikitia	Keri	Ngaire
Arorangi	Hikurangi	Kowhai	Reka
Ataahua	Hine	Kuku	Tui

Boys

Ahi	Maaka	Petera	Taiaha
Amokura	Manaia	Pita	Takawai
Hahona	Manu	Puke	Tamati
Hemi	Marama	Rakaunui	Tane
Henare	Matai	Rangi	Tangaroa
Hone	Maunga	Rata	Tangohia
Huatare	Murihiku	Rawiri	Tipene
Ihi	Ngawari	Rewi	Uenuku
Irirangi	Nui	Riki	Waiariki
Kahurangi	Nukuhia	Rongo	Waihanga
Kapua	Omaka	Ropata	Whatitiri
Kukuwai	Onepu	Rua	Whero

Bethel Hebrew: the house of God. Bethell, Bethelle. *Diminutive*: Beth.

Bethesda Hebrew: a house of mercy. A place mentioned in the Bible.

Bethia Hebrew: the daughter of God.

Beti A Welsh diminutive of Elizabeth.

Betrys Welsh form of Beatrice.

Betsey/Betsy Diminutives of Elizabeth.

Bette/Bettie/Betty/Bettye *See* Elizabeth.

Bettina *See* Elizabeth. *Diminutive*: Tina.

Betula Hebrew: a maiden.

Beulah Hebrew: the married one. A biblical placename.
Beula.

Beverley Old English: from the stream of the beaver.
Beverlee, Beverlie, Beverly.
Diminutive: Bev.

Bevin Irish Gaelic: sweet-voiced, melodious.

Beyoncé The name of a popular American singer and actress.

Bian Vietnamese: secretive, or hidden.

Bianca Italian form of Blanche. Used by Shakespeare for characters in two of his plays. *See also* Blondelle.
Biancah, Bianka, Biankah.

Biba A diminutive of Barbara.

Bibi Arabic: a lady.

Bic Chinese: green, like jade.
Bec.

Bice *See* Beatrice.

Bicetta Italian form of Beatrice.

Biddy Irish diminutive of Bridget.
Biddie.

Bijou French: a jewel.
Bijoux.

Bilinda/Billinda/Billynda *See* Belinda.

Billie Teutonic: a wise ruler or protector. Feminine form of Billy and William, and also a diminutive of Wilhelmina.
Billee, Billi, Billy, Billye.

Bina Hebrew: intelligence, understanding. Also a diminutive of Albina and Sabina.

Bindi From an Aboriginal word, meaning a plant with burrs.
Bindea, Bindee, Bindey, Bindie, Bindy.

Binnie Celtic: a wicker basket.
Binney, Binni, Binny.

Birdie American/Modern English: a little bird.

Birgit/Birgitta/Birgitte/Birkita *See* Bridget.

Björk Icelandic: a birch tree.
Byerk.

Blaike *See* Blake.

Blaine Irish Gaelic: thin, slender.
Blain, Blane, Blayne.

Blair Scottish Gaelic: from the plain. Also a boy's name.
Blaire, Blayr, Blayre.

Blaise Latin: she who stammers.
Blaize, Blasia, Blayze, Blaze.

Blake Old English: pale or fair-haired.
Blaike, Blayke.

Blanche Old French: fair-haired, or of a fair complexion. *See also* Bianca and Blondelle.
Bianca (Italian), Blanca (Spanish), Blanch, Blanchard, Blancharde, Blanka (Czech, Polish), Blinnie (Irish).

Blane/Blayne *See* Blaine.

Blanka *See* Blanche.

Blayke *See* Blake.

Blayr/Blayre *See* Blair.

Blaze Old English: a bright fire or flame. Also a form of Blaise.
Blaize, Blayz, Blayze.

Blenn Welsh: a hill.
Blen, Blenne.

Blessing Middle English: one who brings happiness.

Bless, Blesse.

Bleu French form of Blue.

Blinnie Irish form of Blanche.

Bliss Old English: joy, gladness.
Blisse, Blyss, Blysse.

Blith/Blithe *See* Blythe.

Blodwen Welsh: a white flower or blessed flower.
Blodwyn.

Blondelle French: the little blond or fair one. *See also* Bianca and Blanche.
Diminutive: Blondie.

Blossom Old English: a flower or bloom.

Blue A modern 'colour name'.
Bleu (French), Blu.

Bluebell An unusual 'flower name'.

Blyss/Blysse *See* Bliss.

Blythe Old English: joyous and cheerful.
Blith, Blithe, Blyth.

Bo Chinese: precious. *See also* Beau.

Boann Irish Gaelic: a water goddess.
Boanna, Boanne.

Bobbi/Bobbie/Bobby *See* Roberta.

Bodie A modern, generally male, name.
Bodee, Bodey, Bodhi, Bodi, Bowdey, Bowdi, Bowdie.

Bodil Old Norse: a battle maiden.

Bolero Spanish: a lively dance.
Boleroe.

Bona Latin: good.
Bonne (French).

Bonita Spanish: pretty.
Diminutives: Bonni, Bonnie, Bonny, Nita.

Bonne *See* Bona.

Bonnie English/Scottish: fine, pretty.
See also Bonita.
Bonney, Bonni, Bonny.

Boronia A 'plant name'.

Bouquet French: a bunch of flowers.

Bowdey/Bowdi/Bowdie *See* Bodie.

Bozena Slavic: the favoured one.
Bozenah, Bozenka.

Brady Irish Gaelic: from an old surname.
Bradea, Bradee, Bradie, Braydee, Braydie.

Brandice/Brandie *See* Brandy.

Brandy Dutch: brandy, fine wine.
Also a feminine form of Brandon.
Brandea, Brandee, Brandey, Brandi, Brandice, Brandie.

Branwen Welsh: beautiful, or a holy raven.
Brangwen, Brangwyn, Brangwynne.

Braydee/Braydie *See* Brady.

Breanna/Breanne *See* Briana.

Breda A city in the Netherlands. Also an Irish form of Bridget.
Bredah, Breeda, Breedah.

Bree Originally a diminutive of Bridget and Briana.
Bre, Brea, Brei, Brie.

Breeanna/Bree-Anna *See* Briana.

Breeze From Spanish: a light wind, implying someone who is carefree.
Breese, Breez, Breeza, Breezah.

Brenda Irish Gaelic: a raven. Old Norse: a flaming sword.

Brenley Old Norse: burning wood.
Brenlea, Brenlee, Brenleigh, Brenly, Brinleigh, Brinley.

Brenna Irish Gaelic: raven-haired.

Brettelle A feminine form of Brett,

meaning a Breton.
Bretell, Bretella, Bretelle, Brettell, Brettella.

Briallen Welsh: a primrose.

Briana Celtic: noble, honourable. The feminine form of Brian.
Breanna, Breanne, Breeanna, Bree-Anna, Brianna, Brianne, Briarne, Brienna, Brina, Bryana, Bryanna. *Diminutives*: Bree, Bria, Brie.

Briar Middle English: a thorny plant. Briare, Bryar, Bryare, Bryer.

Brice Celtic: the speckled, or freckled, one. Mainly a boy's name.
Bryce.

Bridey/Bridie *See* Bridget.

Bridget Celtic/Irish Gaelic: strong, spirited; an ancient Celtic goddess. St Brigid is one of Ireland's patron saints.
Berit (Scandinavian), Birgit (Scandinavian), Birgitta (Scandinavian), Birgitte (Scandinavian), Birkita (Basque), Breda (Irish), Bríd (Irish Gaelic), Bridged, Bridgenia, Bridgid, Brigett, Brigette, Brighid (Irish Gaelic), Brigid (Irish), Brigida (Italian, Spanish), Brigidine, Brigit, Brigitta (Scandinavian), Brigitte (French, German), Brita, Britt (Swedish), Brygida (Polish), Piritta (Estonian, Finnish).
Diminutives: Biddie, Biddy, Bree, Bridey (Irish), Bridgie, Bridie (Irish), Brie, Briege (Irish Gaelic), Brydie.

Brie *See* Bree, Briana and Bridget.

Brienna *See* Briana.

Brigette/Brigid/Brigida/Brigitte *See* Bridget.

Brihoney *See* Bryony.

Brina Hebrew: the seventh. *See also* Briana and Bryna.

Brinleigh/Brinley *See* Brenley.

Brionee/Briony *See* Bryony.

Britnee/Britney *See* Brittany.

Britt A Swedish form of Bridget.
Brita, Britta.

Brittany Latin: Britain. The name of a French province.
Britnee, Britney, Britnie, Brittania, Britteny, Brittnee, Brittney, Brittni, Brittnie.

Brodie Irish Gaelic: a ditch.
Brodea, Brodee, Brodey, Brody.

Brona Irish: sorrow.

Bronnen Cornish: a rush.

Brontë English: from the surname of the Brontë sisters, novelists Anne, Charlotte and Emily.
Bronte, Brontee, Brontey, Brontie, Bronty.

Bronwen Welsh: white or fair-breasted.
Bronwenn, Bronwenne, Bronwyn. *Diminutives*: Bron, Bronnie.

Bronya Slavic: armour, protection.

Brook Old English: at the brook or stream.
Brooke.

Brooklyn A New York suburb.
Brooklin, Brooklinn, Brooklinne, Brooklynn, Brooklynne.

Bruella/Bruelle *See* Brunella.

Bruna Teutonic: brown, or dark-haired. The feminine form of Bruno. *See also* Brunella.
Brunah, Brunetta (French), Burnetta.

Brunella Italian/Teutonic: brown-

haired. *See also* Bruna.
Bruella, Bruelle, Brunelle, Brunilla.

Brunhilde Teutonic: an armed warrior maiden. A warrior queen in Germanic legend.
Brunhild, Brunhilda, Brynhild.

Bryana/Bryanna *See* Briana.

Bryar/Bryare/Bryer *See* Briar.

Bryce *See* Brice.

Brydie/Brygida *See* Bridget.

Bryher Celtic: one of the Isles of Scilly, off the coast of Cornwall.

Brylie Possibly a combination of Bryony and Lee, or a variation of Rylie.
Brylea, Brylee, Bryleigh, Bryley.

Bryluen Cornish: a rose.

Bryn Welsh: a hill. Also a boy's name.
Brynn, Brynne.

Bryna Irish: strength.
Brina.

Bryony Greek: a vine-like plant.
Brihoney, Brionee, Brioney, Brionie, Briony, Bryonee, Bryonie.

Buena Spanish: good.
Bueno, Buona.

Buffy Native American: a buffalo. Also a diminutive of Elizabeth.

Bunny English: a little rabbit.
Bunnie.

Bunty Originally a pet name, perhaps meaning a lamb.
Buntee, Buntie.

Buona *See* Buena.

Burnetta *See* Bruna.

Buttercup A 'flower name'.

Butterfly Old English: a brightly coloured insect.

C

Cacelie *See* Cecilia.

Caddie/Caddy *See* Cadence.

Cadence Latin: rhythmic.
Cadena, Cadenza (Italian), Kadence. *Diminutives*: Caddie, Caddy.

Cadi Welsh form of Catherine.

Cailee/Caileigh/Cailey *See* Caley.

Cailin *See* Caillin and Colleen.

Caillin Welsh: the peacemaker.
Cailin, Cailinn, Caillyn, Cailyn.

Cairine *See* Catherine.

Cairistìona Scottish Gaelic form of Christina.

Cairo From Arabic: the capital of Egypt. Also a boy's name.

Cait/Caite *See* Kate.

Caitlin Irish Gaelic form of Catherine. *See also* Kathleen.
Caitlan, Caitlyn, Caitlynn, Catelyn, Kaitlin, Kaitlinn, Kaitlyn, Katelin, Katelyn, Kate-Lynn, Katelynn, Katelynne.

Caitrin Irish Gaelic form of Catherine.

Caja Cornish: a daisy.
Caya, Cayah, Kaia, Kaiah, Kaiya, Kaja, Kaya, Kayaa, Kya, Kyah, Kyha.

Calais A French seaport.

Calandra Greek: a lark.
Calandre (French), Calandria (Spanish), Kalandra.

Calantha Greek: a beautiful blossom.
Calanthe (French), Kalantha.

Caleda *See* Calida.

Caledonia Latin: a woman from

Scotland.
Caledonie.

Caley Irish Gaelic: slender. Also a
boy's name. *See also* Kayley.
Cailee, Caileigh, Cailey, Cailie,
Calee, Calie, Caylee, Cayley, Caylie.

Calico A cotton fabric.
Calicoh, Caliko, Calikoh, Callico.

Calida Latin: warm and loving.
Caleda, Callida.

Calista Greek: the most beautiful
one.
Caliste, Callista, Calliste, Kalista,
Kallista.

Calla Greek: beautiful.

Callia *See* Calliope.

Callidora Greek: the gift of beauty.

Calliope Greek: a beautiful voice. The
muse of poetry in Greek mythology.
Callia, Calliopi, Kalliope (Greek).

Callista/Calliste *See* Calista.

Callisto Greek: a mythological
nymph.

Callula Latin: the beautiful little one.

Caloris Greek: a geographical feature
of the planet Mercury.

Calypso Greek: a legendary sea
nymph. Also a West Indian style of
music.
Kalypso.

Cam Vietnamese: sweet.

Cambelle A feminine form of
Campell, meaning a crooked mouth.
Cambell, Campbelle.

Cambria Latin: an ancient name for
Wales.

Camella *See* Camilla.

Camellia A 'flower name'.
Camelia.

Cameo Italian: an engraved gem.

Cameron Scottish Gaelic: a crooked
nose.
Camren, Camron, Camryn,
Kameron, Kamryn.
Diminutives: Cam, Camm, Cammie,
Kam.

Camilla Latin: from a Roman family
name, possibly meaning noble.
Camella, Camila (Spanish), Camilia,
Camille (French), Kamila (Czech,
Polish).
Diminutives: Milli, Millie, Milly.

Campbelle *See* Cambelle.

Camren/Camryn *See* Cameron.

Canace Greek: the daughter of the
wind.

Canada A 'country name'.

Candace Possibly meaning brilliant
white. The name of several queens
of Ethiopia, and mentioned in the
Bible.
Candice, Candis, Candiss, Candyce,
Candyse, Kandace, Kandice,
Kandyce.
Diminutives: Candi, Candie, Candy,
Kandy.

Candia Greek: an ancient placename.

Candida Latin: white.
Candide (French).
Diminutives: Candi, Candie, Candy.

Candis/Candiss *See* Candace.

Candra Latin: luminescent.

Candy English: the sweet one. Also a
diminutive of Candace and Candida.
Candi, Candie.

Candyce/Candyse *See* Candace.

Canna Latin: a reed. A 'plant name'.

Caoimhe Irish Gaelic: lovely.

Capri An Italian island.

Caprice Italian: unpredictable, whimsical.

Cara Cornish: love. Irish Gaelic: love, or a friend. Italian: the beloved one.
Caragh (Irish Gaelic), Carah, Caralie, Careen, Carina, Carine, Carinna, Carita, Kara, Karah.

Caralyn A combination of Cara and Lynn.

Carden Irish Gaelic: from the black fortress. Also a boy's name.
Cardene, Cardin, Cardine.

Caree *See* Carey.

Careen English: a character in Margaret Mitchell's *Gone With the Wind*. *See also* Cara.

Carel *See* Carol.

Caren/Carin *See* Karen.

Carensa/Carenza *See* Kerensa.

Caressa *See* Caresse and Carissa.

Caresse French: an embrace.
Caress, Caressa, Carezza (Italian).

Carey Celtic: from the river. Cornish: the loved one. Irish: the name of a castle.
Caree, Carie, Cary.

Cari Turkish: flowing like water.

Cariba Probably from Caribbean.
Caribah, Kariba, Karibah.

Caridad/Carita/Caritas *See* Charity.

Carilla *See* Carla and Carol.

Carina The name of a southern constellation. *See also* Cara.
Carinah.

Carine/Carinna *See* Cara.

Carisma *See* Charisma.

Carissa Latin: the most beloved one.
Caressa, Carice, Carisa, Carise, Carisse, Carita, Karisa, Karise.

Carita *See* Cara and Carissa.

Carla A feminine form of Charles, meaning a free man. *See also* Carol, Caroline and Charlotte.
Carilla (Spanish), Carlah, Carlee, Carleen (Irish), Carleigh, Carlene, Carletta, Carlin, Carlita, Karla, Karlah.
Diminutives: Carley, Carlie, Carly, Karly.

Carleen/Carlene *See* Carla and Carlin.

Carleigh/Carley/Carlie/Carly *See* Carla, Caroline and Charlotte.

Carletta *See* Carla.

Carlin Cornish: from the fort by the pool. Irish Gaelic: the little champion. *See also* Carla and Caroline.
Carleen, Carlene, Carlyn.

Carlina/Carline *See* Caroline.

Carlita *See* Carla.

Carlota/Carlotta *See* Charlotte.

Carlyn *See* Carlin.

Carlyon Cornish: from the slate works.
Carleon.

Carma/Carmah *See* Karma.

Carmé Greek: one of Jupiter's satellites.
Karmé.

Carmel Hebrew: a garden or orchard. The name of a mountain in the Bible.
Carmela (Italian), Carmelina (Italian), Carmeline, Carmelita (Spanish), Carmella, Carmen (Spanish), Carmenita, Carmia, Carmiel, Carmina, Carmine,

Carmita, Karmel, Karmen.
Diminutives: Melina, Mell, Melli, Mellie, Melly.

Carmella *See* Carmel.

Carmen/Carmenita *See* Carmel.

Carmia/Carmiel/Carmita *See* Carmel.

Carmine Spanish: crimson. Also a form of Carmel.
Carmena, Carmene, Carmina, Carmyna, Carmyne.

Carna Hebrew: a horn.

Carnation A 'flower name'.

Carnelian A 'gemstone name'.
Cornelian.

Caro Spanish: the dear or beloved one. Also a diminutive of Caroline.

Carol A feminine form of Charles, a free man. *See also* Carla, Caroline and Charlotte.
Carel, Carilla (Spanish), Carola, Carole (French), Carolie, Carroll, Carryl, Caryl, Karel, Karol.

Caroline A feminine form of Charles, a free man. *See also* Carla, Carol and Charlotte.
Carlin (Italian), Carlina (Italian), Carline, Caroleen, Carolin, Carolina (Italian), Carolyn, Carolyne, Charleen, Charlene, Charline, Kararaina (Maori), Karolina (Polish, Scandinavian), Karoline (German), Sharleen, Sharlene.
Diminutives: Carley, Carlie, Carly, Caro, Carrie, Carro, Karrie, Lena, Lina, Lyn, Lynn.

Carolyn *See* Caroline.

Caron From the surname of French 1950s–1960s actress Leslie Caron.
Carone, Caronn, Caronne.

Carrie Originally a diminutive of Caroline.
Carri, Karri, Karrie.

Carro *See* Caroline.

Carrol *See* Carol.

Carryl Welsh: love. *See also* Carol. Caryl.

Carson *See* BOYS.

Carter Old English: a cart maker or driver. More commonly a boy's name.

Cartier A famous French jewellery company.

Cary *See* Carey.

Caryn *See* Karen.

Carys Welsh: the beloved one.
Cerys.

Casey Irish Gaelic: the vigilant one. Also a boy's name.
Casee, Casie, Kasey, Kasie, Kaycee, Kaycie.

Cashmira/Cashmyra *See* Kashmira.

Cass/Cassie *See* Cassandra.

Cassandra Greek: a legendary Trojan princess with the gift of prophecy.
Casandra, Cassandre (French), Kassandra.
Diminutives: Cass, Cassie, Kass, Kassie.

Cassia Hebrew: a tree, a variety of cinnamon. *See also* Kezia.

Cassidy Irish Gaelic: the clever one.
Kassidy.

Cassiel The angel of Saturday.

Casta Latin: pure and modest.

Castalia Greek: a mythological figure.

Caster Old English: a Roman site.

Catalina/Catarina *See* Catherine.

Catalonia A region of Spain.

Cate/Catena/Catey/Cath *See* Catherine and Kate.

Catelyn *See* Caitlin.

Cathay An archaic name for China.

Cathee/Cathie Diminutives of Catherine.

Catherine Greek: pure. A 4th-century saint who was martyred on a wheel. *See also* Caitlin, Katherine and Kathleen.
Cadi (Welsh), Cairine (Gaelic), Caitlin (Irish Gaelic), Caitrin (Irish Gaelic), Catalina (Spanish), Catarina (Portuguese), Caterina (Italian), Catharina, Catharine, Catherina, Catheryn, Catheryne, Cathrine, Cathro, Cathryn, Catrin (Welsh), Catrina, Catriona (Gaelic), Cattarina (Italian), Ekaterina (Russian), Ekaterini (Greek).
Diminutives: Cait (Irish Gaelic), Cate, Catena, Catey, Cath, Cathee, Cathie, Cathy, Catina (Spanish), Cato (Dutch), Caty, Cayt, Cayte, Kate, Kerry, Treena, Trina, Triona.

Cathleen/Cathlene *See* Kathleen.

Cathy A diminutive of Catherine.

Catina/Cato *See* Catherine.

Catrice A modern form of Catherine. Catrece, Katrece, Katrice.

Catrin/Catrina *See* Catherine.

Catriona Gaelic form of Catherine.

Caya *See* Caja.

Caylee/Cayley/Caylie *See* Caley.

Cayt/Cayte Diminutives of Catherine.

Ceara Irish Gaelic: a spear. *See also* Chiara.
Cearah.

Cecilia Latin: the blind one, or the sixth. The feminine form of Cecil and the name of the patron saint of music. *See also* Sheila.
Cacelie (German), Cecelia, Cécile (French), Cecilie, Cecily, Cecilya, Celia, Célie (French), Cicely, Hihiria (Maori), Hiria (Maori), Secilia, Selia, Sheila (Irish), Síle (Irish Gaelic), Sìleas (Scottish Gaelic), Silke (German), Sisilia (Fijian).
Diminutives: Cele, Cissie, Sissey, Sissie, Sissy.

Cecily *See* Cecilia.

Ceilidh Gaelic: a social gathering, involving music and dancing.
Ceili.

Ceinwen Welsh: blessed and fair.

Celandine A 'flower name'.

Celena/Celene/Celina/Celine *See* Selena.

Celeste Latin: heavenly.
Celesta, Celestia, Celestial, Celestina (Italian), Celestine, Celina, Céline (French), Seleste.
Diminutives: Celia, Célie.

Celia/Célie *See* Cecilia and Celeste.

Celina/Céline *See* Celeste.

Cerelia *See* Ceres.

Cerella *See* Ceres and Cyrilla.

Cerena/Cerene *See* Serena.

Cerenitee/Cerenitie/Cerenity *See* Serenity.

Cerentha An unusual name, possibly derived from Ceres.

Ceres Latin: the Roman goddess of corn and tillage.
Cerelia, Cerella.

Ceridwen Welsh: fair poetry.

Ceridwyn, Cerridwen.
Diminutive: Ceri.

Cerise French: cherry red.
Cerrise, Cherise.

Cerys *See* Carys.

Chablis French: a type of white wine.
Chablee, Chabli, Chablie.

Chae/Chay/Chaye *See* Shay.

Chaelen *See* Shaylen.

Chai Hindi: tea.
Chae, Chi, Chih.

Chakra Sanskrit: a wheel. A centre of spiritual power in the body.

Chamba Sherpa/Tibetan: the loved one.

Chamonix A French ski resort.
Chamonee, Chamonie.

Chance *See* BOYS.

Chanda American: possibly a form of Chandra.
Chandah, Chandi, Chandie.

Chandra Sanskrit: the shining moon.

Chanel French: a famous perfume and fashion label.
Chanell, Chanelle, Chenelle, Chennelle, Shanel, Shanell, Shanelle, Shannele, Shannelle.

Chantal French: a stone or boulder. The name has come to mean a little singer.
Chantale, Chantalle, Chantel, Chantelle, Shantal, Shantel, Shantelle.

Chanté From the French word chanter, meaning to sing.
Chantae, Chantay, Shantae, Shantay.

Chara *See* Charis.

Chardonnay French: a type of white wine.
Chardonae, Chardonaie, Chardonay, Chardonnae, Chardonnaie.

Charis Greek: the graceful one.
Chara, Charissa, Charisse.

Charisma Greek: a gift, or healing power. The personification of grace and beauty in Greek mythology.
Carisma, Charis.

Charity Latin: loving and benevolent. One of the three Graces in Greek mythology.
Caridad (Spanish), Carita (Italian), Caritas, Charita, Karita (Scandinavian).
Diminutives: Cherrie, Cherry.

Charleen/Charlene/Charline *See* Caroline.

Charlie A diminutive of Charlotte. *See also* Sharlie.
Charla, Charlah, Charlee, Charleigh, Charley, Charli, Charlise, Charlize, Charly, Charlyse, Charlyze, Tcharli, Tcharlie.

Charlotte A feminine form of Charles, a free man. *See also* Carla, Carol, Caroline and Charlie.
Carlota (Spanish), Carlotta (Italian), Charlot, Charlott, Charlotta, Harata (Maori), Karlotte (German), Sharlot, Sharlott, Sharlotte.
Diminutives: Carleigh, Carley, Carlie, Carly, Charlie, Lotta, Lottie, Lotty, Tottie, Totty.

Charmaine Greek: delightful.
Charmain, Charman, Charmayne, Charmian, Charmion, Sharmaine, Sharman.

Charmian/Charmion *See* Charmaine.

Charnee/Charney *See* Sharney.

Charona/Cherona *See* Sharona.

Chase *See* BOYS.

Chastity Latin: pure and chaste.

Chava Hebrew form of Eve.

Chavaun/Chavaune *See* Siobhán.

Chavi Gypsy: a young girl.
Chavie.

Chayanna/Chayanne *See* Cheyenne.

Chayelen/Chaylen *See* Shaylen.

Cheetah Hindi: an 'animal name'.

Chelle *See* Michelle.

Chelsea A fashionable London
suburb.
Chelse, Chelsee, Chelsey, Chelsi,
Chelsie, Chelsy, Cheltzee, Cheltzi,
Cheltzie.

Chen Chinese: the dawn.

Chenelle/Chennelle *See* Chanel.

Chenoa Native American: a white
dove.

Cher French: the beloved one.
Chere, Cherelle, Cherene, Cheri,
Cherida, Cherie, Cherise, Cherrel,
Cherri, Cherrie, Cherry, Cheryl,
Cheryth, Sher, Sheree, Sherri,
Sherrie, Sherry, Sheryl.

Cherilyn From Cher or Cheryl and
Lynn.

Cherise *See* Cerise and Cher.

Cherish Old French: the treasured
one.

Cherrel/Cheryl *See* Cher.

Cherry *See* Charity and Cher. Also a
'fruit name'.
Cherri, Cherrie, Cherye.

Chesna Slavic: peaceful.
Chezna.

Chevonne *See* Siobhán.

Cheyenne A Native American tribe

and a city in the USA.
Chayanna, Chayanne, Cheyan,
Cheyanne.

Cheylen *See* Shaylen.

Chi/Chih *See* Chai.

Chiara Italian form of Clare.
Ceara, Cearah, Ciara, Ciarah, Ciarra,
Kiara, Kiarah, Kiarra.

Chic French: attractive and stylish.
Chique.

Chiffon French: a sheer fabric,
implying delicacy.

Chika Japanese: near.

Chimena/Chimene *See* Ximena.

China A 'country name'.
Chinah, Chyna, Chynah.

Ching *See* Qing.

Chique *See* Chic.

Chiquita Spanish: the little one.

Chirsty *See* Kirstie.

Chizu Japanese: a thousand storks. A
name that implies longevity.

Chloe Greek: a fertile young maiden.
A New Testament name.
Chloee, Cloe, Cloee, Cloey, Clohee,
Khloe, Khloee, Kloee, Klohe,
Klohee.

Chloris Greek: green; a plant lover.
Cloris.

Cho Japanese: a butterfly. Korean:
beautiful.

Choden Sherpa/Tibetan: the devout
one.

Chora *See* Cora.

Chow Chinese: summer.

Chris/Chrissie *See* Christina.

Chrissanth/Christanta *See*
Chrysantha.

Christabel English: a beautiful Christian. From Christina and Belle. Christabell, Christabella, Christabelle, Christobella, Christobelle, Cristabel, Kristabel, Kristabella, Kristabelle.

Christal/Christel/Christelle *See* Christina and Crystal.

Christie/Christy Diminutives of Christina.

Christina Latin: a follower of Christ, a Christian. *See also* Kirsten and Kirstie.
Cairistìona (Scottish Gaelic), Christa, Christal, Christan, Christel, Christelle (French), Christen, Christiana, Christiane, Christianna, Christine, Christyna, Cristin, Cristina (Italian, Portuguese), Cristine, Crístíona (Irish Gaelic), Cristyna, Kerstin (Swedish), Kirsten (Scandinavian), Kirstin, Kirsty, Kirstyn, Kristeen, Kristel (German), Kristen (Danish), Kristene, Kristie, Kristina (Swedish), Kristine, Kristy, Krystyna (Polish).
Diminutives: Chris, Chrissi, Chrissie, Chrissy, Christie, Christy, Crissie, Crissy, Kirstie (Scottish), Kirsty (Scottish), Kris, Stina, Tina.

Christmas Old English: born at Christmas time.

Christobelle *See* Christabel.

Chrysantha Greek: a golden flower. Chrissanth, Christanta, Chrysanthe.

Chrysilla Greek: golden-haired.

Chrystal *See* Crystal.

Chu Chinese: a pearl. Native American: a rattlesnake.

Chun Chinese: spring.

Chyna *See* China.

Ciana/Ciarna *See* Kiana.

Ciara *See* Chiara and Kiera.

Cicely *See* Cecilia.

Cidney *See* Sidney.

Ciel French: the sky. Ciele, Ciell, Ciella, Cielle.

Cilla A diminutive of Priscilla.

Cincelia A modern name, probably from Cynthia and Celia.

Cinderella French: a maiden of the cinders or ashes.
Diminutives: Cindi, Cindie, Cindy.

Cindy A diminutive of Cinderella, Cynthia and Lucinda (*see* Lucy). Cindee, Cindi, Cindie, Sindy.

Cindylou From Cindy and Louise.

Cinnabar Greek: red. A 'colour name' and also the name of a mineral.

Cinnamon Hebrew: a 'spice name'.

Cintia/Cinzia *See* Cynthia.

Cirilla/Cirille *See* Cyrilla.

Cissie *See* Cecilia.

Citrine Middle English: a pale-yellow gem, a form of quartz.

Claerwen A Welsh placename. Claerwenn, Claerwenne, Claerwyn, Claerwynn, Claerwynne.

Clair/Claire/Clairice *See* Clare and Clarice.

Clancy *See* BOYS.

Clara *See* Clare.

Clarabelle French: bright and beautiful. From Clara and Belle. Clarabella, Claribel.

Clare Latin: bright and famous. The name of an Irish county. *See also* Chiara, Clarice and Clarity.

Chiara (Italian), Clair, Claire (French), Clara, Clareen, Clarenza, Claresta, Clareta, Claretta, Clarette, Clarina, Clarinda, Clarine, Clarista, Clarita (Spanish), Clarona, Klara (German, Scandinavian, Slavic).
Diminutive: Clarrie.

Clarey A modern form of Clare. Clairee, Clairey, Clairy, Clary.

Clarice French from Latin: the little brilliant one. *See also* Clare and Clarity.
Clairece, Clairice, Clarisa (Spanish), Clariss, Clarissa, Clarisse, Clerissa, Klarice, Klarissa (German), Klarisse.
Diminutive: Clarrie.

Clarinda/Clarine *See* Clare and Clorinda.

Clarista/Clarita/Clarona *See* Clare and Clarity.

Clarity From Latin: clearness. *See also* Clare and Clarice.
Clarita (Spanish), Claritas, Claritee, Claritie.

Clarrie *See* Clare and Clarice.

Claude/Claudette *See* Claudia, and Claude in BOYS.

Claudia Latin: the lame one. The feminine form of Claude.
Claude (French), Claudetta, Claudette (French), Claudina, Claudine (French), Klaudia (Polish).
Diminutives: Claud, Claude, Claudie.

Clea/Cleapatra *See* Cleopatra.

Clematis Greek: a climbing plant. A 'flower name'.

Clemence Latin: mild, merciful.
Clemenica, Clemency, Clementia, Clementina (Spanish), Clementine,

Clemenza (Polish), Klementyna (Polish).
Diminutives: Clem, Clemmie.

Clementina/Clementine/Clemenza *See* Clemence.

Cleo/Cleotha *See* Cleopatra and Clio.

Cleopatra Greek: glory of the father. The queen of Egypt from 47–30 BC. Cleapatra, Cleotha, Cliopatra, Kleopatra, Kliopatra.
Diminutives: Clea, Cleo, Clio, Kleo, Klio.

Clerissa *See* Clarice.

Cliantha Greek: a glorious flower. Cleantha, Cleanthe, Clianthe.

Clio Greek: the glorious one; the muse of history in Greek mythology. *See also* Cleopatra.
Cleo.

Cliva Old English: from the cliff. Feminine form of Clive.
Cleva.

Clodagh Irish: the name of a river. Cloda, Clodah.

Cloe/Cloee/Cloey/Clohee *See* Chloe.

Clorinda Persian: of renowned beauty.
Clarinda, Clorina.

Cloris *See* Chloris.

Clotilda Teutonic: a famous battle maiden.
Clothilda, Clothilde (French), Clotilde.

Clova Middle English from Latin: from clove, a spice.
Clovah, Clove.

Clover Old English: a 'flower name'.

Clymene Greek: renowned.

Coco The first name of the famous

fashion designer Chanel.
Koko.

Cody Old English: a pillow or cushion. Also a boy's name.
Codey, Codi, Kodi, Kodie, Kody.

Coleen/Colene *See* Colleen.

Colenso Cornish: from the dark pool.

Colette/Colletta/Collette *See* Nicola.

Colleen Irish Gaelic: a girl.
Cailin (Gaelic), Coleen, Colene, Coline, Collene, Colline, Collyne.

Colombia A South American country.

Columba Latin: dove-like.
Colombe (French), Columbia, Columbina, Columbine.

Columbine A 'flower name'. *See also* Columba.
Columbina.

Comfort A Puritan 'characteristic name'.

Concepción Latin: the beginning. A Spanish name that relates to the Virgin Mary's Immaculate Conception.
Concepta, Conception, Concetta (Italian).
Diminutives: Concha, Conchita.

Concha/Conchita *See* Concepción.

Concordia Latin: the harmonious one.

Condoleeza The name of the former US Secretary of State Condoleezza Rice. It is believed to be from a musical term meaning 'with sweetness'.
Condola, Condoleesa, Condolesa, Condoleeza, Condolezza, Condolisa.

Conni/Connie/Conny *See* Constance.

Constance Latin: steadfast, constant.

Constancia, Constancy, Constantia, Constantina, Konstanze (German).
Diminutives: Con, Conni, Connie, Conny.

Consuela Latin: the comforter. Generally a Spanish name.
Consolata (Italian), Consuelo.
Diminutive: Suela.

Content A Puritan 'characteristic name'.

Cora Greek: a maiden.
Chora, Corella, Coretta, Corette, Corina, Corinna, Corinne, Corissa, Corisse, Correna, Corrine, Corynna, Korinne.

Corabelle A combination of Cora and Belle, meaning a beautiful maiden.
Corabell, Corabella.

Coral Latin: from the sea.
Corale, Coralie, Coralina, Coraline.

Corazón Spanish: the heart. Often used in the Philippines.

Cordelia Celtic: a jewel of the sea. A character in Shakespeare's *King Lear*.
Cordélie (French), Cordella, Kordelia.
Diminutive: Delia.

Corella/Coretta *See* Cora.

Corey Celtic/Gaelic: a dweller in the hollow.
Coree, Cori, Corie, Correy, Corry, Cory, Koree, Korey, Kori, Korie.

Corin *See* BOYS.

Corina/Corinna/Corinne/Corrine *See* Cora.

Corissa/Corisse *See* Cora.

Corky Generally a nickname.
Corkee, Corkey, Corki, Corkie.

Corlette A Manx Gaelic surname,

possibly meaning of Thor's peple.
Corlet, Corlett.

Corliss Old English: the cheerful one.
Corlissa.

Cornelia Latin: a horn. The feminine
form of Cornelius.
Cornela, Cornelie, Cornelietta
(Dutch), Cornelle, Kornelia.
Diminutive: Nelia.

Corona Latin: a crown.

Correy/Cory *See* Corey.

Corsica A Mediterranean island.

Corynna *See* Cora.

Cosette French: of the victorious
army.
Cosetta, Cozette.

Cosima Greek: harmony, perfect
order.

Cotton Middle English: a type of
fabric. Also a boy's name.
Coton.

Courtney Old French: probably
meaning the short-nosed one.
Originally a boy's name.
Courtenay, Courteney, Courtnay,
Courtnee, Courtnie, Kourtnee,
Kourtney, Kourtnie.

Cozette *See* Cosette.

Cressida Greek: the golden one. A
Shakespearean character.
Cressa.

Crida Irish Gaelic: the name of a
saint.

Crisiant Welsh: like a crystal.

Crispina Latin: the curly-haired one.
Feminine form of Crispin.
Crispine.

Cristabel *See* Christabel.

Cristal *See* Crystal.

Cristin/Cristina/Cristine/Crístíona
See Christina.

Crocus Latin: a 'plant name'.

Crystal Greek: as clear as ice. A
'gemstone name'.
Christal, Christel, Christelle
(French), Chrystal, Cristal, Kristal,
Krystal, Krystle.

Csarina/Csarine *See* Tsarina.

Culley Gaelic: from the forest. Also a
boy's name.
Cullee, Culli, Cullie, Cully.

Cumbria An English county.

Curtis Old French: one who is
courteous. Generally a boy's name.
Curtiss, Curtys, Kurtis, Kurtiss,
Kurtys.

Cushla Irish Gaelic: the beat of my
heart.
Cushlah, Quishla, Quishlah.

Cyan Greek: a dark-blue colour.
Cyane, Cyanne.

Cybele/Cybil/Cybill/Cybilla *See*
Sybil.

Cydney *See* Sidney.

Cygnet Middle English: a young
swan.
Cygnett, Cygnette, Cygni, Cygnie.

Cynara Greek: an artichoke or thistle.

Cynthia Greek: of the moon. An
alternative name for the Greek moon
goddess, Artemis.
Cintia (Portuguese), Cinzia (Italian),
Cynthie.
Diminutives: Cindi, Cindie, Cindy,
Cyn.

Cypriana Greek: a woman from
Cyprus.
Cipriana, Cypra, Cyprienne, Cypris.

Cyra Persian: like the sun.

Cyrena Greek: a woman from
Cyrene, an ancient Greek colony in
North Africa.
Cyrene, Cyrenia, Kyrena, Kyrenia.

Cyreta American: possibly the
feminine form of Cyrus.
Cyreeta, Syreeta, Syreta.

Cyrilla Greek: lordly or the proud
one. Feminine form of Cyril.
Cerella, Cirilla, Cirille, Cyria, Cyrille
(French).

Czarina/Czarine *See* Tsarina.

D

Dacey Gaelic: the southerner. Also a
boy's name.
Dacee, Dacie, Dacy, Daycie.

Dacia Greek: a woman from Dacia,
an ancient European country.

Dae Korean: greatness.

Dael *See* Dale.

Daffodil From Greek: the asphodel.
A 'flower name'.

Dafne *See* Daphne.

Dagmar Old Norse: a maiden of the
day.

Dagna Old Norse: a new day.
Dagny.

Dahlia A flower, named after the
Swedish botanist Dahl.
Dahla, Dalia (Arabic), Dalya.

Dai Japanese: great.

Dail/Daile *See* Dale.

Daila Latvian: beautiful.

Daina *See* Dana.

Dairine Irish Gaelic: fruitful.

Daireen, Dairne.

Daisy Old English: the day's eye; a
'flower name'. Also a diminutive of
Margaret.
Daisee, Daisi, Daisie, Daizee, Daizi,
Daizie, Daizy, Daysee, Daysi, Daysie,
Daysy.

Dakota Native American: a friend.
Also a boy's name.
Dakotah.

Dalas *See* Dallas.

Dale Old English/Teutonic: a valley
dweller. Also a boy's name.
Dael, Dail, Daile, Dayle.

Daley *See* BOYS.

Dali After the famous Spanish artist
Salvador Dali.
Dalee, Dalie, Dallie, Dalley, Dally.

Dalia/Dalya *See* Dahlia.

Dalila Swahili: gentle. *See also*
Delilah.

Dalla Icelandic: luminous.

Dallas Celtic: skilled, or from the
field of water. A city in Texas and
also a boy's name.
Dalas, Dalice, Dallis, Dalys.

Damaris Greek: gentle. A New
Testament name.
Damara.

Damiana Greek: tame, domesticated.
The feminine form of Damian or
Damon.
Damiane.

Damika A modern, probably made-
up, name.
Damikah, Dammika, Dammikah.

Damita Spanish: the little noble lady.

Damosel Old English: a damsel, or
young unmarried woman.
Damsel, Damzel.

Dana Czech: God is my judge. Old English: from Denmark.
Daina, Danah, Danuta (Polish), Dayna.

Danaë Greek: the mother of Perseus in Greek mythology.

Dance Middle English: an unusual 'noun name'.
Danse.

Danee *See* Danni.

Danetta/Danette *See* Danielle.

Dani *See* Danielle and Danni.

Danielle Hebrew: God is my judge; the feminine form of Daniel. *See also* Danni.
Danell, Danella, Danelle, Danetta, Danette (French), Daniela (Czech, Polish), Daniele, Daniella, Danila, Danneal, Dannealle, Danniel, Dannielle, Danya.
Diminutives: Dani, Danni, Danny.

Danika Slavic: the morning star.
Danica.

Danila/Dannielle *See* Danielle.

D'Ann *See* Diana.

Danni Originally a diminutive of Danielle.
Danee, Dani, Dania, Danie, Danii, Dannee, Dannie, Danny, Dany.

Danu Gaelic: the goddess of fruitfulness.

Danuta Polish: a little deer. *See also* Dana.

Danya *See* Danielle.

Daphne Greek: the laurel. In Greek mythology, a nymph who was transformed into a laurel tree.
Dafne, Daphna, Daphnie, Daphney.

Dara Arabic: a halo. Hebrew: compassion, wisdom.

Darah, Darra.

Darby Irish Gaelic: free from envy. Also a boy's name.
Darbee, Darbi, Darbie, Derby.

Darcy Old French: an old Norman family name.
Darcee, Darcey, Darcia, Darcie, D'Arcy, Darsey, Darsy.

Daria Greek: wealthy. The feminine form of Darius and the name of a saint.
Darea, Dariah, Darian, Darice, Darie, Daris, Darya (Russian).

Darilynn *See* Darlene.

Darlene From Old French: the beloved one. *See also* Darrelle.
Darilynn, Darla, Darleen, Darline.

Darrelle Old French: the beloved one. The feminine form of Darrell. *See also* Darlene.
Darel, Darelle, Daryl, Daryll, Darylle.

Darrene English: a feminine form of Darren.
Daron, Daryn, Daryne.

Darsey/Darsy *See* Darcy.

Darya *See* Daria.

Davida Hebrew: beloved. A feminine form of David. *See also* Davina.
Davita.
Diminutive: Vida.

Davina Hebrew: the beloved one. A feminine form of David. *See also* Davida.
Davene, Davinia, Devina.

Dawa Sherpa/Tibetan: born on a Monday. Also a boy's name.

Dawn English: daybreak, dawn.
Dawna, Dawne.

Dayan *See* Diana.

Daycie *See* Dacey.

Dayle *See* Dale.

Dayna *See* Dana.

Daysee/Daysie/Daysy *See* Daisy.

Deahna/Deana/Deanna/Deanne *See* Dena and Diana.

Deandra *See* Diana.

Deborah Hebrew: a bee, an industrious woman. A biblical name.
Debor, Debora, Debra, Devora (Jewish), Devorah (Jewish), Devore, Tepora (Maori).
Diminutives: Deb, Debbi, Debbie, Debby, Debs.

Debra *See* Deborah.

Dechen Sherpa/Tibetan: health and happiness. Originally a Bhutanese name.
Dichen.

Decima Latin: the tenth.

Dedra *See* Deirdre.

Dee A diminutive of names such as Audrey, Deirdre, Delia and Diana.
Dede, Deedee, Dee Dee, Didi.

Deena *See* Diana.

Deeta *See* Perdita.

Deirdre Celtic: sorrow. A character in Irish legend.
Dedra, Deidhre, Deidra, Deidre, Deirdra, Dierdra, Dierdre.
Diminutives: Dede, Dee, Deedee, Didi.

Dela/Delah *See* Della.

Delaney Gaelic: the challenger's descendant.
Delaina, Delaine, Delainey, Delainy, Delany, Delayne.
Diminutives: Del, Dell, Delle.

Delcine *See* Dulcie.

Delen Cornish: a petal.
Dellen.

Delfina/Delfine *See* Delphine.

Delia Greek: another name for Artemis, the Greek moon goddess. *See also* Cordelia and Della.
Deliah.
Diminutive: Dee.

Delicia Latin: delight.
Delica, Délice (French), Delight, Delise, Delissa, Delite.

Delilah Hebrew: a beautiful temptress. The lover of Samson in the Bible.
Dalila, Delila, D'Lila, D'Lilah.
Diminutives: Lila, Lilah.

Dell/Delle Diminutives of names such as Delaney and Della.

Della Probably from Delia or Delilah and Ella. Also a diminutive of Adelaide and Adèle.
Dela, Delah, Dell, Dellah, Delle.
Diminutives: Del, Dell, Delle.

Delma Spanish: of the sea.
Delmah, Delmar.

Delora/Delores *See* Dolores.

Delphine Latin: a woman from Delphi, or a 'flower name' (from delphinium).
Delfina (Italian, Spanish), Delfine, Delpha, Delphia, Delphina, Delphinia, Delvene, Delvine.

Delta Greek: the fourth, as in fourth child.

Delvene/Delvine *See* Delphine.

Delwyn Welsh: neat and fair.
Delwen.

Delyth Welsh: neat and pretty.

Demelza Cornish: from a placename. The heroine of Winston Graham's

Poldark novels.

Demetria Greek: from Demeter, the goddess of fertility.
Demeter, Demetra, Dimitra, Dimitria.
Diminutive: Demi.

Demi Latin: half. *See also* Demetria.

Dena Old English: from the valley. The feminine form of Dean. Also a diminutive of Adina.
Deana, Deanna.

Deni/Denice *See* Denise.

Denise French from Greek: a lover of wine. A feminine form of Dennis.
Denice, Denisa, Denize, Denyse, Dionyse, Dionyza .
Diminutives: Deni, Dennie, Denny.

Denver *See* BOYS.

Derby *See* Darby.

Derica A feminine form of Derek, ruler of the people.
Dereka, Derrica.

Derry A diminutive of names such as Derryn and Derryth.

Derryn From an old Welsh name.
Derren, Derrin, Deryn.
Diminutive: Derry.

Derryth Welsh: of the oak.
Diminutive: Derry.

Dervla Irish Gaelic: the daughter of the poet.
Dervila.

Derya Hawaiian: the ocean.

Desdemona Greek: ill-fated. A Shakespearean character who was murdered by her husband Othello.
Desmona.
Diminutives: Desda, Desi, Desie.

Desi/Desie Diminutives of names such as Desdemona and Desiree.

Desiree Latin: the desired one.
Deseray, Desiderata, Desideria, Desirata, Desire, Desirée (French), Desirita (Spanish), Desrae, Desray, Desree, Desrey.
Diminutives: Desi, Desie.

Desma Greek: a pledge.

Desta Ethiopian: happiness.

Destiny Old French: fate. A popular name in the USA.
Destina, Destine, Destinee, Destiney, Destinia, Destinie.

Destry The name of a 1950s movie.
Destree, Destrey, Destri, Destrie.

Deva/Devah *See* Devi and Diva.

Devi Sanskrit: godlike, a goddess.
Deva, Devanee, Devee, Devina.

Devika Sanskrit: a little goddess.

Devina *See* Davina and Devi.

Devine *See* Divine.

Devona Old English: from the county of Devon.

Devora/Devorah/Devore *See* Deborah.

Dewi Indonesian: a goddess.
Dewee.

Dexter *See* BOYS.

Dextra Latin: right-handed, dextrous. The feminine form of Dexter.

Dhani Hindi/Nepali: prosperous.

Dharma Hindi: religion, or the religious one. Also a boy's name.

Dhyann *See* Diana.

Dia Spanish: the day.
Diah.

Diamanta French from Latin: adamant, like a diamond.
Diamanda, Diamante, Diamantina, Diamond.

Diana Latin: the divine one. The goddess of hunting and the moon in Roman mythology.
D'Ann, Dayan, Deahna, Deana, Deandra, Deanna, Deanne, Deena, Dhyann, Dhyanne, Diahann, Dian, Diandra, Diane (French), Dianna, Dianne, Dyan, Dyana, Dyane, Dyanna, Dyanne, Riana (Maori).
Diminutives: Dee, Di, Didee.

Diandra/Diane/Dianne *See* Diana.

Dianella A genus of flowering plants.
Dianelle.

Diantha Greek: a divine flower.
Dianthe, Dianthia.

Dichen *See* Dechen.

Didi *See* Dee and Deirdre.

Dido Greek: a queen of Carthage.

Didrika Teutonic: the people's ruler.

Diella Latin: one who worships God.
Diellah, Dielle.

Dierdra/Dierdre *See* Deirdre.

Diki Sherpa/Tibetan: healthy and wealthy.

Dilan/Dillon/Dillyn *See* Dylan.

Dilys Welsh: true, steadfast.

Dimitra/Dimitria *See* Demetria.

Dimity Greek: a thin cotton material.
Dimitee, Dimiti, Dimitie, Dymitee, Dymity.

Dina The angel of wisdom and the law. *See also* Adina and Dinah.
Dinah, Dinara.

Dinah Hebrew: judgement. A biblical name.
Dina, Dyna, Dynah.

Dion *See* Dione, and Dion in BOYS.

Dione Greek: the daughter of heaven. A goddess in Greek mythology.
Dion, Diona, Dioni, Dionna, Dionne.

Dionyse/Dionyza *See* Denise.

Dior French: the golden one. A legendary French fashion and perfume company.
Diora, Diore.

Disa Greek: double. Old Norse: lively.

Dita *See* Edith and Perdita.

Diva Latin: a goddess.
Deva, Devah, Divah.

Divine Middle English: the heavenly one.
Devine.

Dixie French: the tenth. Also a girl from the American south.
Dixee, Dixey, Dixy.

Diza Hebrew: joy.

D'Lila/D'Lilah *See* Delilah.

Dobrila Slavic: kind, good.

Dodie Hebrew: beloved. *See also* Dorothy.
Dodi.

Doina Romanian: a type of folk song.

Dolkar Sherpa/Tibetan: a Buddhist goddess.

Dollie/Dolly *See* Dolores and Dorothy.

Dolma Sherpa/Tibetan: a female deity.

Dolores Spanish: sorrow. From the seven sorrows of the Virgin Mary.
Delora, Delores, Deloris, Dolora, Dolorita, Dolour, Dores (Portuguese).
Diminutives: Dollie, Dolly, Lola, Lolita.

Dominica Latin: belonging to the

Lord. The feminine form of Dominic.
Domenica (Italian), Domeniga,
Domina, Dominga (Spanish),
Domini, Dominica, Dominique
(French).
Diminutive: Dom.

Dominique French form of
Dominica.

Domino Latin. A popular game.

Dona/Donah *See* Donna.

Donalda Scottish Gaelic: the ruler
of the world. The feminine form of
Donald.
Donna, Donella, Donelle, Donia.

Donata Latin: given by God, a gift.
Donatella (Italian), Donetta,
Donette, Donica.

Donella/Donelle *See* Donalda.

Donetta/Donette *See* Donata.

Donia *See* Donalda and Donla.

Donica *See* Donata.

Donla Irish Gaelic: a brown lady.
Donia, Donlah.

Donna Italian: a lady; a short form
of Madonna. *See also* Donalda and
Ladonna.
Dona, Donah, Donnah.

Doone Irish Gaelic: a placename.
Doon.

Dora Greek: a gift. Originally a
short form of Dorothy, Isadora and
Theodora.
Dorah, Doralea, Doreen, Dorelia,
Dorella, Dorelle, Dorena, Dorene,
Doretta, Dorette, Doria, Dorian,
Dorinda, Dorine, Dorita.
Diminutives: Dorey, Dory.

Dorcas Greek: a gazelle or doe. *See
also* Tabitha.

Dorcia.

Doré French: golden. *See also* Dory.
Dore, Dorée.

Doreen *See* Dora.

Dorelia/Dorella/Dorelle *See* Dora.

Dores *See* Dolores.

Dorete/Doretta *See* Dora and Dorothy.

Doria The feminine form of Dorian.
See also Dora and Doris.
Dorian, Doriane.

Dorian *See* Dora and Doria.

Dorigen A character from one of
Chaucer's *Canterbury Tales*.
Dorigan, Dorrigan, Dorrigen.

Dorinda Greek: a beautiful gift. Also
a variation of Dora.

Doris A Greek goddess of the sea.
Doria, Dorice, Dorisa, Dorise, Dorit
(Polynesian), Dorita, Dorris.
Diminutives: Dorri, Dorrie, Dory.

Dorita *See* Dora and Doris.

Dorothy Greek: the gift of God. *See
also* Dora and Theodora.
Dorete (Danish), Doretta, Dorosia
(Polish), Dorota (Czech), Dorotea
(Italian, Spanish), Dorothea (Dutch,
German), Dorothée (French),
Dorothya, Tarati (Maori).
Diminutives: Dodie, Dollie, Dolly,
Dorrie, Dot, Dottie, Thea.

Dory French: the golden-haired one.
See also Dora, Doré and Isadora.
Dorey, Dori, Dorie.

Dot/Dottie *See* Dorothy.

Douce French: gentle, sweet.

Doutzen Dutch: the feminine form
of Douwe, meaning a dove.
Doutzan, Doutze.

Dova Teutonic: peace, a dove.

Dovah, Dove.

Drew A diminutive of Andrew, but occasionally given to girls.
Dru, Drue.

Druella Teutonic: an elfin vision.

Drusilla Latin: from an old Roman family name.
Drucilla.

Duana Irish Gaelic: a little dark maiden.
Duanna, Dwana, Dwanna.

Duena Spanish: a chaperone.
Duenna.

Duessa Celtic: black.

Dulcie Latin: sweet.
Delcine, Dulce, Dulcea, Dulcia, Dulciana, Dulcine, Dulcinea (Spanish), Dulcyna (Polish).

Dulcyna *See* Dulcie.

Dumaka Nigerian: the helper.

Durga Sanskrit: unattainable. A Hindu goddess.

Dusana Czech: a spirit, a soul.

Dusk Old English: twilight.
Duske, Dusky.

Dusty The feminine form of Dustin.
Dustine, Dustyn, Dustyne.

Dwana/Dwanna *See* Duana.

Dyan/Dyana/Dyane *See* Diana.

Dyani Native American: a deer.

Dylan Welsh: from the sea. Generally a boy's name.
Dilan, Dillon, Dillyn, Dilyn, Dyllan, Dyllon.

Dymitee/Dymity *See* Dimity.

Dymphna Irish Gaelic: a fawn.
Dympna.

Dyna Greek: powerful. *See also*

Dinah.
Dynah.

Dysis Greek: the sunset.

Dyta *See* Edith and Perdita.

E

Eadrea *See* Edrea.

Eadwina/Eadwine/Eadwyne *See* Edwina.

Earla/Earlene/Earline *See* Erline.

Eartha Old English: of the earth.
Erda, Erta, Ertha, Herta, Hertha.

Easter Old English: born at Easter time.
Eastre.

Ebanee/Ebanie *See* Ebony.

Ebba Old English: from the rich fortress.

Eberta Teutonic: bright, brilliant.

Ebony Greek: a black wood.
Ebanee, Ebani, Ebanie, Ebany, Ebonee, Eboni, Ebonie.

Ebrel/Ebril Cornish and Welsh forms of April.

Echo Greek: a repeating sound. A nymph in Greek mythology.
Ecco.

Eclipse Middle English: something that obscures, as in an eclipse of the moon.
Eklipse.

Eda Old English: prosperous.
Edah, Edda, Eddah.

Edain *See* Etain.

Edana Gaelic: fiery. *See also* Aidan.
Edann, Edanna, Eidan, Eidann.

Edeline *See* Adelaide.

Edellion One of the names of British Prime Minister David Cameron's daughter. Meaning unknown.

Eden Hebrew: a place of pleasure, as in the Garden of Eden. Irish Gaelic: fiery. Old English: a bear cub.
Edenn, Edin.

Edena *See* Edwina.

Edeva Old English: a rich gift.

Edin *See* Eden.

Edina *See* Edwina.

Edith Old English: prosperity, or a gift.
Edita (Italian), Editha, Edithe, Ediva, Edyta (Polish), Edyth, Edythe.
Diminutives: Dita, Dyta, Edie, Edy, Eydie.

Edlyn Old English: a noble maiden.
Edelyn.

Edmé Scottish: a variation of Esmé, and a feminine form of Edmund.
Edmée.

Edmonda Old English: a rich protector. A feminine form of Edmund.
Edmondia, Edmunda.

Edna Hebrew: renewal, rejuvenation. Also a form of Eithne.

Edrea Old English: prosperous, powerful.
Eadrea, Edra.

Edrey Old English: probably a form of Edrea.
Edree, Edri, Edrie, Edris, Edry.

Edwardina Old English: a prosperous guardian. The female form of Edward.
Edwarda, Edwarde, Edwardine.

Edwige *See* Hedwig.

Edwina Old English: a prosperous friend. The feminine form of Edwin.
Eadwina, Eadwine, Eadwyne, Edena, Edina, Edweana, Edweena, Edwine, Edwinna.
Diminutives: Ed, Eddie, Win, Winnie.

Edyta/Edyth/Edythe *See* Edith.

Eeve *See* Eve.

Efa Welsh form of Eve.

Effie/Effy *See* Euphemia.

Egeria Greek: a wise adviser.

Eglantine A 'flower name', from Old French.
Eglantina, Eglantyne.

Ehetere Maori form of Esther.

Eibhlin Irish Gaelic: beautiful.

Eidan A form of Aidan and Edana.

Eiddwen Welsh: the beloved fair one.

Eila A Finnish name of uncertain meaning.

Eileen Irish Gaelic: the light of the sun. The Irish form of Helen.
Aileen (Scottish), Ailene, Aisleen (Scottish), Aleen, Alene, Aline, Ayleen, Aylene, Eilene, Eiline, Eily (Irish Gaelic), Eleen, Elene, Ileana, Ilena, Ilene, Isleen.
Diminutives: Ailee, Aili, Ailie.

Eilis Irish Gaelic form of Elizabeth.

Eilish *See* Ailis.

Eir Old Norse: the goddess of healing.

Eira Welsh: snow.

Eireen/Eirena/Eirene *See* Irene.

Eirian Welsh: silver.

Eirwen Welsh: as white as snow.

Eister *See* Esther.

Eithne Irish Gaelic: ardent, fiery. *See also* Aine and Ena.
Edna, Eithna, Enya, Ethene, Ethna, Ethne, Etna.

Ekaterina/Ekaterini *See* Catherine.

Eklipse *See* Eclipse.

Ekore Maori: will not.

Ela/Elah *See* Ella.

Elaida A name from *The Wheel of Time* series of fantasy novels.
Elaidah, Elayda, Elaydah.

Elaine From the Old French form of Helen.
Alaine, Elaina, Elana, Elane, Elayna, Elayne, Ilayne.
Diminutives: Laine, Lainey.

Elan Hebrew: a tree. Native American: the friendly one.

Elana *See* Elaine and Ilana.

Elanor/Elanore *See* Eleanor.

Elara Greek: a satellite of the planet Jupiter.

Elata Latin: exalted, of high birth.

Elayda/Elaydah *See* Elaida.

Elayna/Elayne *See* Elaine.

Elberta/Elbertina/Elbertine *See* Alberta.

Elda Italian form of Hilda.

Eldora Spanish: the golden one.

Eleanor Old French: the light of the sun. A form of Helen. *See also* Leonora.
Elanor, Elanora, Elanore, Eleanora, Eleanore, Elenora, Eleonora (Italian), Eleonore (French, German), Elinor, Elinora, Elinore, Ellenor, Ellinor, Leanor (Spanish), Lennore, Lenora, Lenore, Leonora, Leonore.

Diminutives: Ella, Elli, Ellie, Elly, Nell, Nelly, Nora (Scandinavian), Norah, Noreen.

Elecia/Eleesha *See* Alicia.

Electra Greek: brilliant.
Electre, Elektra, Elettra (Italian).

Eleen/Elene *See* Eileen.

Eleganza Italian: one who is elegant.
Eleganze.

Elen/Elena/Eleni *See* Helen.

Elenora/Eleonora/Eleonore *See* Eleanor.

Eleri Welsh: the name of a river.

Eletta/Elette *See* Ella.

Eleu Hawaiian: alert and lively.

Elf Dutch/German: eleven. Old English: a sprite or a fairy.
Elfa, Elfe, Elfene, Elfine.

Elfreda/Elfreida/Elfrida *See* Alfreda.

Elga *See* Olga.

Éliane Latin: from the Greek word for the sun.
Elian, Eliana, Eliann, Elianne.

Elicia *See* Alicia.

Elida *See* Alida.

Elika An attractive Persian name.
Elikaa, Elikah.

Elin Swedish form of Helen.

Elinor/Elinore *See* Eleanor.

Eliora Hebrew: God is my light.
Eleora.

Elisa/Elise/Elissa *See* Elizabeth.

Elisabet/Elisabeth *See* Elizabeth.

Elissa Greek: a mythological figure.

Elita Old French: the chosen one. *See also* Alida.

Elitsa Bulgarian: a little fir tree.
Elitza.

Eliza *See* Elizabeth.

Elizabeth Hebrew: consecrated to God. A name from the Bible. *See also* Isabel and Lisa.
Eilis (Irish Gaelic), Elisa (Italian), Elisabet (Scandinavian), Elisabeth, Elisabetta (Italian), Elisavetta (Russian), Elise (French), Elissa, Eliza, Ellissa, Elsa, Elsbeth, Else (Danish, German), Elspeth, Elysa, Elysabeth, Elyse, Elyssa, Elyzabeth, Elzira (Portuguese), Erihapeti (Maori), Ilisapeci (Fijian), Ilisapesi (Polynesian), Ilsa, Ilse (German), Irihapeti (Maori), Leisel (German), Liese (German), Liesl, Lisa, Lisabet, Lisabeth, Lisbet, Lisbeth, Lise (Scandinavian), Liza.
Diminutives: Bess, Bessie, Bessy, Bet, Beth, Bethan (Welsh), Beti (Welsh), Betsey, Betsy, Bette, Bettie, Bettina, Betty, Bettye, Buffy, Ella, Elsie, Libby, Lili, Lilibet, Lisette (French), Liz, Lizette, Lizzie, Lizzy, Lysette, Lyz, Zizi (Hungarian).

Elka Polynesian: black.
Elkah.

Elke Teutonic: noble.
Elkee, Elkie, Elkey.

Ella Old English: elfin, a fairy maiden. Also a diminutive of Eleanor, Elizabeth, Ellen and Helen.
Ela, Elah, Eletta, Elette, Ellah, Ellana, Ellanna.
Diminutives: Elli, Ellie, Elly, Ellye.

Ellamay A 'combination name'.

Elle French: she, a woman.

Ellecia *See* Alicia and Ellice.

Ellen A form of Helen.
Ellin, Ellyn, Elyn, Elynn.
Diminutives: Ella, Elli, Ellie, Elly, Nell.

Ellenor/Ellinor *See* Eleanor.

Elli/Ellie Diminutives of Alice, Eleanor, Ella, Ellen and Helen.

Ellice Greek: Jehovah is God. The feminine form of Elias.
Ellecia, Ellicia, Ellis, Ellise, Ellyce.

Ellicia/Ellisha *See* Alicia and Ellice.

Ellis *See* Ellice.

Ellisa *See* Elizabeth.

Elloise/Ellouise *See* Eloise.

Ellora Ancient caves in southern India.
Ellorah.

Ellula *See* Elula.

Elly/Ellye Diminutives of Alice, Eleanor, Ella, Ellen and Helen.

Ellyce *See* Ellice.

Ellyn *See* Ellen.

Elma Greek: pleasant, amiable.

Elmas Armenian/Turkish: a diamond.
Elmas, Elmaz, Elmaza.

Elmira Old English: noble.

Elodia/Elodie *See* Alodie.

Eloise Teutonic: healthy.
Elloisa, Elloise, Ellouise, Eloisa, Elouise, Heloise.

Elowen Cornish: an elm tree.

Elrica Teutonic: the ruler of all.

Elsa/Else/Elsie *See* Alice and Elizabeth.

Elspeth *See* Elizabeth.

Elula From Elul, the sixth lunar month of the Hebrew calendar, corresponding to the zodiac sign of Virgo.
Ellula.

Eluned Welsh form of Lynn and Lynette (*see* Linnet).

Elva *See* Alfreda and Elvina.

Elvina Old English: the friend of the elves.
Alvina, Elva, Elvine.

Elvira Latin: the fair one. Teutonic: a true stranger.
Alvira, Elvera, Elvire.

Elwyn Welsh: white- or fair-browed.
Elwin, Elwine, Elwinn, Elwinne, Elywne, Elwynn, Elwynne.

Elyn/Elynn *See* Ellen.

Elysa/Elysabeth/Elyse/Elyssa *See* Alicia and Elizabeth.

Elyshia *See* Alicia.

Elysia Latin: blissful.

Elyzabeth *See* Elizabeth.

Elzira Portuguese form of Elizabeth.

Ema Polynesian/Samoan: beloved. Also a form of Emma.
Emah.

Emajen/Emajin *See* Imogen.

Emalee/Emali/Emalia/Emalie *See* Emily.

Emba Swahili form of Amber. *See also* Ember.

Ember Old English: the glowing remains of a fire. Also a form of Amber.
Emba, Embah, Embar, Embere, Embeur, Embr, Embry, Embur

Emblyn Cornish form of Amelia.

Emelda *See* Imelda.

Emelia/Emelie/Emelina/Emelye *See* Emily.

Emer Irish Gaelic: a traditional name.

Emerald A 'gemstone name'.
Emerant, Emeraude (French), Emmerald, Emrallt (Welsh), Esmeralda (Spanish), Esmerelda.

Diminutives: Meraud, Meraude.

Emere Maori form of Emily.

Emerson The son (or daughter) of Emery, meaning an industrious ruler. Generally a boy's name.
Emmasen, Emmason, Emmasyn, Emersen, Emmersen, Emmerson.

Emery Teutonic: an industrious ruler. More commonly a boy's name.
Emmery, Emmory, Emory, Emrey.

Emiko Japanese: a smiling child.

Emili/Emilia/Emilie *See* Emily.

Emily Teutonic: industrious. *See also* Amelia.
Emalee, Emali, Emalia, Emalie, Emelia, Emelie, Emelina, Emeline, Emely, Emelye, Emelyn, Emere (Maori), Emilee, Emiley, Emili, Emilia (Italian), Emiliana, Émilie (French), Emilie, Emmalee, Emmily.
Diminutives: Em, Emme, Emmi, Emmie, Emmy.

Emina Latin: a noble or lofty maiden.

Emma Teutonic: the healer of the universe.
Ema, Emah, Emmah, Emmalene, Emmaline, Emmelene, Emmeline, Emmelyn.
Diminutives: Em, Emme, Emmi, Emmie, Emmy.

Emmalee/Emmily *See* Emily.

Emmanuelle Hebrew: God is with us. The feminine form of Emmanuel.
Emanuela, Emanuelle, Emmanuela, Manuela (Spanish), Manuella, Manuelle.

Emmasen/Emmason *See* Emerson.

Emme/Emmi/Emmy *See* Emily and Emma.

Emmelene/Emmeline/Emmelyn *See*

Emma.

Emmerald *See* Emerald.

Emmery/Emory/Emrey *See* Emery.

Emmylou From Emily and Louise.

Emogen/Emogene/Emojen *See* Imogen.

Emrallt Welsh form of Emerald.

Ena Irish Gaelic: ardent. A variation of Aine and Eithne.

Enaki Hawaiian: the fiery sea.

Enda Irish: a bird.

Endocia Greek: of unquestionable reputation.
Eudocia, Eudocie.

Endora Hebrew: a fountain.

Engelberta Teutonic: a bright angel.

Engracia *See* Grace.

Enid Celtic: a pure soul.

Ennis Celtic: from the island. More commonly a boy's name.
Enis, Enys, Ennys.

Ennor Cornish: honour.
Enor.

Enora Greek: light.

Enrica Italian and Spanish form of Henrietta.

Enya A form of Eithne.

Eowyn A name from *The Lord of The Rings*, probably invented by the author, J R R Tolkien.

Ephemia *See* Euphemia.

Epiphany From Greek: an appearance or revelation. A Christian festival held on 6 January. *See also* Theophania and Tiffany.
Epifanee, Epifhanie, Epifhany, Epiphanee, Epiphanie.

Eran *See* Erin.

Eranthe Greek: a flower of spring.

Erda *See* Eartha.

Erena/Erene *See* Irene.

Erica Old Norse: a powerful ruler. The feminine form of Eric.
Ericah, Erika (German, Scandinavian), Erikah, Eryka, Erykah.

Erihapeti A Maori form of Elizabeth.

Erin Irish Gaelic: from Ireland.
Eran, Erina, Erinn, Erinna, Erinne, Erran, Errin, Erryn, Eryn.

Eris Greek: the goddess of discord.

Erline Old English: a noblewoman. The feminine form of Earl.
Earla, Earlene, Earline, Erlene.

Erma Teutonic: a maiden of the army; a feminine form of Herman. *See also* Armina.
Ermina, Erminia, Erminie, Irma.

Ermine Old French: a type of fur.
Ermina, Erminia.

Ernestine Teutonic: serious, earnest. The feminine form of Ernest.
Erna, Ernesta, Ernestina, Ernestyna.

Errin/Erryn *See* Erin.

Erta/Ertha *See* Eartha.

Erwina Teutonic: an honourable friend.

Erykah *See* Erica.

Eryn *See* Erin.

Esara Hebrew: our treasure.
Esarah.

Esha Sanskrit: a wish or desire.

Eshtar *See* Ishtar.

Esmé Old French: the loved one. *See also* Edmé.
Esma, Esmae, Esmah, Esmay, Esmeh, Esmey.

Esmerelda A form of Emerald.
Esmeralda (Spanish).

Esperance Latin: hope.
Esperanza (Spanish).

Esprit French from Latin: wit, lively
intelligence or spirit.
Espree, Esprie.

Esrela/Esrella *See* Ezrela.

Essence Middle English from Latin:
that which is essential, or the true
nature of something.

Esta Italian: from the east. *See also*
Esther.

Estefania *See* Stephanie.

Estelle French from Latin: a star. *See
also* Esther and Stella.
Estée (French), Estell, Estella,
Estrella (Spanish).
Diminutives: Stella, Stelle.

Esther Hebrew: a star. *See also* Estelle,
Hesper and Stella.
Ehetere (Maori), Eister (Irish Gaelic),
Esta, Ester, Esterre (Italian), Eszter
(Hungarian), Hadassa (Jewish),
Hadassah (Jewish), Hester, Hesther.
Diminutives: Essie, Etty, Hettie,
Hetty.

Estrella Spanish form of Estelle.

Esyllt Welsh form of Isolde.

Etain Irish: shining, bright.
Aideen, Edain, Etaoin.

Eternity Middle English: endless,
forever.
Eternal, Eternité.

Ethel Teutonic: a noble maiden.
Etel, Ethelda, Ethelinda, Etheline,
Ethelyn, Ethyl.

Ethene *See* Aine and Eithne.

Ethna/Ethne/Etna *See* Eithne.

Étienette French from Greek: a
garland or crown; the feminine form
of Étienne. *See also* Stephanie.

Etsu Japanese: delight.

Etta/Ettie *See* Henrietta.

Euclea Greek: glory.

Eudocia/Eudocie *See* Endocia.

Eudora Greek: a wonderful gift.

Eufamie/Eufemia *See* Euphemia.

Eugenia Greek: noble, well-born. The
feminine form of Eugene.
Eugene, Eugénie (French).
Diminutives: Gena, Gene, Genia,
Genie.

Eulalia Greek: the well-spoken one.
Eulalie (French), Eulaylia, Olalla
(Spanish), Ulalia.

Euna *See* Úna.

Eunice Greek: victorious.
Unice.

Euphemia Greek: of good reputation.
Ephemia, Eufamie, Eufemia (Italian,
Spanish, Portuguese), Euphémie
(French).
Diminutives: Effie, Effy.

Euphrasia Greek: joy, delight.

Eurwen Welsh: fair.
Eurwyn.

Eurydice The goddess of the
underworld in Greek mythology.
Euridice.

Eustacia Greek: fruitful. The
feminine form of Eustace.
Eustacie.
Diminutives: Stacey, Stacie, Stacy.

Eva/Evah *See* Eve.

Evadne Greek: fortunate.

Evaleen/Evalyn *See* Evelyn.

Evaleigh *See* Eveleigh.

Evana *See* Ivana and Jane.

Evangeline Greek: the bearer of good news.
Evangela, Evangelia, Evangelina, Ivangela, Ivangelia, Ivangelina.

Evania Greek: peaceful, tranquil.

Eve Hebrew: life-giving. *See also* Evelyn.
Chava (Hebrew), Eeve, Efa (Welsh), Eva, Evah, Evva (Russian), Ewa (Polish), Hava (Jewish), Havva (Turkish), Yeva (Russian), Yiva, Yva, Yve.
Diminutives: Evey, Evie, Evita (Spanish), Evy.

Eveleigh A combination of Eve and Leigh, or a form of Evelyn.
Evaleigh, Everleigh, Everley, Everly, Evley.

Everild/Everilda *See* Averil.

Evelyn English: from an old surname, but also related to Eve.
Aveline, Evaleen (Irish), Evalyn, Eveleigh, Evelen, Evelene, Evelin, Evelina, Eveline, Evelinn, Evelinn, Evelyne, Evelynn, Evelynne, Everlyn, Everlynne, Evlyn, Evyleen, Evlyn.
Diminutives: Evey, Evie, Evy.

Ever Always, at all times.
Everr.

Everild/Everilda *See* Averil.

Everleigh/Everley/Everly *See* Eveleigh.

Everlyn/Everlynne *See* Evelyn.

Evetta/Evette *See* Yvette.

Evie/Evita *See* Eve and Evelyn.

Evley/Evlyn *See* Eveleigh and Evelyn.

Evoke To call up, as in a memory, or cause to appear.

Evon/Evonne *See* Yvonne.

Evva/Ewa *See* Eve.

Evy/Evyleen/Evlyn *See* Eve and Evelyn.

Ewalani Hawaiian: a heavenly woman.

Exene American. A modern made-up name.

Exodus Middle English from Greek: to leave or go out. The second book of the Old Testament. Also a boy's name.
Exodos.

Eydie A diminutive of Edith.

Eyota Native American: the greatest.

Ezrela Feminine form of Ezra, the helper.
Esrela, Esrella, Ezra, Ezrah, Ezrella.

F

Fabia Latin: a bean grower. Feminine form of Fabian.
Fabiana, Fabienne (French), Fabiola (Spanish).

Fabiola Spanish form of Fabia.

Fabrianne Latin: resourceful, or a craftswoman.
Fabriane, Fabrianna, Fabrienne (French).

Fadila Arabic: generous and distinguished.

Fae/Faeth/Faethe/Fai/Faie *See* Faith and Fay.

Faerie/Faery *See* Fairy.

Faine Old English: joyful.
Faina, Fayna, Fayne.

Fair Middle English: beautiful, or of light or pale colouring.
Faire, Fayr, Fayre.

Fairley Old English: a clearing in the woods. Also a boy's name.
Fairlee, Fairleigh, Fairlie.

Fairy Middle English: a supernatural being.
Faerey, Faerie, Faery, Fairee, Fairey, Fairie.

Faith Trusting in God, having faith. *See also* Fidela.
Faeth, Faethe, Faithe, Faithi (African), Fayth, Faythe.
Diminutives: Fae, Fai, Faie, Fay, Faye.

Faiza Arabic: victorious.
Faizah, Fayza.

Falda Icelandic: with folded wings.

Fallon Irish: a leader. Also a boy's name.
Fallan, Fallyn.

Fame *See* Fayme.

Fanchon *See* Frances.

Fannie/Fanny *See* Frances.

Farah Arabic: happiness. *See also* Farrah.
Fariha.

Farica/Farika *See* Frederica.

Farida Arabic: unique.
Faridah, Faride.

Fariha *See* Farah.

Farrah Old English: beautiful.
Fara, Farah, Farra.

Fatima Arabic: a woman who abstains, or weans a child. A daughter of the prophet Muhammad.
Fatimah, Fatma.

Faun/Fauna/Faunia *See* Fawn.

Faustine Latin: the fortunate one.
Fausta, Faustina, Faustyna.

Fawn Old French: a young deer.
Faun, Fauna, Faunia, Fawna, Fawnia.

Fay From Old French: a fairy or magical creature. *See also* Faith.
Fae, Faye, Fayette, Fayine, Fey.

Fayme Latin: of high reputation, renowned.
Fame, Faym.

Fayna/Fayne *See* Faine.

Fayr/Fayre *See* Fair.

Fayth/Faythe *See* Faith.

Fayza *See* Faiza.

Fearn/Fearne *See* Fern.

February The second month of the year; from the Latin word februare (purification).
Februar (Danish, German), Februari (Swahili), Februaria.

Fedelma *See* Fidelma.

Federica *See* Frederica.

Fedora A Russian form of Theodora. Also a type of hat.
Fedorah.

Feebee/Feebi/Feebie *See* Phoebe.

Felda Teutonic: from the field.

Felice/Felicia *See* Felicity.

Felicity Latin: lucky, fortunate. The feminine form of Felix.
Felica, Felice, Felicia, Feliciana, Felicidad (Spanish), Felicie (German), Felicita (Italian), Felicitas, Félicité (French), Felis, Felita, Feliza, Felizia.
Diminutive: Flick.

Felipa *See* Philippa.

Felita/Feliza/Felizia *See* Felicity.

Felix *See* BOYS.

Fenella Gaelic: the white- or fair-shouldered one.
Finella, Finola, Fionnuala, Fionola,

Fynella.

Fennagh An Irish placename.
Fenagh, Fenna, Fennah.

Feodora *See* Theodora.

Feona/Feonah *See* Fiona.

Ferida Turkish: unique.
Feridah, Feride.

Fern Old English: fern-like. A 'plant name'.
Fearn, Fearne, Ferne.

Fernanda Teutonic: prepared for the journey; a traveller or adventurer. The feminine form of Ferdinand.
Ferdinanda, Fernande (French), Fernandina.

Feronia Latin: a mythological goddess.

Fey *See* Fay.

Ffion Welsh form of Fiona.

Fhebee/Fheebi/Fheebie *See* Phoebe.

Fidela Latin: faithful. *See also* Faith.
Fidele, Fidelia, Fidelita, Fidelity.

Fidelma Irish Gaelic: the name of a saint.
Fedelma.

Fifi *See* Josephine.

Fig Middle English: a 'fruit name'.

Filberta/Filbertha *See* Philberta.

Filippa *See* Philippa.

Filomena/Filomene *See* Philomena.

Fina *See* Fiona.

Finella/Finola/Fionola *See* Fenella.

Finesse French: skill or elegance.
Finess.

Finlay Scottish Gaelic: a fair warrior. More commonly a boy's name.
Findlay, Findley, Finley, Finnlay, Finnley.

Fiona Irish Gaelic: a vine. Scottish Gaelic: the fair one.
Feona, Feonah, Ffion (Welsh), Fina (Irish), Fionah, Fione, Fionn, Fionna, Fyona, Fyonah.
Diminutive: Fee.

Fiora *See* Flora.

Fiore Italian: a flower.
Fioray, Fioreh, Fiorina, Fiorine.

Fiorella Italian: a little flower.

Fiorenza Italian form of Florence.

Fire *See* BOYS.

Flair Latin: elegance and style.
Flaire, Flayr, Flayre.

Flame Middle English: something that burns or blazes.
Flaime, Flayme.

Flanna Gaelic: red-haired. The feminine form of Flannan.

Flannery *See* BOYS.

Flavia Latin: the golden-haired one.
Flavie (French).

Flax Middle English: a 'plant name'.
Flaxen.

Flayme *See* Flame.

Flayr/Flayre *See* Flair.

Fleur Old French: a flower. *See also* Fiore and Flora.
Fleura, Fleure.
Diminutive: Fleurette.

Flo *See* Flora and Florence.

Flora Latin: a flower. The Roman goddess of flowers and the spring. *See also* Fiore and Fleur.
Fiora, Florah, Flore (French), Florea, Florella, Florette, Floria.
Diminutives: Flo, Florrie.

Florence Latin: blossoming, flourishing.

Fiorenza (Italian), Florance, Florancia, Florencia, Florentia, Florentina, Florentyna, Florinda.
Diminutives: Flo, Florrie, Flossie.

Floria *See* Flora.

Folole A Samoan name of uncertain meaning.

Fonda Latin: affectionate.

Fontaine French: a spring or fountain.
Fontana (Italian), Fontayne.

Fortuna Latin: the fortunate one.
Fortunata, Fortune.

Fosetta French: the dimpled one.

Fotini Greek: light.
Photini.

Franca Italian form of Frances.

Frances Latin: from France, or a free woman. The feminine form of Francis.
Franca (Italian), Francene, Francesca (Italian), Francess, Francette, Francina (Dutch), Francine (French), Francisca (Spanish), Françoise (French), Franka (Russian), Franziska (German).
Diminutives: Fanchon (French), Fannie, Fanny, Fran, France, Franci, Francie, Frankie, Frannie.

Francesca/Francisca *See* Frances.

Francine *See* Frances.

Françoise *See* Frances.

Frangipani French: a scented flower.
Frangipanie, Frangipanni, Frangipannie.

Franka/Frankie *See* Frances.

Frayda/Frayde *See* Freyde.

Freda A diminutive of names such as Alfreda, Frederica and Winifred.

Fredah, Freida, Freide (German), Frida, Frieda, Friede.

Frederica Teutonic: a peaceful ruler. The feminine form of Frederick.
Farica, Farika, Federica, Fredericka, Frédérique (French), Frerika, Friederike (German), Frydryka (Polish).
Diminutives: Freda, Freddie, Friede (German), Fritzi (German).

Freema The name of a British actress (Freema Agyeman), best known for her role as Martha Jones in the *Doctor Who* TV series.
Frema, Frima.

Freesia A fragrant flower.

Freya Old Norse: a lady. The goddess of love in Scandinavian mythology.
Freja (Swedish), Freyja.

Freyde Yiddish: joy.
Frayda, Frayde, Freyda.

Frida/Frieda/Friede *See* Alfreda, Freda, Frederica and Halfrida.

Friday The day of Freya, the Norse equivalent of the Roman god Venus.

Fritzi *See* Frederica.

Fronde Latin: a fern leaf.
Frond.

Fuchsia An unusual 'flower name', after the German botanist Leonhard Fuchs.
Fushia.

Fuki Japanese: joy.
Fukie.

Fulvia Latin: tawny-haired. The wife of Mark Antony.

Fynella *See* Fenella.

Fyona/Fyonah *See* Fiona.

G

Gabbie/Gabi/Gabie *See* Gabrielle.

Gabrielle Hebrew: a woman of God. The feminine form of Gabriel.
Gabrell, Gabrella, Gabrelle, Gabriela (Polish), Gabriele (Czech, German), Gabriella (Italian), Gabrilla, Gavrielle, Gavrila.
Diminutives: Gabbie, Gabe, Gabi, Gabie, Gaby.

Gada Hebrew: lucky.

Gadar Armenian: perfection.

Gae/Gai *See* Gay.

Gael *See* Abigail and Gail.

Gaenor Welsh form of Gaynor.

Gaia The earth goddess in Greek mythology.
Gaea, Gaya.

Gail A diminutive of Abigail.
Gael, Gaila, Gailene, Gailin, Gaille, Gale, Gayla, Gayle, Gayleen, Gaylene.

Gainor *See* Gaynor.

Gala Italian: a festival or celebration. Also a diminutive of Galina.

Galatea Greek: milky-white. A sea nymph in Greek mythology.

Galaxy Middle English from Greek: a star system.
Galaxi, Galaxia, Galaxie, Galaxye.

Gale *See* Gail.

Galena Latin: a lead-like metal.

Galia Hebrew: a wave.

Galiena Teutonic: a lofty maiden.
Galiana.

Galilee A region of northern Israel.

Galina Russian from Greek: calm. *See also* Helen.
Halina (Polish).
Diminutive: Gala.

Galya Hebrew: God has redeemed.

Gana Hebrew: a garden.
Ganah, Gania, Ganya.

Garcelle A feminine form of garçon, French for a boy.
Garcel, Garcela, Garcell, Garcella.

Gardenia A 'flower name'.

Gari Feminine form of Gary, a spearman.
Garee, Garie.

Garland Old French: a crown or wreath of flowers.

Garner Old French: one who tends a garden. Also a boy's name.
Gardner.

Garnet Old French: dark red, from the colour of pomegranates. Also a 'gemstone name'.
Garnett, Garnetta, Garnette.

Gavrielle *See* Gabrielle.

Gavrila Hebrew: a heroine. *See also* Gabrielle.
Gavrilla.

Gay Old French: blithe, cheerful.
Gae, Gai, Gaye.

Gaya *See* Gaia.

Gayle/Gayleen/Gaylene *See* Gail.

Gaynor Welsh: fair and soft. *See also* Guinevere.
Gaenor (Welsh), Gainor, Gaynore.

Gazelle French: a small antelope.
Gazella, Gazellah, Ghazal (Arabic), Ghazella, Ghazelle.

Geena *See* Gina.

Geeta *See* Gita.

Geerta *See* Gertrude.

Gelasia Greek: laughing, like a bubbling spring.
Gelasie.

Gemina Greek: a twin.
Gemini, Geminia, Geminie.

Gemma Italian: a jewel or gem.
Gemmah, Jemma, Jemmah.

Gen Japanese: the source.

Gena *See* Eugenia and Gina.

Gene/Genia *See* Eugenia, Gina and Jean.

Genesia Latin: the newcomer.
Genesa, Genisia.

Genette *See* Genevieve and Jeannette.

Geneva A city in Switzerland. *See also* Genevieve.
Geneve.

Genevieve Old French: a woman of the people. The patron saint of Paris.
Genavieve, Geneva, Genevra, Ginevra (Italian), Jenevieve.
Diminutives: Genette, Ginette, Veva, Vevette (French).

Genista Latin: the broom plant.

Genna/Gennah *See* Jenna.

Gennifer/Genny *See* Jennifer.

Genowefa A form of Guinevere and Jennifer.

Georgeanne/Georgena/Georgene *See* Georgina.

Georgette French form of Georgina.

Georgia Originally a diminutive of Georgina. Also a state in the USA and a region of the former USSR. *See also* Jorja.
Georga, Georgah, Georgi, Georgiah,
Georgie, Georja, Georjia, Giorga, Giorgia, Giorja, Giorjia.

Georgina Greek: a girl from the farm; the feminine form of George. *See also* Georgia.
Georgeanne, Georgeina, Georgena, Georgene, Georgette (French), Georgia, Georgiana, Georgienne (French), Georgine (French), Giorgetta (Italian).
Diminutives: George, Georgie, Georgy, Gigi (French), Gina.

Georja/Georjia *See* Georgia.

Geraldine From Old French: a noble spear carrier. The feminine form of Gerald. *See also* Gerarda.
Geralda, Geraldeine, Geraldina, Giralda (Italian), Giraldina, Giraldine, Jeraldine.
Diminutives: Geri, Gerri, Gerry, Jerri, Jerry.

Geranium Greek: a 'flower name'.

Gerarda From Old French: a brave spear woman. The feminine form of Gerard. *See also* Geraldine.
Jerarda.

Gerda Old Norse: protected. Also a diminutive of Gertrude.
Gerd (Scandinavian), Gerde (German).

Geri/Gerri/Gerry *See* Geraldine.

Gerlinde Teutonic: of the weak spear.
Gerlina, Gerlinda.

Germaine French: the name of a saint.
Germain, Germana, Germane, Germayne, Jermain, Jermaine, Jermayne.

Gertrude Teutonic: a spear maiden.
Geerta (Dutch), Gertraud (German), Gertrud (German), Gertruda.

EARLY SETTLERS' NAMES

New Zealand's first European settlers bore, by today's standards, a very limited range of first names. The settlers were overwhelmingly English (by 1840 there were about 2000 British subjects in New Zealand), but the first ships also brought people of Irish, Welsh, Scottish and French origins. These are some of the most common early settlers' names.

Girls		Boys	
Ann	Louisa	Arthur	John
Catherine	Margaret	Benjamin	Joseph
Eliza	Martha	Edward	Richard
Elizabeth	Mary	George	Robert
Emma	Rebecca	Harry	Samuel
Harriet	Sarah	Henry	Thomas
Jane	Susannah	James	William

Diminutives: Gerda, Gert, Gertie, Truda, Trudi, Trudie, Trudy.

Gessica/Gessika *See* Jessica.

Ghada Arabic: graceful.

Ghazal/Ghazella/Ghazelle *See* Gazelle.

Ghislain/Ghislaine *See* Giselle.

Ghita *See* Gita.

Gia Italian: a diminutive of Gianna and Giovanna (*see* Jane).
Giah, Giya, Giyah.

Giaan *See* Jane.

Giacinta Italian form of Hyacinth.

Giada Italian form of Jade.

Gian/Gianina/Gianna Italian forms of Jane.

Gigi French: a diminutive of Georgina, Gilberta and Virginia.

Gilana Hebrew: joy.
Gilah.

Gilberta Teutonic: a bright or famous pledge. The feminine form of Gilbert.
Gilberte, Gilbertha, Gilbertina, Gilbertine.
Diminutives: Berta, Gigi, Gillie, Gilly.

Gilda Teutonic: a sacrifice.

Gillian Latin: from a Roman family name. The feminine form of Julian and a derivative of Julia.
Gilian, Gillane, Gillianne, Jillian.
Diminutives: Gill, Gilly, Jill, Jilli, Jillie, Jilly.

Gina A diminutive of names such as Georgina and Regina.
Geena, Gena, Gene, Ginah.

Ginette/Ginevra *See* Genevieve.

Ginger A diminutive of Virginia. Also a 'spice name'.
Ginjer.
Diminutives: Gini, Ginnie, Ginny.

Gioia Italian: joy.

Giorga/Giorja *See* Georgia.

Giorgetta *See* Georgina.

Giovanna An Italian form of Jane.

Gipsy *See* Gypsy.

Giralda/Giraldina/Giraldine *See* Geraldine.

Giselle Teutonic: a pledge.
Ghislain, Ghislaine (French), Gisela (Dutch, German), Gisèle (French), Giselia, Gisella, Gizela, Gizelle.

Gita Sanskrit: a song.
Geeta, Ghita.

Gitana Spanish: a gypsy.

Giulia/Giulietta Italian forms of Julia.

Giuseppina Italian form of Josephine.

Giya/Giyah *See* Gia

Gizela/Gizelle *See* Giselle.

Gladi Hawaiian form of Gladys.

Gladys Welsh: possibly a form of Claudia.
Gladdis, Gladi (Hawaiian), Gladis, Gleda, Gwladys (Welsh).

Gleda *See* Gladys.

Glen Gaelic/Welsh: from the valley or glen. *See also* Glenda and Glenys.
Glenn, Glenne, Glennette.

Glenda Welsh: pure and good. *See also* Glenys.
Glendah, Glenna.
Diminutives: Glen, Glenn.

Glenice/Glenis/Glenise *See* Glenys.

Glenna *See* Glenda.

Glenys Welsh: holy, pure. *See also* Glenda.
Glenice, Glenis, Glenise, Glennis, Glynis, Glynnis.
Diminutives: Glen, Glenn.

Gloria Latin: glorious.

Gloriana, Gloriane, Glorianna, Glorianne, Glorien, Glory.

Glynis/Glynnis *See* Glenys.

Goda *See* Guda.

Godiva Old English: the gift of God.

Golda/Golden *See* Goldie.

Goldie English: the golden one.
Golda (Yiddish), Golden, Goldey, Goldi, Goldina, Goldine.

Grace Latin: graceful.
Engracia (Spanish), Graça (Portuguese), Gracela, Gracele, Gracell, Gracella, Gracia (Spanish), Graciela (Spanish), Gracielle, Graice, Gratia (Dutch, German), Grayce, Grazia (Italian), Graziella (Italian), Grazina.
Diminutives: Gracee, Gracey, Graci, Gracie.

Gracious Middle English: one who has grace or elegance.

Grainne *See* Grania.

Grania Irish Gaelic: a figure in Irish legend.
Grainne (Irish Gaelic), Granya.

Gratia Dutch and German form of Grace.

Grayce/Grazia/Graziella/Grazina *See* Grace.

Grayson *See* BOYS.

Greer/Grier *See* Gregoria.

Gregoria Greek: watchful, vigilant.
Greer (Scottish), Grier (Scottish), Grigoria.

Greta/Gretchen/Grete/Gretel *See* Margaret.

Griselda Teutonic: the grey battle heroine.
Griselde, Grizel (Scottish), Grizelda.

Diminutives: Selda, Zelda.

Gryffyn *See* BOYS.

Guadalupe Arabic: the river of the wolf. Generally a Spanish name.

Guan-yin Chinese: the goddess of mercy.

Guda Old English: good.
Goda.

Gudrun Old Norse: divine lore or wisdom.

Guida Latin: the guide.

Guin/Guinn/Guinne *See* Gwyn.

Guinevere Welsh: fair and soft. The wife of King Arthur. *See also* Gaynor, Jennifer and Vanora.
Gaenor (Welsh), Gaynor, Genowefa, Guenevere, Guinever, Gweniver (Cornish), Gwenore.

Gunda *See* Gunnhild.

Gunnel The upper part of a boat.
Gunnell.

Gunnhild Old Norse: a maiden of battle.
Gunda, Gunhild, Gunhilda, Gunhilde, Gunilla.

Gussie/Gusta Diminutives of Augusta.

Gwen Welsh: fair or blessed. *See also* Gwendolen, Gwyn and Gwyneth.
Gwynne.

Gwendolen Welsh: a white ring or brow.
Gwenda, Gwendolene, Gwendolin, Gwendolina, Gwendoline, Gwendolyn, Gwendolyne.
Diminutives: Gwen, Gwennie.

Gweniver Cornish form of Guinevere.

Gwenllyn A combination of two Welsh names, Gwen (fair or blessed) and Llyn (a lake).

Gwenllynn, Gwenllynne, Gwenlyn, Gwenlynn, Gwenlynne.
Diminutive: Gwen.

Gwennap Cornish: the name of a saint and a placename.

Gwenor *See* Guinevere.

Gwinau Welsh: brown.
Gwynau.

Gwladys *See* Gladys.

Gwyn Welsh: white. Also a diminutive of Gwyneth.
Guin, Guinn, Guinne, Gwen, Gwinn, Gwinne, Gwynn, Gwynne.

Gwyneth Welsh: from a region of north Wales.
Gweneth, Gwenneth, Gwenith, Gwenyth, Gwynneth.
Diminutives: Gwen, Gwyn.

Gwynne *See* Gwen and Gwyn.

Gypsy Old English: a wanderer.
Gipsy.

Gytha Old English: warlike.

H

Habiba Arabic: the beloved.
Habibah, Haviva.

Hadassa/Hadassah Jewish forms of Esther.

Hadil Arabic: cooing like a dove.

Hadiya Arabic/Swahili: a gift.

Hadley *See* BOYS.

Hadria *See* Adriana.

Hadya Arabic: a leader or guide.
Huda.

Haeata Maori: dawn or a beam of light.

Hafwen Welsh: as beautiful as summer.

Hagar Hebrew: forsaken, or taking flight.
Hagir (Arabic), Hajar (Arabic).

Hahana Maori: radiant or glowing.

Haidee Greek: modest.

Hailee/Haileigh/Hailey *See* Hayley.

Haimi Hawaiian: the seeker.
Haimee.

Haiven *See* Haven.

Haiz/Haize *See* Haze.

Hajar *See* Hagar.

Haki Maori form of Jackie. *See* Jacqueline.

Hala Arabic: a halo around the moon.

Halaina *See* Helen.

Halcyone Greek: a kingfisher.
Halcyon.

Haldana Old Norse: half Danish.

Halee/Haleigh/Haley *See* Hayley.

Halfrida Teutonic: a peaceful heroine.
Diminutives: Frida, Frieda, Friede.

Halia Hawaiian: fond remembrance.
Halea, Haleia.

Halima Arabic: kind, gentle.

Halina Polish form of Helen and Galina.

Halle/Hallie *See* Hayley.

Halo Latin: a circle of light.
Haloe, Halow.

Halona Native American: fortunate.

Hama Japanese: a child of the shore.

Hana Arabic: bliss, happiness. Czech form of Joanne. Maori: to glow. Also a form of Hannah.

Hanai Hawaiian: lucky.

Hanan Arabic: the tender affectionate one.

Hannabeth A combination of Hannah and Beth (*see* Elizabeth).
Hannahbeth.

Hannah Hebrew: favoured by God, or graceful. *See also* Anne.
Hana, Hania (Polish), Hanna.

Hanne German form of Joanne.
Hannelore, Hanni (Swiss).

Hansine German from Hebrew: God is gracious. A feminine form of Hans.

Hapai Polynesian: a legendary figure.

Happy English: bright and cheerful.
Happi, Happie, Happye.

Haralda Old English: the ruler of the army. The feminine form of Harold.
Harelda, Harolda, Haroldina.

Harata Maori form of Charlotte.

Hariata Maori and Polynesian form of Harriet.

Hariet/Hariett/Hariette *See* Harriet.

Harika Turkish: beautiful.

Harikoa Maori: happy.

Harley Old English: from the meadow of the hares, or from the grey wood. *See also* Hartley.
Harlea, Harlee, Harleigh, Harlene, Harlie, Harly.

Harlow Old English: a meeting place. The surname of a legendary 1920s–1930s actress (Jean Harlow).
Harlo, Harloe, Harlowe.

Harmony Greek: concordant, in harmony.
Harmonee, Harmoney, Harmoni, Harmonia, Harmonie.

Harolda/Haroldina *See* Haralda.

Harper Old English: a harp maker or player.
Harpa, Harpah.

Harriet Teutonic: the ruler of the home. A feminine form of Harry and Henry. *See also* Henrietta.
Hariata (Maori, Polynesian), Hariet, Hariett, Hariette, Harried (Breton), Harriett, Harrietta, Harriette, Harriot.
Diminutives: Hattie, Hettie, Hetty.

Harris *See* BOYS.

Hartley Old English: from the meadow of the hare or stag. *See also* Harley.
Hartlea, Hartlee, Hartleigh, Hartlie, Hartly.

Haruko Japanese: spring.

Hasika Sanskrit: laughter.

Hasina Swahili: good.

Hathor Ancient Egyptian: the goddess of love and joy.

Hattie *See* Harriet and Henrietta.

Hauku Maori: dew.

Haurahi Maori: dew.

Hava/Havva *See* Eve.

Havana Spanish: the capital of Cuba.
Havanah, Havanna, Havannah.

Haven Middle English: a place of safety or shelter.
Haiven, Havenn, Hayven.

Haviva *See* Habiba.

Haya Hebrew: life.
Hayat (Arabic).

Hayden *See* BOYS.

Hayfa Arabic: slender, delicate.

Hayley Old English: a high clearing or meadow.

Hailea, Hailee, Haileigh, Hailey, Halee, Haleigh, Haley, Halle, Hallie, Haylea, Haylee, Hayleigh, Haylie, Hayly, Heylea, Heylee, Heyleigh, Heyley, Heylie.

Hayven *See* Haven.

Haze A type of mist.
Haiz, Haize, Hayz, Hayze.

Hazel Old English: from the hazel tree.
Hayzel, Hayzell, Hayzelle, Hazell, Hazelle.

Heather Old English: a 'flower name'.

Heavenly Middle English: blissful, resembling heaven.
Heaven, Heavenlea, Heavenlee, Heavenlie, Hevenly.

Hebe Greek: youthful. A goddess of youth in mythology.

Hebron Hebrew: an Israeli city, mentioned in the Bible.

Hedda *See* Hedwig.

Hedea Greek: pleasing.
Hedia, Hedya.

Hedwig Teutonic: the contentious one; a fighter. The name of a saint.
Edwige (French), Hedvig (Scandinavian), Hedviga (Hungarian), Jadwiga (Polish).
Diminutives: Hedda (Scandinavian), Hedy (Scandinavian).

Hedya *See* Hedea.

Heidi Swiss diminutive of Adelheid (*see* Adelaide), well known from Johanna Spyri's classic children's book.
Heide, Heidee, Heidie.

Heledd Welsh: a traditional name.
Hyledd.

Helen Greek: the light of the sun. *See also* Eileen, Elaine, Eleanor and Ellen.
Alena (Lithuanian), Elen (Welsh), Elena (Italian, Portuguese, Spanish), Eleni (Greek), Elin (Swedish), Galina (Russian), Halaina, Halina (Polish), Helaine, Helayna, Helayne, Helena, Helene (German), Hélène (French), Helenka (Polish), Hellen, Ileana (Romanian), Illona (Irish), Ilona (Hungarian), Jelena (Slavic), Léan (Irish Gaelic), Olena (Ukrainian), Yelena (Russian).
Diminutives: Ella, Elli, Ellie, Elly, Hels, Ilka (Hungarian), Lana, Lena, Lene (Dutch, German), Nell, Nellie, Nelly.

Helena/Helene *See* Helen.

Helga Old Norse: successful, prosperous. *See also* Olga.
Hella.

Helia Greek: the sun.

Helice Greek: a spiral.
Helica.

Hella *See* Helga.

Hellen *See* Helen.

Helma/Helmine German diminutives of Wilhelmina.

Heloise *See* Eloise.

Helvetia Latin: a woman from Switzerland.

Hendrika *See* Henrietta.

Heni Maori form of Jane.

Henrietta Teutonic: the ruler of the home. A feminine form of Henry. *See also* Harriet.
Enrica (Italian, Spanish), Hendrika (Dutch), Henrieta, Henriette (French), Henrika (Swedish), Henrike (German), Henryka (Polish).
Diminutives: Etta, Ettie, Hattie, Hettie, Hetty, Netta, Nettie, Netty, Yetta.

Henrika/Henrike/Henryka *See* Henrietta.

Hera Greek: a queen. The wife of Zeus, ruler of the heavens, in Greek mythology. Also a Maori form of Sarah.

Herma/Hermia/Hermina *See* Hermione.

Hermione Greek: the feminine form of Hermes, the messenger of the gods in Greek mythology.
Herma, Hermia, Hermina, Hermine (German), Herminia.

Hermosa Spanish: beautiful.

Hero A priestess of Aphrodite, the goddess of love in Greek mythology.

Herta/Hertha *See* Eartha.

Heshu Chinese: a star in the constellation of Canis Minor.

Hesper Greek: the evening star. *See also* Esther.
Hespera, Hesperia.

Hester/Hesther *See* Esther.

Hestia Greek: the goddess of the hearth in Greek mythology.

Hettie/Hetty Diminutives of Esther, Harriet and Henrietta.

Heulwen Welsh: sunshine.
Heulwyn, Heulyn.

Hewlett The feminine form of Hewett (little Hugh).
Hewlet, Hewlette, Hewlit, Hewlitt, Hewlitte.

Heylee/Heyleigh/Heylie *See* Hayley.

Hibernia Latin: a woman from Ireland.
Hiberna.

Hibiscus Greek: a 'flower name'.

Hidé Japanese: excellent, fruitful.

Hihiria Maori form of Cecelia.

Hika Polynesian: a daughter.

Hikitia Maori: to lift by the arms.

Hikurangi Maori: a sacred mountain on the North Island's East Cape.

Hilaire *See* Hilary.

Hilary Latin: the cheerful one. Originally a boy's name.
Hilaire (French), Hilaria (Spanish), Hilery, Hillary.

Hilda Teutonic: a battle maiden.
Elda (Italian), Hilde (German), Hillda, Hylda.

Hildegard Teutonic: a battle stronghold.
Hildegarde.

Hildemar Teutonic: battle celebrated.

Hina Japanese: like the sun. Polynesian: the wife of Maui, a legendary hero.

Hina-Uri Polynesian: the goddess of the moon.

Hinda Jewish: a female deer.
Hinda, Hinde.

Hine Maori/Polynesian: a maiden.

Hinemoa Polynesian: a girl from legend.

Hinengaro Maori: conscience.

Hippolyta Greek: she who frees the horses.

Hira Maori form of Jean. Also a shield.

Hiria Maori form of Celia.

Hiriwa Polynesian: silver.

Hiroko Japanese: generous.

Hiwa Hawaiian: jet-black, or choice.

Hiwakea Hawaiian: black and white.

Hjördis Old Norse: a sword goddess.

Hoala Hawaiian: to agitate.

Hokaka Maori: desired or wished for.

Hoki Maori: also, because.

Hoku Polynesian: a star.

Holda Teutonic: concealed. *See also* Hulda.
Holde, Holle.

Holea/Holee/Holeigh/Holi *See* Holly.

Holiday *See* BOYS.

Holland Old English: from the enclosed or sacred ground. A 'country name'.
Holand, Hollan.

Holle *See* Holda.

Holly Old English: a type of tree. Suitable for a child born around Christmas.
Holea, Holee, Holeigh, Holi, Holie, Hollea, Hollee, Holleigh, Holley, Holli, Hollie.

Honey Old English: the sweet one.
Honee, Honi, Honie.

Honeyblossom The unusual name of one of Bob Geldof's daughters.

Honeysuckle Middle English: a fragrant flower.
Honiesuckle.

Honour Latin: honourable.
Honor, Honora, Honorata (Italian), Honore (French), Honoria, Honorine (French), Onóra (Irish Gaelic).

Hoong Chinese: pink.
Hong.

Hope Old English: hopeful,
optimistic.

Horatia Latin: from a Roman family
name. The feminine form of Horace.
Horacia.

Hortense Latin: the garden lover.
Hortencia, Hortensia, Hortenze,
Ortense (Italian), Ortensia (Italian).

Hosanna Latin: in praise of God.
Hosana, Osana, Osanna.

Hoshi Japanese: a star.

Hotoke Maori: winter.

Hua Chinese: a flower.

Huberta Teutonic: a brilliant mind.
The feminine form of Hubert.
Hubertha, Huberthe.

Huda *See* Hadya.

Huette French from Teutonic: heart
and mind. The feminine form of
Hugh.
Huetta, Hughetta, Hughette,
Hughina (Scottish), Hughine,
Huguette (French).

Hughette/Hughina *See* Huette.

Huhana Maori form of Susannah.

Huia Maori: an extinct native New
Zealand bird

Hula Polynesian: a Hawaiian dance.

Hulda Hebrew: a prophetess. Old
Norse: lovable.
Holda, Huldah.

Humarie Maori: a peaceful person.

Hune Maori form of June.

Hunter *See* BOYS.

Huntress Middle English: a female
hunter.

Hunteress, Hunteresse, Huntresse.

Hura Maori form of Jude. *See* Judith.

Huria Maori form of Julia.

Huriana Maori form of Juliana.

Hurihia Maori: changeable.

Hweiling Chinese: infinite wisdom.

Hyacinth Greek: young and
beautiful; a 'flower name'. *See also*
Jacinta.
Giacinta (Italian), Hyacintha,
Hyacinthe (French), Hyacinthia.

Hylda *See* Hilda.

Hyledd *See* Heledd.

Hypatia Greek: the highest.

I

Ianthe Greek: a violet-coloured
flower. *See also* Iolanthe.
Iantha, Ianthina, Janthina, Janthine.

Iben A popular Danish name.

Ida Old Norse: diligent. Teutonic:
happy, or youthful.
Idah, Idalia, Idalina, Idaline, Idella,
Idelle, Idette (German).

Idalia Spanish: the sun.

Idelia Teutonic: noble.

Idella/Idelle/Idette *See* Ida.

Idona A Norse goddess who was in
charge of the apples of eternal youth.
Idonea, Idonia, Idonie, Idony, Iduna,
Idunn.

Idra Aramaic: a fig tree.

Idylla Greek: perfect.
Idyll, Idylle, Idyllia.

Ierne Latin: from Ireland.

Ieshia Swahili: life, or lively.
Iesha, Ieysha.

Ignatia Latin: ardent, fiery. The feminine form of Ignatius.
Ignacia, Ignazia (Italian), Iniga.

Igrayne The mother of King Arthur.
Igraine, Ygraine, Ygrayne.

Ihipera Maori form of Isabel.

Iku Japanese: nourishing.

Ila Old French: from the island. *See also* Isla.
Ilah.

Ilana Hebrew: a tree.
Elana.

Ilayne *See* Elaine.

Ileana Greek: from the city of Ilion (Troy). Also a form of Eileen and Helen.
Ilia, Iliana, Ilyana.

Ilena/Ilene *See* Eileen.

Ilia/Iliana *See* Ileana.

Ilisapeci Fijian form of Elizabeth.

Ilisapesi Polynesian form of Elizabeth.

Ilka *See* Ilona.

Illona Irish form of Helen.

Illusion Middle English: something that is not quite real.

Ilma Finnish: like the air.

Ilona Hungarian form of Helen.
Diminutive: Ilka.

Ilsa *See* Alice and Elizabeth.

Ilse German diminutive of Elizabeth.

Ilyana *See* Ileana.

Ima Japanese: now, the present.

Iman Arabic: a believer in God.

Imelda Italian/Spanish: a fighter.
Emelda, Imalda.

Diminutive: Melda.

Immacolata Italian: after the Immaculate Conception.
Immaculada (Spanish), Immaculata.

Imogen Celtic: a girl or maiden. Latin: the image of her mother.
Emajen, Emajin, Emogen, Emogene, Emojen, Emojin, Imagen, Imagin, Imajin, Imijin, Imojin, Imogene, Imogine.

Impala Zulu: an African antelope.
Impalah, Impalla, Impallah.

Imperia Latin: imperious, the imperial one.
Imperio (Spanish).

Ina Polynesian: a moon goddess. *See also* Agnes.

Inara A goddess in Hittite mythology, similar to Artemis, the Greek goddess of the moon.
Inarah, Innara, Innarah.

Inari Finnish: a lake. Also a Japanese rice goddess.

Inas Polynesian: the wife of the moon.

Inbar Hebrew form of Amber.

Inca Spanish: a Peruvian tribe.
Inka.

Indara The earth goddess of the Indonesian island of Sulawesi.

India A 'country name'.
Indea, Indeah, Indiah, Indiella, Indya, Indyah.

Indiana A state of the USA. Also a boy's name.
Indeana, Indeanna, Indianna, Indi-Anna, Indie-Anna, Indyana, Indyanna, Indy-Anna.
Diminutives: Indee, Indey, Indie, Indy.

63

Indie A genre of alternative rock music. Also diminutive of Indiana and similar names.
Indee, Indey, Indi, Indy.

Indigo Latin: a deep blue-violet colour.

Indira Sanskrit: an alternative name for Lakshmi, wife of the god Vishnu.

Indya/Indyah *See* India.

Ines/Inez *See* Agnes.

Inga/Ingaberg/Inge/Inger *See* Ingrid.

Ingrid Old Norse: the hero's daughter.
Inga, Ingaberg, Inge, Ingeborg, Inger, Inkeri (Finnish).

Iniga *See* Ignatia.

Iniki Hawaiian: a famous hurricane.

Inka *See* Inca.

Innara/Innarah *See* Inara.

Innes Celtic/Gaelic: an island in the river, or from the island.
Iniss, Inness, Innis.

Innocentia Latin: innocent.
Inocencia (Spanish), Inocenta (Polish).

Inoki Hawaiian: devoted.

Iokina Hawaiian: God will develop.

Iola Greek: violet-coloured.
Iolanda, Iole.

Iolana Hawaiian: to soar like a hawk.

Iolanthe Greek: a violet flower. *See also* Ianthe, Violet and Yolanda.

Iona Hawaiian: a dove. Scottish: a Hebridean island.

Ione Greek: a violet-coloured stone.

Iphigenia Greek: the daughter of Agamemnon in Greek mythology.
Iphigénie (French).

Ipo Hawaiian: a sweetheart.

Ira Polynesian: a sky goddess.

Ireland Old English: the land of the Irish.

Irene Greek: peace.
Airini (Maori), Eireen, Eirena, Eirene, Erena, Erene, Ireen, Irena (Slavic), Irène (French), Irina (Russian), Irine.

Ireta Latin: angry, enraged.

Iriaka Maori: a hanging vine.

Irihapeti A Maori form of Elizabeth.

Irina/Irine *See* Irene.

Iris Greek: a rainbow. A 'flower name'.
Irisa (Russian), Irise, Irissa, Irris.

Irma Latin: noble. Teutonic: whole, strong. *See also* Erma.
Erma, Irmina, Irmine.

Irvette Old English: a friend from the sea.
Irva, Irvetta.

Isa Teutonic: strong-willed.

Isabel Spanish: a form of Elizabeth, meaning consecrated to God. *See also* Belle and Isabella.
Ihipera (Maori), Isabeau (French), Isabelita (Spanish), Isabell, Isabella (Italian, Spanish), Isabelle (French), Isbel (Scottish), Iseabail (Scottish Gaelic), Iseabel, Ishbel, Isobel, Isobell, Isobelle, Issabel, Issabell, Issabella, Issabelle, Izabel, Izabele, Izabella, Izabellah, Izabelle, Ysabel (Spanish), Ysobel.
Diminutives: Bel, Bella, Belle, Issie, Izzie, Izzy, Sabella, Sabelle.

Isabella A very popular name; the Italian and Spanish form of Isabel.
Isabellah, Isobella, Isobellah, Issabella, Issabellah, Izabella,

Izabellah.

Isabeth A combination of Isabel and Beth (*see* Elizabeth).

Isadora Greek: the gift of Isis. The feminine form of Isidore.
Isadore, Isidora, Isidore, Izadora.
Diminutives: Dora, Dory.

Isbel/Ishbel *See* Isabel.

Isel/Isell *See* Izel.

Iseult *See* Isolde.

Ishana Sanskrit: desirable.
Ishanna, Ishara.

Ishi Japanese: a stone.

Ishtar The Babylonian goddess of love and fertility; the equivalent of the Greek goddess Aphrodite and the Roman goddess Venus.
Eshtar.

Isi Native American: a deer.

Isidora/Isidore *See* Isadora.

Isis Ancient Egyptian: the goddess of fertility; the supreme goddess.
Iside (Italian).

Isla The name of a Scottish island. Spanish: an island.
Ila, Ilah, Islah, Islay.

Isleen *See* Eileen.

Ismena Greek: learned.
Ismenia.

Isobel/Isobelle *See* Isabel.

Isobella *See* Isabella.

Isola Latin: isolated; a loner.

Isolde Welsh: the fair one.
Esyllt (Welsh), Iseult, Isoda, Isolda, Yseult, Yseulte, Ysolda, Ysolde.

Isra Arabic: journeying by night.
Thai: freedom.

Issabel/Issabella/Issabelle/Issie *See*

Isabel and Isabella.

Ita Irish Gaelic: thirsty. The name of a 6th-century saint.
Ite, Itta, Yootha, Ytha.

Italia Latin: from Italy.
Itala.

Iva Old French: a yew tree. *See also* Ivana.

Ivalo Greenlandic: possibly meaning a sinew or tendon. Also a Lapland placename.
Ivalu.

Ivana Slavic form of Jane and a feminine form of Ivan.
Evana, Ivanka (Czech), Ivanna, Ivanovna, Iveta (Slavic), Yvana, Yvanna.
Diminutives: Iva, Ivka.

Ivangela/Ivangelina *See* Evangeline.

Ivanka/Iveta/Ivka *See* Ivana.

Ivelisse An unusual Spanish name.

Ivory Latin: from the tusks of an elephant.
Ivoree, Ivorey, Ivori, Ivorie.

Ivy Old English: a 'plant name'.
Ivee, Ivey, Ivie, Ivye.

Iwi Maori: a tribe.

Izabel/Izabella/Izabelle *See* Isabel.

Izadora *See* Isadora.

Izanami Japanese: she who invites you to enter.

Izel A Turkish name of uncertain meaning.
Isel, Isell, Izell.

Izett A modern name, a combination of Isabel and the feminine 'ette'.
Izet, Izette.

Izzie/Izzy *See* Isabel.

J

Jaala/Jaalah *See* Jala.

Jaçana Portuguese: a type of bird.

Jacaranda A tropical tree with lavender-coloured flowers.
Jacarandah.

Jacenta *See* Jacinta.

Jacey Native American: the moon.
Jacee, Jaci, Jacie, Jacy, Jaycee, Jayci, Jaycie.

Jacilyn *See* Jacqueline.

Jacinta Spanish from Greek: beautiful. Also a form of Hyacinth.
Jacenta, Jacinda (Greek), Jacinna, Jacinte, Jacinth, Jacintha, Jacinthe (French), Jacinthia, Jasinta, Jesinta.

Jacinth Greek: a purple-coloured gemstone. *See also* Jacinta.
Jacintha, Jacinthe (French), Jacynth.

Jacki/Jackie/Jacky/Jacklyn *See* Jacqueline.

Jacoba Hebrew: the supplanter. A feminine form of Jacob.
Jacobella (Italian), Jacobina, Jacobine, Jakoba, Jakuba (Polish).

Jacqueline French from Hebrew: the supplanter. The feminine form of Jacob and James.
Jacilyn, Jackeline, Jackelyn, Jacklyn, Jackolin, Jaclyn, Jacquelina, Jacquelyn, Jacquetta (French), Jacquette, Jaklyn, Jaklynn, Jaquenetta, Jaquenette, Jaquet (Cornish), Jaquiline.
Diminutives: Haki (Maori), Jack, Jacki, Jackie, Jacky, Jacqui, Jacquie.

Jacy *See* Jacey.

Jacynth *See* Jacinth.

Jada Hebrew: the wise one.
Jadah, Jahda, Jaida, Jaidah, Jayda, Jaydah.

Jade Spanish: a 'gemstone name'.
Giada (Italian), Jaed, Jaedd, Jaedde, Jaede, Jaid, Jaide, Jayd, Jayde, Jaydie.

Jadwiga *See* Hedwig.

Jae *See* Jay.

Jael *See* Yael.

Jaela/Jaelah *See* Jayla.

Jaffa Hebrew: beautiful.
Jaffe, Jafit, Yaffa, Yaffah.

Jahda *See* Jada.

Jahmila *See* Jamila.

Jahnaya/Jahneya *See* Janaya.

Jai/Jaie *See* Jay.

Jaid/Jaida/Jaide *See* Jada and Jade.

Jaila/Jailah *See* Jayla.

Jaime A modern feminine form of James. Also from j'aime, French for I love you. *See also* Jamesina.
Jaimee, Jaimey, Jaimi, Jaimia (Polynesian), Jamey, Jamie, Jamiee, Jaymee, Jaymi, Jaymie.

Jain/Jaina/Jaine *See* Jane.

Jakeah A feminine form of Jake (*see* Jacob in BOYS).
Jaikea, Jaikeah, Jakea.

Jaklynn *See* Jacqueline.

Jakoba/Jakuba *See* Jacoba.

Jala Arabic: clarity, shining.
Jaala, Jaalah, Jalah.

Jamaica A Carribbean island.
Jamaika, Jamayca, Jamayka.

Jamal Arabic: comely.
Jamala, Jamalah.

Jameela/Jamella *See* Jamila.

Jamesina Hebrew: the supplanter.
A feminine form of James. *See also*
Jaime.
Jamesetta, Jamesette, Jamesine.

Jamey/Jamie *See* Jaime.

Jamieson *See* BOYS.

Jamila Arabic/Swahili: beautiful.
Jahmila, Jameela, Jamella, Jamilah,
Jamilia.

Jamima *See* Jemima.

Jan/Jana *See* Jane, Janet and Joanne.

Janaya A modern name, derived from
Jan or Janet.
Jahnaya, Jahneya, Janayah.

Jancis A combination of Jane and
Frances.
Jances, Jancess, Janciss.

Jane Hebrew: God is gracious. A
feminine form of John, and one
of the most popular female names
for centuries. *See also* Janelle, Janet,
Janice, Janine, Jean, Jenna, Joan,
Joanne, Shane, Sheena, Sian and
Siobhán.
Evana (Slavic), Giaan, Gianina
(Italian), Gianna (Italian), Giovanna
(Italian), Heni (Maori), Ivana
(Czech), Ivanna (Russian), Jain,
Jaina, Jaine, Jana (Czech, Polish),
Janna, Janneke (Dutch), Jannike
(Scandinavian), Jayn, Jayna, Jayne,
Jeanne (French), Jehanne (French),
Jenna (Cornish), Juana (Spanish),
Juanita (Spanish), Seini (Tongan),
Shane (Irish Gaelic), Shaun, Shauna,
Shawn, Shawna, Sheena, Sheenah,
Shena, Shevaun (Irish), Shivaun
(Irish), Sian (Welsh), Siobhán (Irish
Gaelic), Soana (Tongan).
Diminutives: Gia (Italian), Gian
(Italian), Ivanka (Czech), Jan, Janey,

Janie, Jaynie, Nita (Spanish).

Janelle A combination of Jane and
the feminine elle suffix.
Janel, Janella, Jannel, Jannelle, Jenel,
Jenelle.

Janet *See also* Jane, Jeannette and
Sinéad.
Janeth, Janett, Janetta, Janette,
Jeanette, Jeannette, Jenette, Sinéad
(Irish Gaelic), Sioned (Welsh).
Diminutives: Jan, Jann.

Janice A form of Jane.
Janis, Janise.

Janine A form of Jane.
Janina (Polish), Janita, Janyne,
Jeannine (French).

Janna Hebrew: flourishing. *See also*
Jane.
Jannah.

Janne *See* Joanne.

Jannel/Jannelle *See* Janelle.

Jannike *See* Jane.

Janthina/Janthine *See* Ianthe.

Janti A modern name, probably
derived from Jan, Jane or Janet.
Jantee, Janti, Jantie, Jantina, Jantine,
Jantti, Janty.

January The first month of the year.
After Janus, the Roman god of
beginnings and endings.
Januar (German), Januarea, Januari
(Swahili), Januaria, Januarie, Janvier
(French).

Japonica Latin: a shrub with pink,
red or white flowers.
Japonika.

Jaquenette/Jaquet/Jaquiline *See*
Jacqueline.

Jarah Hebrew: honey.

Jarita Sanskrit: a legendary bird.

Jarka Slavic: spring-like.

Jarmila Slavic: the grace of spring.

Jarrah *See* BOYS.

Jarvia Teutonic: as sharp or keen as
a spear.
Jarvinia.

Jasinta *See* Jacinta.

Jaslyn A modern name, possibly a
combination of Jasmine and Lyn (a
waterfall).
Jasleen, Jaslene, Jaslin, Jaslynn,
Jaslynne, Jazlyn, Jazlyne, Jazlynn,
Jazlynne.
Diminutives: Jas, Jassie, Jaz, Jazz,
Jazzie, Jazzy.

Jasmine Persian: a fragrant flower.
Jasmin, Jasmina, Jasminah, Jasminka,
Jasmyn, Jasmyne, Jazmin, Jazmina,
Jazmine, Jazmyn, Jazmyne, Jazzmin,
Jazzmine, Jazzmyn, Jazzmyne,
Jessamin, Jessamina, Jessamine,
Jessamyn, Yasmeen (Arabic), Yasmin
(Arabic), Yasmina, Yasmine, Yassmin,
Yassmine.
Diminutives: Jas, Jassie, Jaz, Jazz,
Jazzie, Jazzy, Jess.

Jasvinder Sikh: the glory of the Lord.
Jasvinda, Jasvindah.

Jati An unusual name from Cyprus.

Javiera *See* Xaviera.

Jaxi A modern made-up name.
Jaxee, Jaxey, Jaxie, Jaxy.

Jay Old English: a bird. *See also*
BOYS.
Jae, Jai, Jaie.

Jaya Sanskrit: victory. The name of a
Buddhist goddess.

Jaycee/Jayci/Jaycie *See* Jacey.

Jayd/Jayda/Jayde *See* Jada and Jade.

Jayla A modern name, derived from
Jay, or a variation of Kayla.
Jaela, Jaelah, Jaila, Jailah, Jaylah.

Jaymee/Jaymie *See* Jaime.

Jayn/Jayna/Jayne/Jaynie *See* Jane.

Jazlyn/Jazlyne *See* Jaslyn.

Jazmin/Jazmine/Jazmyn *See* Jasmine.

Jazz A musical genre. Also a
diminutive of Jaslyn and Jasmine.
Jaz, Jazann, Jazra, Jazza, Jazzah, Jazze,
Jazzi, Jazzie, Jazzra, Jazzy.

Jazzmin/Jazzmyne *See* Jasmine.

Jean A form of Jane.
Gene, Genia, Hira (Maori), Jeana,
Jeane, Jeanella, Jeanna, Jeanne, Jeen,
Jeene, Jenella.
Diminutives: Jeanie, Jeannie.

Jeanne/Jehanne *See* Jane.

Jeannette A form of Janet.
Genette, Jeanette, Jenette, Jennet,
Jennette.
Diminutives: Jeanie, Jeannie.

Jeannine *See* Janine.

Jedda Aboriginal: a beautiful girl.
Jeda, Jedah, Jeddah.

Jedna *See* Jenna.

Jeen/Jeene *See* Jean.

Jehan Arabic: a beautiful flower.

Jelena *See* Helen.

Jelissa Possibly derived from Melissa.
Jelissah, Jelyssa, Jelyssah.

Jemima Hebrew: a dove. A biblical
name.
Jamima, Jehmima, Jemiah, Jemimah,
Jemmima.

Jemma *See* Gemma.

Jen/Jennie/Jenny Diminutives of

Jennifer.

Jenaya A modern name, probably a form of Jennifer.
Jenaia, Jeneya, Jenya.

Jenel/Jenella/Jenelle *See* Janelle and Jean.

Jenevieve *See* Genevieve.

Jendaya African: thankful.
Jendayah.

Jenna A Cornish form of Jane. Also a diminutive of Jennifer.
Genna, Gennah, Jedna (Cornish), Jennah.

Jennalyn A combination of Jennifer (the fair one) and Lynn (a waterfall).
Jenalin, Jenalyn, Jennalin, Jenna-Lin, Jenna-Lyn, Jenna-Lynn, Jenna-Lynne.

Jennifer Cornish/Welsh: fair and soft. A form of Guinevere.
Gennifer, Genowefa, Jenafer, Jenifa, Jenifer (Cornish), Jennefer, Jenniva.
Diminutives: Genny, Jen, Jeni, Jenna, Jenni, Jennie, Jenny.

Georgia/Jeorgiah *See* Jorja.

Jeraldine/Jerri/Jerry *See* Geraldine.

Jerarda *See* Gerarda.

Jeremia Hebrew: appointed by God. The feminine form of Jeremiah and Jeremy.
Jeremiah, Jeremie, Jeremya.

Jermain/Jermaine/Jermayne *See* Germaine.

Jerusha Hebrew: the married one.

Jesica/Jesika/Jessa *See* Jessica.

Jesinta *See* Jacinta.

Jesmond A suburb of Newcastle upon Tyne, England. The name possibly means the hill of Jesus.
Jesmonde, Jezmond, Jezmonde.

Jess *See* Jasmine and Jessica.

Jessa A form of Jess or Jessica.
Jessah, Jessay.

Jessalin/Jessalynn *See* Jessica.

Jessamin/Jessamyn *See* Jasmine.

Jesse A diminutive of Jessica. Also a boy's name from the Bible, meaning God's gift.
Jessie, Jessye.

Jessica Hebrew: wealthy. A character in Shakespeare's *The Merchant of Venice*.
Gessica, Gessicah, Gessika, Gessikah, Jesica, Jesicah, Jesika, Jesikah, Jeska, Jessa, Jessaca, Jessacah, Jessalin, Jessalynn, Jessicah, Jessika, Jessikah, Jesska, Jesslyn.
Diminutives: Jess, Jesse, Jessi, Jessie, Jessye.

Jesslyn/Jessye *See* Jesse and Jessica.

Jet Latin: black; a material used for making jewellery.
Jeta, Jett, Jetta, Jette.

Jetsun Bhutanese/Tibetan: venerable.

Jetty Middle English: a wharf or pier.
Jetee, Jetey, Jeti, Jetie, Jettee, Jettey, Jetti, Jettie.

Jeudi French: Thursday.

Jeune French: young.
Jeunesse.

Jewel Old French: a gemstone; or the precious one.
Jewell, Jewelle, Jewels.

Jezebel A Hebrew name from the Old Testament.
Jezabel, Jezabell, Jezabelle, Jezebell, Jezebelle.

Jezmond/Jezmonde *See* Jesmond.

Jie Chinese: pure.

Jill/Jilli/Jillie/Jillian/Jilly *See* Gillian.

Jimena Spanish form of Ximena.

Jin Chinese: golden. Korean: a jewel. Jing.

Jo/Jo-Ann/Joanna/Jo-Anne *See* Joanne and Josephine.

Joan *See* Jane and Joanne.

Joanne A form of Jane. *See also* Hanne. Hanne (German), Janne (Scandinavian), Joan, Joana, Joann, Jo-Ann, Joanna, Jo-Anne, Joeanna, Joeanne, Johana (Czech), Johanna (Dutch, German, Scandinavian), Johanne, Joina, Jone, Jonella, Jonna (Danish), Seònaid (Scottish), Shona (Scottish), Siôna (Welsh), Soana (Tongan).
Diminutives: Hana (Czech), Jana, Jo, Joanie, Joni, Jonie.

Jobina Hebrew: the persecuted one. The female form of Job. Jobie, Jobinah, Joby, Jobyna.

Jocasta Greek: the shining moon. The mother of Oedipus in Greek mythology.

Jocelyn Latin: the merry one. Jocelin, Joceline, Jocelyne, Jocelynne, Joscelin, Josceline, Joscelyn, Joslin, Josline, Josselin, Josselyn, Josslyn. *Diminutive*: Joss.

Jocosa Latin: humorous, playful. Joccoa.

Jocunda Latin: cheerful, merry.

Jodie A diminutive of Judith. Jodee, Jodene, Jodette, Jodey, Jodhi, Jodi, Jodia, Jody, Johdee, Johdi, Johdie, Johdy.

Joelle French from Hebrew: the Lord is God. The feminine form of Joel. Joeli, Joell, Joella, Jo-Elle, Joellen, Joely, Joellyn.

Joette *See* Josephine.

Johana/Johanna/Johanne *See* Joanne.

Johdee/Johdi/Johdie *See* Jodie.

Johnna A feminine form of John, meaning God is gracious. *See also* Jonica and Jovana. Johna, Johnetta, Johnette, Johnnetta, Johnnette, Jonetta, Jonette, Jonna, Jonnah.

Joi *See* Joy.

Joice *See* Joyce.

Joina *See* Joanne.

Jolan/Jolanda/Jolani/Jolanta *See* Yolanda.

Jolanka Hungarian: one who is good. Jola, Jolah, Jolan.

Jolene An American 'combination name', perhaps of Jo and Marlene. Joleen, Joline.

Jolie French: pretty. Joli, Joliette, Joly.

Jone/Jonella *See* Joanne.

Joni/Jonie *See* Joanne.

Jonica A feminine form of John. *See also* Johnna and Jovana. Jonicah, Jonika, Jonikah, Jonnica, Jonnicah, Jonnika, Jonnikah.

Jonina Hebrew: a dove. The feminine form of Jonah. Jona, Jonah, Jonia, Joniah, Joninah.

Jonna/Jonnah *See* Joanne and Johnna.

Jonquil A 'flower name', from the Latin word for a reed.

Jora Hebrew: autumn rain.

Jordan Hebrew: flowing down, as in the River Jordan. Also a boy's name.

Jordaine, Jordana, Jordane, Jordann, Jordanne, Jordayne, Jordena, Jordin, Jordyn, Jourdan, Jourden.
Diminutives: Jordi, Jordie, Jordy, Jori, Jory.

Jori/Jory *See* Jordan.

Jorja A modern form of Georgia.
Jeorgia, Jeorgiah, Jorgia, Jorgiah, Jorjah, Jorjia, Jorjiah,
Diminutives: Jeorgi, Jeorgie, Jorji Jorjie.

Joscelin/Joslin *See* Jocelyn.

Josée French form of Josephine.

Josephine Hebrew: God shall add. The feminine form of Joseph.
Giuseppina (Italian), Joette, Josanna, Josée (French), Josefina (Spanish), Josefine, Josepha, Josèphe (French), Josephina, Josetta, Josette, Josiane (French), Jozefa (Slavic), Jozefina, Jozefine, Jozetta, Jozette, Sosefina (Tongan).
Diminutives: Fifi, Jo, Joe, Josee, Josey, Josie, Pepa (Spanish), Pepita (Spanish), Posy.

Josetta/Josette/Josiane *See* Josephine.

Joss Originally a diminutive of Jocelyn.
Josonia, Josse, Jossonia.

Josslyn *See* Jocelyn.

Jourdan/Jourden *See* Jordan.

Jovana Slavic: a feminine form of John.
Jovanah, Jovanna, Jovannah.

Jovita Latin: the joyful one.

Joy Latin: joyful.
Joi, Joie, Joya, Joye, Joyita.

Joyanne A combination of Joy and Anne.
Joyan, Joyann, Joy-Ann, Joy-Anne.

Joyce Middle English from Breton: a lord. Originally a male name.
Joice, Joyous.
Diminutive: Joycie.

Joyita *See* Joy.

Jozefa/Jozefine/Jozette *See* Josephine.

Juana/Juanita Spanish forms of Jane.
Diminutive: Nita.

Jubilee Middle English: a celebration.
Jubilie.

Judah/Jude/Judeen/Judetta/Judie *See* Judith.

Judith Hebrew: a woman from Judea, or the praised one. A name from the Bible. *See also* Jodie.
Juda, Judah, Judeen, Judetta, Judina, Judit (Spanish), Judita (Czech, Spanish), Juditha, Judithe (French), Judyth, Judythe, Siobhán (Irish), Siubhan (Scottish), Turuhira (Maori), Yehudit (Hebrew).
Diminutives: Hura (Maori), Jodie, Jude, Judi, Judie, Judy, Jutta (German), Jutte (Dutch).

Julea/Jules *See* Julia.

Julia Latin: from a Roman family name, possibly meaning youthful. *See also* Gillian.
Giulia (Italian), Giulietta (Italian), Huria (Maori), Huriana (Maori), Julea, Juli (Hungarian), Juliana, Juliane, Juliann, Julianna (German), Julie (French), Julieanne, Julienne, Juliet, Julietta (Spanish), Juliette (French), Julina, Juline, Julita (Filipina, Spanish), Julitta, Julya (Russian).
Diminutives: Jill, Jules.

Julie/Juliet/Juliette *See* Julia.

Julina/Juline/Julita/Julitta *See* Julia.

July A 'month name'.
Juillet (French), Julai (Swahili), Juli (Dutch, Swedish).

Julya *See* Julia.

Jumah Arabic: Friday.
Juma, Jumaa (Swahili).

Jumoke Nigerian: the beloved one.

Jun Chinese: the truth. Nepali: moonlight.

June A 'month name'.
Hune (Maori), Juen, Juna, Junella, Junelle, Junetta, Junette, Juni (Danish, Swahili), Junia, Junie, Junina, Junine, Junita.

Juneau A city in Alaska.
Juneaux, Junot.

Juni/Junia/Junina/Junita *See* June.

Juniper Latin: a 'plant name'.

Junko Japanese: an obedient child.

Juno Latin: the heavenly one, the wife of Jupiter in Roman mythology. Also a form of Úna.

Jura A mountain range in France.
Jurah.

Jurisa Slavic: a storm.
Jurisah, Jurise.

Jurnee A modern name, probably derived from the word journey.
Jurney, Jurni, Jurnie.

Justice Middle English: rightness. *See also* Justine.
Justica, Justicia, Justisa, Justise, Justyce, Justyse.

Justine Latin: fair, just. The feminine form of Justin.
Justa, Justicia, Justina, Justyna, Justyne.

Jutta/Jutte *See* Judith.

Jyoti Sanskrit: light.

K

Kaaren/Kaarena/Kaarin *See* Karen.

Kabira Arabic: powerful.

Kade Indonesian: a popular girl's name.

Kadence *See* Cadence.

Kadira *See* Qadira.

Kae *See* Kay.

Kaela *See* Kaila.

Kaer Breton form of Katherine.

Kagami Japanese: a mirror.

Kahili Hawaiian: a feather.

Kahla *See* Kala.

Kahu Maori: a cloak.

Kai Native American: a willow. *See also* Kay.
Kaie, Khi, Ki, Kie, Ky, Kye.

Kaia/Kaiya *See* Caja.

Kaikala Hawaiian: sea and sun.

Kaiko Japanese: forgiveness.

Kaila Hebrew: crowned with laurel.
Kaela, Kaelah, Kailah, Kayla, Kaylah.

Kailana Hawaiian: the adored one.

Kailani Hawaiian: the sea and sky.

Kailmana Hawaiian: a diamond.

Kaimana Hawaiian: the power of the sea.

Kaisa Finnish: pure.

Kaisha *See* Keisha.

Kait/Kaite *See* Kate.

Kaitlin/Kaitlyn *See* Caitlin.

Kaja *See* Caja.

Kaku Maori: a hawk.

Kala Hawaiian: the sun. *See also* Kali. Kahla.

Kalama Hawaiian: a flaming torch. Kalamah.

Kalan *See* BOYS.

Kalandra *See* Calandra.

Kalani Hawaiian: the sky. Kaliani.

Kalantha *See* Calantha.

Kalauni Tongan: a crown.

Kalea Hawaiian: bright.

Kaleesha/Kalesha *See* Kalisha.

Kalei Hawaiian: a flower wreath, or the beloved one.

Kalena Hawaiian form of Karen.

Kaleria An unusual name of Russian origin.

Kaley *See* Kayley.

Kali Sanskrit: black. Kala.

Kalika Greek: a rosebud.

Kalila Arabic: beloved.

Kalinda Sanskrit: the sun.

Kalinn Scandinavian: a river. Kalin, Kalyn, Kalynn.

Kalisha A modern, generally American, name. Kaleesha, Kalesha, Kalysha.

Kalista/Kallista *See* Calista.

Kalli Greek: a lark. Kallie, Kally.

Kalliope *See* Calliope.

Kaloni Hawaiian: the sky, or a chieftain.

Kalpana Sanskrit: a fantasy.

Kalyani Sanskrit: auspicious, beautiful.

Kalyn/Kalynn *See* Kalinn.

Kalypso *See* Calypso.

Kalysha *See* Kalisha.

Kam *See* Cameron.

Kama Sanskrit: love.

Kamal Perfection. The name of a Baha'i month that encompasses 1–19 August, so suitable for a Leo child.

Kamala Sanskrit: a lotus. Kamal (Nepali), Kamalika.

Kamaria African: of the moon.

Kamea Hawaiian: the one and only.

Kameko Japanese: the child of the tortoise, implying longevity.

Kameron/Kamryn *See* Cameron.

Kamila Czech and Polish form of Camilla.

Kamilah Arabic: the perfect one.

Kamini Sanskrit: desirable.

Kanani Hawaiian: beauty.

Kanapa Maori: radiant.

Kandace/Kandice/Kandy *See* Candace.

Kaneli Tongan: canary yellow.

Kani Hawaiian: sound.

Kanika African: a black cloth.

Kaniva Polynesian: the Milky Way. Kanivah.

Kanoa Polynesian: free.

Kanti Sanskrit: lovely.

Kanuha Hawaiian: the sulky one.

Kanya Sanskrit: pure; the Hindu name for the zodiac sign of Virgo. Thai: a young lady. Kanyana.

Kapua Hawaiian: a flower.

Kara/Karah *See* Cara.

Kararaina Maori form of Caroline.

Karel *See* Carol.

Karen Danish form of Katherine.
Caren, Carin, Caryn, Kaaren, Kaarena, Kaarin, Kalena (Hawaiian), Kareen, Kareena, Karena, Karin (Swedish), Karina, Karine, Karyn.

Karensa/Karenza *See* Kerensa.

Karewa Maori: a buoy.

Kariba/Karibah *See* Cariba.

Karima Arabic: noble, generous.

Karin/Karina/Karine *See* Karen.

Karisa/Karise *See* Carissa.

Karita Scandinavian form of Charity.

Karla/Karly *See* Carla and Karli.

Karli Turkish: the girl of the snow.
Karlea, Karlee, Karleigh, Karlie, Karly, Karlye.

Karlotte *See* Charlotte.

Karma Sanskrit: fate or destiny. Sherpa/Tibetan: a star. Also a boy's name.
Carma, Carmah, Karmah.

Karmé *See* Carmé.

Karmel/Karmen *See* Carmel.

Karol *See* Carol.

Karolina/Karoline *See* Caroline.

Karrie *See* Carrie.

Karsha *See* Keisha.

Karyn *See* Karen.

Kasey/Kasie *See* Casey.

Kashmira From Kashmir, an Indian state.
Cashmira, Cashmyra, Kashmirah, Kashmyra.

Kass/Kassandra/Kassie *See* Cassandra and Katherine.

Kassidy *See* Cassidy.

Katalin *See* Katherine.

Kataraina/Katarina/Katerina/ Katerine *See* Katherine.

Kate A diminutive of Catherine and Katherine.
Cait (Irish), Caite, Cate, Kait, Kaite, Kayt, Kayte.

Katelin/Katelyn/Kate-Lynn *See* Caitlin.

Katherine Greek: pure. A 4th-century saint who was martyred on a wheel. *See also* Catherine, Karen, Kate, Kathleen, Katya and Kay.
Kaer (Breton), Karen (Danish), Katalin, Kataraina (Maori), Katarina (Swedish), Katerina (Czech, Russian), Katerine (Czech, Russian), Katharine, Katharyn, Katherina (German), Kathleen (Irish), Kathri (Swiss), Kathrin, Kathrina (Danish), Kathrine, Kathryn, Kathryne, Katja (German), Katra (Slavic), Katren, Katrien (Dutch, German), Katrin, Katrina (German, Scandinavian), Katrine (Dutch, German), Katriona, Katryn, Kattalin (Basque), Katya (Russian).
Diminutives: Kass, Kate, Kath, Kathe, Kathee, Kathie, Kathy, Katie, Katy, Katye, Kay, Kaye, Kerry, Kit, Kitty, Treena, Trina.

Kathleen Irish form of Katherine. *See also* Catherine and Caitlin.
Caitlin, Cathleen, Cathlene, Kateleen, Kathlene, Katyleen.
Diminutives: Kath, Kathy, Katie, Katy.

Kathri/Kathrin/Kathryn *See* Katherine.

Katia/Katiah/Katiya *See* Katya.

Katie *See* Katherine and Kathleen.

Katja/Katra *See* Katherine and Katya.

Katrece/Katrice *See* Catrice.

Katren/Katrin/Katrina/Katrine *See* Katherine.

Kattalin Basque form of Katherine.

Katy *See* Katherine and Kathleen.

Katya A Russian form of Katherine. Katia, Katiah, Katiya, Katja (German), Katyah.

Kaula Polynesian: a prophet.

Kaulana Polynesian: famous.

Kawena Hawaiian: glowing like a fire or the sunset.

Kay A diminutive of Katherine. Kae, Kai, Kaie, Kaye, Kayla, Kaylene.

Kaya *See* Caja.

Kaycee/Kaycie *See* Casey.

Kayla/Kaylah *See* Kaila, Kay and Kayley.

Kayley Irish Gaelic: slender. *See also* Caley. Kaley, Kayla, Kaylee, Kayleigh, Kaylie.

Kayna Cornish: a saint's name.

Kayscha/Kaysha *See* Keisha.

Kayt/Kayte *See* Kate.

Kazia *See* Kezia.

Kea Maori: a mountain parrot.

Keala Hawaiian: a pathway.

Kealee/Kealeigh/Kealie *See* Keeley.

Keana/Keanna/Kearna *See* Kiana.

Keara/Kearah *See* Kiera.

Kearoa Polynesian: a legendary figure.

Keatyn Old English: from the place of the kites or hawks. Keatin, Keating, Keaton, Keetyn, Keyton, Keytyn.

Kedra A modern American name.

Kedrah, Khedra, Khedrah.

Keeley Irish Gaelic: beautiful or handsome. Can also be a boy's name. Kealee, Kealeigh, Kealey, Keali, Kealie, Kealy, Keelah, Keelee, Keeleigh, Keeli, Keelie, Keely.

Keera/Keerah *See* Kiera.

Keesha *See* Keisha.

Keetyn *See* Keatyn.

Kei Hawaiian: dignified or glorious.

Keiko Japanese: the beloved or adored one.

Keilani Hawaiian: glorious.

Keira/Keirah *See* Kiera.

Keiri/Keirie *See* Kerry.

Keisha Contemporary American: possibly from Keshia (the favourite). *See also* Lakeisha. Kaisha, Karsha, Kayscha, Kaysha, Keesha, Kesha, Keysha, Keyshia, Kiesha.

Keitha Celtic: from the forest. A feminine form of Keith. Keithia.

Keiva Possibly a feminine form of Keith, meaning from the forest. Keivah, Keva, Kevah.

Kelda Old Norse: a fountain or mountain spring.

Kelila Hebrew: a crown of laurel.

Kellina *See* Kelly.

Kelly Irish Gaelic: a warrior maid. Kelee, Keli, Kelle, Kellee, Kelley, Kelli, Kellie, Kellina. *Diminutive*: Kell.

Kelsey Old Norse: the dweller on the island, or by the water. Generally a Norwegian name. Kelsee, Kelsi, Kelsie, Kelsy.

Keltie *See* BOYS.

Kenda African: a child of the water. Also a feminine form of Ken (handsome and fair).

Kendall English: from the bright valley.
Kendal, Kendel, Kendell.

Kendra Celtic: a hill. Old English: royal power. The feminine form of Kendrick.

Kenisha American: the beautiful one.
Kenecia, Keneesha, Kenesha, Keneshah, Kenicia, Kenishah.

Kenna Celtic: love.
Kennah, Kenia, Kennia.

Kennedy *See* BOYS.

Kensa Cornish: the first.

Kenwyn Cornish/Welsh: the name of a saint. Also a boy's name.
Kenwyne, Kenwynn, Kenwynne.

Kenya An African country.

Kenzie A modern name, a diminutive of the popular Mackenzie.
Kenza, Kenzah, Kenzee, Kenzey, Kenzi, Kenzy.

Keona Hawaiian: God's precious gift.

Kerala A state in southern India.
Keralah, Keralla, Kerallah.

Kerani Sanskrit: sacred bells.

Keren Hebrew: a ray, or a horn. A biblical name.
Kerena, Kerin.

Kerensa Cornish: love.
Carensa, Carenza, Karensa, Karenza, Kerenza.

Kereru Maori: a wood pigeon.

Kerewin Maori: the main character of Keri Hulme's novel *The Bone People*.

Kerezen Cornish: a cherry.

Keresen.

Keri Maori: skin. *See also* Kerry.
Kerie.

Kerin *See* Keren.

Kerith Hebrew: a stream mentioned in the Bible.

Kerra Cornish: one who is dear.
Kerrah.

Kerrera Scottish Gaelic: an island in the Inner Hebrides.

Kerry Irish Gaelic: dark; the name of an Irish county. Also a diminutive of Catherine and Katherine.
Keiri, Keirie, Keri, Kerie, Kerre, Kerrey, Kerri, Kerrie, Kerryn, Kery, Kierry.

Kerry-Ann A 'combination name'.
Kerri-Ann, Kerry-Anne.

Kersti/Kerstie/Kersty *See* Kirstie.

Kerstin/Kerstyn *See* Kirsten.

Kesang Sherpa/Tibetan: of the golden age.

Kesha *See* Keisha.

Keshia African: the favourite. *See also* Keisha.
Kesha.

Kesia/Kesiah *See* Kezia.

Kestrel English: a small falcon.
Kestrell, Kestrelle.

Keturah Hebrew: fragrant incense.
Ketura.

Ketzia *See* Kezia.

Keva/Kevah *See* Keiva.

Keverne Irish Gaelic: beloved, lovable. Feminine form of Kevin.

Keyna Welsh: a jewel.

Keysha/Keyshia *See* Keisha.

Keyt/Keyte *See* Kite.

Keyton/Keytyn *See* Keatyn.

Kezia Hebrew: a cassia tree. A daughter of Job in the Old Testament. *See also* Cassia. Kazia, Kesia, Kesiah, Ketzia, Keziah. *Diminutives*: Kez, Kezzie, Kezzy.

Khalida Arabic: eternal.

Khedra/Khedrah *See* Kedra.

Khi/Ki/Kie *See* Kai.

Khloe/Khloee *See* Chloe.

Khym *See* Kim.

Kiana Irish Gaelic: ancient. Ciana, Cianna, Ciarna, Ciarni, Keana, Keanna, Kearna, Kianna, Kiannah, Kiarna, Kiarni, Kinna, Kinnah, Kyana, Kyanah, Kyanna, Kyannah.

Kiara The name of an Irish saint. *See also* Chiara. Kiarah, Kiarra, Kiarrah.

Kichi Japanese: fortunate.

Kidani Swahili: a bracelet.

Kiele Hawaiian: a gardenia.

Kiera Irish Gaelic: dark, black. The feminine form of Kieran. Ciara (Irish), Keara, Kearah, Keera, Keerah, Keira, Keirah, Kierah, Kierra, Kira.

Kierry *See* Kerry.

Kiesha *See* Keisha.

Kiki Egyptian: from the castor plant.

Kiku Japanese: a chrysanthemum.

Kilea/Kilee/Kiley *See* Kylie.

Kilia Hawaiian: heaven.

Kim The hero in Rudyard Kipling's novel. Vietnamese: the golden one. Also a diminutive of Kimberley. Khym, Kimm, Kimya, Kyhm, Kym, Kymm. *Diminutives*: Kimmi, Kimmie, Kimmy.

Kimana African: a butterfly. Kimama, Kimanna.

Kimberley Old English: from the meadow. Kimberlee, Kimberlie, Kimberly, Kimbra, Kymberlie. *Diminutives*: Kim, Kym.

Kimbra *See* Kimberley.

Kimiko Japanese: heavenly.

Kimm/Kimmie *See* Kim.

Kin Japanese: golden.

Kineta Greek: active.

Kini Polynesian: God is gracious.

Kinna/Kinnah *See* Kiana.

Kiona Native American: from the brown hills. Kionah.

Kira Japanese: dark. Persian: the sun. *See also* Kiera. Kirah, Kirra, Kyra, Kyrah.

Kiran Sanskrit: a ray of light. Kirran.

Kirby Old Norse/Teutonic: from the church town. Kirbea, Kirbee, Kirbeigh, Kirbi, Kirbie.

Kiri Polynesian: the bark of a tree. Kirri, Kirry.

Kirilee A modern 'combination name' from Kiri and Lee. Kirilly, Kirrilly.

Kirimei A Maori name of uncertain meaning.

Kirsten Scandinavian form of Christina. Kerstin (Swedish), Kerstyn, Kirstin,

Kirstyn, Kjersti (Norwegian).

Kirstie Scottish form of Christina.
Chirsty, Kersti, Kerstie, Kersty,
Kirsti, Kirsty.

Kismet Persian: destiny.

Kit/Kitty *See* Katherine.

Kita Japanese: from the north.

Kite Middle English: a type of hawk.
Also a boy's name.
Keyt, Keyte, Kyte.

Kiwa Polynesian: a figure from
mythology.
Kiwah.

Kiyoko Japanese: clear.

Kjersti *See* Kirsten.

Klara German, Scandinavian and
Slavic form of Clare.

Klarice/Klarissa/Klarisse *See* Clarice.

Klaudia *See* Claudia.

Klementyna *See* Clemence.

Kleo/Kleopatra/Klio/Kliopatra *See*
Cleopatra.

Kloee/Klohe/Klohee *See* Chloe.

Koanga Maori: spring, or happiness.

Kodi/Kodie/Kody *See* Cody.

Kohana Japanese: a little flower.

Kohia Polynesian: a passionflower.

Koko Japanese: a stork. Native
American: of the night. *See also*
Coco.

Kolina Greek: pure. Swedish: a
maiden.

Kolohe Hawaiian: a rascal.

Kona Hawaiian: a lady. Sanskrit: a
name for the planet Saturn.
Konah.

Kono Polynesian: a basket.

Konstanze *See* Constance.

Kopu The Maori name for Venus.

Kordelia *See* Cordelia.

Koren Greek: a maiden.

Korey/Kori/Korie *See* Corey.

Kori Maori: exercise.

Korinne *See* Cora.

Kornelia *See* Cornelia.

Koula Tongan: golden.

Kourtnee/Kourtney/Kourtnie *See*
Courtney.

Kowhai Maori: yellow.

Kris/Kristel *See* Christina.

Krishna Sanskrit: black or dark.

Kristabel *See* Christabel.

Kristal/Krystal/Krystle *See* Crystal.

**Kristeen/Kristen/Kristie/Kristina/
Kristine** *See* Christina.

Krystyna *See* Christina.

Krythia An unusual classical-
sounding name.

Kuine Maori form of Queenie. *See*
Queena.
Kuini (Samoan).

Kuku Maori: a dove.

Kumari Sanskrit: a girl or daughter.

Kumi Japanese: a braid.

Kumiko Japanese: a beautiful child.

Kura Maori: treasure. Polynesian: red.

Kuri Japanese: a chestnut.

Kurtis/Kurtiss/Kurtys *See* Curtis.

Kyana/Kyanah/Kyanna *See* Kiana.

Ky/Kye *See* Kai.

Kyhm *See* Kim.

Kyla Scottish Gaelic: from the narrow
strait. The feminine form of Kyle.
Kylah, Kyle.

Kylie Aboriginal: a boomerang.
Kilea, Kilee, Kileigh, Kiley, Kylea,
Kylee, Kyleigh, Kyli, Kyliee, Kyly.

Kylli Finnish: a name from a legend.

Kym/Kymm *See* Kim.

Kymberlie *See* Kimberley.

Kyna Irish Gaelic: wise.

Kyoko Japanese: a mirror.

Kyon Korean: brightness.

Kyra/Kyrah *See* Kira.

Kyrena/Kyrenia *See* Cyrena.

Kyria Greek: ladylike.

Kyte *See* Kite.

L

Lacey Old French: lace.
Lace, Lacie, Lacy.

Ladonna Modern American: a lady;
a combination of Donna and la, the
French feminine form of 'the'.
La Donna.

Ladybird A colourful beetle, or the
bird of our Lady (the Virgin Mary).
Ladibird, Ladibyrd, Ladybyrd.

Lael *See* BOYS.

Laetitia Latin: happiness.
Latisha, Leticia (Spanish), Letitia,
Lettice.
Diminutives: Lettie, Letty.

Lahela Hawaiian form of Rachel.

Lahnee/Lahni/Lahnie *See* Lani.

Laila/Lailah *See* Layla and Leila.

Laine/Lainey *See* Elaine and Lane.

Laione Polynesian form of Leona.

Laka Hawaiian: gentle.

Lakah.

Lake Old English: the original
meaning was a stream rather than a
pool or pond.
Laik, Laike, Layk, Layke.

Lakeisha American: possibly from
Keshia (the favourite) or Aisha (life).
See also Keisha, Ladonna, Lakena and
Laneka.
Lakaisha, Lakeshia, Lekaisha,
Lekeisha, Lekeshia.

Lakena Another modern American
'La name'. *See also* Lakeisha.
Lakeena, Lakeenah, Lakenah,
Lakhena.

Lakshmi Sanskrit: a lucky omen; the
Hindu goddess of beauty and wealth.
See also Indira.
Lakmé, Laxmi.

Lakya Hindi: born on a Thursday.

Lala Slavic: a tulip.
Lalah, Lalla, Lallah.

Lalage Greek: chatter, babble.

Lali Hindi: red. Polynesian: the
highest point of the heavens.
Lalli, Lally.

Lalita Sanskrit: playful, charming.

Lamorna Cornish: a placename.

Lan Vietnamese: an orchid.

Lana Spanish: wool. Also a
diminutive of Alana, Helena and
Svetlana.
Lanah, Lanna, Lannah.
Diminutives: Lanni, Lannie, Lanny.

Lane English: from the narrow road.
See also Alana.
Laine, Lainey, Laney, Layne.

Laneka A modern American 'La
name'. *See also* Lakeisha.

Laneeka, Laneekah, Lanekah,
Laneke, Lanneka, Lannekah,
Lanneke.

Lani Polynesian: the sky. *See also* Larni.
Lahnee, Lahni, Lahnie, Lanee, Lania,
Lanie.

Lanikais Hawaiian: the heavenly sea.

Lanna/Lannah *See* Alana and Lana.

Lara Russian: a diminutive of Larissa.

Laraine/Larayne/Lareine/Lareyne
See Lorraine.

Larida/Laridah *See* Lerida.

Larissa Russian from Greek: cheerful,
lighthearted.
Larisa, Larisse, Laryssa, Larysse.
Diminutives: Lara, Larah.

Lark English: a songbird.

Larni Possibly a variation of Lani, a
Polynesian name meaning the sky.
Larne, Larnee, Larney, Larnie, Larny.

Laryn/Larynn *See* Lauren.

Lasca Latin: weary.

Lassie English/Scottish: a little girl.

Lastri Indonesian: a common girl's
name.

Latai A figure in Polynesian mythology.

Latasha A modern American 'La name'.
LaTasha, La Tasha.

Latifa Arabic: kind and gentle.
Lateefa.

Latisha *See* Laetitia.

Latonia Latin: the mother of Diana
in Roman mythology.
Latona, Latonya.

Latoya Spanish: victorious. A popular
name in the USA.
La Toya, Latoyah, La-Toyah.
Diminutives: Toya, Toyah.

Launa/Launah *See* Lorna.

Laura Latin: a laurel wreath or tree.
See also Lauren and Lorenza.
Laurah, Laurana, Laure (French),
Laureen, Laurel, Laurelle, Laurene,
Lauretta (Italian), Laurette, Lauria,
Laurian, Lauriane, Laurice, Lauris,
Lora (German), Lore (German),
Lorelle, Lorena, Lorenza (Italian),
Lores, Loretta, Lorinda, Loris, Lorita,
Lowri (Welsh).
Diminutives: Lauri, Laurie, Lori,
Lorri, Lorrie.

Laure/Laurel/Laurelle/Lauretta *See*
Laura and Lorelle.

Lauren English: a feminine form of
Laurence. Originally made popular
by the actress Lauren Bacall. *See also*
Laura.
Laryn, Larynn, Lauran, Laureen,
Laureena, Laurena, Laurence,
Laurene, Laurenn, Laurenne,
Laurentia (Italian), Laurentina
(Italian), Laurin, Laurine, Lauryn,
Lawren, Lawrenn, Lawrenne, Loreen,
Loreena, Loren, Lorena, Lorene,
Lorin, Lorine, Lorren, Lorrin,
L'Wren, L'Wrenn, L'Wrenne.
Diminutives: Lauri, Laurie, Lori,
Lorri, Lorrie.

Laurenza *See* Lorenza.

Lauria/Laurian/Laurice *See* Laura.

Laurin/Laurine/Lauris/Lauryn *See*
Laura and Lauren.

Laveda Latin: one who is purified or
innocent.

Lavena/Lavenia *See* Lavinia.

Lavender From Latin: a 'plant name'.
Lavenda, Lavendah.

Laverne French: spring-like, or from

the alder tree. Popular in the USA.
Lavern, Laverna, LaVerne.
Diminutives: Vern, Verna, Verne.

Lavinia Latin: a lady, or a mother of
Rome.
Lavena, Lavenia, Lavina, Levina,
Levinia, Livinia.
Diminutives: Vina, Vinia, Vinny.

Lawren/Lawrenn *See* Lauren.

Laxmi *See* Lakshmi.

Layk/Layke *See* Lake.

Layla Arabic: as intoxicating as wine.
Laila, Lailah, Laylah, Leyla, Leylah.

Layne *See* Lane.

Le Vietnamese: a pearl.

Lea Hawaiian: the goddess of canoe
builders. *See also* Leah, Leandra and
Lee.

Leah Hebrew: languid, weary. The
wife of Jacob in the Bible.
Lea, Leaha, Leea (Finnish), Leia,
Leigha, Leya, Leyah, Lia (Italian),
Liah, Lija, Lijah, Lijia.

Leala French: the loyal one.

Léan Irish Gaelic form of Helen.

Leandra Latin: like a lioness. The
female version of Leander. *See also*
Leona and Lionelle.
Leanda, Leandah, Leandrah.
Diminutive: Lea.

Leanna *See* Leanne and Liana.

Leanne A combination of Lee and
Anne.
Leane, Leanna, Leighanne.

Leanor *See* Eleanor.

Leda Greek: the mother of Helen of
Troy. *See also* Alida.

Lee Old English: a meadow or a
clearing. Also a Chinese family

name.
Lea, Leigh, Leigha.

Leea Finnish form of Leah.

Leela Sanskrit: playful.
Leelah.

Leelee A 'combination name'.

Leena/Leenah *See* Lena.

Leesa/Leeza *See* Lisa.

Leeston A modern name, derived
from Lee. Also a boy's name.
Leesten, Leestyn, Leisten, Leiston,
Leistyn.

Lei Hawaiian: a flower garland.

Leia/Leigha *See* Leah.

Leigh *See* Lee.

Leighanne *See* Leanne.

Leighton *See* BOYS.

Leila Arabic: dark as the night.
Laila, Lela, Lelah, Lila, Lilah.

Leilani Hawaiian: a heavenly flower.

Leisel German form of Elizabeth.

Leisten/Leiston/Leistyn *See* Leeston.

Leith *See* BOYS.

Lekaisha/Lekeisha/Lekeshia *See*
Lakeisha.

Lemuela Hebrew: devoted to God.
The feminine form of Lemuel.

Lena A diminutive of Caroline,
Helen and other names.
Leena, Leenah, Lenah, Lene (Danish,
German), Leni (German), Lina,
Linah.

Lencey A modern name, possibly a
form of Lena.
Lencee, Lenci, Lencie, Lency.

Lene German/Scandinavian: a
diminutive of Helen and Magdalene
(*see* Madeline). *See also* Lena.

Leni *See* Lena.

Lenis Latin: gentle and smooth.
Leneta, Lenita.

Lennora/Lennorah *See* Leonora.

Lenora/Lenore *See* Eleanor and
Leonora.

Leoda Teutonic: a woman of the
people.
Leola, Leota.

Leoma Old English: light, bright.

Leona Latin: a lioness. A feminine
form of Leo or Leon. *See also*
Leandra, Leonarda and Leontine.
Laione (Polynesian), Leonarda,
Leone, Leonee, Leonelle, Leoni,
Leonia, Leonice, Leonie, Léonne
(French), Leontia, Liona.
Diminutive: Loni.

Leonarda Old French: a brave lioness.
The feminine form of Leonard. *See
also* Leona.

Leonia/Leonice/Leonie *See* Leona.

Leonora A form of Eleanor.
Lennora, Lennorah, Lenora, Lenore,
Leonore.

Leontine Latin: like a lion. *See also*
Leona.
Leontina, Leontyne.

Leora Greek: light.
Leor, Leorah, Leore.

Lerida From Rida, an Arabic name
meaning the favoured one.
Larida, Laridah, Leridah.

Leroy *See* BOYS.

Lesley Scottish Gaelic: from an
ancient surname. Also a boy's name.
Leslea, Leslee, Lesleigh, Leslie, Lesly,
Lezli, Lezlie, Lezly.
Diminutive: Les.

Leta Swahili: to bring.

Letha Greek: from Lethe, the river of
forgetfulness.
Leithia, Lethia.

Leticia/Letitia/Lettice *See* Laetitia.

Letta/Lettah Diminutives of Violetta
(*see* Violet).

Levana Latin: the rising sun.
Levania, Levanna, Levona.

Levia Feminine form of Levi,
meaning united.

Levina Old English: a bright flash.
See also Lavinia.
Levinia.

Levona *See* Levana.

Lewanna Hebrew: the moon.

Lex/Lexa/Lexie/Lexine/Lexy *See*
Alexandra.

Leya/Leyah *See* Leah.

Leyla/Leylah *See* Layla.

Lezli/Lezlie/Lezly *See* Lesley.

Lhakpa Sherpa/Tibetan: born on a
Wednesday. Also a boy's name.

Lhamu Sherpa/Tibetan: a goddess.

Li Chinese: plum blossom.

Lia/Liah *See* Leah.

Lian Chinese: a graceful willow.

Liana French: to bind like a vine.
Leanna, Liane, Lianna, Lianne.

Libby A diminutive of Elizabeth and
Sybil.

Liberty Latin: freedom.
Libertee, Libertey, Liberti, Libertie.

Lida Slavic: loved by the people. A
form of Ludmila and Lydia.
Lidah.

Lidia/Lidya *See* Lydia.

Lien Chinese: a lotus.

Liese/Liesl German forms of Elizabeth.

Lija/Lijah/Lijia *See* Leah.

Lil/Lill Diminutives of Lillian and Lily.

Lila German: mauve. Spanish: a lilac flower. *See also* Delilah and Leila. Lilah.

Lilac Persian: a mauve flower.

Lilea/Lilee *See* Lily.

Lili *See* Elizabeth, Lillian and Lily.

Li-Li Chinese: a beautiful plum blossom.

Lilia/Lilian/Lilias *See* Lillian and Lily.

Lilibet A diminutive of Elizabeth.

Lilie/Lilija *See* Lily.

Lilith Arabic/Hebrew: dark, a woman of the night.

Lillea/Lilley/Lilli *See* Lily.

Lillian A diminutive of Elizabeth. *See also* Lily.
Lilian, Liliana, Liliane (French), Liliann, Lilias (Scottish), Lillyn, Lilyan, Lilyann, Lilyanne.
Diminutives: Lil, Lili, Lill, Lilli, Lily.

Lilo Hawaiian: generous.

Lily Latin: a 'flower name', a symbol of purity. *See also* Lillian.
Lilea, Lilee, Lili, Lilia (Hawaiian), Lilias, Lilie (German), Lilija (Icelandic), Lillea, Lillee, Lilley, Lilli, Lillia, Lillie, Lillis, Lilly, Lyli, Lylie, Lylli, Lyllie, Lys (French).
Diminutives: Lil, Lill.

Lilyan/Lilyann/Lilyanne *See* Lillian.

Lin Chinese: a jade stone. Also a diminutive of Linda and similar names.

Lina/Linah *See* Caroline and Lena.

Linda Spanish: pretty. Also a diminutive of names such as Belinda and Melinda.
Lindah, Lindy, Lynda, Lyndey.
Diminutives: Lin, Lindie, Linn, Lyn.

Lindal/Lindall *See* Lyndal.

Linden Old English: a 'tree name'.
Lindan, Lindon, Lindyn.

Lindsey Originally a Scottish surname.
Lindsay, Linzi, Lyndsey, Lynsey.

Lindy *See* Linda.

Linetta/Linette *See* Linnet.

Ling Chinese: delicate.

Linley Old English: from the field of flax. Also a boy's name.
Linleigh, Linnley, Lynleigh, Lynley, Lynnley.

Linnea Old Norse: a lime tree or lime blossom.
Linea, Lynea, Lynnea.

Linnet Old French: a small bird.
Eluned (Welsh), Linetta, Linette, Linnette, Lynetta, Lynette, Lynnetta, Lynnette.

Linzi *See* Lindsey.

Liona *See* Leona.

Lionelle Old French: a young lion. The feminine form of Lionel. *See also* Leandra, Leona, Leonarda and Leontine.
Lionella, Lyonella, Lyonelle.

Lisa A diminutive of Elizabeth.
Leesa, Leeza, Lisah, Liza.

Lisabet/Lisabeth/Lisbet/Lisbeth *See* Elizabeth.

20th-CENTURY NAMES

Here are some of the most popular New Zealand girls' and boys' names for several decades of the 20th-century. For an interesting comparison, refer to Early settlers' names on page 55 and 21st-century names on page 105.

Girls   Boys

1980s–1990s

Brianna	Laura	Adam	Hayden
Brittany	Lauren	Andrew	Jared
Caitlin	Melissa	Bradley	Kyle
Chelsea	Nicole	Brandon	Matthew
Danielle	Rose	Christopher	Sean

1970s

Belinda	Lisa	Benjamin	Jason
Catherine	Michelle	Cameron	Michael
Joanne	Natalie	Craig	Nicholas
Jodie	Simone	Damian/	Shane
Kellie/	Tania/	Damien	Stephen/
Kelly	Tanya	James	Steven

1950s

Ann/Anne	Lynn/Lynne	Andrew	Iain/Ian
Denise	Margaret	Bruce	John
Diane/Dianne	Pamela	David	Patrick
Jennifer	Robyn	Gary/Garry	Philip/Phillip
Kerrie/Kerry	Suzanne	Graeme	Thomas

1930s

Audrey	Marjorie	Alan	Leslie
Beryl	Mary	Dennis	Neil
Doreen	Norma	Eric	Peter
Elizabeth	Patricia	James	Richard
Joyce	Shirley	Kenneth	Ronald

Early 1900s

Annie	Gladys	Albert	George
Daisy	Lilian	Arthur	Harold
Edith	Olive	Cecil	Reginald
Edna	Phyllis	Francis	Stanley
Florence	Winifred	Frederick	Walter

Lise/Lisette *See* Elizabeth.

Lissa *See* Melissa.

Lita *See* Alida.

Liv Old Norse: defence, protection. Lieve.

Livana Hebrew: of the moon.

Livia A diminutive of Olivia. Also an ancient Roman family name. Liviah, Liviana, Livija, Liviya, Liviyah, Livvie, Livvy.

Livinia *See* Lavinia.

Liz/Lizette/Lizzie/Lizzy *See* Elizabeth.

Liza *See* Elizabeth and Lisa.

Lizanne A combination of Liz and Anne. Lizana, Lizann, Lizanna.

Llawella Welsh: lion-like, a leader. The feminine form of Llewellyn. Llawela.

Llyn Welsh: a lake. Llyne, Llynn, Llynne.

Lobelia Latin: a 'flower name'. Lobeliah, Lobellia, Lobelliah.

Lobsang Sherpa/Tibetan: the kind-hearted one. Also a boy's name.

Lodema Old English: a guide or leader.

Loella/Loelle *See* Louella.

Lois Greek: agreeable. A name from the New Testament. Loida (Spanish), Loise, Loiss, Loisse.

Loise *See* Lois and Louise.

Lokelani Hawaiian: a heavenly rose.

Lola Spanish: a diminutive of Dolores. Lolah. *Diminutive*: Lolita.

Lolo Probably a variation of Lola or Lulu.

Lona English/Spanish: solitary. Polynesian: a moon goddess.

Loni Hawaiian: the sky, or heaven. *See also* Leona.

Lora/Lore *See* Laura.

Loralee/Loralei *See* Lorelei.

Loreen/Loreena *See* Lauren.

Lorelei German: alluring. A river goddess who lured sailors to their death. Loralee, Loralei, Lorelia, Lorelie, Lorilee, Lurleen, Lurlene, Lurline.

Lorelle A combination of Laura and Elle. Laurella, Laurelle, Lorella.

Loren The surname of a famous Italian actress (Sophia Loren). *See also* Lauren. Lorenn, Lorenne.

Lorena/Lorene/Loretta *See* Laura and Lauren.

Lorenza Italian: from the laurel tree; the feminine form of Lorenzo. *See also* Laura. Laurenza.

Lores/Lori/Loris *See* Laura and Lauren.

Lorin/Lorinda/Lorine/Lorita *See* Laura and Lauren.

Lorna Invented by R D Blackmore for the heroine of his 1860s novel *Lorna Doone*, possibly derived from a Scottish placename. Launa, Launah, Lornah.

Lorne A Scottish placename. Also a boy's name.

Lorrae Australian: from Lorraine and Rae.

Lorraine Old German: a province on

the border of France and Germany.
Laraine, Larayne, Lareine, Lareyne,
Larraine, Lorain, Loraine, Lorane,
Lorrayne.
Diminutives: Raine, Rayne.

Lorren/Lorri/Lorrin *See* Laura and
Lauren.

Losa Polynesian: a rose.

Lotta/Lottie/Lotty *See* Charlotte.

Lotus Greek: a 'flower name'.

Lou/Loucee/Louci/Loucie *See*
Louise and Lucy.

Louanna/Louanne *See* Luana.

Louella A combination of Louise and
Ella.
Loella, Loelle, Louelle, Luella, Luelle.
Diminutives: Lou, Lu, Lulu
(German).

Louisa/Louisanna *See* Louise.

Louise Teutonic: a famous warrior
maiden. The feminine form of Louis.
Aloisa, Aloysia, Aloyza, Loise, Louisa,
Louisanna, Louisetta, Louisette,
Louisiana, Louisse, Louize, Lovisa
(Swedish), Loyce, Luisa (Italian,
Spanish), Luise (German), Luiza,
Luize, Ruiha (Maori), Ruihia
(Maori).
Diminutives: Lou, Lova (Swedish),
Lu, Lulu (German), Luu.

Louisiana A state of the USA and
also a form of Louise.
Louisianna, Luisiana, Luisianna.

Loula A form of either Lou or
Louella.
Loulah, Loulia, Loulla.

Loulou/Lou-Lou *See* Lulu.

Lourdes French/Spanish: a pilgrimage
town in southern France.

Lova *See* Louise.

Love *See* Lovella.

Loveday Old English: dear day.
Lovda, Loveda, Lowdy (Cornish).

Lovella A modern name, derived
from the word love.
Love, Lovell, Lovelle, Lovetta,
Lovette.

Lovisa *See* Louise.

Lowdy Cornish form of Loveday.

Lowenna Cornish: joyful.
Lowena, Lowenek.
Diminutive: Wenna.

Lowri Welsh form of Laura.

Loyal Old French: true and faithful.
Loyale, Loyla, Loylah, Loyola,
Loyolah.

Loyce *See* Louise.

Luana Hawaiian: happy. Old
German: a graceful warrior maiden.
Louanna, Louanne, Luane, Luanna,
Luwana, Luwanna.

Luba Russian/Slavic: a lover.
Lubica, Luby.

Luca A form of Luke, one of Christ's
apostles. More commonly a boy's
name.
Lucah, Luka, Lukah.

Lucci/Luce/Lucee/Lucette *See* Lucy.

Lucia/Luciana/Lucie *See* Lucy.

Lucienne French from Latin: light.
The feminine form of Lucian.
Lucian, Luciana (Italian), Luciann,
Lucianna, Lucianne, Lucien,
Lucienn, Lucienna.

Lucilla/Lucille *See* Lucy.

Lucina Latin: the Roman goddess
of childbirth and the moon. *See also*
Lucy.

Lucinda/Lucinde *See* Lucy.

Lucine Armenian form of Lucy.

Lucretia Latin: reward, riches.
Lucrece, Lucrecia (Spanish), Lucrezia (Italian).

Lucy Latin: light. The feminine form of Lucius and Luke.
Loucee, Loucey, Louci, Loucie, Lucci, Luccie, Luce (French, Italian), Lucee, Lucetta, Lucette, Lucey, Lucia (Italian, Spanish), Luciana (Italian), Lucida, Lucie, Lucienne (French), Lucija (Slavic), Lucile, Lucilla, Lucille, Lucina, Lucinda, Lucinde (French), Lucine (Armenian), Lucita, Lucya (Polish), Lucyl, Lucylle, Lucyna, Lucyne, Luiseach (Irish Gaelic), Lusi, Lusia, Lusie, Luzia (Italian), Luzie (German), Ruhia (Maori), Ruihi (Maori).
Diminutives: Cindi, Cindie, Cindy, Lou, Lu, Luciella (Italian), Luu.

Luda *See* Ludmila.

Ludella Old English: an elf or pixie maiden.

Ludmila Slavic: loved by the people.
See also Lida and Mila.
Ludmilla.
Diminutives: Luda, Mila.

Ludo A popular board game.
Ludoe, Ludow.

Luella/Luelle *See* Louella.

Luisa/Luise/Luize *See* Louise.

Luiseach *See* Lucy.

Luisiana/Luisianna *See* Louisiana.

Luka/Lukah *See* Luca.

Lula Eritrean: a little sister.

Lulu Arabic/Swahili: a pearl. Also a diminutive of Louella and Louise.
Loulou, Lou-Lou, Luletta, Lulette, Lu-Lu, Lulua (Arabic).

Luna Latin: the moon.
Lunah, Luneta, Lunetta, Lunette.

Lupe Tongan: a pigeon.

Lupi Tongan: a ruby.
Lupia, Lupiah, Lupie.

Lurleen/Lurlene/Lurline *See* Lorelei.

Lusi/Lusie *See* Lucy.

Luu A diminutive of Louise and Lucy.

Luvena Latin: the little beloved one.

Luwana/Luwanna *See* Luana.

Luzanne Spanish: a lady of light.
Luzan, Luzann.

Luzia/Luzie *See* Lucy.

L'Wren/L'Wrenn/L'Wrenne *See* Lauren.

Lydia Greek: a woman from Lydia, an ancient kingdom in Asia Minor.
Lida (Czech), Lidia (Italian, Polish), Lidya, Lyddie, Lydie (French).

Lyle *See* BOYS.

Lyli/Lylie/Lyllie *See* Lily.

Lyn *See* Caroline, Linda and Lynn.

Lynda/Lyndey *See* Linda.

Lyndal Australian/English: probably from Lynn and Dale.
Lindal, Lindall, Lindell, Lyndall, Lyndell.

Lyndsey *See* Lindsey.

Lynetta/Lynette/Lynnette *See* Linnet.

Lynleigh/Lynley/Lynnley *See* Linley.

Lynn Old English: a waterfall. Also a diminutive of names such as Carolyn.
Eluned (Welsh), Lin, Linn, Lyn, Lynelle, Lynne.

Lynnea *See* Linnea.

Lynsey *See* Lindsey.

Lynx From Greek: a North American wild cat.

Lyonella/Lyonelle *See* Lionelle.

Lyra A northern constellation.
Lyrah.

Lyris Greek: she who plays the harp or lyre.
Lyre, Lyric, Lyrique.

Lys French form of Lily.

Lysandra Greek: the liberator.

Lysette *See* Elizabeth.

Lystra Greek: free.

Lyz A diminutive of Elizabeth.

M

Maarit Finnish form of Margaret.

Maata A Maori form of Martha.

Mab *See* Maeve.

Mabel Old French: amiable, lovable.
See also Amabel.
Mabe, Mabele, Mabell, Mabella, Mabelle, Mable, Mabli (Welsh), Maybel, Maybelle.

Mabyn Cornish/Welsh: the name of a saint and a placename.

Macaria Greek: a mythological figure.

Macey Old English: little Matthew.
Macee, Maci, Macie, Macy.

Machiko Japanese: fortunate.

MacKenna Irish Gaelic: the son or daughter of Ken or Kennedy.
Mackenna, McKenna, Makenna.

Mackenzie Scottish Gaelic: the son or daughter of the handsome one. *See also* Kenzie.
Mackensie, MacKenzie, Makenzee, Makenzie, Makenzy, McKenzie, Mekenzie, Mekenzie, Mekenzy.

Mackinley Scottish Gaelic: the son or daughter of Finlay.
Mackinlay, Mackinlee, Mackinleigh, McKinlay, McKinley.

Maclean Scottish Gaelic: the son or daughter of the follower of St John.
Maclaine, MacLaine, Maclayne, McLaine, McLane, McLean.

Macy *See* Macey.

Madalen/Madalena *See* Madeline.

Maddeson/Maddison *See* Madison.

Maddi/Maddie/Maddy *See* Madeline and Madison.

Madeira Portuguese: an island off the African coast. Also a fortified wine.

Madel/Madelia/Madeliene *See* Madeline.

Madeline From the biblical name Magdalene, meaning a woman from the village of Magdala. *See also* Marlene.
Madalaine, Madalen, Madalena (Spanish), Madalene, Madaline, Madalyn, Maddalena (Italian), Madel, Madelaine, Madeleine (French), Madelia, Madeliene, Madelin, Madelina, Madella, Madelle, Madelon (French), Madelyn, Madlen, Madlena (German), Madlin, Madlon, Madlyn, Madolene, Madoline, Magdala, Magdalen, Magdalena, Magdalene, Magdalina (Russian), Magdalone (Danish), Magdolen, Magdolene, Magdolin, Magdoline, Makarena (Maori), Malena, Malene

(Danish), Malina, Modlen (Welsh).
Diminutives: Alena (Czech, German), Alenka (Slavic), Lena, Lene (German), Madi, Maddi, Maddie, Maddy, Magda (German), Mala, Malin (Swedish).

Madge *See* Margaret and Marjorie.

Madhuri Sanskrit: sweet. Madhu, Madhur.

Madison Old English: the son of Maud or Matthew. Also a boy's name.
Maddeson, Maddison, Maddyson, Madisen, Madisyn, Madysen, Madysin, Madyson.
Diminutives: Maddi, Maddie, Maddy.

Madlen/Madlena/Madlin/Madolene *See* Madeline.

Madonna Italian: my lady. A title of the Virgin Mary.
MaDonna.

Madrona Latin: a lady or noblewoman. A Jewish name.
Madra (Spanish), Madrun, Matrona (Russian), Matryona (Russian).

Madura An Indonesian island.

Madysen/Madyson *See* Madison.

Mae *See* May.

Maeko Japanese: truthful, or joyous.

Maeve Irish Gaelic: intoxicating. A queen in Irish legend.
Mab, Mave, Meave.

Magali A popular Turkish name.

Magda/Magdala/Magdalen/Magdalene *See* Madeline.

Magena Native American: the coming moon.

Magenta Italian: a town in Italy and a 'colour name'.

Maggi/Maggie *See* Margaret.

Magna Latin: great. Norwegian: strength.

Magnolia French: a 'flower name', after the French botanist Pierre Magnol.

Magryta Lithuanian form of Margaret.

Mahalia Hebrew: tenderness. Mahala, Mahalah, Mahila, Mehalia.

Mahesa Sansksrit: the feminine form of Mahesh, a great ruler.

Mahia Maori: a deed or act.

Mahina Hawaiian/Polynesian: the moon.

Mahira Hebrew: energetic.

Mahogany A 'tree name'.

Mahrie/Mahry *See* Mary.

Mahuika The goddess of fire in Maori mythology.

Mahuru Polynesian: the goddess of spring.

Mai Swedish diminutive of Margaret and Mary. *See also* May.

Maia The most beautiful of the mythological nymphs, the Pleiades. *See also* Mary and Maya.
Maija, Maya.

Maida Old English: a maiden. Maide, Maidel, Maidie (Irish, Scottish), Mayda.

Maile Hawaiian: a type of vine.

Maili Polynesian: a summer breeze.

Mair/Maire/Mairee/Mairi *See* Mary.

Mairead Irish and Scottish form of Margaret.

Mairin Irish Gaelic form of Maureen.

89

Mairwen Welsh: a combination of Mair (Mary) and Gwen (fair or blessed).
Mairwenn, Mairwenne.

Maisie Scottish diminutive of Margaret.
Maisee, Maisey, Maizee, Maizey, Maizie.

Maja *See* Maya.

Majella Italian: the name of an Italian saint.

Majesta Latin: the majestic one.

Majida Arabic: illustrious.

Majoli Possibly from majolica, a type of Italian pottery.
Majolee, Majolie, Majoly.

Makaela/Makayla *See* Michaela.

Makala Polynesian: the myrtle tree.

Makana Polynesian: a gift.

Makani Polynesian: the wind.

Makarena Maori form of Magdalen.
See Madeline.

Makareta Maori form of Margaret.

Makenna *See* MacKenna.

Makenzee/Makenzie/Makenzy *See* Mackenzie.

Maku Maori: wet.

Mala Sanskrit: a necklace. *See also* Madeline.

Malak Arabic: an angel.

Malana Hawaiian: light or buoyant.
Malanah, Malanna, Malannah.

Malara The morning star (Venus) in New Guinea legend.

Malati Sanskrit: a jasmine flower.

Malaya Spanish: free. A 'country name'.

Malena/Malene *See* Madeline.

Malerie A form of Valerie.

Mali Thai: a flower. Welsh: a form of Mary and Molly.
Malie.

Malia Hawaiian form of Mary.

Malika Arabic: the feminine form of Malik, the master.

Malin Swedish diminutive of Madeline.

Malina Hawaiian: calming. *See also* Madeline.

Malinda/Malynda *See* Melinda.

Malise Gaelic: the servant of God.

Malissa *See* Melissa.

Malkah Hebrew: a queen.
Malka, Malkeh.

Mallory Old French: unlucky. Also a boy's name.
Mallorey, Mallorie, Malorey, Malorie, Malory.

Malva Greek: soft and tender.
Malvah, Melva, Melvah.

Malvina Gaelic: the smooth-browed one.
Malvena, Melvena, Melvina.

Mame A diminutive of Margaret and Mary.
Mamie.

Mana Hawaiian: heavenly. Maori: power.

Manamea Samoan: unparalleled beauty.

Manar *See* Munira.

Manawa Maori: the heart.

Manawaroa Maori: a big heart.

Manda/Mandie/Mandy *See* Amanda.

Mandala Sanskrit: a circle. A mystic

symbol of the universe in the Hindu religion.

Mandara Sanskrit: the name of a tree.

Mandela An attractive name, in honour of the legendary South African activist and politician Nelson Mandela. Mandella.

Mandisa African: sweet.

Mandolin A stringed musical instrument.
Mandolina, Mandoline, Mandolinne, Mandolyn, Mandolynne.

Mangu Maori: a big heart.

Mani Sanskrit: a jewel.

Manon French diminutive of Marie (*see* Mary).

Mantra Sanskrit: a prayer or incantation.
Mantrah.

Manuela/Manuella/Manuelle *See* Emmanuelle.

Maple An unusual 'plant name'.
Mapel, Mapell, Mapelle.

Mara Hebrew: bitter; the original form of Mary. Maori: a garden. Also a diminutive of Tamara.
Marah.

Marabel A combination of Mary and Belle.

Maralyn *See* Marilyn.

Marama Maori: the moon. Polynesian: radiant.

Maran *See* Maren.

Maranda *See* Miranda.

Marcella Latin: belonging to Mars. The feminine form of Marcus and Mark. *See also* Marcia and Martina.
Marcela (Czech), Marcelia, Marcelle

(French, Spanish), Marcellina, Marcelline, Marchelle, Marsell, Marsella, Marselle.
Diminutives: Marci, Marcie, Marcy.

Marchesa/Marchessa *See* Marquise.

Marcia Latin: belonging to Mars. *See also* Marcella and Martina.
Marcea, Marsha, Marsia, Martia.
Diminutives: Marci, Marcie, Marcy.

Mardi The French name for Tuesday.
Mardee, Mardey, Mardie, Mardy.

Mardrea An unusual name from the West Indies.

Marea/Maree *See* Mary.

Mareikura Maori: a female supernatural being.

Marelda Teutonic: a famous battle maiden.

Maren Basque: from the sea.
Maran, Marenn, Marenne, Marin, Maron.

Marene *See* Maureen.

Maresa *See* Maris.

Marganit Hebrew: a lovely flower.

Margaret Latin: a pearl. *See also* Margot, Marguerite, Marion and Megan.
Maarit (Finnish), Mairead (Irish, Scottish), Magryta (Lithuanian), Makareta (Maori), Marganita (Jewish), Margareta, Margaretha (German), Margaretta, Margarida (Portuguese), Margarita (Spanish), Marged (Welsh), Marget, Margette, Margherita (Italian), Margit (Hungarian, Swedish), Margitta, Margret (German), Margreta, Margrethe (Danish), Margriet (Dutch), Margrit, Marguerita, Marguerite (French), Mari

(Bohemian), Marjeta (Czech), Marketta (Finnish), Megan (Welsh). *Diminutives*: Daisy, Greta (German, Swedish), Gretchen (German), Grete, Gretel (Swiss), Madge, Maggi, Maggie, Mags, Mai (Swedish), Maisie (Scottish), Mame, Mamie, Marge, Margie, Margot (French), May, Meg, Meggie, Peg, Peggie, Peggy, Rita.

Margaux *See* Margot.

Marged/Marget/Margette/Margit *See* Margaret.

Margerie/Margery *See* Marjorie.

Margot Originally a diminutive of Margaret.
Margo, Margaux.

Marguerite *See* Margaret. Also a 'flower name'.
Marguerita.

Mari *See* Margaret and Mary.

Maria/Mariah *See* Mary.

Mariam/Mariamne *See* Miriam.

Marian/Mariana/Marianne *See* Marion.

Maribel Spanish: a combination of Maria and Belle or Isabel.
Maribell, Maribella, Maribelle, Marybella, Marybelle.

Marie Maori: peaceful. Also the French form of Mary.

Mariea/Mariee *See* Mary.

Marie-Claire A 'combination name'.

Marieke *See* Mary.

Mariel *See* Marielle, Mary and Muriel.

Marielle French: a form of Marie. *See* Mary.
Mariel, Mariell, Mariella (Italian).

Marietta Italian form of Maria. *See* Mary.
Maretta, Marette, Mariet (Dutch), Marieta (Spanish), Mariette, Marita (Spanish).

Marigold Old English: a golden flower.
Marygold.

Marika Maori: quiet and careful. Slavic: a form of Mary.

Mariko A popular Japanese name.

Marilia Portuguese form of Mary.

Marilyn A combination of Mary and Lynn.
Maralyn, Marilene, Marilynn, Marylin, Marylyn.

Marin *See* Maren.

Marina Latin: of the sea. *See also* Maris and Mary.
Mareena, Marinah, Marine (French), Marna (Swedish), Maryna, Marynah, Merina, Merinah.
Diminutives: Marne, Marnie.

Marini Swahili: pretty.

Marion Originally a French diminutive of Marie. *See also* Mary.
Marian, Mariana, Mariane (German), Marianna, Marianne (French), Marionne, Maryon, Mereanna (Maori).

Mariquita Spanish form of Mary.

Maris Latin: of the sea. *See also* Marina and Mary.
Maresa, Marice, Marisa, Marise, Marissa, Marisse, Marris, Meris, Merisa, Merissa.

Marita *See* Marietta and Mary.

Mariya/Mariyah/Marja *See* Mary.

Marjani Swahili: coral.

Marjeta Czech form of Margaret.

Marjorie From the herb name, marjoram.
Margerie, Margery, Margory, Marjery, Marjolaine (French), Marjory.
Diminutives: Madge, Marge, Margie, Marj, Marji, Marjie.

Marketta Finnish form of Margaret.

Markisa/Markise *See* Marquise.

Marla *See* Marlene and Mary.

Marlea/Marlee *See* Marlene and Marley.

Marlene German: a combination of Maria (*see* Mary) and Magdalene.
Marla, Marlane, Marlee, Marleen, Marlena, Marlina, Marlyne.

Marley Old English: from the pleasant meadow.
Marlea, Marlee, Marleigh, Marli, Marlie, Marly.

Marlies Dutch: a combination of Maria and Elisabeth.
Marleis.

Marlon *See* BOYS.

Marlow Old English: from the lake or pond. Also a boy's name.
Marlowe.

Marmara Greek: radiant.

Marna *See* Marina.

Marne/Marnie Diminutives of Marina and other names.

Maron *See* Maren.

Marquise The feminine form of Marquis, French for a nobleman.
Marchesa (Italian), Marchessa, Markisa, Markise, Marquess, Marquesse, Marquisa.

Marsala Italian: a town, and a sweet fortified wine.

Marsell/Marsella/Marselle *See* Marcella.

Marsena Persian: worthy, or dignified. Also a boy's name.

Marsha/Marsia *See* Marcia.

Marta/Marte *See* Martha.

Marter *See* Martyr.

Martha Aramaic: a lady. A name from the Bible.
Maata (Maori), Marta (Italian, Spanish), Marte (Scandinavian), Martella, Marthe (French, German), Mata (Maori).
Diminutives: Marti, Martie, Martita (Spanish), Marty.

Marti/Martie/Marty *See* Martha and Martina.

Martia *See* Marcia.

Martina Latin: of Mars, the Roman god of war. A feminine form of Martin. *See also* Marcella and Marcia.
Martine (French), Martyna (Polish), Martyne.
Diminutives: Marti, Martie, Marty.

Martyr An unusual modern name, implying someone with strong convictions.
Marter.

Maru Polynesian: gentle.

Marula A southern African shrub.

Marvel Latin: a wonderful thing.
Marva, Marvela, Marvella, Marvelle.

Mary Hebrew: bitter, as in a bitterly wanted child. Latin: the star of the sea. From the same root as Miriam, and one of the most enduringly popular female names. *See also* Mara, Marina, Marion, Marlene, Maureen,

Mia, Miriam, Moira and Molly.
Mahrie, Mahry, Mair (Welsh), Maire
(Irish Gaelic), Mairee, Mairi, Mairie
(Irish Gaelic), Malia (Hawaiian),
Mara (Hebrew), Marah, Marea,
Maree, Maretta, Marette, Mari,
Maria, Mariah, Marie (French,
Maori), Mariea, Mariee, Marieke
(Dutch), Mariel, Mariella (Italian),
Marielle (French), Marieta (Spanish),
Marietta (Italian), Mariette, Marika
(Slavic), Marilia (Portuguese),
Mariquita (Spanish), Marisa, Marita
(Spanish), Mariya (Russian), Mariyah,
Marja (Finnish), Marla (Bavarian),
Marya (Cornish, Russian), Marye,
Maryse (French), Maureen (Irish),
Mele (Tongan), Mere (Polynesian),
Meri (Polynesian), Meria, Meriah,
Mhairi, Moira (Irish Gaelic).
Diminutives: Mai (Swedish), Maia,
Maja, Mali (Welsh), Mame, Mamie,
Manon (French), Masha (Russian),
May, Maya, Mia (Danish, Swedish),
Mimi (Italian), Mitzi (Swiss), Molli,
Mollie, Molly, Polly, Ria (Spanish).

Marya Arabic: white and pure.
Cornish: a form of Mary.

Maryam *See* Miriam.

Maryann A 'combination name'.
Mary-Ann, Maryanna, Maryanne,
Mary-Anne, Miriama (Maori).

Marybella/Marybelle *See* Maribel.

Mary-Ellen From Mary and Ellen.

Mary-Jane From Mary and Jane.

Marylou From Mary and Louise.

Marylyn *See* Marilyn.

Maryna/Marynah *See* Marina.

Maryon *See* Marion.

Maryse *See* Mary.

Maryvonne French: from Marie and
Yvonne.

Masa Japanese: straightforward.

Mascot Something that brings good
luck.
Mascott, Mascotte.

Masha Russian diminutive of Mary.

Masika Swahili: the rainy season.

Masina Samoan: the moon.

Mata A Maori form of Martha.

Matilda Teutonic: the mighty battle
maiden.
Matelda, Mateldah, Mathilda,
Mathilde (French), Matila, Matildah,
Matilde (Italian), Matylda (Czech,
Polish), Maud, Maude, Maudie,
Mechteld (Dutch).
Diminutives: Matti, Mattie, Tilda,
Tillie, Tilly.

Matina Of the morning. Also a
feminine form of Matt (Matthew),
meaning a gift of God. *See also*
Mattea.
Matinah, Mattina, Mattinah,
Mattyna, Mattynah, Matyna,
Matynah.

Matisse An unusual name; after
Henri Matisse, a famous French
painter and sculptor.
Matise, Matyse, Matysse.

Matrika Hindi: a mother.

Matrona/Matryona *See* Madrona.

Matsu Japanese: a pine tree.
Matsuko.

Mattea Hebrew: the gift of God. The
feminine form of Matthew.
Matthea, Matthia, Mattia.

Matti/Mattie Diminutives of Matilda.

Matylda *See* Matilda.

Matyse/Matysse *See* Matisse.

Maud/Maude/Maudie *See* Matilda.

Maura Celtic: a 5th-century saint.
Maure, Mora.

Maureen Irish form of Mary. *See also* Moira.
Mairin (Irish Gaelic), Marene, Maurene, Maurine, Maurn, Moirean, Moreen, Morena, Moryne.
Diminutive: Mo.

Mauve French from Greek: violet-coloured.
Mauv.

Mave *See* Maeve and Mavis.

Mavis French: a songbird.
Diminutive: Mave.

Maweke Polynesian: a sea breeze.

Maxelle A feminine form of Max, meaning the greatest.
Maxcel, Maxcell, Maxcella, Maxcelle, Maxel, Maxell, Maxella.

Maxine Latin: the greatest. The feminine form of Maximilian.
Maxeen, Maxene, Maxyne.
Diminutives: Max, Maxi, Maxie, Maxy.

Maxwell *See* BOYS.

May A diminutive of Margaret and Mary. Also a 'month name'.
Mae, Mai, Maye, Mei (Maori).

Maya Latin: the great one. The name of Roman and Hindu goddesses and a diminutive of Maria. *See also* Maia and Mary.
Maia, Maija, Maja, Mayaa, Mayah, Mya, Myah.

Maybell/Maybelle *See* Mabel.

Mayda *See* Maida.

Maysa Arabic: she who walks gracefully.

Mc names – *see* Mac.

Mea/Meah *See* Mia.

Meadow Middle English: a small grassy field.
Meadowe, Meddow, Meddowe.

Meagan/Meaghan *See* Megan.

Meave *See* Maeve.

Mechel/Mechelle *See* Michelle.

Mechteld Dutch form of Matilda.

Medea Greek: a princess in mythology.

Medina Arabic: a city in Saudi Arabia.

Medley Middle English: a mixture.
Medlee, Medlie, Medly.

Medusa Greek: a character from mythology.

Mee Chinese: beautiful.
Mei.

Meena Sanskrit: a precious gem or a fish. The name represents the zodiac sign Pisces.
Mina, Minah.

Meera Sanskrit: a devotee of the god Krishna.
Meerah.

Meesha *See* Misha.

Meg/Meggie Diminutives of Margaret and Megan.

Megan Welsh form of Margaret.
Meagan, Meagen, Meaghan, Meegan, Meegen, Megann, Megen, Meghan, Meghann, Meigan.
Diminutives: Meg, Meggie.

Megara Greek: a mythological figure.

Megumi Japanese: blessing.

Mehalia *See* Mahalia.

Mehitabel Hebrew: God is our joy.

Mei *See* Mee. Also the Maori form of May.

Meiko Japanese: a bud.

Meila/Meilah *See* Mela.

Mei-Lin Chinese: a beautiful lotus.

Meiling Chinese: the name of a princess.
Mei-Ling.

Meinwen Welsh: fair and slender.

Meisha *See* Misha.

Mei-Yu Chinese: beautiful jade.

Meizhen Chinese: possibly meaning a precious plum.

Mekenzee/Mekenzie/Mekenzy *See* Mackenzie.

Mel *See* Amelia, Carmel, Melanie, Melinda and Melissa.

Mela Sanskrit: a fair or festival. *See also* Melanie.
Meila, Meilah, Melah.

Melanie Greek: the dark or black one.
Mela, Melaine, Melan, Melanee, Melani, Melania, Melany, Melloney (Cornish), Mellony, Melony.
Diminutives: Mel, Melli, Mellie, Melly.

Melantha Greek: a dark flower.
Melanthe.

Melati Indonesian: a jasmine flower.

Melba English: after the famous opera singer Dame Nellie Melba.

Melda *See* Imelda.

Mele Tongan form of Mary.

Melek Arabic: an angel.

Meli Hawaiian: honey.

Melia Greek: a mythological nymph.

Melicent *See* Millicent.

Melina Greek: gentle. *See also*

Carmel.

Melinda A combination of Melanie or Melissa and Linda.
Malinda, Malynda, Melynda.
Diminutives: Linda, Mel, Melli, Mellie, Melly.

Melisanda/Mélisande *See* Millicent.

Melissa Greek: the honey bee.
Malissa, Melesa, Melisa, Melisah, Melita, Melitta, Mellissah, Millissa.
Diminutives: Lissa, Mel, Melli, Mellie, Melly.

Melita/Melitta *See* Melissa.

Mell/Melli/Mellie/Melly *See* Amelia, Carmel, Melanie, Melinda and Melissa.

Mellicent/Mellisent *See* Millicent.

Mellin/Mellyn *See* Melyn.

Melloney/Mellony/Melony *See* Melanie.

Melody Greek: like a song.
Melodee, Melodi, Melodia, Melodie, Melodye.

Melora A daughter of King Arthur in Celtic mythology.
Mellora, Mellorah, Melorah.

Melva Welsh: a sweet place. *See also* Malva.
Melvah.

Melvena/Melvina *See* Malvina.

Melwyn Cornish: as fair as honey.
Melwynn, Melwynne.

Melyn Welsh: yellow.
Mellin, Mellyn, Melynn, Melynne.

Melynda *See* Melinda.

Melys Welsh: sweet.
Melyss.

Memphis *See* BOYS.

Menorah Hebrew: the seven-branched candelabra of the Jewish religion. Menora.

Menta *See* Minta.

Menuha Hebrew: tranquillity.

Meraud/Meraude *See* Emerald.

Mercedes Spanish: merciful. From a title of the Virgin Mary. Mercede (Italian), Mercey, Merci, Mercia, Mercie, Mercy.

Mercuria Latin: the feminine form of Mercury, a planet and the messenger of the gods in Roman mythology. Mercurina, Mercurine.

Mercy *See* Mercedes.

Mere A Polynesian form of Mary.

Mereanna Maori form of Marianne. *See* Marion.

Meredith Old Welsh: lordly. Also a boy's name. Meredeth, Meredyth, Merideth, Meridith, Meridyth. *Diminutives*: Merrie, Merry.

Meren Breton form of Merryn.

Merette From French words meaning a little sea. Meretta.

Meri Finnish: the sea. Polynesian: a form of Mary.

Meria/Meriah *See* Mary.

Meriam *See* Miriam.

Meridee/Meridie *See* Merridee.

Meriel *See* Muriel.

Merika A name from the *Dragonriders of Pern* series of fantasy novels. Mereeka, Mereekah, Merikah.

Merilyn From Merry and Lynn.

Merin/Merinah *See* Marina and Merryn.

Meris/Merisa/Merissa *See* Maris.

Merivale Old English: a pleasant valley. Also a boy's name. Merrivale, Merryvale, Meryvale.

Merkaba Hebrew: a chariot. Merkabah.

Merle Old French: a blackbird. Also a diminutive of Muriel. Merl, Merla, Meryl, Meryle, Myrle.

Merlin Old Welsh: from the fort by the sea, or the falcon. Also a boy's name. Merlina, Merlinda, Merline, Merlinn, Merlinne, Merlyn, Merlynda, Merlynn, Merlynne.

Merna *See* Myrna.

Merpati Indonesian: a dove.

Merridee A combination of Merry and Dee. *See also* Merry. Meridee, Meridie, Meridy, Merridie, Merridy.

Merrill *See* Muriel.

Merry Old English: joyful, happy. *See also* Meredith and Merridee. Merilyn, Merrey, Merri, Merrie, Merrie, Merrilee, Merrilie, Merrily.

Merryn Cornish: a saint's name and a placename. Also a boy's name. Meren (Breton), Merin (Welsh), Merran, Merren, Merrin, Meryn.

Merryvale/Meryvale *See* Merivale.

Mertice Old English: pleasant and famous. Mertyce.

Mertle *See* Myrtle.

Merva A feminine form of Mervyn, meaning a famous friend. Mervah, Mervorna, Mervyn,

Mervynn, Mervynne.

Merwenna *See* Morwenna.

Meryem Turkish form of Miriam.

Meryl/Meryle *See* Merle.

Meshel/Meshelle *See* Michelle.

Messina Latin: the middle child.

Meta Latin: the ambitious one.

Metis Greek: the wise one.
Metys.

Mhairi *See* Mary.

Mia Scandinavian diminutive of
Mary.
Mea, Meah, Miah, Miia (Finnish),
Mija, Miya, Miyah, Mya, Myah.

Michaela Hebrew: like the Lord. A
feminine form of Michael. *See also*
Michelle and Mikaedy.
Makaela, Makayla, Micaela, Micaila,
Micayla, Michaele, Michaelie,
Michaelina, Michaeline, Michala,
Michayla, Michella, Mikaela,
Mikaella, Mikaila, Mikala, Mikayla,
Mychaela, Mykaela.
Diminutives: Micki, Mickie, Micky,
Mikki.

Michal Hebrew: a brook. A biblical
name.

Michala/Michella *See* Michaela and
Michelle.

Michelle French from Hebrew:
like the Lord. A feminine form of
Michael. *See also* Michaela.
Mechel, Mechell, Mechelle, Meshel,
Meshell, Meshelle, Michel, Michele,
Michelina, Micheline (French),
Michell, Michella, Mishelle.
Diminutives: Chelle, Shell, Shelley,
Shelli, Shellie, Shelly.

Michiko Japanese: the righteous way.

Michi.

Micki/Mickie/Micky Diminutives of
Michaela.

Midori Japanese: green.

Mietta French: a sweet little thing.
Miette.

Miffany *See* Myfanwy.

Mignon French: sweet and dainty. *See
also* Minette.
Mignone, Mignonette.

Miia/Mija *See* Mia.

Mika Japanese: the new moon.

Mikaedy A modern version of
Michaela.
Mikadee, Mikadi, Mikadie, Mikayde,
Mikaydi, Mikaydie.

Mikaela/Mikala/Mikayla/Mikki *See*
Michaela.

Miki Hawaiian: quick and nimble.
Japanese: a stem.

Miko Japanese: virginal.

Mila A short form of Ludmila (loved
by the people) and Milena (the
favoured one).
Milah, Milia, Miliah, Milla, Millah,
Myla, Mylah.

Milana From Milan, an Italian city.
Milan, Milanah, Milann, Milanna,
Milannah.

Mildred Old English: strong yet
gentle.
Milda, Mildrid.
Diminutives: Milli, Millie, Milly.

Milena Czech: the favoured one.
Mila, Milana, Milenna, Millena,
Millenna.

Miley A modern name, made popular
by the singer and actress Miley Cyrus.

Milea, Milee, Milei, Mileigh, Milie, Mylea, Mylee, Mylei, Myleigh, Myley, Mylie.

Miliani Hawaiian: a gentle caress.

Milla *See* Mila.

Milli/Millie/Milly Diminutives of Amelia, Camilla, Mildred and Millicent.

Millicent Teutonic: strong and industrious.
Melicent, Melisanda, Mélisande (French), Mellicent, Mellisent, Milicent, Milissent.
Diminutives: Milli, Millie, Milly.

Millissa *See* Melissa.

Mimi Italian diminutive of Maria. *See* Mary.

Mimosa Latin: a 'plant name'.

Mina A diminutive of several names. *See also* Meena.

Minerva Latin: the goddess of wisdom.

Minette A diminutive of Mignonette. *See* Mignon.
Minetta, Mynette.

Ming Chinese: light or enlightenment.

Mink A weasel-like animal, famous for its highly prized fur.
Minke, Mynk, Mynke.

Minks/Minkse *See* Minx.

Minna Teutonic: love. Also a diminutive of Wilhelmina.
Minne.

Minnie *See* Wilhelmina.

Minta Greek: of the mint plant.
Menta, Mintah, Mintha.

Minuet French: a type of dance.
Minuett, Minuette.

Minx A flirtatious girl.
Minks, Minkse, Minxe, Mynx, Mynxe.

Mira Slavic: the famous one. *See also* Myra.

Mirabelle Latin: lovely.
Mirabel, Mirabella, Mireille (French), Mirella (Italian).

Miraca From miracle, meaning a marvel or a wonderful thing.
Miracca, Miracle, Miraka, Mirakka.

Mirage French: an illusion; something unreal.
Mirag, Miraj, Miraje.

Miranda Latin: the admired one. Probably invented by Shakespeare for the heroine of *The Tempest*.
Maranda, Marandah, Mirandah, Myranda, Myrandah.
Diminutives: Randa, Randie, Randy.

Mireille/Mirella *See* Mirabelle.

Miriam Hebrew: a biblical name meaning bitter. *See also* Mary.
Mariam, Mariamne (Hebrew), Maryam (Arabic), Meriam, Meryem (Turkish), Miriama (Maori), Miriamu (African), Miriana (Slavic), Miriyana, Myriam.

Miriama Maori form of Maryann and Miriam.

Mirka Czech: tranquil.

Mirna *See* Myrna.

Miromiro Maori: a tomtit (bird).

Mirren The surname of a famous British actress (Dame Helen Mirren).

Misha A diminutive of Michelle or Michael, meaning like the Lord.
Meesha, Meisha, Mischa (Russian).

Mishelle *See* Michelle.

Missy A young lady.
Missie.

Mistic/Mistique *See* Mystic.

Misty Old English: of the mist.
Mysti.

Mitzi Swiss diminutive of Maria. *See*
Mary.

Miya Japanese: a temple. *See also* Mia.
Miyah.

Moana Maori/Polynesian: the sea.
Moanah.

Moata Maori: early.

Modesty Latin: the moderate or
modest one.
Modest (Russian), Modesta,
Modeste, Modestia, Modestine,
Modesto (Italian).

Modlen Welsh form of Madeline.

Moe Maori: sleep.

Moerangi Maori: the sleepy sky.

Moetuma Polynesian: a figure from
legend.

Mohana Sanskrit: bewitching; the
enchantress.
Mohini.

Moina *See* Mona.

Moira Irish Gaelic form of Mary. *See
also* Maureen.
Maura, Maurya, Moirah, Mora,
Moyra, Moyrah.

Moirean *See* Maureen.

Mokai Maori: a pet.

Moko Maori: a personal mark.

Molly A diminutive of Mary.
Mali (Welsh), Mollee, Molley, Molli,
Mollie, Polly.

Momi Hawaiian: a pearl.

Mona Irish Gaelic: the noble one.
Also a diminutive of Monica.
Moina, Monah, Moya, Moyna.

Monday Middle English: the day of
the moon.
Mondae, Mondai, Mondaye.

Monet After the French Impressionist
artist Claude Monet.
Monay, Monée.

Monica Latin: an adviser or
counsellor. The name of a saint.
Monika (German, Slavic), Monike,
Moniqua, Monique (French),
Mo'Nique, Mo'nique.
Diminutive: Mona.

Monique French form of Monica.

Monroe *See* BOYS.

Montana Latin: from the mountains; a
state of the USA. Also a boy's name.
Montanah, Montanna, Montannah.

Moon Middle English: a heavenly
body. Suitable for a Cancerian child
as Cancer is ruled by the moon.
Moone.

Mo'onia The unusual name of an
Australian netball star (Mo'onia
Gerrard).

Mora *See* Maura and Moira.

Morag Scottish Gaelic: the great one.
Moreen.

Moray A region of Scotland.
Morae, Morai.

Moreau French. Probably after the
actress Jeanne Moreau.
Moreaux.

Moreen *See* Maureen and Morag.

Morena *See* Maureen.

Morenwyn Cornish: a fair maiden.

Morgan Welsh: the bright sea. Also a

boy's name.
Morgaine, Morgana, Morganna,
Morganne, Morgayne, Morgen,
Morgenne, Morgwn.

Moriah Hebrew: God is my teacher.
An Old Testament placename.
Moria.

Morin/Morinn/Morinne *See* Moryn.

Morna *See* Myrna.

Morva Cornish: a placename.
Morvah.

Morven Gaelic: a region of Scotland.
Morvan, Morvenn, Morvenne.

Morwenna Cornish/Welsh: a maiden.
The name of a saint.
Merwenna, Morwen, Morwenn,
Morwenne, Morwyn (Welsh).

Moryn Welsh: the sea.
Morin, Morinn, Morinne, Moryne,
Morynne.

Moryne *See* Maureen and Moryn.

Moselle French from Egyptian:
probably meaning delivered or saved.
The feminine form of Moses.
Mosella, Mozella, Mozelle.

Moxie A modern name of uncertain
meaning.
Moxee, Moxey, Moxi, Moxy.

Moya/Moyna *See* Mona.

Moyra/Moyrah *See* Moira.

Muirenn Irish Gaelic: the fair or
white one from the sea.
Muireann.

Muirne *See* Myrna.

Muka Maori: flax fibre.

Muna Arabic: a hope, or a wish.

Munira Arabic: the luminous one.
Manar, Munirah.

Mura Japanese: from the village.

Murasaki Japanese: lavender.

Muriel Gaelic: of the bright sea.
Mariel, Meriel, Merrill, Muireall
(Scottish Gaelic), Murial, Muriele,
Murielle, Muiriol (Irish Gaelic),
Murial.
Diminutive: Merle.

Murphy Irish Gaelic: a warrior of the
sea. More commonly a boy's name.
Murphey.

Musetta Greek: a little muse.
Musette.

Musika Tongan: like music.

Mya/Myah *See* Maya and Mia.

Myall *See* BOYS.

Mychaela/Mykaela *See* Michaela.

Myfanwy Welsh: the beloved one.
Miffany, Myvanwy.

Myla/Mylah *See* Mila.

Mylee/Myleigh/Mylie *See* Miley.

Mynette *See* Minette.

Mynk/Mynke *See* Mink.

Mynx/Mynxe *See* Minx.

Myra Greek: fragrant; from myrrh,
an aromatic shrub. *See also* Myron in
BOYS.
Mira, Mirah, Myrah.

Myranda *See* Miranda.

Myri Possibly a form of Myra.
Myree, Myreen, Myrene, Myrie,
Myrine.

Myriad Greek: many, innumerable.

Myriam *See* Miriam.

Myrle *See* Merle.

Myrna Irish Gaelic: beloved.
Merna, Mirna, Morna, Muirne
(Gaelic), Myrnah.

Myron *See* BOYS.

Myrtle Greek: a 'plant name'.
Mertle, Myrta, Myrtell, Myrtis.

Mysti *See* Misty.

Mystic Latin: from the word meaning
secret.
Mistic, Mistique Mystik, Mystike,
Mystique (French).

N

Nabila Arabic: noble.
Nabeela.

Nada Arabic: the generous one.

Nadia Slavic: hope.
Nadeen, Nadeena, Nadene, Nadiah,
Nadina, Nadine (French), Nadiya,
Nadya (Russian).

Nadira Arabic: precious.

Nadya *See* Nadia.

Nahla/Nahlani *See* Nalani.

Naia Polynesian: a dolphin.
Naya.

Naida Greek: a water nymph.
Naiad, Nayad, Nyad.

Naiki/Naikie *See* Nike.

Nairne Scottish Gaelic: from the
river.
Nairn.

Nakeita/Nakita *See* Nikita.

Nalani Hawaiian: the calm of the skies.
Nahla, Nahlani, Nala, Nalah.

Nami Japanese: a wave.
Namiko.

Nan A diminutive of Anne, Nancy
and Nanette.

Nana *See* Anne and Nancy.

Nanaia Maori. A biblical name.

Nanala Polynesian: a sunflower.

Nancy Originally a diminutive of
Anne.
Nancee, Nancey, Nanci, Nancie,
Nancye, Nanette.
Diminutives: Nan, Nana, Nance.

Nanette *See* Nancy. Also a French
diminutive of Anne.
Diminutive: Nan.

Nani Polynesian: beautiful.

Nanine/Nanna *See* Anne.

Nanon French diminutive of Anne.

Nanook Eskimo: a bear god,
representing noble strength and
purpose.

Naomi Hebrew: pleasant. A biblical
name, and the feminine form of
Noam.
Naoma, Naomee, Naomie, Neomi,
Neomie, Niomi, Niomie, Noemi,
Noemia (Portuguese), Noemie.

Napea Latin: a girl of the valley.

Nara Japanese: an oak tree. Old
English: the nearest and dearest one.

Narada Japanese: the messenger
of the gods, the equivalent of the
Roman god Mercury.
Naradah.

Narcisse French from Latin: the
narcissus or daffodil flower.
Narcisa, Narcise, Narciss, Narcissa.

Narda Latin: a fragrant ointment or
perfume.

Narelle Australian: probably from
Nara and Elle.

Nariel The angel of the midday
winds.
Narielle.

Nariko Japanese: humble.

Narisa/Narissa *See* Nerissa.

Nasia Hebrew: God's miracle. Nasya.

Nasrin Persian: a wild rose. Nasreen, Nesrin (Turkish).

Nastasia/Nastya *See* Anastasia.

Nata Sanskrit: a dancer.

Natalie Latin: born at Christmas. Natala, Natale, Natalee, Natalia, Natalina (Italian), Nataly, Natalya (Russian), Natalye, Nathalia, Nathalie (French).
Diminutives: Natasha (Russian), Nattie, Nettie, Talia (Russian), Talya (Russian).

Natasha Russian diminutive of Natalie. Natarsha, Natasa, Natascha, Natashya.
Diminutive: Tasha.

Nathalia/Nathalie *See* Natalie.

Nathania Hebrew: a gift of God. The feminine form of Nathan. Natania, Natanya, Nathene.

Natividad Spanish: the nativity.

Navana A modern American name. Navanah, Navanna, Navannah, Navianah, Navianna, Naviannah.

Navy Either a 'colour name' or referring to a fleet of ships. Navee, Navey, Navie.

Nawal Arabic: a gift.

Naya *See* Naia.

Nayad *See* Naida.

Nazaret Spanish: of Nazareth. Nazareth.

Nea *See* Neala and Nova.

Neala Irish Gaelic: the champion. The feminine form of Neal or Neil. *See also* Nola. Neale, Nealina, Neela, Neelah, Neila, Neilina (Scottish).
Diminutives: Nea, Nia.

Neave Old English: a nephew. Also a boy's name. Neava, Neavah, Neaves, Neiv, Neive, Neve.

Nebula Latin: a cluster of stars in astronomy. Also cloud or mist.

Neco *See* Nico.

Neda Slavic: born on Sunday. Nedda.

Neela/Neelah/Neila/Neilina *See* Neala and Nila.

Neena/Neenah *See* Nina.

Neesha *See* Nisha.

Neiv/Neive *See* Neave.

Neka Native American: a wild goose.

Neko *See* Nico.

Nelda Old English: of the elder tree.

Nelia A diminutive of Cornelia.

Nell A diminutive of Eleanor, Ellen and Helen. Nella, Nelli, Nellie, Nelle, Nelley, Nelly.

Nellwyn Old English: a bright companion.

Nena/Nenah *See* Nina.

Neola Greek: the young one.

Neoma Greek: the new moon.

Neomi/Neomie *See* Naomi.

Neptunia Latin: from Neptune, a planet and the Roman god of the sea. Neptuna.

Nereida *See* Nerina.

Nerida Aboriginal: a flower.
Nerada, Neradah, Nereda, Neredah, Neridah.

Nerina Greek: a sea nymph. *See also* Nerissa.
Nereida, Nerice, Nerine, Nerita.

Nerissa Probably a form of Nerina.
Narisa, Narissa, Nerisa.

Neroli The name of an Italian princess.
Nerolee, Nerolia, Nerolie.

Nerys Welsh: a lady.

Nesrin Turkish form of Nasrin.

Nessa Cornish: the nearest one. Also a diminutive of Agnes and Vanessa.
Nessi, Nessie.

Nesta Welsh form of Agnes.

Netta/Nettie/Netty Diminutives of Antonia, Henrietta and many names ending with etta and ette.

Nevada Spanish: snow, or as white as snow. A state of the USA.
Neva, Nevah, Nevadah.

Nevaeh A modern made-up name, heaven spelt backwards.
Neveah.

Nevan Irish: holy, or a little saint.
Neven, Nevyn.

Neve *See* Neave.

Neysa/Neza *See* Agnes.

Nga Maori: a witch.

Ngahere Maori: a forest.

Ngahiwi Maori: many hills.

Ngahuia Maori: prized feathers.

Ngahuru Maori: autumn.

Ngaio Maori: a native tree.

Ngaire Maori: flaxen.

Ngaere, Niree, Nyree.

Ngoikore Maori: the weak one.

Nia *See* Neala and Nova.

Niamh Irish Gaelic: beautiful, bright. The daughter of a sea god in Irish mythology.
Niam.

Niccola/Niccole *See* Nicola.

Nichelle A variation of Michelle.

Nick/Nicky Diminutives of Nicola.

Nico A diminutive of Nicola.
Neco, Neko, Niko.

Nicola Latin: the victory of the people. The feminine form of Nicholas.
Niccola, Niccole, Nichola, Nichole, Nicholette, Nicholina, Nickola, Nickole, Nicla (Italian), Nicole (French), Nicolette (French), Nicolina, Nicoline, Niki (Greek), Nikola.
Diminutives: Colette (French), Colletta, Collette, Nick, Nicky, Nico, Nikki.

Nicole/Nicolette/Nicolina *See* Nicola.

Nidia *See* Nydia.

Nigella The feminine form of Nigel.

Nikau Maori: a palm tree.

Nike A winged maiden, the goddess of victory in Greek mythology (the equivalent of the Roman goddess Victoria).
Naiki, Naikie, Nikey.

Niki/Nikki/Nikola *See* Nicola.

Nikita Russian: unconquerable. Traditionally a boy's name, but now given to girls.
Nakeita, Nakeitah, Nakita, Nakitah, Niketa, Niketah, Nikitah.

21st-CENTURY NAMES

The 'Top-30' boys' and girls' names for 2015 are listed on page xvi. In addition, here are some other very popular 21st-century names for New Zealand babies.

Girls

Aaliyah	Jorja		
Abigail	Katie		
Addison	Kayla		
Alexandra	Keira		
Alyssa	Mackenzie		
Amber	Madeleine		
Amy	Mikayla		
Anna	Molly		
Aria	Nevaeh		
Ashleigh	Peyton		
Brooke	Phoebe		
Catherine	Rachel		
Courtney	Rebecca		
Eden	Samantha		
Elizabeth	Sarah		
Evie	Stella		
Hayley	Summer		
Ivy	Tayla		
Jade	Victoria		
Jasmine	Zara		

Boys

Alex	Jaxon
Ashton	Jesse
Bailey	Joel
Beau	Jonathan
Ben	Jordan
Braxton	Joseph
Caleb	Levi
Callum	Logan
Cameron	Luke
Cody	Michael
Connor	Mitchell
David	Nathan
Dylan	Nicholas
Edward	Oscar
Eli	Patrick
Finn	Reuben
Hamish	Riley
Harrison	Toby
Harry	Xavier
Jake	Zachary

Niko *See* Nico.

Nikoda A modern name, possibly derived from Nikita.
Nikodah.

Nila Hindi: blue, or a sapphire.
Neela, Neelah, Nihla, Nilah, Nilo

(Nepali).

Niley A modern name, possibly a form of Miley.
Nilee, Nileigh, Nilie, Nylee, Nyeleigh, Nyley, Nylie.

Nima Sherpa/Tibetan: born on a

Sunday. Also a boy's name.

Nimfa/Nimfea/Nimfia *See* Nymphea.

Nina Spanish: a girl. *See also* Anne
and Antonia.
Neena, Neenah, Nena, Nenah,
Ninah, Ninetta, Ninette.

Ninon French diminutive of Anne.

Niomi/Niomie *See* Naomi.

Nira Modern Hebrew: of the loom.

Niree *See* Ngaire.

Nirvana Sanskrit: happy, or a
heavenly state.
Nirvanah, Nirvanna, Nirvannah.

Nisha Sanskrit: the night.
Neesha.

Nissa Scandinavian: a friendly elf. *See
also* Nyssa.
Nisa, Nissah, Nyssa.

Nita Native American: a bear. Also
a Spanish form of Anne, and a
diminutive of Anita, Bonita, Juanita
and other names.
Nitah.

Nitika The angel of precious stones.
Nitikah.

Nixie German: a water sprite.
Nixee, Nixey, Nixi, Nixy.

Nizana Hebrew: a flower bud.
Diminutive: Zana.

Noa A feminine form of Noah,
a Hebrew name meaning rest or
comfort.
Noah, Noha.

Noe Hawaiian: misty rain.

Noelani Hawaiian: a beautiful girl
from heaven.

Noeline *See* Noelle.

Noelle Old French: Christmas, or

born at Christmas. The feminine
form of Noel.
Noel, Noeline, Noell, Noella, Noëlle,
Noellyn, Noleen, Nolene.

Noemi/Noemia/Noemie *See* Naomi.

Noha *See* Noa.

Nohea Hawaiian: lovely.

Noilani A popular Thai name.

Nola Irish Gaelic: the champion,
or the fair-shouldered one. *See also*
Neala and Nuala.
Nolah.

Noleen/Nolene *See* Noelle.

Noleta Latin: unwilling.
Nolita.

Nona Latin: the ninth, as in the ninth
child.
Noni, Nonie.

Noni/Nonie Diminutives of Nona
and Nora.

Nonna Russian: the name of a saint.

Noomi An unusual Scandinavian
name.
Noomie.

Noor Arabic: light or fire.
Nour, Noura, Nur, Nura.

Nora A diminutive of Eleanor. Also a
Scottish feminine form of Norman.
Norah, Noreen, Norelle, Norlene.
Diminutives: Noni, Nonie.

Nordica Teutonic: from the north.
Nordika.

Noreen *See* Nora.

Nori Japanese: a doctrine.
Diminutive: Noriko.

Norlene *See* Nora.

Norma Latin: a rule or standard;
the perfect girl or woman. Also a

Scottish feminine form of Norman.

Normandy A French province.
Normandea, Normandee,
Normandey, Normandie.

Norna Old Norse: the goddess of fate.

Nour/Noura *See* Noor.

Nouvelle French: the newcomer. *See
also* Nova.
Nouveau (French), Nouveaux, Nouvel,
Nouvella, Novella, Novellah, Novelle.

Nova Greek: new, the newcomer.
Nea, Nia, Novah, Novia, Novella,
Novelle.

Nu Burmese: tender.

Nuala Irish Gaelic: the fair-
shouldered one. *See also* Nola.
Nula.

Nuna Native American: the land.

Nur/Nura *See* Noor.

Nuray Turkish: a bright moon.
Nureil.

Nya Thai: from the north.
Nyah.

Nyad *See* Naida.

Nydia Latin: a refuge or nest.
Nidia.

Nylee/Nyeleigh/Nylie *See* Niley.

Nymphea Greek: a maiden.
Nimfa (Polish, Spanish), Nimfea,
Nimfia, Nymfa, Nymfea, Nymfia,
Nymph, Nympha, Nymphia.

Nyoko Japanese: a gem or treasure.

Nyree *See* Ngaire.

Nyssa Greek: the beginning. *See also*
Nissa.
Nissa, Nissah, Nysa, Nyssah.

Nyx Latin: white-haired.
Nyxie.

O

Oba Nigerian: an ancient river goddess.

Obelia Greek: a pillar or needle.

Oceana Greek: of the sea.
Oceanea, Oceania, Oceanna.

Octavia Latin: the eighth.
Octava, Octavie (French), Ottavia
(Italian).
Diminutive: Tavia.

Oda Teutonic: rich.

Odela/Odele/Odella *See* Odile.

Odelia Hebrew: I will praise God. *See
also* Odile.

Odessa Greek: a long journey.

Odette French: a home lover.
Odett, Odetta.

Odile French: riches, prosperity. A
feminine version of Otto.
Odela, Odele, Odelia, Odelie,
Odelinda, Odell, Odella, Odilia,
Odilla, Ottilie, Ottoline.

Odina Native American: a mountain.
Odena.

Odrey Probably a modern form of
Audrey.
Odree, Odri, Odrie, Odry.

'Ofa Tongan: love.

Ofelia/Ofilia *See* Ophelia.

Ofra/Ofrah *See* Ophrah.

Ohara Japanese: a field.

Ohorere Maori: suddenly.

Okalani Hawaiian: from heaven.

Okeroa Maori: a long search.

Oki Japanese: from the ocean.

Oksana An exotic Russian name, possibly meaning a treasure. Oksanna, Oxana, Oxanna.

Ola Old Norse/Scandinavian: a descendant. The feminine form of Olaf.

Olalla Spanish form of Eulalia.

Olathe Native American: beautiful.

Oleander Greek: an evergreen tree. Olea, Oleanda, Oleandah, Oliana (Polynesian).

Olena Hawaiian: turmeric. Also the Ukrainian form of Helen. Olina.

Olenka *See* Olga.

Olethea Latin: truth. Oleta.

Olga Russian: the holy one. The feminine form of Oleg. Elga, Helga (Scandinavian), Olenka, Olia, Olienka, Olva, Olya.

Oli/Olie Diminutives of Olivia.

Olia A form of Olga.

Oliana Polynesian form of Oleander.

Olien Russian: like a deer.

Olimpia/Olimpie *See* Olympia.

Olina *See* Olena.

Olinda Latin: fragrant. Olynda.

Olive *See* Olivia.

Olivia Latin: an olive tree or branch; a symbol of peace and the feminine form of Oliver. A character in Shakespeare's *Twelfth Night*. *See also* Livia. Alivia, Alivya, Alivyah, Allivia, Oliva, Olive, Olivette, Oliviah, Oliviana, Olivya, Olivyah, Ollivia, Ollivya, Olyve, Olyvia, Olyviah, Olyvya.

Diminutives: Livia, Livvie, Livvy, Oli, Olie, Ollie.

Olva/Olya *See* Olga.

Olwen Welsh: white or fair footprints. A character in Welsh legend. Olwyn.

Olympia Latin: the heavenly one; from the home of the gods. Olimpia (Italian), Olimpias, Olimpie, Olympe (French), Olympias.

Olynda *See* Olinda.

Olyve/Olyvia/Olyvya *See* Olivia.

Oma Arabic: long-lived. The feminine form of Omar.

Omaka Maori: the place where the stream flows.

Ombra Italian: shade or a shadow. Ombrah.

Omega Greek: the last.

Ona Lithuanian form of Anne. *See also* Úna.

Onawa Native American: one who is wide awake.

Ondine Latin: a water sprite. Ondina, Undine.

Onida Native American: the expected or awaited one. Oneida.

Onike Tongan form of Onyx.

Ono Hawaiian: sweet or delicious.

Onóra Irish Gaelic form of Honour.

Onyx Greek: a semi-precious stone. Onike (Tongan), Ónix (Spanish), Onixe, Onyxe.

Oona/Oonagh *See* Úna.

Opal Sanskrit: a jewel or precious stone.

Opale, Opalina, Opaline (French), Opeli (Tongan).

Ophelia Greek: a helper. A character in Shakespeare's *Hamlet*.
Ofelia (Spanish), Ofilia, Ophélie (French).
Diminutive: Phelia.

Ophrah Hebrew: a fawn, or a lively maiden.
Ofra, Ofrah, Ophra, Oprah, Orpah.

Ora Latin: light, golden.
Orah.

Oralee/Oralia/Oralie/Orelia *See* Aurelia.

Orange A 'colour name'.
Orancia (Italian), Oranje, Orena (Welsh).

Orchid Latin: a 'flower name'.
Orcid, Orkid.

Ordelia Teutonic: the spear of the elf.
Ordella.

Orea Greek: the maid of the mountains.

Orena *See* Orange.

Oriana Latin: to rise. An Italian name.
Oriane (French).

Oriel The angel of destiny. *See also* Aurelia.

Orinda Hebrew: a pine tree.

Oriole Latin: a golden bird.

Orissa A state in eastern India.

Orkid *See* Orchid.

Orla Irish Gaelic form of Aurelia.
Orlagh, Orlah.

Orlanda The feminine form of Orlando (from the famed land).

Orna Hebrew: light. Irish Gaelic: pale.

Ornella Italian: a flowering ash tree.

Ornetta, Ornette (French).

Orpah *See* Ophrah.

Orsa/Orseline/Orsola *See* Ursula.

Orsina The feminine form of Orson, a little bear.

Ortense/Ortensia *See* Hortense.

Orvokki Finnish form of Violet.

Orysia An unusual Ukrainian name.

Osana/Osanna *See* Hosanna.

Ostara The Anglo-Saxon goddess of the moon and dawn.

Otira Maori: but, however.

Ottavia *See* Octavia.

Ottilie/Ottoline *See* Odile.

Ottobra The Italian word for October, so suitable for a Libra or Scorpio child.
October, Octobra, Octobre (French), Octobria, Oktoba (Swahili), Oktober (Dutch, German, Norwegian).

Ourania *See* Urania.

Owena Welsh: well born. The feminine form of Owen.

Oxana/Oxanna *See* Oksana.

Ozora Hebrew: the strength of the Lord.

P

Pacifica Latin: calm, as in the Pacific Ocean.
Pasifiki (Tongan).

Padma Sanskrit: a lotus.
Padmah, Padmini.

Paget A little page. *See also* Paige.
Padget, Padgett, Padgette, Paget,

Pagette.

Paige Old English: a young child. Also a boy's name.
Page, Paig, Paij, Paije, Payg, Payge.

Painter Middle English: one who paints pictures.
Paynter, Peinter, Peynter.

Paisley A Scottish town, after which the paisley pattern was named.
Paislea, Paislee, Paisleigh, Paisly.

Paiten/Paiton/Paityn *See* Payton.

Palila Hawaiian: a bird.

Pallas Greek: knowledge and wisdom.

Palma Latin: a palm tree. A town in Majorca.
Palmah, Palmira, Palymyra.

Paloma Spanish from Latin: a dove.
Palomah, Palometa, Palomita.

Pamela English: a name invented by the 16th-century poet Sir Philip Sidney, possibly based on the Greek word for sweetness or honey.
Pamala, Pameela (Sanskrit), Pamelia, Pamelina, Pamella, Pamina, Pamla.
Diminutives: Pam, Pammi, Pammie, Pammy, Pani (Maori).

Pamina/Pamla *See* Pamela.

Pandita Sanskrit: a scholar.

Pandonia Latin: a 10th-century saint.

Pandora Greek: all-gifted, talented. A figure from Greek mythology.

Pani Maori form of Pam. *See* Pamela.

Pania Maori: a mythological sea maiden.

Panna Hindi: an emerald. Also the Hungarian form of Anne.

Pansy Old French: thoughts; a 'flower name'.
Pansee, Pansey, Pansi, Pansie.

Panthea Greek: all of the gods.

Paola/Paolina *See* Paula.

Paquita Spanish: one who is free.
Pequita.

Pare Maori form of Polly.

Parirau Maori: the wing of a bird.

Paris Greek: a character in mythology. Also the capital of France. Originally a boy's name.
Parise, Parris, Parisse, Parrys, Parys, Paryse.

Parisa Persian: fairy-like.
Parysa.

Parker *See* BOYS.

Parnella Old French: a little rock. *See also* Peta, Petronel and Pierre.
Parnell, Parnelle.

Parthenia Greek: maidenly, virginal.

Parvati Sanskrit: the daughter of the mountain.

Parys/Paryse *See* Paris.

Parysa *See* Parisa.

Pasang Sherpa/Tibetan: born on a Friday. Also a boy's name.

Pascale French from Latin: Easter, or born at Easter.
Pasca (Cornish), Pascal, Pascaline, Pascall, Pascalle, Paschale, Pascoe (Cornish), Pascuala (Spanish), Pasquelina (Italian), Pasquette (French).
Diminutives: Pasca, Pascha, Pasqua.

Pascoe Cornish form of Pascale.

Pashmina Hindi from Persian: a fine woollen fabric.
Pashmeena, Pashmena.

Pasifiki Tongan form of Pacifica.

Pasqua/Pasquelina/Pasquette *See* Pascale.

Pat/Patsy/Pattie *See* Patricia.

Patience English: one of the seven virtues.
Paciencia (Spanish), Pazienza (Italian).

Paton *See* Payton.

Patrea *See* Patricia.

Patrice French form of Patricia.

Patricia Latin: noble, well-born. The feminine form of Patrick.
Patrea, Patria, Patrice (French), Patrisha, Patrizia (Italian).
Diminutives: Pat, Patsy, Patti, Pattie, Patty, Tricia, Trish, Trisha.

Paula Latin: small. The feminine form of Paul.
Paola (Italian), Paolina, Paule, Pauletta, Paulette (French), Paulina (Spanish), Pauline (French), Paulita, Pavla (Czech).

Pauline French form of Paula.

Pavla *See* Paula.

Pax Latin: peace. *See also* Peace.
Paz (Spanish), Pazia, Pazita.

Payg/Payge *See* Paige.

Paynter *See* Painter.

Payton Old English: from the warrior's farm.
Paiten, Paiton, Paityn, Paton, Payten, Peyton.

Peace Middle English: the peaceful one. *See also* Pax.

Peaches Middle English: a 'fruit name'.
Peach, Pêche (French).

Pearl Old French: a little sphere. A 'gem name'.
Pearla, Pearle, Pearlie, Pearline, Perl (Welsh), Perla (Italian, Spanish),

Perle, Perlette (French), Perlina.

Peata Maori form of Beatrice.

Peg/Peggie/Peggy Diminutives of Margaret.

Pega An 8th-century saint.

Peinter *See* Painter.

Peita *See* Peta.

Pelagia Greek: from the sea.

Pele Hawaiian: a goddess of fire.

Pema Sherpa/Tibetan: a lotus.

Penelope Greek: the weaver. A character in mythology.
Diminutives: Pen, Pennee, Penni, Pennie, Penny.

Penni/Pennie/Penny *See* Penelope.

Penthea Greek: the fifth.
Penthia.

Peony Latin: healing. A 'flower name'.

Pepa/Pepita Spanish diminutives of Josephine. *See also* Pepper.

Pepe Tongan: a butterfly.

Pepper Middle English: a 'spice name'.
Pepa, Pepah, Peppa, Peppah.

Pequita *See* Paquita.

Perdita Latin: the lost one. A name invented by Shakespeare for a character in *The Winter's Tale*.
Perditah.
Diminutives: Deeta, Dita, Dyta.

Perette *See* Peta.

Peridot Arabic: a green gemstone.

Perl/Perla/Perle/Perlina *See* Pearl.

Peronel/Peronella *See* Petronel.

Perouze Armenian: turquoise.

Perpetua Latin: continuing,

enduring. The name of a saint.

Perry Old English: from the pear tree. Perrey, Perri, Perrie, Perrin, Perryn.

Persephone Greek: the goddess of the underworld.

Persia A 'country name'.

Persis Latin: a woman from Persia. A New Testament name.

Peta Greek: a rock or stone. A feminine form of Peter. *See also* Parnella, Petronel and Pierre. Peita, Perette (French), Petah, Petra, Petrea, Petrina, Petrine (Danish), Pier, Pierette, Pierina, Pieta, Pietah, Pietra (Italian).

Petal From Latin: part of a flower. Petall.

Petra/Petrea/Petrina/Petrine *See* Peta.

Petronel Latin: the name of an early saint, and related to the boy's name Peter. *See also* Parnella, Peta and Pierre. Peronel, Peronella, Petronella, Petronelle, Petronilla.

Petula Possibly from the Latin word for to ask, or to seek. Petulia. *Diminutive*: Pet.

Petunia A 'flower name'.

Peynter *See* Painter.

Peyton *See* Payton.

Phaedra Greek: the bright one. The wife of Theseus in Greek mythology. Phaidra, Phedra.

Phebe/Phebee/Phebie *See* Phoebe.

Phelia *See* Ophelia.

Philadelphia Greek: brotherly love. A city in the USA.

Philana Greek: a friend of mankind.

Philantha Greek: a lover of flowers. Philanthe.

Philberta Old English: very brilliant. Filberta, Filbertha, Philbertha.

Philida/Phillida/Phillis *See* Phyllis.

Philippa Greek: a lover of horses. The feminine form of Philip and Phillip. Felipa (Spanish), Filippa (Italian), Philipa, Philippina, Philippine (French, German), Phillippa. *Diminutives*: Phil, Philly, Pip, Pippa.

Philomela Greek: a lover of song. Philomel.

Philomena Greek: a lover of the moon. Filomena, Filomene, Philomene.

Phiper *See* Piper.

Phoebe Greek: radiant and bright like the sun. The name of a Greek deity and mentioned in the New Testament. Feebee, Feebi, Feebie, Fhebee, Fheebi, Fheebie, Phebe (Italian), Phebee, Phebie, Phoebee, Phoebie.

Phoenix *See* BOYS.

Photini *See* Fotini.

Phyllis Greek: a green bough or branch. A character in mythology. Philida, Philis, Phillida, Phillis, Phylis, Phyllida, Phyllys.

Phyper *See* Piper.

Pia Latin: pious, devout. An Italian and Spanish name.

Piaf French: the surname of a legendary singer (Édith Piaf). It is believed to mean a sparrow or little bird in French slang.

Piaff.

Pier/Pierette/Pierina *See* Peta and Pierre.

Pierre The French version of Peter. More commonly a boy's name, but sometimes used for girls.
Pier, Piera, Pierina, Pierine, Pierr, Pierra.

Pieta/Pietah/Pietra *See* Peta.

Piki Maori: a fig.

Pilar Spanish: supportive, a pillar.

Piltti An unusual Finnish name.

Pina Spanish: a pine tree.
Pinah, Pine, Pineta, Pinetah.

Pink A 'colour name'.
Pinke, Pynk, Pynke.

Pip A diminutive of Philippa.

Piper Middle English: a pipe player. Also a boy's name.
Phiper, Phyper, Pipa, Pipah, Pipere, Pyper.

Pipi Maori: a shellfish.

Pippa A diminutive of Philippa.
Pippah, Pippi.

Piritta Estonian and Finnish form of Bridget.

Pisces Latin: fishes. The last sign of the zodiac.
Piscea, Piscia.

Pixie Celtic/English: a fairy or sprite.
Pixee, Pixey, Pixy.

Placida Latin: peaceful, serene. Feminine form of Placido.
Placidia, Placidina.

Platona Greek: wise, broad-shouldered.

Pleasance One who is pleasant.
Plaisance (French).

Plutia From Pluto, the mythological god of the underworld, and the planet that rules the zodiac sign of Scorpio.
Pluta, Pluto.

Poet Middle English: one who writes poetry.
Poete, Poett, Poette.

Polly A form of Molly.
Pare (Maori).

Pollyanna A 'combination name'.

Pomona Latin: fertile, fruitful.

Pony A small horse.
Ponee, Poney, Poni, Ponie.

Poppy Old English: a 'flower name'.
Poppee, Poppey, Poppi, Poppie.

Portia Latin: an offering. The heroine of Shakespeare's *The Merchant of Venice*.
Porcha, Porchia, Porsha, Porshia.

Posy A bunch of flowers. Also a diminutive of Josephine.
Posee, Posey, Posie.

Pounamu Maori: greenstone. *See also* Waipounamu.

Prada A famous Italian fashion label.
Pradah, Prahda.

Praise Middle English: one who deserves approval or admiration.
Praiz, Praize, Prayse, Prayze.

Precious Middle English: something of great value.

Prema Sanskrit: love, affection.

Presley Old English: from the priest's meadow. More often a boy's name.
Preslea, Preslee, Presleigh, Presly.

Prima Latin: the firstborn.

Primavera Spanish: springtime or a

child of the spring.

Primrose Latin: the first rose; a 'flower name'. *See also* Primula.

Primula A 'flower name', an alternative name for a primrose.

Prioska Hungarian: the blushing one.

Priscilla Latin: from a Roman family name.
Prisca (Spanish), Prisilla.
Diminutives: Cilla, Pris, Prissie, Silla.

Priya Sanskrit: beloved.
Priyah, Priyanka.

Prize Middle English: a reward.
Pryse, Pryze.

Proserpina The Roman equivalent of Persephone, the Greek goddess of the underworld.
Proserpine.

Prospera Latin: favourable.

Provence A region of France.

Providence Middle English: foresight, or divine protection or care.
Providenca, Providenza, Provydence.

Prudence Middle English: one who shows careful foresight.
Prudencia, Prudentia.
Diminutives: Pru, Prue.

Prunella Latin: a little plum.
Prunelle.
Diminutives: Pru, Prue.

Pryse/Pryze *See* Prize.

Psyche Greek: the immortal, or the soul.

Pualani Hawaiian: a heavenly flower.

Pualena Hawaiian: yellow.

Puanani Hawaiian: a beautiful flower.

Puatara Polynesian: a legendary figure.

Puma Spanish: an American wild cat.

Pumah.

Puna Finnish: red. Hawaiian: a child of the moon. Maori: a spring.

Puntira An attractive Thai name.

Pupuhi Maori: the wind.

Pura Latin: the pure one.

Purnima Sanskrit: the night of the full moon.
Diminutive: Purni.

Putiputi Maori: a flower.

Pynk/Pynke *See* Pink.

Pyper *See* Piper.

Pyrena Greek: the fiery one.
Pyrenia.

Pythia Greek: a prophet.
Pythea.

Q

Qadira Arabic: powerful.
Kadira.

Qing Chinese: greenish-blue.
Ching.

Quaile Manx Gaelic: the son or daughter of Paul. Also a boy's name.
Quail, Quale, Quayl, Quayle.

Quarta Latin: the fourth, or fourth child.
Quartana, Quartia.

Queena Old English: a woman.
Kuine (Maori), Kuini (Samoan), Queen, Queenie.

Queenan An Irish Gaelic surname.
Quenan.

Quella English: to pacify.

Quenby Scandinavian: womanly.

Quendryth An unusual Welsh name.
Quendreth, Quendrethe, Quendrith,
Quendrithe, Quendrythe.

Quentin Latin: the fifth, as in the
fifth-born child. *See also* Quinta.
Quenten, Quenton, Quentyn,
Quinten, Quinton, Quintyn.

Querida Spanish: the beloved one.

Questa French: the searcher.

Quiana A modern name, derived
from either Queenie or Quinn.
Quianah, Quianna, Quiannah,
Quinna, Quinnah.

Quilla The moon goddess of the
Incas.

Quincy *See* Quinta. Also a boy's
name.
Quincey.

Quinette *See* Quinta.

Quinn Irish Gaelic: wise and
intelligent. Also a boy's name.
Quin, Quinne.

Quinta Latin: the fifth, as in the
fifth-born child. *See also* Quentin
and Quincy.
Quincy, Quincey, Quinette,
Quintana, Quintilla, Quintina.

Quinten/Quinton *See* Quentin.

Quintessa Latin: the essence.
Quentessa.

Quirina Spanish and Italian: the
feminine form of Quirino (*see* Corin
in BOYS).

Quirita Latin: a citizen.

Quishla/Quishlah *See* Cushla.

Quona The name of a medieval noble
Italian family.
Qona.

R

Ra Maori/Polynesian: the sun.

Rabia Arabic: the harvest, or the
spring.
Rabea, Rabeah, Rabi'a, Rabiah,
Rabiya, Rabiyah,

Rachel Hebrew: a ewe. The wife of
Jacob and mother of Joseph in the
Bible.
Lahela (Hawaiian), Rachael,
Rachela (Polish), Rachele (Italian),
Rachelle, Raghnaid (Scottish Gaelic),
Raghnailt (Irish Gaelic), Rahel
(Hebrew), Rahela, Rahera (Maori),
Rakel (Scandinavian), Rakelle,
Raquel (Spanish), Raquelle, Rashell,
Rashelle, Raychel, Raychelle.
Diminutives: Rae, Ray, Shelley.

Racine A French surname, best
known through Jean Racine, a
17th-century dramatist.
Raceen, Raceene.

Rada Slavic: glad.

Radella Old English: an elfin adviser.
Radelle.

Radha Sanskrit: success. The name of
a Hindu goddess.
Radhia (Arabic).

Radinka Slavic: joyful, active.

Radmilla Slavic: a worker for the
people.

Rae English: a doe. *See also* Rachel
and Raelene.
Rai, Raie, Ray, Raye.

Raelene An Australian made-up name.
Raeline.
Diminutives: Rae, Ray.

Raemonda *See* Ramona.

Rafaela/Rafaella/Raffaela *See* Raphaella.

Raghnailt Irish Gaelic form of Rachel.
Raghnaid (Scottish Gaelic).

Rahel/Rahela *See* Rachel.

Rahera Maori form of Rachel.

Rahnee/Rahni *See* Rani.

Rai/Raie *See* Rae.

Rain Middle English: water that falls from the sky. *See also* Raine.

Raina Polish and Czech form of Regina.

Rainbow Old English: an array of bright colours.
Rainbowe, Rainebow, Rainebowe.

Raine Old German: advice, decision. Also a diminutive of Lorraine.
Rain, Rainn, Rainne, Rayn, Rayne, Reine, Rhain, Rhaine, Rhane, Rhayne.

Raisa Russian from Greek: adaptable.

Raissa Old French: the believer.
Raisse.

Raiven/Raivenne *See* Raven.

Raiza Hebrew form of Rose.

Raja Arabic: the hopeful one.
Rajah, Rajia, Rajya.

Rajani Sanskrit: dark, of the night.

Rakel Scandinavian form of Rachel.

Ramla Swahili: one who predicts the future.

Ramona Spanish: a wise protector. The feminine form of Ramón and Raymond.
Raemonda, Ramonah, Ramonda, Ramonde, Ramone, Rayma, Raymona.

Rana Arabic: beautiful to gaze upon. *See also* Rani. Ranya.

Randa/Randie/Randy *See* Miranda.

Rangi Maori/Polynesian: the sky.

Rangimarie Maori: peaceful.

Rani Sanskrit: a queen.
Rahnee, Rahni, Rana, Ranee.

Raniya Arabic: one who gazes.
Rania, Raniyah.

Ranya *See* Rana.

Raphaela Hebrew: the divine healer, or healed by God. The feminine form of Raphael.
Rafaela, Rafaella, Rafaelle, Raffaela, Raffaele, Raphael, Raphaella, Raphaelle.

Raquel/Raquelle/Rashell/Rashelle *See* Rachel.

Rashida Arabic: righteous.

Rata Maori: a tree with large red flowers.

Rati Sanskrit: love.

Raukura Maori: a plume of feathers.

Ravel A French composer.
Ravell, Ravella, Ravelle, Ravello.

Raven Middle English: a 'bird name'.
Raiven, Raivenne, Ravenn, Ravenne, Rayven, Rayvenne.

Ravenna A city in Italy.

Ray/Raye *See* Rachel and Raelene.

Raychel/Raychelle *See* Rachel.

Rayma/Raymona *See* Ramona.

Rayn/Rayne *See* Lorraine and Raine.

Rayna *See* Regina.

Rayven/Rayvenne *See* Raven.

Rea *See* Rhea.

Reagan/Reagen *See* Regan and Regina.

Reanna *See* Rhiannon.

Reba *See* Rebecca.

Rebecca Hebrew: possibly meaning a heifer or a knotted cord. The wife of Isaac in the Bible.
Rebbeca, Rebbeka, Rebeca (Spanish), Rebecka, Rebeka, Rebekah, Rebekka (German), Reveka (Greek), Ripeka (Maori), Rivka (Hebrew), Robecca, Robeccah, Robecka, Robeckah.
Diminutives: Bec, Becca, Becci, Beck, Becka, Becki, Beckie, Becky, Bek, Beki, Bekki, Reba, Riba.

Rebeka/Rebekah/Rebekka *See* Rebecca.

Rebel Latin: the rebellious one. Also a boy's name.
Rebele, Rebell, Rebelle.

Reece From Welsh: ardent.
Rees, Reese, Rhys (Welsh), Rhyse.

Reena *See* Rena.

Reeta/Reetah *See* Rita.

Reeves *See* BOYS.

Regan Irish Gaelic: the descendant of a king. A character in Shakespeare's *King Lear*. *See also* Regina.
Reagan, Reagen, Régan, Regann, Reganne, Regen, Regenn, Regenne, Reigan, Reigen, Rhegan, Rhegen.

Regina Latin: a queen.
Raina (Czech, Polish), Rayna, Reagan, Regan, Regia, Régine (French), Reina, Reine (French), Réjeanne (French), Renia (Polish).
Diminutives: Gina, Reg, Reggie, Rina.

Rehua The Polynesian goddess of the stars.

Reigan/Reigen *See* Regan.

Reiko Japanese: grateful.

Reiley/Reilley *See* Riley.

Reina/Reine *See* Raine and Regina.

Réjeanne French form of Regina.

Reka Maori: sweet.

Rémy French from Latin: an oarsman, one who rows. Generally a boy's name.
Remee, Remey, Remi, Remia, Remie, Remy, Remya.

Ren Japanese: a waterlily.

Rena Hebrew: a joyous song.
Reena, Rina.

Renata Latin: one who is reborn. Originally an Italian name.
Renae, Renate (German), Renay, Rene, Renée (French), Rennae, Rennay.
Diminutives: Renni, Rennie, Renny.

Renay/Rene/Renée *See* Renata.

Renia Polish form of Regina.

Renita Latin: a rebel.

Renny Irish Gaelic: small but powerful. *See also* Renata.
Reni, Renie, Renney, Rennie.

Rere Maori: a waterfall.

Reseda Latin: a mignonette flower.

Reta/Retah *See* Rita.

Reva Latin: renewed strength. *See also* Riva.

Reveka Greek form of Rebecca.

Revel Old French: a rebel, or one who makes merry. Also a boy's name.
Revell, Revelle, Revil, Revill, Reville.

Rewa Polynesian: slender.

Rex *See* BOYS.

Rexana Latin: regally graceful.
Rexann, Rexanna, Rexanne.

Rez Hungarian: red- or copper-coloured.
Rezia.

Rhaine/Rhane/Rhayne *See* Raine.

Rhea Greek: a stream, or a mother.
Rea.

Rhegan/Rhegen *See* Regan.

Rhian/Rhiarne *See* Ryan.

Rhiannon Welsh: a nymph, or a queen. A Celtic goddess associated with the moon.
Reanna, Rheanna, Rheannon, Rhian, Rhiann, Rhianna, Riana, Rianna, Riannon.

Rhianwen Welsh: a blessed or pure maiden.
Rhianwyn, Rhianwynne.

Rhoda Greek: a rose, or a woman from the island of Rhodes. A New Testament name.
Rhodah, Rhodia, Roda, Rodah.

Rhodanthe Greek: like a rose.

Rhona *See* Rona.

Rhonda Welsh: the name of a valley.
Rhondda, Ronda, Rondah.

Rhonwen Welsh: a white lance, or white hair.

Rhose/Rhosyn/Rhoze *See* Rose.

Rhubee/Rhubie *See* Ruby.

Rhyan/Rhyana *See* Rihana and Ryan.

Rhylea/Rhylee/Rhyleigh *See* Riley.

Rhymer One who rhymes.

Rhys/Rhyse *See* Reece.

Ria Spanish: of the river. Also a short form of Maria (*see* Mary).
Riaa, Riah.

Riahn/Rian/Rianne *See* Ryan.

Riana *See* Rhiannon. Also the Maori form of Diana.

Rianna/Riannon *See* Rhiannon.

Riba A diminutive of Rebecca.

Ricarda A feminine form of Richard.
Richarda, Richarde, Richella, Richelle.

Ricki/Rickie/Ricky/Rikki/Rikky Diminutives of several names.

Rida Arabic: the favoured one.

Rider *See* BOYS.

Rien *See* Ryan.

Rihana Arabic: sweet basil.
Rhyana, Rhyanna, Rihan, Rihanah, Rihann, Rihanna, Rihannah.

Rikka Finnish: the feminine form of Richard.

Riley Irish Gaelic: valiant. Old English: a rye meadow.
Reiley, Reilley, Reilly, Rhlye, Rhylea, Rhylee, Rhyleigh, Rielly, Riely, Rilea, Rilee, Rileigh, Rylea, Rylee, Ryleigh, Rylie, Rylye.

Rilla Teutonic: a stream.

Rima Maori: five.
Rimah.

Rimu Polynesian: a tree.

Rina *See* Regina and Rena.

Rindill Icelandic: a wren.
Rindil.

Rinzen Sherpa/Tibetan: the holder of intellect. Also a boy's name.

Rion *See* Ryan.

Riona Irish Gaelic: a queen.
Rionah.

Ripeka Maori form of Rebecca.

Ripley Old English: from the meadow of the shouter or loud one.
Riplea, Riplee, Ripleigh, Riply.

Risa Latin: laughter.

Rita A short form of Margarita (*see* Margaret).
Reeta, Reetah, Reta, Retah, Ritah.

Riva French from Latin: the shore or a riverbank.
Reva, Revah, Rivah.

River Middle English: a watercourse.
Rivera, Rivier, Riviera, Rivière (French).

Rivka Hebrew form of Rebecca.

Roan/Roann *See* Rowan.

Roanna Latin: gracious. Also a combination of Rose and Anna. *See also* Rosanna and Rowan.
Roana, Roane, Roanne.

Robalyn From Robin and Lynn.
Robalin.

Robbi/Robbie/Robby Diminutives of Roberta and similar names.

Robecca/Robecka *See* Rebecca.

Robena *See* Robin.

Roberta Old English/Teutonic: bright fame, famous. A feminine form of Robert. *See also* Robin.
Roberte, Robertha, Ruperta (German). *Diminutives*: Berta, Bertha, Bobbi, Bobbie, Bobby, Robbi, Robbie, Robby.

Robin English: originally a diminutive of Roberta.
Robena, Robina, Robine (French), Robinette, Robinia, Robyn, Robyna, Robyne.

Rochelle French: a small rock. Also from La Rochelle, a French fishing port.
Rochella, Rochette, Roshelle.

Roda/Rodah *See* Rhoda.

Roderica Teutonic: a famous ruler. The feminine form of Roderick.
Roderika, Roderyka.

Rodica Romanian: one who is fertile.
Rodika.

Roenah *See* Rowena.

Rohan Sanskrit: ascending. More commonly a boy's name.

Rohana Sanskrit: sandalwood.

Rohesia *See* Rose.

Roimata Maori: tears.

Róis/Róisín Irish Gaelic forms of Rose.

Rokeya/Rokia *See* Roqia.

Roksana *See* Roxana.

Rolanda Teutonic: from the famed land. Feminine form of Roland.
Rolande.

Roma Latin: from Rome.
Romaine, Romana, Romane, Romella, Romelle, Romola.

Romany A gypsy.
Romain, Romaine, Romanee, Romani, Romanie, Rommanee, Rommany.

Romella/Romelle *See* Roma.

Romilda Teutonic: a glorious warrior maiden.
Romelda, Romilde. *Diminutives*: Romi, Romy.

Romola *See* Roma.

Romy German diminutive of Rosemary. *See also* Romilda.

Rona Maori: the female moon. Scottish: the name of an island.
Rhona, Ronah.

Ronalda Old Norse: powerful. Also a feminine form of Ronald.

Ronan *See* BOYS.

Ronda *See* Rhonda.

Rongo Maori: to obey.

Rongopai Maori: the gospel.

Ronni/Ronnie/Ronny Diminutives of Veronica.

Roqia Persian: the dawn.
Rokeya, Rokeyah, Rokia, Rokiah, Roquia.

Rory *See* BOYS.

Ros *See* Rosalind and Rosamond.

Rosa Italian and Spanish form of Rose. *See also* Rosalia.
Rosah, Roza (Polish), Rozah.

Rosabelle Latin: a beautiful rose.
Rosabel, Rosabella.

Rosalba Italian: a white rose.

Rosaleen Irish form of Rosalind.

Rosalia Latin: a form of Rosa. The name of a 12th-century saint.
Rosalea, Rosalee, Rosa Lee, Rosalie, Rozalia, Rozalie.

Rosalind Latin: a beautiful rose. Old German: from the word for a horse. Shakespeare's heroine in *As You Like It*. *See also* Rosamond.
Rosaleen (Irish), Rosalin, Rosalinda, Rosalinde, Rosaline, Rosalyn, Rosalynd, Rosalynne, Roseline, Roslind, Roslyn, Rozalin, Rozaline, Rozlin, Rozlind.
Diminutives: Ros, Roz.

Rosamond Latin: a pure rose, or the rose of the world. Old German: from the word for a horse. *See also* Rosalind.
Rosamund, Rosemonda, Rosemonde (French), Rosemund, Rosmunda (Italian), Rozamond.
Diminutives: Ros, Roz.

Rosanna A combination of Rose and Anna.
Roanna, Roanne, Rosanne, Roseann, Roseanna, Roseanne, Rosena, Rozanna, Rozanne.

Rosario Spanish: a rosary.
Rosaria.

Rose Latin: a 'flower name' (from rosa). *See also* Rhoda, Rosa, Rosalia, Rosamond and Rosemary.
Raiza (Hebrew), Rhose, Rhosyn (Welsh), Rhoze, Rohesia, Róis (Irish Gaelic), Rosa (Italian, Spanish), Rosea, Rosel, Rosen (Cornish), Rosena, Rosene, Roseta (Portuguese), Rosetta (Italian), Rosette (French), Rosia, Rosina (Italian), Rosine, Rosita (Spanish), Roskia (Hungarian), Roze, Rozea, Rozen (Cornish), Rozena, Rozene, Rozia, Rozina (Slavic), Rozita.
Diminutives: Róisín (Irish Gaelic), Rosheen (Irish), Rosie, Rosine (French), Rosy, Rozie, Rozy, Ruzena (Czech), Zita (Italian, Spanish).

Roseanne *See* Rosanna.

Roselani Hawaiian: a heavenly rose.

Roseline *See* Rosalind.

Roselle A combination of Rose and Elle.
Rosella, Rozella, Rozelle.

Rosemary Latin: dew of the sea; a 'herb name'. Also a form of Rose.
Rosamaria, Rosamarie, Rosamaree, Rosemaria, Rosemarie.
Diminutives: Romy (German), Rosie, Rosy.

Rosemund *See* Rosamond.

Rosen A Cornish form of Rose.

Rosena/Rosene *See* Rosanna and Rose.

Rosenwyn Cornish: a fair rose.

Roseta/Rosetta/Rosette *See* Rose.

Rosevear Cornish: from the moorland.

Roshan Persian: splendid. Also a boy's name.
Roshana, Roshann, Roshanna.

Rosheen Irish Gaelic form of Rose.

Roshelle *See* Rochelle.

Rosia/Rosina/Rosine *See* Rose.

Rosie/Rosy *See* Rose and Rosemary.

Rosita *See* Rose.

Roskia Hungarian form of Rose.

Roslind/Roslyn *See* Rosalind.

Roubee/Roubi/Rouby *See* Ruby.

Rouge French: red.

Rowan Irish Gaelic: the little red-haired one. More commonly a boy's name.
Roan, Roann, Roanna, Roanne, Rowann, Rowanna, Rowanne, Rowen.

Rowena Celtic: the white-haired one. Old English: a well-known friend.
Roenah, Rowenah.

Roxana Persian: dawn. The wife of Alexander the Great.
Roksana (Russian), Roxane, Roxanna, Roxanne, Roxene, Roxine. *Diminutives*: Roxi, Roxie, Roxy.

Royale Old French: the regal one. A feminine form of Roy.
Royal, Royall, Royalle.

Roz *See* Rosalind and Rosamond.

Roza/Roze/Rozen/Rozena *See* Rosa and Rose.

Rozalie/Rozalie *See* Rosalia.

Rozalin/Rozaline/Rozlin *See* Rosalind.

Rozamond *See* Rosamond.

Rozanna/Rozanne *See* Rosanna.

Rozella/Rozelle *See* Roselle.

Rozia/Rozie/Rozina/Rozita/Rozy *See* Rose.

Ruange Polynesian: a legendary figure.

Rubey/Rubi/Rubie/Rubina *See* Ruby.

Ruby Latin: a precious stone.
Rhubee, Rhubi, Rhubie, Rhuby, Rouba, Roubee, Roubey, Roubi, Roubia, Roubie, Rouby, Roubye, Ruba, Rubea, Rubeah, Rubeena, Rubetta, Rubette, Rubey, Rubi (Spanish), Rubia, Rubie, Rubina, Rubinia, Rubye.

Rudelle Teutonic: the famous one.
Rudella.

Rue Old English from Greek: an aromatic medicinal plant. *See also* Ruth.

Ruella A combination of Ruth and Ella.

Rufina Latin: red-haired. The feminine form of Rufus.

Ruhia/Ruihi Maori forms of Lucy.

Ruiha/Ruihia Maori forms of Louise.

Rukmini Sanskrit: the wife of Lord Krishna. Often used in Indonesia.

Rula Latin: a ruler. A popular Polish name.

Rumer English: a gypsy.
Ruma, Rumah.

Runa Old Norse: secret lore.

Ruperta *See* Roberta.

Ruri Japanese: an emerald.

Rusalka Czech: a wood nymph. Russian/Slavic: a fairy or mermaid.
Rusalkah, Ruzalka, Ruzalkah.

Diminutives: Rusa, Rusah, Ruza, Ruzah.

Ruth Hebrew: beautiful and compassionate. A biblical name.
Rut (German, Scandinavian), Rutu (Maori).
Diminutives: Rue, Ruthie, Ruthy.

Rutu Maori form of Ruth.

Ruza/Ruzalka *See* Rusalka.

Ruzena *See* Rose.

Ryan Irish Gaelic: a little king. More commonly a boy's name.
Rhian, Rhiarne, Rhyan, Riahn, Rian, Rianne, Rien, Rion, Ryann, Ryanne, Ryen, Ryenne, Ryon.

Rylea/Rylee/Ryleigh/Rylie *See* Riley.

S

Sabah Arabic: the morning.
Saba.

Sabbathe Hebrew: born on the Sabbath.
Sabada, Sabas (Hebrew), Sabata, Sabath, Sabbata, Sabbath, Sabbatha.

Sabella/Sabelle *See* Isabel.

Sabena/Sabene *See* Sabina.

Sabia Irish: the sweet one.

Sabina Latin: a Sabine woman (from central Italy). The name of a saint.
Sabena, Sabene, Sabienne, Sabine (French), Sabinella, Sabyna, Sabyne, Savina (Russian).
Diminutives: Bina, Saba (Slavic).

Sabira Arabic: the patient one.
Sabirah.

Sabiya Arabic: of the morning.

Sable Middle English: black, or very dark.
Sabel, Sabelle.

Sabra Hebrew: a thorny cactus, or to rest.

Sabrina Celtic: a legendary character, after whom the River Severn in Britain is named.
Sabreena, Sabrine, Sabrinna, Sabryna, Zabrina.

Sabyna/Sabyne *See* Sabina.

Sacha *See* Sasha.

Sachi Japanese: joy.

Sachiko Japanese: a joyful child.

Sadie A diminutive of Sarah.
Sadee, Sadye, Saidee, Zadee, Zadie.

Sadira Persian: a lotus.

Safari *See* BOYS.

Saffi Danish form of Sophie. *See also* Saffron.

Saffir/Saffira/Safira *See* Sapphira.

Saffron Arabic: a 'spice name'.
Saffra, Safra, Safron.
Diminutives: Saffi, Saffy.

Safia Arabic: the confidante, or the pure one.
Safina, Safiyya.

Saga Swedish: a Norse goddess.
Sagah.

Sagan After the French novelist Françoise Sagan.
Sagann, Saganne.

Sage Old French: wise. Also a 'herb name'.
Saige, Sayge.

Sahar Arabic: dawn.

Sahara Arabic: the name of a desert.

Sahira Sanskrit: a mountain.

Saidee *See* Sadie.

Saige *See* Sage.

Sailor Middle English: one who sails.
Sailer, Sayla, Saylah, Sayler, Saylor.

Sakti *See* Shakti.

Sakura Japanese: cherry blossom.

Salama *See* Salima.

Salena *See* Salina.

Salima Arabic: safe, secure. The
feminine form of Salim.
Salama, Salema, Salma, Selima,
Selma, Zelma.

Salina Latin: solemn.
Salena.

Sally Originally a diminutive of
Sarah.
Sali, Salie, Sallee, Salli, Sallie, Sallye,
Saly.
Diminutives: Sal, Sall.

Salma *See* Salima.

Salome Hebrew: peace. A biblical
name.
Saloma, Salomea (Polish), Salomeh.

Salote Polynesian: a lady.
Saloteh.

Salvia Latin: a 'plant name'.
Salvina.

Sam A diminutive of Samantha and
Samuela.

Samala/Samella *See* Samuela.

Samantha Aramaic: she who listens.
Semantha, Symantha.
Diminutives: Sam, Sammi, Sammie,
Sammy.

Samara Hebrew: guarded by God.
Samar.

Samaria Hebrew: a biblical placename.

Samedi The French name for Saturday.

Samira Arabic: one who entertains.
Sameera (Sanskrit), Sameerah,
Samirah, Zameera, Zameerah,
Zamira, Zamirah.

Sammi/Sammie/Sammy Diminutives
of Samantha and Samuela.

Samoa Polynesian: a Pacific Ocean
country.

Samuela Hebrew: asked of God. The
feminine form of Samuel.
Samala, Samella, Samelle, Samuele,
Samuelle.
Diminutives: Sam, Sammi, Sammie,
Sammy.

Sana Arabic: radiant. Hebrew: a lily.

Sanaz Persian: graceful.

Sancia Latin: sacred.
Sancha, Sanchia, Sancya.

Sandi/Sandie/Sandy Diminutives of
Alexandra and Sandra.

Sandra A diminutive of Alexandra.
Sandrah, Sandria, Sandrine, Saundra,
Sondra, Zandra.
Diminutives: Sandi, Sandie, Sandy.

Sangmu Sherpa/Tibetan: the kind-
hearted one.

Sanna A diminutive of Susannah.

Santina Italian/Spanish: saint-like.
Santinah, Santine, Santyna, Santyne.

Saoirse Irish Gaelic: freedom.

Sapphira Greek: deep blue. A
'gemstone name'. *See also* Zafira.
Saffir (Welsh), Saffira, Safira, Saphira,
Saphyre, Sapphire.

Sarah Hebrew: a princess. The wife of
Abraham and mother of Isaac in the
Bible. *See also* Sadie, Sally and Zara.
Hera (Maori), Sara (Arabic, French,
German), Sarai, Saraid (Irish Gaelic),

Sarena, Sarene, Saretta, Sarette,
Sari, Saria, Sariah, Sarina (Hebrew),
Sarine, Sarita, Sarka (Czech), Sarra,
Sarrah, Sela (Tongan), Sharee, Shari,
Zara, Zarah, Zaria.
Diminutives: Sadie, Sal, Sally, Zadee,
Zadie, Zaidee.

Sarahanna A combination of Sarah
and Hannah (graceful).
Sarahana, Sarahannah, Saranna.

Sarai/Saraid *See* Sarah.

Sarala Sanskrit: honest.

Sarea A mythological angel.

Sarena/Saretta *See* Sarah.

Sari Hindi: after the dress of Indian
women. *See also* Sarah.
Saria, Sarie, Sary, Sarye.

Saril Turkish: flowing water.

Sarina/Sarita *See* Sarah.

Sarisha Sanskrit: charming.

Sarka Czech form of Sarah.

Saroja Sanskrit: born in a lake.

Sarona Samoan form of Sharon.

Sarra/Sarrah *See* Sarah.

Sary/Sarye *See* Sari.

Sasha Russian diminutive of
Alexandra.
Sacha (French), Sascha (German),
Sashi, Sashie, Sashka.

Saskia Dutch: a Saxon.

Satarah Hebrew: a princess. Persian:
a star.
Satara, Sataria.

Satine Middle English: a smooth silky
fabric.
Satin, Satina, Satinah, Satinea.

Saturday Middle English: a 'day
name'. After Saturn, a planet and

the Roman god of agriculture and
fertility.
Samedi (French), Satordi (Basque),
Satordie.

Saturnia Latin: of Saturn, the Roman
god of agriculture.

Saundra *See* Sandra.

Savanna Spanish: from the grasslands
or open plains.
Savana, Savanah, Savannah,
Zavanna, Zavannah.

Saviera *See* Xaviera.

Savina *See* Sabina.

Sawsan Arabic form of Susannah.

Saxona Teutonic: a Saxon.

Sayge *See* Sage.

Sayla/Sayler/Saylor *See* Sailor.

Scarlett Old French: a 'colour name'.
Originally made popular by Margaret
Mitchell's *Gone With the Wind*.
Scarlet, Scarlette.

Schanee/Schaney/Schanie *See*
Sharney.

Schapelle A modern made-up name,
utilising the feminine elle suffix.
Schapell, Shapell, Shapelle.

Schuyla/Schuyler/Schyler *See* Skylar.

Scotland A modern 'country name'.

Scout Middle English: one who
observes and reports.
Scoute, Scoutt, Scoutte, Scowte.

Sean *See* Shaun.

Seana/Seanna *See* Siana.

Season Latin: the time of sowing.

Sebastiana Latin: a woman from
Sebasta. The feminine form of
Sebastian.
Sebasta, Sebastia, Sebastianne,

Sebastienne (French).

Sebila *See* Sybil.

Seble African: born in autumn.

Secilia *See* Cecilia.

Secunda Latin: the second child.

Seela/Seelah *See* Sela.

Seeta *See* Sita.

Segovia A Spanish town, and the surname of a famous classical guitarist.

Seini Tongan form of Jane.

Seirian Welsh: sparkling.

Seiriol Welsh: the bright one.

Sela Hebrew: a rock. An Old Testament placename. Also the Tongan form of Sarah.
Seela, Seelah, Selah.

Selby *See* BOYS.

Selda *See* Griselda.

Selena Greek: the goddess of the moon.
Celena, Celene, Celina, Celine, Selene, Selenia, Selina, Selinda, Selyna, Selyne, Zelena.

Seleste *See* Celeste.

Selia *See* Cecilia.

Selina *See* Selena.

Selma A diminutive of Anselma. *See also* Salima.
Selmah, Zelma, Zelmah.

Semantha *See* Samantha.

Semele A figure from Greek mythology.
Semelia.

Semira Hebrew: the uppermost part of the heavens.
Semirah.

Senga Scottish Gaelic: the slender one.

Seònaid Scottish Gaelic form of Joanne.
Seona, Shona.

Septima Latin: the seventh-born.

Sequoia Native American: a large coniferous tree.
Sequoya.

Sera *See* Seraphina.

Seraphina Hebrew: the ardent burning one. The Seraphim are an order of angels in the Bible.
Serafima (Russian), Serafina (Italian, Spanish), Serafine, Seraphine (French).
Diminutive: Sera.

Seren Welsh: a star.
Serren, Steren (Cornish).

Serena Latin: calm, serene. *See also* Serenity.
Cerena, Cerene, Serene, Serina, Serine.

Serenity One who is serene. *See also* Serena.
Cerenitee, Cerenitie, Cerenity, Serenitee, Serenitie.

Serica Latin: the silken one.

Serilda Teutonic: the armoured battle maiden.
Serilde.

Serina *See* Serena.

Seven *See* BOYS.

Severina Latin: the stern or severe one.
Séverine (French).

Sevilla Spanish: the name of a city.
Seville.

Shaan *See* Sian.

Shade Middle English: comparative darkness. Also a boy's name.

SURNAMES AS FIRST NAMES

A modern trend is to use surnames as first names, so here is a selection. Many of these are 'occupation names', such as Cooper, Fletcher, Hunter, Mason and Taylor. Brand names like Armani, Chanel and Hurley are popular, as are celebrity surnames – including Aniston, Arquette, Beckham, Cruz and Jagger.

Many of the names are suitable for both boys and girls, but most of the meanings will be found in the Boys A–Z.

Aniston	Clooney	Hunter	Nelson
Armani	Cohen	Hurley	O'Neil
Arquette	Connor	Huxley	O'Shea
Asher	Cooper	Jackson	Presley
Ashton	Cruz	Jagger	Preston
Austin	Dali	Jensen	Quinn
Bardot	Dawson	Jovi	Rafferty
Baxter	Deacon	Kiernan	Ravel
Beckham	Denver	Kingston	Reeves
Bracken	Dior	Ledger	Rider
Branagh	Driver	Lennon	Rix
Brando	Duffy	Lincoln	Sagan
Brock	Dyson	Logan	Sheraton
Bronson	Elliott	Loren	Sullivan
Brooke	Finn	Mackinley	Taylor
Brosnan	Fletcher	Madison	Tennyson
Bryson	Flynn	Maddox	Travers
Callaghan	Fox	Marlow	Trudeau
Cameron	Fraser	Mason	Truman
Caron	Harlow	Matisse	Walker
Carter	Harrison	Mirren	Wills
Cartier	Hendrix	Monet	Wycliff
Cash	Heston	Moreau	Zappa
Chanel	Hilton	Nash	Zidane

Shady, Shadye, Shaida, Shaide, Shayda, Shayde.

Shae/Shai/Shaie *See* Shay.

Shaelen/Shailen *See* Shaylen.

Shahira Arabic: famous.

Shahnaz Persian: the pride of the emperor.

Shaida/Shaide *See* Shade.

Shain/Shaine *See* Shane.

Shaina Hebrew: beautiful.
Shayna.

Shaka Zulu: the founder. Also a boy's name.

Shakila Arabic: the feminine form of Shakil (handsome).
Shakala, Shakeela, Shaquila.

Shakira Arabic: thankful.
Shakeera, Shakeira, Shakera, Shakiera, Shaquira.

Shakti Sanskrit: the powerful one.
Sakti.

Shakuntala Sanskrit: a bird.

Shalaila A modern, probably made-up, name.
Shalailah.

Shalini Sanskrit: modest.

Shamal Iraqi: the constant one.

Shamarnie A modern made-up name, possibly a variation of Sharney.
Shamarnee, Shamarney, Shamarni, Shamarny.

Shamarra Arabic: one who is ready for battle.
Shamara, Shamarah, Shamarrah, Shamra, Shanara, Shanarah, Shanarra, Shanarrah, Shanra, Shanrah.

Shan *See* Sian.

Shana *See* Shannah.

Shane From Irish Gaelic: a variation of Sean (John), and so a form of Jane. *See also* Shaun and Shay.
Shain, Shaine, Shayn, Shayne, Sheyne.

Shanel/Shanelle *See* Chanel.

Shani Hebrew: red. Swahili: wonderful. Also a form of Sian. *See also* Sharney.
Shanee, Shanie, Shanyi, Sharney, Sharni, Sharnie.

Shania A name made popular by the Canadian country singer Shania Twain.
Shanaya, Shanayah, Shanaye, Shaniah.

Shannah Irish Gaelic: from an old surname.
Shana, Shanna, Shannagh.

Shannele/Shannelle *See* Chanel.

Shannon A river in Ireland. Also a boy's name.
Shannan, Shannen, Shannone, Shannyn, Shanon, Shanyn.

Shanra/Shanrah *See* Shamarra.

Shanta *See* Shanti.

Shantae/Shantay *See* Chanté.

Shantal/Shantel/Shantelle *See* Chantal.

Shanti Sanskrit: the tranquil one.
Shanta.

Shapell/Shapelle *See* Schapelle.

Shaquila/Shaquira *See* Shakila and Shakira.

Sharan *See* Sharon.

Sharee/Shari *See* Sarah.

Sharen/Sharenne *See* Sharon.

Sharifa Arabic: the honourable one.
The feminine form of Sharif.

Sharleen/Sharlene *See* Caroline.

Sharlie A variation of Charlie, a diminutive of Charlotte.
Sharla, Sharlee, Sharleigh, Sharley, Sharli, Sharly.

Sharlot/Sharlott/Sharlotte *See* Charlotte.

Sharmaine/Sharman *See* Charmaine.

Sharmila Sanskrit: the protected one.

Sharney A modern name, probably from Shani or Sharon.
Charnee, Charney, Schanee, Schaney, Schanie, Sharna, Sharnae, Sharnah, Sharnee, Sharni, Sharnie, Sharnnie, Sharnye.

Sharon Hebrew: a flat plain; a biblical placename. *See also* Sharona.
Sarona (Samoan), Sharan, Sharen, Sharenne, Sharona, Sharonda, Sharone, Sharonne, Sharron, Sharyn. *Diminutives*: Sharney, Sharni, Sharnie, Shaz, Shazza.

Sharona A form of Sharon.
Charona, Cherona, Sharonah, Sharonna, Sherona, Sheronah.

Shaun From the boy's name Sean. *See also* Jane and Shane.
Sean, Shauna, Shaune, Shaunelle, Shawn, Shawna, Shawnelle.

Shavaun/Shavon/Shavonne *See* Siobhán.

Shawn/Shawna *See* Shaun.

Shay Tibetan: crystal. Also a form of Shane.
Chae, Chay, Chaye, Shae, Shai, Shaie, Shaye, Shaylee, Shayleigh, Shaylie, Shea.

Shayda/Shayde *See* Shade.

Shaylen A modern form of Shay.
Chaelen, Chayelen, Chaylen, Cheylen, Shaelen, Shailen, Shayelen, Sheylen.

Shaylie A form of Shay.
Shayla, Shaylah, Shaylee, Shaylei, Shayleigh, Shayli, Shayly.

Shayn/Shayne *See* Shane.

Shayna *See* Shaina.

Shea *See* Shay.

Sheba Greek: a woman of Sheba, an ancient Arabian country.

Sheela Sanskrit: of good character. *See also* Sheila.
Sheelah, Shila, Shilah.

Sheelagh/Sheelah *See* Sheela and Sheila.

Sheena Scottish Gaelic form of Jane.
Sheenah, Shena, Shenah.

Sheera *See* Shira.

Sheila Irish form of Cecilia.
Sheela, Sheelagh, Sheelah, Sheilah, Shela, Shelagh (Irish), Síle (Irish Gaelic), Sìleas (Scottish Gaelic).

Shelby Old English: the dweller at the ledge estate.
Shelbee, Shelbey, Shelbi, Shelbie.

Sheldon Old English: from the steep valley.
Sheldan, Shelden.

Shelley Old English: from the wood, or the meadow's edge. Also a diminutive of Michelle and Rachel.
Shell, Shellee, Shelli, Shellie, Shelly.

Shenaid/Shenaide/Shenayd *See* Sinéad.

Shenay A contemporary American name, of uncertain meaning.
Shenae, Shenaye, Shennay, Shennaye, Shinae, Shinay, Shinaye.

Sher/Sheree *See* Cher.

Sheraton An English surname, and a famous chain of hotels.
Sheraten, Sheratin, Sheratyn.

Sheraz *See* Shiraz.

Shereen *See* Shirin.

Sheridan Irish Gaelic: the wild one.
Sheriden, Sheridon, Sheridyn.

Sherleen/Sherley *See* Shirley.

Sherona/Sheronah *See* Sharona.

Sherri/Sherry/Sheryl *See* Cher.

Shevaun/Shivaun *See* Siobhán.

Sheylen *See* Shaylen.

Sheyne *See* Shane.

Shifra Hebrew: beauty and grace. A biblical name.
Shiphrah.

Shila/Shilah *See* Sheela.

Shiloh Hebrew: a place of rest. A biblical name.
Shila, Shilah, Shilo, Shyla, Shylah, Shylo, Shyloh.

Shima Japanese: an island.

Shina Japanese: virtuous.

Shinae/Shinay *See* Shenay.

Shine Middle English: a glow, or to excel.
Shyne.

Shira Hebrew: my song.
Sheera, Shirah, Shiri.

Shiraz A city in Iran, and a type of red wine.
Sheraz.

Shiri *See* Shira.

Shirin Persian: charming.
Shereen, Shireen, Shirrin.

Shirley Old English: from the bright meadow. Originally a boy's name.
Sherleen, Sherley, Shirlee, Shirleen,
Shirlene, Shirlie.
Diminutives: Sherl, Shirl.

Shobhana Sanskrit: beautiful.
Shoba.

Shona A southern African people. *See also* Joanne and Seònaid.

Shondelle A modern name, possibly a form of Chantal.
Shondal, Shondall, Shondalle, Shondel, Shondell, Shontal, Shontalia, Shontall, Shontalle, Shontel, Shontell, Shontelle.

Shoshana Hebrew: a lily, or a rose.
See also Susannah.

Shrine Middle English: something that is sacred.
Shryne.

Shuang Chinese: bright and clear.

Shui Chinese: water.

Shulamit Hebrew: peacefulness.
Shula, Shulamite, Shulamith.

Shyla/Shylo/Shyloh *See* Shiloh.

Shyne *See* Shine.

Sian Welsh form of Jane.
Shaan, Shan, Shani, Siahn, Siân, Siani.

Siana A modern name, possibly a variation of Siena.
Seana, Seanna, Sianna, Siannah, Sianne.

Sibel/Sibella/Sibyl/Sibylla *See* Sybil.

Sidney Old English: from the riverside meadow. Old French: from St Denis.
Cidney, Cydney, Sidnee, Sidnei, Sidni, Sidnie, Sidny, Sydnee, Sydnei, Sydney, Sydnie, Sydny.

Sidonie Latin: a woman from Sidon, in modern-day Lebanon.

Sidonia, Sidony, Sydonia, Sydonie.

Sidra Latin: of the stars.
Sidrah, Sidria, Sidriah.

Siena Italian: a city in Tuscany. *See also* Siana.
Sienah, Sienna, Siennah.

Sierra Latin: from the mountains.
Siera, Sierah, Sierrah.

Signy Old Norse: a new victory.
Signe, Signi.

Sigourney Old Norse: the conqueror.

Sigrid Old Norse: a beautiful victory.
Sigrud.
Diminutive: Siri.

Sigrun Old Norse: a secret victory.

Síle/Sileas *See* Cecilia and Sheila.

Silk Middle English: a fine fabric.
Silke, Silkee, Silkey, Silkie, Silky, Sylk, Sylke.

Silke German form of Cecilia.

Silla *See* Priscilla.

Silva/Silvana *See* Sylvia.

Silver Old English: the fair or silvery one.
Silva, Silvah.

Silvestra Latin: of the woods. The feminine form of Silvester. *See also* Sylvia.
Sylvestra.

Silvi/Silvia/Silvie *See* Sylvia.

Simin Persian: silvery.

Simone Hebrew: the listener. The feminine form of Simon.
Simonn, Simmone, Simona, Simonetta (Italian), Simonette (French), Simonne, Symona, Symone, Symonn, Symonne.

Sina A moon goddess in Samoan mythology.

Sindy *See* Cindy.

Sinéad Irish Gaelic form of Janet.
Shenaid, Shenaide, Shenayd, Shenayde.

Siobhán Irish Gaelic form of Jane and Judith.
Chavaun, Chavaune, Chevonne, Shavaun, Shavaune, Shavon, Shavonne, Shevaun, Shivaun, Siubhan (Scottish Gaelic).

Sion *See* Zion.

Siôna Welsh form of Joanne.

Sioned Welsh form of Janet.

Siran Armenian: alluring.

Sirena Greek: a sea nymph. In mythology, the Sirens lured mariners to their death through seductive singing.
Siren, Sirène (French), Sirine, Syren, Syrena.

Siri *See* Sigrid.

Sirikit Thai: the name of a queen.

Sirkka Finnish: she who makes music.
Sirka.

Sisilia Fijian form of Cecilia.

Sissey/Sissie/Sissy Diminutives of Cecilia.

Sistine The Pope's chapel in the Vatican.
Sisteen, Sistyne, Systeen, Systine, Systyne.

Sita Sanskrit: a furrow. The Hindu goddess of the harvest.
Seeta.

Sitara Sanskrit: a star.

Siubhan *See* Siobhán.

Siùsan *See* Susannah.

Sjonia *See* Sonia.

Sky Middle English: the heavens. *See also* Skye.

Skye Scottish: an island in the Inner Hebrides.
Sky, Zky, Zkye.

Skylar From a Dutch word for a scholar or schoolmaster. Also a boy's name.
Schuyla, Schuyler (Dutch), Schylar, Schyler, Skuyla, Skuylar, Skyla, Skylah, Skyler, Skylor, Skyyla, Skyyla, Skyylah.

Slaney *See* BOYS.

Sloan *See* BOYS.

Soana Probably the Tongan form of Jane and Joanna.

Soffea/Soffia *See* Sophia.

Sofi/Sofia/Sofie/Sofya *See* Sophia.

Solae/Solai *See* Soleil.

Solana Latin: the sun. Generally a Spanish name.
Sol, Solina, Solita, Soluna.

Solange Latin: the solemn one. A French name.
Solangia.

Soledad Spanish: good health.

Soleil French: the sun.
Solae, Solai, Solaie, Solay, Solaye, Solei.

Solina/Solita/Soluna *See* Solana.

Solrun Norwegian: derived from sol, meaning the sun.

Solveig Old Norse: from the strong house; generally a Norwegian name.
Solvig (Swedish).

Somer/Sommer *See* Summer.

Sona/Sonah *See* Sonora.

Sonam Sherpa/Tibetan: the fortunate one. Also a boy's name.

Sonata Italian: a musical composition. Sonnata.

Sondai/Sonday/Sondie *See* Sunday.

Sondra *See* Sandra.

Song Old English: a musical composition. Also a Korean name.
Songe.

Sonia A form of Sophia.
Sjonia, Sonicka, Sonika, Soniya, Sonja (Scandinavian), Sonje (Scandinavian), Sonnya, Sonya (Russian).

Sonnet From French: a type of poem.
Sonet, Sonett, Sonnett, Sonnette.

Sonnie/Sonny *See* Sunny.

Sonnya/Sonya *See* Sonia.

Sonora From Latin: a loud or resonant sound.
Sona, Sonah, Sonorah, Sonore, Sonoria.

Soo Korean: a long life.

Sophalia A modern form of Sophia.
Sophalie, Sophallia, Sophallie, Sophally, Sophaly.

Sophee/Sophie *See* Sophia.

Sophia Greek: wisdom. *See also* Sonia.
Saffi (Danish), Sofea, Soffea, Soffia, Sofi (Greek), Sofia (Norwegian, Swedish), Sofie (Danish, Dutch), Sofina, Sofine, Sofya (Russian), Sophea, Sophee, Sophie, Sophina, Sophine, Sophy, Sopia, Te Paea (Maori), Zofia (Polish), Zofie (Czech), Zofja (Slavic), Zosia (Polish).

Sophronia Greek: sensible.

Sora Native American: a songbird.

Soraya Persian: seven stars.

Sorcha Gaelic: brightness.
Sorka.

Soren *See* BOYS.

Sorina Romanian: of the sun.
Sorana.

Sorrel Old French: bitter. A 'plant name'.
Sorel, Sorell, Sorelle, Sorrell, Sorrelle.

Sosefina Tongan form of Josephine.

Sousan *See* Susan.

Sousanna/Sousanne *See* Susannah.

Souzana Persian: fire.
Souzan, Souzanah, Souzann, Souzanna, Souzannah.

Spencer *See* BOYS.

Spring A 'season name'.

Stacey Diminutive of Anastasia and Eustacia. Also a boy's name.
Stacee, Staci, Stacia, Stacie, Stacy, Stasya (Russian).

Star A star. *See also* Stella.
Starla, Starlia, Starlie, Starr, Starre.

Stefania/Stefanie/Steffanie/Steffany *See* Stephanie.

Steffi/Steffie/Steffy *See* Stephanie.

Stella Latin: a star. *See also* Estelle, Esther and Star.
Stellah, Stellar, Stelle.

Stephanie Greek: a garland or crown. The feminine form of Stephen.
Estefania (Spanish), Étienette (French), Stefanee, Stefani, Stefania (Italian, Greek, Polish), Stefanie, Steffanie, Steffany, Stepania, Stephana, Stephane, Stephania, Stéphanie (French), Stephanine (German), Stephena, Stephenie,

Stevana, Stevania, Stevena, Tapania (Finnish).
Diminutives: Stef, Steffi (German), Steffie, Steffy, Steph, Stevi, Stevie.

Steren Cornish form of Seren.

Stevana/Stevania/Stevena/Stevie *See* Stephanie.

Stina A diminutive of Christina.

Stockard An English surname. Also a boy's name.

Storey/Story *See* BOYS.

Storm Old English: a tempest. Also a boy's name.
Storme.

Su/Sue Diminutives of Susan and Susannah.

Suela *See* Consuela.

Suellen American: from Susan and Ellen.
Sue-Ellen.

Sujata Sanskrit: of noble birth.

Sujatmi Indonesian: a popular girl's name.

Suki Japanese: beloved. *See also* Susan.
Sukey, Sukie.

Sula Icelandic: the sun. Welsh: Sunday.

Sulema *See* Zulema.

Sultana Arabic: a queen or empress.

Suma/Sumah *See* Summer.

Sumalee Thai: a beautiful flower.

Sumi Japanese: the refined one.

Summer Old English: a 'season name'.
Somer, Sommer, Suma, Sumah, Sumer, Sumher, Summa, Summah, Summar, Zommer (German).

Sun Korean: goodness.

Sunday Old English: a 'day name',

literally the day of the sun.
Sondai, Sondaie, Sonday, Sondi,
Sondie, Sundai, Sundaie, Sundaye,
Sundi, Sundie.

Sunee Thai: good.

Sunflower A yellow flower of the sun.

Sunita Sanskrit: of good conduct.

Sunniva Old English: the gift of the
sun. The name of a saint.

Sunny English: bright, cheerful.
Sonnie, Sonny, Sunni, Sunnie.

Sunshine The brightness and radiance
of the sun.
Sunshyne.

Surata Sanskrit: bliss.

Suri Japanese: a princess. Persian: a
red rose.
Suree, Surey, Surie, Sury, Surye.

Surya Nepali: the sun. Sanskrit: a sun
god.
Suraya, Suria, Suriaya.

Susan Hebrew: a lily. *See also*
Susannah.
Sousan, Susen, Suska (Slavic), Suzan,
Suzen, Xuxa (Brazilian).
Diminutives: Su, Sue, Sukey, Suki,
Sukie, Suse, Susi, Susie, Susy, Suze,
Suzie.

Susannah Hebrew: a lily. The original,
biblical, form of Susan.
Huhana (Maori), Sawsan (Arabic),
Shoshana (Hebrew), Siùsan (Scottish
Gaelic), Sousanna, Sousanne,
Susana (Spanish), Susanna, Susanne
(German), Susette, Sussana, Suzana,
Suzanna, Suzannah, Suzanne (French),
Suzetta, Suzette (French), Zuzana
(Czech), Zuzanna (Latvian, Polish).
Diminutives: Sanna, Su, Sue, Susi,
Susie, Susy, Suzie, Suzsi, Zanna, Zsa

Zsa (Hungarian).

Susette *See* Susannah.

Susi/Susie/Susy Diminutives of
Susan and Susannah.

Suska Slavic form of Susan.

Suyin The surname of a well-known
Chinese author (Han Suyin).

Suzan/Suzen/Suzie *See* Susan.

Suzanna/Suzannah/Suzanne *See*
Susannah.

Suzetta/Suzette/Suzsi *See* Susannah.

Suzu Japanese: a little bell.
Suzuki.

Svea Swedish: a woman of Sweden.

Svetlana Slavic: light. Generally a
Russian name.
Svetla (Czech).
Diminutive: Lana.

Swan Old English: a 'bird name'.
Swann, Swanne.

Swanhild Teutonic: a swan of battle.
Svanhild, Swanhilda, Swanhilde.

Sweeney *See* BOYS.

Sybil Greek: the prophetess. A name
from Greek mythology.
Cybele (French), Cybil, Cybill,
Cybilla, Cybille, Sebila, Sibel, Sibella,
Sibelle, Sibil, Sibilla, Sibille, Sibyl,
Sibylla, Sibylle (German), Sybella,
Sybelle, Sybilla, Sybille (French).
Diminutives: Libby, Sib, Syb.

Sydnee/Sydney/Sydny *See* Sidney.

Sydonia/Sydonie *See* Sidonie.

Sylk/Sylke *See* Silk.

Sylph Greek: a spirit of the air and
the protector of young maidens,
sometimes appearing as a butterfly.
Sylf.

Sylvestra *See* Silvestra.

Sylvette/Sylvie *See* Sylvia.

Sylvia Latin: from the forest. *See also* Silvestra.
Silva, Silvana (Italian), Silvi, Silvia, Silvie, Silvija, Silvy, Sylva, Sylvana, Sylvania, Sylvanna, Sylvette, Sylvie (French).

Symantha *See* Samantha.

Symona/Symone/Symonne *See* Simone.

Syna Greek: together.

Syon *See* Zion.

Syreeta/Syreta *See* Cyreta.

Syren/Syrena *See* Sirena.

Syria Aramaic: a Middle Eastern country.

Systeen/Systine/Systyne *See* Sistine.

T

Tabea German form of Tabitha.

Tabitha Aramaic: a doe or gazelle; a biblical name. *See also* Dorcas.
Tabatha, Tabea (German), Tabetha.

Tacita Latin: silent or peaceful.
Tacey, Tacitah, Tacye.

Taheisha A variation of Taleisha.
Taheesha, Tahesha, Tahiesha, Tahisha.

Tahira Arabic: pure and virtuous.

Tahiti Polynesian: sunrise. A 'country name'.

Tahnia/Tahnya *See* Tanya and Tatyana.

Tahuri Maori: to start.

Tai Polynesian: the ocean.

Taie, Ty, Tye.

Taila/Tailah/Tailer/Tailor *See* Taylor.

Tailin/Tailyn/Tailynn *See* Taylin.

Taimana Maori: a diamond.

Taka Japanese: tall, or honourable. Polynesian: a name from legend.

Takara Japanese: a treasure.

Takeisha A modern American 'Ta name', a variation of Keisha.
Takeesha, Takesha, Takiesha, Takisha.

Taki Japanese: a waterfall.

Talaine A 'Ta name', possibly from Elaine.
Talaina, Talayna, Talayne.

Taleisha Contemporary American: possibly from Aisha (life).
Taleesha, Taleeshia, Talisa, Talisha, Talishia, Talissa.

Talia Greek: flourishing. Hebrew: dew. *See also* Natalie and Talya.
Taliah, Thalia.

Talitha Aramaic: a little girl or maiden. A biblical name.
Taletha, Talita.

Tallulah Native American: running water.
Talloulah, Talula.

Talulla Irish Gaelic: a prosperous lady.

Talwyn Cornish: a fair brow.

Talya Hebrew: a lamb. Russian: a diminutive of Natalya.
Talia, Talyah.

Tam Vietnamese: of the heart. *See also* Tamara and Tamsin.

Tama Japanese: a jewel.

Tamahine Maori: a girl.

Tamar Jewish form of Tamara.

Tamara Hebrew: a palm tree. A popular name in Germany and Russia.
Tamar (Jewish), Tamarah, Tamarra, Tamarrah, Tamaya, Tamayah, Tameea, Tameeah, Tamina, Taminah, Tamira, Tamirah, Tamora, Tamorah, Tamra, Tamrah, Tamryn.
Diminutives: Mara, Tam, Tammi, Tammie, Tammy.

Tamarind A tropical tree.
Tamarinde, Tamarynd, Tamarynde.

Tamarine An unusual name from Thailand.
Tamarin, Tammarin, Tammarine.

Tamasina/Tamasine *See* Tamsin and Thomasina.

Tameka Hebrew: a twin. A feminine form of Thomas. *See also* Tamsin and Thomasina.
Tameika, Tameikah, Tamekah, Tamika, Tamikah, Tomeika, Tomeikah.

Tamiko Japanese: a child of the people.

Tamina/Tamira *See* Tamara.

Tammi/Tammie/Tammy *See* Tamara and Tamsin.

Tamora/Tamra/Tamryn *See* Tamara.

Tamsin Cornish: a feminine form of Thomas. *See also* Tameka and Thomasina.
Tamasin, Tamazin, Tamsine, Tamsyn, Tamsyne, Tamzin, Tamzine.
Diminutives: Tam, Tammi, Tammie, Tammy.

Tan *See* Thanh.

Tandy A modern name, possibly a diminutive of Andrew or Andy.
Tandee, Tandey, Tandi, Tandie.

Tanedra The name of an American actress (Tanedra Howard).

Tanedrah, Tanidra, Tanidrah.

Taneisha/Tanesha *See* Tanisha.

Taneka A modern American 'Tan name'. *See also* Tanisha.
Taneeka, Tanekah, Tanika, Tanikah, Tanike.

Tang A popular Chinese name.

Tangiwai Maori: a type of greenstone.

Tango Spanish: a dance.
Tangoe.

Tani Japanese: from the valley.
Taniko.

Tania *See* Tanya, Tatyana and Titania.

Tanisha African: born on a Monday.
Taneisha, Tanesha, Tanishe, Tanissa, Tanisse, Tannisha, Tannissa, Teneisha, Tenisha.

Tanja *See* Tanya and Tatyana.

Tansy Greek: immortal. A 'flower name'.
Tansie, Tanzey.

Tanya Russian: a diminutive of Tatyana. *See also* Titania.
Tahnia, Tania, Tanja (German).

Tanzey *See* Tansy.

Tao Chinese: long life.

Tapairo Polynesian: a legendary figure.

Tapania Finnish form of Stephanie.

Tapora Maori: a placename.

Tara Irish Gaelic: a rocky hill; the ancient home of Ireland's kings. Polynesian: a sea goddess. Sanskrit: a star; the name of a Buddhist goddess. *See also* Tarin.
Tarah, Tarra, Tarrah.

Tarah Hebrew: an Old Testament placename. *See also* Tara.

Tarama An unusual name that may be derived from Tara.

Taran/Taren *See* Tarin.

Taranga Polynesian: a figure from legend.

Tarati Maori form of Dorothy.

Tarika Hindi: a star
Tareka.

Tarin A modern name, probably a form of Tara.
Taran, Taren, Tarran, Tarren, Tarrin, Tarryn, Tarrynn, Taryn, Taryna, Tarynn.

Tarita A Polynesian name of uncertain meaning.

Tarna A name from *The Wheel of Time* series of fantasy novels.
Tarnah.

Tarra/Tarran/Tarrin/Taryn *See* Tara and Tarin.

Tasha A diminutive of Natasha.

Tashi Sherpa/Tibetan: prosperity. Also a boy's name.

Tasma The feminine version of Tasman (*see* BOYS), a name derived from Tasmania and the explorer Abel Tasman.
Tasmah, Tasman, Tasmin, Tasmyn, Tazma, Tazmah, Tazman, Tazmin, Tazmyn.

Tatania/Tatiana *See* Tatyana.

Tate Old Norse: cheerful. Also a diminutive of Tatum.
Tait, Taite, Tayt, Tayte.

Tatum Old English: from Tate's homestead. Also a boy's name.
Diminutive: Tate.

Tatyana Latin: silver-haired. A popular Russian name. *See also* Tanya.
Tatania, Tathiana (Italian), Tatia, Tatiana, Tatienne (French), Tatjana, Tatjanna, Tatyanna.
Diminutives: Tahnee, Tahnia, Tahnya, Tania, Tanja (German), Tanya.

Tautiti Polynesian: a graceful dancer.

Tavake Polynesian: a daughter in legend.

Tavia *See* Octavia.

Tawny Old French: with yellowish-brown hair.
Tawna, Tawnee, Tawney, Tawni, Tawnie.

Taylin A combination of Taylor and Lin.
Tailin, Tailinn, Tailyn, Tailynn, Tailynne, Taylinn, Taylyn, Taylynn, Taylynne.

Taylor Old French: a tailor.
Taila, Tailah, Tailer, Tailor, Talor, Tayla, Taylah, Tayleh, Tayler, Taylour.

Tayt/Tayte *See* Tate.

Tazma/Tazman/Tazmin/Tazmyn *See* Tasma.

Tcharli/Tcharlie *See* Charlie.

Tea/Téa/Téah *See* Tia and Tiara.

Teagan/Teaghan *See* Tegan and Tegen.

Teague Irish Gaelic: a philosopher or poet. Generally a boy's name.
Teag, Teage, Teigue.

Teal A waterbird.
Teale.

Tean Cornish: one of the Isles of Scilly, off the coast of Cornwall.
Tehan.

Teana/Teanna/Teannah *See* Tianna.

Tearra *See* Tiara.

Te Atawhai Maori: to look after.

Te Awatea Maori: the dawning.

Teea/Teeah *See* Tia.

Tegan Welsh: of doe-like beauty.
Teagan, Teaghan, Teigan, Teigen,
Teighan, Tigan.

Tegen Cornish: a pretty little thing.
Teagan, Teegen.

Tegwen Welsh: beautiful and blessed.

Teigue *See* Teague.

Teina Maori: the youngest.

Tekiya A modern name, popular in
the USA.
Tekeya, Tekeyah, Tekiyah.

Tekla *See* Thecla.

Telma *See* Thelma.

Temepara Maori: a temple.

Te Mira Polynesian: a flour miller.

Temperance Latin: moderate.

Tempest Old French: stormy.
Tempeste.

Tenaya Native American: the name
of a chief.
Tenai, Tenaia, Tenayah, Teniya,
Teniyah.

Teneisha/Tenisha *See* Tanisha.

Tenley A modern name, probably
from an English surname.
Tenlea, Tenlee, Tenleigh, Tenli,
Tenlie, Tenly.

Tennessee A state of the USA. Also a
boy's name.
Tenessee, Tennesee.

Tennille A city in Georgia, USA.
Teneal, Teneale, Teneel, Teneele,
Teniell, Tenille, Tenneal, Tennealle,
Tenneel, Tenneele, Tenniel, Tennielle.

Teodora *See* Theodora.

Teofilia *See* Theophilia.

Te Paea Maori form of Sophia.

Tepora Maori form of Deborah.

Te Puna Maori: the spring.

Terehia Maori form of Teresa.

Terencia Latin: smooth and polished.
A feminine form of Terence.
Terentia, Terenzia.

Teresa Greek: the harvester or reaper.
Tereasa, Terehia (Maori), Terese,
Teresia, Teresina (Italian), Teresinha
(Portuguese), Teresita (Spanish),
Teressa, Tereza (Breton), Terezia
(Hungarian), Terezon (French),
Theresa, Therese, Theresia (German),
Treasa (Irish Gaelic), Tressa, Treza.
Diminutives: Teri, Terri, Terry, Tess,
Tessa, Tessie, Tree.

Tereza/Terezia/Terezon *See* Teresa.

Teri/Terri/Terry Diminutives of
Teresa.

Terra Latin: the earth.

Tertia Latin: the third child.

Terza *See* Thirza.

Tess/Tessa/Tessie Diminutives of
Teresa.

Tetsu Japanese: like iron.

Teya/Teyah *See* Tia.

Thaddea Greek: courageous.
Thada, Thadda, Thadine.

Thalassa Greek: from the sea.

Thalia *See* Talia.

Thana Arabic: gratitude.

Thandi Zimbabwean: beloved.
Thandie, Thandiwe.

Thanh Vietnamese: brilliant.
Tan.

Thao Vietnamese: one who respects

her parents.

Thea Greek: a goddess. Also a diminutive of Alethea, Althea, Anthea, Dorothy and Theodora. Thia.

Theano Greek: a divine name. Theana.

Thecla Greek: the glory of God. Tekla (Scandinavian), Thekla.

Theda Teutonic: of the people. *See also* Theodora.

Thelma Greek: a wish, or will. Telma, Thelmae.

Theodora Greek: the gift of God. The feminine form of Theodore. *See also* Dora and Dorothy.
Fedora (Russian), Feodora (Russian), Teodora (Italian, Polish, Spanish), Theadora.
Diminutives: Dora, Thea, Theda, Theo.

Theodosia Greek: God-given.

Theophania Greek: a manifestation of God. A suitable name for a girl born on 6 January, the Epiphany. *See also* Epiphany and Tiffany.
Théophanie (French), Tifaine (French), Tiffany, Tiphani, Tiphanie.
Diminutives: Tiff, Tiffi, Tiffy.

Theophilia Greek: divinely loved. Teofilia, Theofila, Theophila.

Theora Greek: a thinker or watcher.

Thera Greek: wild. The name of an island.

Theresa/Therese/Theresia *See* Teresa.

Thetis Greek: positive, determined. Thetys.

Thia *See* Thea.

Thirza Hebrew: pleasant.

Terza, Thirzah, Thyrza, Tirtza, Tirza, Tirzah.

Thistle Middle English: a 'plant name'. Thystle.

Thomasina Greek: a twin. A feminine form of Thomas. *See also* Tamsin. Tamasina, Tamasine, Thomasa, Thomasin, Thomasine, Tomasa, Tomase, Tomasina, Tomasine.
Diminutives: Tommi, Tommie, Tommy.

Thora Old Norse: thunder. A feminine form of Thor.
Tora.

Thorberta Old Norse: the brilliance of Thor.

Thordis Old Norse: the spirit of Thor. Thordia.

Thursday Middle English: literally the day of Thor. A 'day name'.

Thyra Greek: a shield-bearer.

Tia A popular contemporary name; probably a diminutive of Tianna and Tiara. Maori: the abdomen.
Téa, Téah, Teea, Teeah, Teya, Teyah, Tiah, Tiala, Tialah.

Tiaki Maori: to look after.

Tianna A popular modern name. Possibly a short form of Christiana or Tatyana, or just a variation of Anna. Teana, Teanna, Teannah, Tiaana, Tiahn, Tian, Tiana, Ti'ana, Tianah, Tianne, Tiarn, Tiarna, Tiarne, Tyana, Tyanah, Tyanna, Tyannah.

Tiara Latin: a crown or coronet. Tearra, Tiarah, Tiarra.
Diminutives: Tea, Tia.

Tiarne Probably from Tianna. Tiarn, Tiarna, Tiarnan.

Tiberia Latin: after the River Tiber.

Tien Chinese: heavenly. Vietnamese: the first. Also a boy's name.

Tierney Irish Gaelic: the descendant of a lord.

Tifaine *See* Theophania.

Tiffany Old English form of Theophania.
Tiffanee, Tiffani, Tiffanie, Tiphani, Tiphanie, Tyfany, Tyffany.
Diminutives: Tiff, Tiffi, Tiffy.

Tigan *See* Tegan.

Tigerlily A 'flower name'.
Tiger-Lily, Tigerlilly, Tiger-Lilly.

Tihi Maori: the summit.

Tila/Tilah/Tilar/Tiler *See* Tyler.

Tilda/Tillie/Tilly Diminutives of Matilda.

Timandra A name used by Shakespeare in one of his plays.

Timora Hebrew: tall.

Timothea Greek: honouring God, or honoured by God. The female form of Timothy.
Timathea, Timea, Timeah.
Diminutives: Tim, Timmie, Timmy.

Tina A diminutive of names such as Bettina, Christina and Valentina.

Tiphani/Tiphanie *See* Theophania and Tiffany.

Tirion Welsh: gentle.

Tirza/Tirzah *See* Thirza.

Titania Greek: the great one. The fairy queen in Shakespeare's *A Midsummer Night's Dream*.
Diminutives: Tania, Tanya.

Tivoli An Italian town.
Tivolie.

Tivona Hebrew: a lover of nature.

Tizane Hungarian: a gypsy.

Toakase Tongan: a woman of the sea.

Tobie Hebrew: God is good. A feminine form of Tobias. *See also* Tuvia.
Toba, Tobah, Tobee, Tobey, Tobi, Tobia, Tobiah, Toby.

Toinette *See* Antonia.

Toku Japanese: virtuous.

Tomasa/Tomasina *See* Thomasina.

Tomeika/Tomeikah *See* Tameka.

Tomiko Japanese: happy.

Tonga Polynesian: a 'country name'.

Tongatea Polynesian: a woman from Tonga.

Toni/Tonia/Tonie/Tonya *See* Antonia.

Topaz Greek: a 'gemstone name'.
Topaze, Topazz, Topazze.

Tora Japanese: a tiger. *See also* Thora and Torah.

Torah Hebrew: teaching. The basis of the Jewish doctrine and religion.
Tora.

Tori/Torie/Tory *See* Victoria.

Tosca An opera by the Italian composer Puccini.
Toscah, Toska, Toskah.

Toscana *See* Tuscany.

Tottie/Totty *See* Charlotte.

Toula Greek: light or brightness.

Tourmaline Singhalese: a 'gemstone name'.

Tova The name of a saint.

Toya/Toyah Diminutives of Latoya.

Tracey Old French: a placename.
Tracee, Traci, Tracie, Tracy, Tracye.

Traviata Italian: one who wanders.

Traylor Old French: a hunter or tracker. Also a boy's name.
Trayler.

Treasa *See* Teresa.

Treena *See* Trina.

Trelise Cornish: the homestead by the court or hall.
Trelease, Treleaze, Trelize, Trelys, Trelyse, Trelyze.

Tress Middle English: a lock of hair.
Tresse.

Tressa Cornish: the third. *See also* Teresa.

Trevena Cornish/Welsh: a homestead on the hill.
Treveena, Treveenah, Trevenah, Trevenna, Trevennah, Trevina, Trevinah.

Treza *See* Teresa.

Tricia *See* Patricia.

Trieste An Italian seaport.

Trilby Italian: sings with trills.
Trilbee, Trilbey, Trilbi, Trilbie.

Trina Greek: pure. Also a diminutive of Catherine, Katherine and Katrina.
Treena.

Trinidad Spanish: a Caribbean island. Also a boy's name.

Trinity Latin: a trio or triad, as in the Holy Trinity.
Trinety, Trini, Trinitey, Triniti, Trinita (Italian), Trinitie, Trynity.

Triona A diminutive of Catriona.

Trish/Trisha Diminutives of Patricia.

Trista Latin: the melancholy one.

Tristanne A feminine form of Tristan or Tristram, a Celtic name meaning the noisy one.
Tristaine, Tristan, Tristane, Tristann, Tristanna, Tristian, Tristianne, Trystan, Trystane, Trystann, Trystanne.

Trix/Trixi/Trixie/Trixy *See* Beatrice.

Trudi/Trudie/Trudy *See* Gertrude.

True Old English: genuine or real.
Tru, Truea, Truett, Truetta, Truette.

Trynity *See* Trinity.

Tsarina The feminine form of tsar, a Russian emperor.
Csarina, Csarine, Czarina, Czarine, Tsara, Tsarah, Tsarine, Tzara, Tzarah, Tzarina, Tzarine.

Tseten Sherpa/Tibetan: the defender of religion. Also a boy's name.

Tshering Sherpa/Tibetan: long life. Also a boy's name.

Tu Chinese: jade.

Tuesday Old English: a 'day name'. *See also* Mardi.

Tui Maori: a native bird.

Tula Sanskrit: the Hindu name for the zodiac sign of Libra.
Tulah.

Tulip Turkish: a 'flower name'.
Tulipan (Spanish), Tulipe, Tulipp, Tulippe.

Tullia Irish Gaelic: peaceful.

Tully *See* BOYS.

Tulsa A city in Oklahoma, USA. Also a boy's name.
Tulsah.

Tumanako Maori: hope.

Tupelo A city in the state of Mississippi, USA.

Turquoise Old French: a precious stone. Also a 'colour name'.

Turua Polynesian: beautiful.

Turuhira Maori form of Judith.

Tuscany A region of Italy.
Toscana (Italian), Tuscana.

Tuti Indonesian: an unusual girl's
name.

Tuvia Hebrew: God is good. A female
form of Tobias. *See also* Tobie.

Twyla Old English: woven with
double thread.
Twila.

Ty/Tye *See* Tai.

Tyana/Tyanna/Tyannah *See* Tianna.

Tyfany/Tyffany *See* Tiffany.

Tyler Old English: a tiler or tile
maker.
Tila, Tilah, Tilar, Tiler, Tyala, Tyalah,
Tyla, Tylah, Tylar.

Tympani Latin: a set of drums.
Tympanee, Tympanie.

Tynan *See* BOYS.

Tyne The name of an English river.
Also a boy's name.

Tyson *See* BOYS.

Tzara/Tzarina/Tzarine *See* Tsara.

U

Uaina Maori: to rain.

Uda Teutonic: prosperous, rich. *See
also* Ute.
Udah, Udele, Udella, Udelle.

Ude/Udele/Udelle *See* Uda and Ute.

Uilani Hawaiian: heavenly beauty.

Ula Celtic: a jewel of the sea.
Cornish: an owl.

Ulalia *See* Eulalia.

Uland/Ulanda/Ulande *See* Yolanda.

Ulani Polynesian: cheerful,
lighthearted.

Ulima Arabic: wise, learned.
Ulema, Ulimah.

Ulla Old Norse: will. *See also* Ulrike.

Ulma Latin: of the elm tree.

Ulrike Scandinavian/Teutonic: the
ruler of all. The feminine form of
Ulrich.
Ulrica, Ulrika (Russian), Ulryka
(Polish).
Diminutives: Ricki, Ricky, Rikki,
Rikky, Ulla (Scandinavian).

Ultima Latin: the greatest, the most
distant.

Ultra Latin: something that is
beyond; the ultimate.
Ultrah.

Ululani Hawaiian: heavenly
inspiration.

Ulva Teutonic: a she-wolf, brave.

Ulyana An unusual name of Russian
origin.

Uma Hebrew: the nation. Sanskrit:
light, peace; a goddess in Hindu
mythology.

Umei Polynesian: a mythological
figure.

Umeko Japanese: the child of the
plum blossom.
Umeyo.

Umiko Japanese: a child of the sea.

Úna Irish Gaelic: a traditional name,
possibly meaning a lamb. Latin: one.
See also Juno.
Euna (Scottish), Ona, Oona (Irish),
Oonagh (Irish), Oonah, Una, Unah.

Undine *See* Ondine.

Unice *See* Eunice.

Unity Oneness. From the Latin word unus, meaning one.
Uneta, Unetta, Unety, Unita.

Unna Icelandic/Teutonic: a woman.

Urania Greek: heavenly. The muse of astronomy in mythology.
Ourania.

Urbana Latin: courteous, belonging to the city.

Ursa Latin: a bear. The name of two northern constellations: Ursa Major and Ursa Minor, the Great Bear and Little Bear respectively. *See also* Ursula.
Ursah, Ursina.

Ursel/Ursela/Urseline/Ursella *See* Ursula.

Ursell Cornish: from the bottom of the hill.

Ursula Latin: a female bear. A 4th-century saint who was martyred in Germany.
Orsa, Orseline, Orsola, Ursa, Ursel, Ursela, Urseline, Ursella, Urshula, Ursola, Ursule, Ursulette, Ursuline.
Diminutives: Ursie, Uschi (German), Ushi.

Uschi *See* Ursula.

Usha Sanskrit: the Hindu goddess of the dawn.
Ushas.

Ushi Chinese: an ox. *See also* Ursula.

Utah A state of the USA.

Ute Teutonic: prosperity. *See also* Uda.
Ude, Uta.

Utina Native American: a woman of my country.

V

Vaila Old Norse: one of the Shetland Islands, off the coast of Scotland.
Vailah.

Val A diminutive of names such as Valda, Valentina and Valerie.

Vala Teutonic: the chosen one.

Valaree *See* Valerie.

Valda Teutonic: a ruler, a battle heroine.
Valdah, Valma, Velda, Walda.
Diminutive: Val.

Valdis Icelandic: a goddess.

Valentina Latin: strong and healthy. A popular name in Eastern Europe.
Valeda, Valencia, Valensia, Valentia, Valentine, Valentyna.
Diminutives: Tina, Val.

Valerie French: strong.
Valaree, Valeree, Valeri, Valeria (Italian), Valeriana (Spanish), Valérie (French), Valery, Valeska (Polish), Vallery.
Diminutive: Val.

Valeska Polish form of Valerie.

Vallery *See* Valerie.

Valletta The capital of Malta.
Valetta.

Valma *See* Valda.

Valmai Welsh: a mayflower.

Valonia Latin: from the valley.
Valona.

Valora Latin: brave.

Van/Vanna Diminutives of Vanessa.

Vana Polynesian: a sea urchin. Also a

diminutive of Vanessa.

Vanda *See* Wanda.

Vanessa A name invented by the 18th-century poet and writer Jonathan Swift.
Vanesa, Vanessah, Vanetta, Venessa. *Diminutives*: Nessa, Nessi, Nessie, Van, Vana, Vanna, Vanni.

Vanetta *See* Vanessa.

Vanilla From a Spanish word; a 'plant name'.
Vanila, Vanilah, Vanillah.

Vanja Scandinavian: the feminine form of Vanya, a Russian diminutive of Ivan.
Vania, Vanya.

Vanka Russian diminutive of Anne.

Vanni Italian diminutive of Anne. *See also* Vanessa.

Vanora Celtic: a white wave. A form of Guinevere.
Vannora, Vanorah, Vanore.

Vanya *See* Vanja.

Varda Hebrew: a rose.
Vardah, Vardia, Vardice, Vardis.

Varina *See* Varvara.

Varley *See* BOYS.

Varuna Sanskrit: the god of the night sky.
Varunah, Varuni.

Varvara Russian form of Barbara. *Diminutive*: Varina.

Vasanti Sanskrit: spring.

Vashti Persian: the beautiful one. An Old Testament name.

Veda Sanskrit: wisdom and knowledge.

Vedette Italian/Old French: a sentinel.
Vedetta.

Vega Arabic: a falling star.

Vela Latin: a sail. A constellation in the Milky Way.
Velah.

Velda *See* Valda.

Veleda Teutonic: inspired wisdom.

Velika Slavic: the great one.

Velma A diminutive of Wilhelmina.
Vilma.

Velvet A soft fabric.
Velvett, Velvette.

Venessa *See* Vanessa.

Venetia Latin: a lady of Venice. *See also* Venice.
Veneta, Venezia.

Venice Anglicised form of Venezia, an Italian city. *See also* Venetia.

Venisa/Venita *See* Venus.

Venla Finnish: a wanderer.

Ventura Spanish: good luck, happiness.

Venus Latin: beautiful. A planet and the Roman goddess of beauty and love.
Venisa, Venita, Venusa, Vinita.

Vera Latin: true. Russian: faith. A common name in Eastern Europe.
Verah, Vere, Verla, Verra (Slavic), Viera (Czech).
Diminutive: Verushka (Czech).

Verbena Latin: a sacred bough or plant.
Vervain.

Verda Latin: fresh. *See also* Verna.

Verdi Latin: green.
Verdey, Verdia, Verdie, Verdis, Verdy.

Vere *See* Vera.

Verena Swiss: a 3rd-century saint.

Verene, Verina, Verine.
Diminutive: Vreni.

Verginia *See* Virginia.

Verity Old French from Latin: truth.
Verita, Veritah.

Verla *See* Vera.

Verna Latin: spring-like, fresh. The
feminine form of Vernon. *See also*
Laverne and Verda.
Verda, Verne, Verneta, Vernice,
Vernita.
Diminutive: Vern.

Verona Latin: an Italian city. Also a
variation of Veronica.

Veronica Latin: a true likeness or
image. Also a variation of Berenice.
Verona, Veronika (Hungarian,
Scandinavian), Veronike (German),
Véronique (French).
Diminutives: Ronni, Ronnie, Ronny,
Vonni, Vonnie, Vonny.

Véronique French form of Veronica.

Verra *See* Vera.

Verran Cornish: the short one.
Verren, Verrin, Verryan, Veryan.

Verushka *See* Vera.

Vervain *See* Verbena.

Vesna Slavic: spring.

Vespera Latin: an evening star.

Vesta Latin: a guardian of the sacred
fire. The Roman goddess of the
hearth.

Veta *See* Vita.

Veva/Vevette *See* Genevieve.

Vevila Irish Gaelic: melodious.
Vevina.

Vicki/Vicky/Vikki *See* Victoria.

Victoria Latin: victory, the victorious
one. A Roman goddess.
Victoire (French), Victorie, Victorine
(French), Victory, Victorya,
Viktoria (German, Scandinavian),
Vitoria (Spanish), Vittoria (Italian),
Vyktoria, Wikitoria (Maori).
Diminutives: Tori, Torie, Tory, Vicki,
Vicky, Vikki.

Vida Hebrew: the beloved one. A
short form of Davida, the feminine
version of David.
Vidah, Videtta, Vidette.

Vidonia Portuguese: a vine branch.

Vidya Sanskrit: knowledge.

Vienna Anglicised form of Wien, an
Austrian city.

Viera *See* Vera.

Vigilia Latin: alert, vigilant.

Viktoria *See* Victoria.

Vilhelmina *See* Wilhelmina.

Vilma *See* Velma.

Vimala Sanskrit: pure.

Vina Spanish: from the vineyard. Also
a diminutive of Lavinia.
Vinia, Vinna, Vinnia.

Vincentia Latin: the conqueror. The
feminine form of Vincent.
Vincencia, Vincenta, Vincenza
(Italian).
Diminutive: Vincie.

Vine Middle English: a 'plant name'.
Vyne.

Vinita *See* Venus.

Viola A name from Shakespeare's play
Twelfth Night. *See also* Violet.
Violah, Violanta, Violenta.

Violet Latin: a 'flower name'. *See also*
Iolanthe and Yolanda.

Orvokki (Finnish), Viola (Italian), Violah, Violante (Spanish), Violeta (Spanish), Violett, Violetta (Italian), Violette (French), Vyolet, Vyolett, Vyoletta, Vyolette.
Diminutives: Letta, Lettah, Vi, Vye.

Viorica Romanian: a bluebell.
Viorika.

Virgilia Latin: a staff-bearer.
Virgila, Virgilie.

Virginia Latin: maidenly, pure.
Verginia, Virginie (French), Virginnia.
Diminutives: Gigi (French), Ginger, Ginnie, Ginny, Vergie.

Virgo Latin: a virgin. A zodiac sign and the Roman goddess of justice. *See also* Virginia.
Virgoe, Virgonia.

Virida Latin: green.
Viridiana, Viridienne (French), Viridis.

Virna A popular Italian name.

Vita Latin: life.
Veta, Vitah, Vitia.

Vitoria/Vittoria *See* Victoria.

Vivaldi After the Italian composer, Antonio Vivaldi.

Viveka Scandinavian: lively.
Viveca, Vivica.

Vivien Latin: full of life, vital. *See also* Vyvyan.
Vivia, Vivian, Viviana (Italian), Vivianne, Vivienne (French), Vivyan.
Diminutives: Viv, Vivi.

Vogue French: a fashion or style.

Voile French: a fine fabric.
Voila, Voyla, Voyle.

Volante Latin: the flying one.

Voletta Greek/Old French: veiled.
Voleta.

Von/Vonne/Vonni/Vonnie/Vonny Diminutives of Veronica and Yvonne.

Vonda From Von, a diminutive of Yvonne (an archer).
Vondah.

Voyla/Voyle *See* Voile.

Vreni *See* Verena.

Vyktoria *See* Victoria.

Vyne *See* Vine.

Vyolet/Vyolette *See* Violet.

Vyoma Sanskrit: the sky.

Vyvyan Cornish: from an old surname. Also a form of Vivien.

W

Wahiba Arabic: the generous one.

Wahida Arabic: unique.

Wailana Hawaiian: calm waters.

Waimarama Maori: clear waters.

Waipounamu Maori: a type of greenstone. *See also* Pounamu.

Waipuna Maori: a spring (water).

Walda *See* Valda.

Walida Arabic: the newborn girl.

Wallis Old French: a foreigner, particularly a woman from Wales.
Wallace, Wallice.

Wanda Teutonic: a Slavic woman, or a wanderer.
Vanda, Wandah, Wandis.

Wanetta Old English: pale.
Waneta, Wanette.

Wanika Hawaiian: God's gracious gift.

Wasima Arabic: graceful, pretty. The feminine form of Wasim.

Wednesday Middle English: the day of Odin, also known as Woden or Wotan.
Wenesdae, Wednesdai, Wensdae, Wensdai, Wensday.

Weka Maori: a wood hen.

Welma *See* Wilhelmina.

Wendy A name invented by J M Barrie in the early 1900s for his play *Peter Pan*.
Wenda, Wende, Wendee, Wendeline, Wendey, Wendi, Wendie.

Wenfreda *See* Winifred.

Wenna Diminutive of Lowenna.

Wenona/Wenonah *See* Winona.

Whetu Maori: a star.

Whetuaroha Maori: the shining moon.

Whetumarama Maori: shining love.

Whina Maori: a helper.

Whitney Old English: from the white island. Also a boy's name.
Whitnee, Whitnie, Whitny, Witnee, Witney, Witnie, Witny.

Wikitoria Maori form of Victoria.

Wilda Teutonic: the untamed one.

Wilfreda Teutonic: desiring peace. The feminine form of Wilfred.
Wilfrieda.

Wilhelmina Teutonic: the resolute protector. A feminine form of William.
Vilhelmina, Welma, Wilhelma, Wilhelmine (German), Willamina, Willette, Wilmena.

Diminutives: Billie, Billy, Helma (German), Helmine (German), Mina, Minna (German), Minne, Minnie, Velma, Vilma, Willa, Willie, Wilma.

Willa A diminutive of Wilhelmina.

Willette *See* Wilhelmina.

Willow Old English: a 'tree name'.
Willo, Willoe, Willowe, Wyllow, Wyllowe.

Wilma A diminutive of Wilhelmina.
Wilmetta, Wilmette, Wylma.

Wilmena *See* Wilhelmina.

Wilona Old English: desired.

Win/Winn/Winne/Winnie *See* Edwina, Winifred and Wynne.

Winema Native American: a female chief.

Wini Maori: a window.

Winifred Teutonic: a peaceful friend. Welsh: joyful peace.
Wenfreda, Winfred, Winifreda, Winifrida.
Diminutives: Freda, Win, Winn, Winne, Winnie, Wynn.

Winona Native American: the firstborn daughter. A town in Minnesota.
Wenona, Wenonah, Winonah, Wynona.

Winsome English: pleasant and attractive.

Winter Old English: born in the winter months.
Winta, Wintah, Winters, Wynter, Wynters.

Wisteria A 'plant name'.
Wistaria, Wistariah, Wisteriah.

Witnee/Witney/Witnie *See* Whitney.

CELEBRITIES' KIDS' NAMES – GIRLS

Unusual names from the past include Bob Geldof's Peaches Honeyblossom and Demi Moore's Scout LaRue. Chef Jamie Oliver is a modern-day 'serial weird-namer', with Daisy Boo Pamela, Petal Blossom Rainbow and Poppy Honey Rosie, while other odd celebrity names include Apple, Exodus and Maxwell. Here are some examples of what famous people have called their daughters (*see* page 170 for boys' names).

Adelaide	Rachel Griffiths	Jazz	George Gregan
Anais	Noel Gallagher	Judah	Ziggy Marley
Apple	Gwyneth Paltrow	Lily-Rose	Johnny Depp
Arabella	Ivanka Trump	Lola	Kate Moss
Ava	Hugh Jackman	Louisanna Ray	Leelee Sobieski
Bailey	Stella McCartney	Lourdes	Madonna
Blue Ivy	Beyoncé	Malia	Barack Obama
Carys	Catherine Zeta-Jones	Marlowe	Sienna Miller
Chance	Sean (Diddy) Combs	Matisse	Ricky Ponting
Clementine	Claudia Schiffer	Maxwell Drew	Jessica Simpson
Coco Riley	Courteney Cox	Mia	Kate Winslet
Cosima	Nigella Lawson	Monroe	Mariah Carey
Daisy True	Meg Ryan	Myla	Roger Federer
Destry	Stephen Spielberg	Nahla Ariela	Halle Berry
Ella	Ben Stiller	Olive	Drew Barrymore
Elula	Sasha Baron Cohen	Penelope	Kourtney Kardashian
Emme	Jennifer Lopez	Piper	Sarah Palin
Ethel	Lily Allen	Ramona	Maggie Gyllenhaal
Ever	Milla Jovovich	Ruby	Jude Law
Exodus	Mike Tyson	Sam	Tiger Woods
Felicity-Amore	Keisha Castle-Hughes	Scarlet	Sylvester Stallone
Gia	Matt Damon	Seraphina	Ben Affleck
Gianna	Kobe Bryant	Shiloh Nouvel	Brad Pitt
Harlow	Nicole Richie	Stella	Matt Damon
Harper Seven	David Beckham	Summer	Shane Warne
Hattie	Tori Spelling	Suri	Tom Cruise
Haven Garner	Jessica Alba	Tabitha	Sarah Jessica Parker
Hazel	Julia Roberts	Theodora	Robbie Williams
Indigo	James Packer	Vida	Matthew McConaughey
Isabella	Princess Mary	Willow Sage	Pink
Isadora Barney	Björk	Zahara Marley	Angelina Jolie

Wraith A spirit.
Wraithe, Wrayth, Wraythe.

Wren Old English: a tiny bird.
Wrenn, Wrenna, Wrenne.

Wyanet Native American: beautiful.

Wylie *See* BOYS.

Wyllow/Wyllowe *See* Willow.

Wylma *See* Wilma.

Wynne Cornish/Welsh: fair or blessed.
Also a diminutive of Winifred.
Winn, Winne, Wyn, Wynette, Wynn.

Wynona *See* Winona.

Wynter/Wynters *See* Winter.

Wyomia From Wyoming, a state of
the USA.
Wyomea, Wyomeah, Wyomiah.

Xamia A type of butterfly.
Xamiah, Zamia, Zamiah.

Xandra A diminutive of Alexandra.

Xanthe Greek: yellow, bright or
golden-haired.
Xanthea, Xanthi, Xanthia, Xanthie,
Zanthe, Zanthea, Zanthi, Zanthia,
Zanthie.

Xara/Xarah *See* Zara.

Xaviera Arabic: brilliant, bright.
Spanish: of the new house; the
feminine form of Xavier.
Javiera, Saviera, Xaverie, Xavière
(French), Zaviera.

Xenia Greek: hospitable, welcoming.
Xena, Xene, Zena, Zenia.

Xiang Chinese: the fragrant one.
Ziang.

Xiaoli Chinese: morning jasmine.

Ximena Basque: the feminine form of
Ximeno (*see* Simon in BOYS).
Chimena, Chimene (French), Jimena
(Spanish), Ximene.

Xingxing Chinese: twin stars.

Xiomara Portuguese: famous in war.

Xochi Mexican: a flower.

Xuan Vietnamese: springtime.
Zuan.

Xuela *See* Zuela.

Xuxa Brazilian form of Susan,
meaning a lily.
Xuxah, Zuza, Zuxah.

Xylia Greek: from the woods.
Xylina, Xylona.

Yachi Japanese: eight thousand. A
'number name'.
Yachiko.

Yael Hebrew: a wild goat. Also a boy's
name.
Jael, Yaelle.

Yaffa/Yaffah *See* Jaffa.

Yakira Hebrew: precious.
Yakirah.

Yalanda *See* Yolanda.

Yalda Persian: an ancient festival.
Yaldah.

Yamuna Hindi: a sacred river.

Yangchen Sherpa/Tibetan: the sacred
one.

Yangzom Sherpa/Tibetan: an
accomplished woman.

Yannah The feminine form of Yann,

the Breton version of John.
Yan, Yana, Yanah, Yanina, Yannina.

Yardley *See* BOYS.

Yasmin/Yasmina/Yasmine/Yassmin *See* Jasmine.

Yasu Japanese: tranquil.

Yedda Old English: a singer, one with a melodious voice.

Yehudit A Jewish form of Judith.

Yelena Russian form of Helen.

Yetta Old English/German: to give. Also a diminutive of Henrietta.

Yetunde A contemporary American name.

Yeva/Yiva *See* Eve.

Ygraine/Ygrayne *See* Igrayne.

Yi Chinese: happy.

Yin Chinese: the moon, or silvery. Yin is the feminine, passive principle in Chinese philosophy, the opposite of Yang.

Ynes/Ynez Spanish forms of Agnes.

Yoko Japanese: good.

Yola African: a firefly. Yolah.

Yolanda Greek/Old French: a violet flower. *See also* Iolanthe and Violet. Jolan (Hungarian), Jolana, Jolanda (Italian), Jolande, Jolani, Jolania, Jolanta (Polish), Uland, Ulanda, Ulande, Yalanda, Yolana, Yoland, Yolandah, Yolande (French), Yolandita (Spanish), Yolane, Yolanta, Yolanthe, Yollanda, Yollandah.

Yon Korean: a lotus blossom.

Yona Hebrew: a dove. The feminine form of Jonah. Yonah, Yonina, Yonita.

Yootha/Ytha *See* Ita.

Yori Japanese: trustworthy.

Yoshi Japanese: good. Also a boy's name. Yoshiko.

Yovela Hebrew: rejoicing.

Ysabel/Ysobel *See* Isabel.

Yseult Medieval French form of Isolde. Yseulte.

Ysolda/Ysolde *See* Isolde.

Yu Chinese: jade. Tibetan: turquoise.

Yue Chinese: the moon.

Yuki Japanese: lucky, or from the snow.

Yumi Japanese: like an arrow.

Yuri Japanese: a lily. Yuriko.

Yusra Arabic: the prosperous one.

Yva/Yve *See* Eve.

Yvana/Yvanna *See* Ivana.

Yvette French diminutive of Yvonne. Evetta, Evette, Yvett, Yvetta.

Yvona *See* Yvonne.

Yvonne French: an archer. Greek: the wood of the yew tree. Evon, Evonne, Yvon, Yvona, Yvonn. *Diminutives*: Von, Vonn, Vonne, Vonni, Vonnie, Vonny, Yvetta, Yvette.

Z

Zabrina *See* Sabrina.

Zada Arabic: the lucky one. Zadah, Zaida, Zayda.

Zadee/Zadie/Zaidee Diminutives of Sarah. *See also* Sadie.

Zafira Spanish: a sapphire. *See also* Sapphira.
Zafera (Greek), Zaffira, Zaffirah, Zafirah.

Zagir Armenian: a flower.

Zahara/Zahira/Zahra *See* Zara.

Zahava Hebrew: golden.

Zahnee/Zahni *See* Zani.

Zaida *See* Zada.

Zaira *See* Zara.

Zali A modern name, possibly made-up.
Zalee, Zalie, Zalih.

Zalika Arabic/Swahili: well-born.

Zameera/Zamira *See* Samira.

Zamia/Zamiah *See* Xamia.

Zana *See* Nizana.

Zandra *See* Alexandra and Sandra.

Zaneta Hebrew: the grace of God.
Zanetta.

Zani A modern name, possibly a feminine form of Zane.
Zahnee, Zahni, Zahnie, Zanee, Zanie, Zanni, Zannie.

Zanna A modern diminutive of Suzanna.

Zanthe/Zanthi/Zanthie *See* Xanthe.

Zara Arabic: a blossom or flower. Hebrew: the bright dawn. *See also* Sarah.
Xara, Xarah, Zahara, Zahira, Zahra, Zaira, Zarah, Zareena, Zaria, Zarina, Zarra, Zarrah, Zhara, Zhra.

Zareena *See* Zara.

Zaria *See* Azaria, Sarah and Zara.

Zarifa Arabic: graceful.

Zarina/Zarra *See* Zara.

Zavanna *See* Savanna.

Zaviera *See* Xaviera.

Zayda *See* Zada.

Zaynab Arabic: a perfumed flower.
Zayneb, Zaynep.

Zea Latin: ripened grain.
Zeah, Zia, Ziah.

Zeena/Zeenah/Zeina *See* Zena.

Zelah Hebrew: a side. Also a Cornish placename.

Zelda A diminutive of Griselda.
Zeldah.

Zele *See* Zelia.

Zelena *See* Selena.

Zelia Greek: zealous, devoted to one's duty.
Zele, Zélie (French), Zelina.

Zelina *See* Zelia.

Zelma/Zelmah *See* Anselma, Salima and Selma.

Zen Japanese: a Buddhist sect. Also a boy's name.
Zenn, Zenne.

Zena Scottish: short form of Alexina (*see* Alexandra). *See also* Xenia and Zenobia.
Zeena, Zeenah, Zeina, Zeinah, Zenah.

Zenaida *See* Zenobia.

Zenda Persian: a sacred woman.
Zendah, Zendaia, Zendaya.

Zenia *See* Xenia and Zenobia.

Zenith Arabic: the highest point.
Zenithe, Zenyth, Zenythe.

Zenna *See* Zenobia.

Zennor Cornish: the name of a village.

Zenobia Greek: given life by Zeus.
Zena, Zenaida, Zenia, Zenna, Zenobie (French), Zenovia (Russian).

Zenyth/Zenythe *See* Zenith.

Zephyr Greek: a breeze. The feminine form of Zephyrus, the god of the west wind in mythology.
Zephir, Zephira, Zephra, Zephrina, Zephrine, Zephyra, Zephyrina, Zephyrine.

Zeporah *See* Zippora.

Zerla *See* Zerlina.

Zerlina Teutonic: serene beauty.
Zerla, Zerlinda, Zerline.

Zeta Greek: the sixth letter of the Greek alphabet.
Zita, Zitah, Zetah.

Zeva Greek: a sword.

Zezia A modern name of uncertain origin.

Zhang A popular Chinese name.

Zhara/Zhra *See* Zara.

Zia *See* Zea.

Ziang *See* Xiang.

Zigana Hungarian: a gypsy.

Zillah Hebrew: shade or a shadow. A biblical name.
Zila, Zilah, Zilla.

Zilpah A biblical name.
Zilpa, Zylpa, Zylpah.

Zina *See* Alexandra.

Zinnia Latin: a 'flower name'.
Zinia.

Zion A hill in Jerusalem, the site of a holy temple. Also a name for the Jewish people.
Sion, Syon, Zyon.

Zippora Hebrew: a little bird, a sparrow. A biblical name.
Zeporah, Zipporah.

Zita Italian: a 13th-century Tuscan saint. Also a diminutive of Rosita (*see* Rose) and *see* Zeta.

Ziva Hebrew: brightness.

Zivka Slavic: life, or lively.

Zizi Hungarian diminutive of Elizabeth.

Zky/Zkye *See* Skye.

Zoë Greek: life.
Zoa, Zoee, Zoelle, Zoey, Zoi, Zoia (Russian), Zoie, Zooey, Zoya.

Zofeya Hebrew: God sees.
Zofeyah.

Zofia/Zofie/Zofja *See* Sophia.

Zohra Arabic: blooming.

Zoi/Zoia/Zoie *See* Zoë.

Zola A modern name, probably derived from Zoë. Also after Emile Zola, a 19th-century French author.
Zolah.

Zommer German form of Summer.

Zooey *See* Zoë.

Zora Slavic: dawn.
Zorah, Zorana, Zorina, Zorine.

Zorina/Zorine *See* Zora.

Zosia Polish form of Sophia.

Zoya *See* Zoë.

Zsa Zsa Hungarian diminutive of Susannah.

Zuan *See* Xuan.

Zuela Spanish: possibly a variation of Suela, a diminutive of Consuela.
Xuela.

Zuleika Persian: brilliant beauty.

Zulema Arabic/Hebrew: peace.
Sulema, Zulima.

Zuri Swahili: beautiful.

Zuza/Zuzah *See* Xuxa.

Zuzana/Zuzanna *See* Susannah.

Zylpa/Zylpah *See* Zilpah.

Zyon *See* Zion.

Boys

A

Aaden/Aadyn *See* Aden.

Aaron Hebrew: exalted. The brother
of Moses in the Bible.
Aaran, Aarone, Aarron, Aaryn,
Aharon (Hebrew), Aron, Arone,
Aronne (German, Italian), Arran,
Arron, Arryn, Eron, Erron, Haroun
(Arabic), Harun (Arabic).
Diminutives: Ari, Arie.

Abad *See* Abbott.

Abaddon Hebrew: destruction.

Abasi *See* Abbas.

Abba Hebrew: a father.

Abban Latin: white.

Abbas Arabic: stern.
Abasi (Swahili).

Abbott Old English: the father of the
abbey.
Abad (Spanish), Abbe, Abboid
(Gaelic), Abbot (French).

Abdiel Hebrew: the servant of God, a
faithful servant.

Abdul Arabic: the son of, or servant
of.
Abdal, Abdel.

Abdullah Arabic: the servant of
Allah.

Abe/Abie *See* Abel and Abraham.

Abel Hebrew: breath, or the son. A
son of Adam and Eve in the Bible.
Diminutives: Abe, Abie.

Abelard Teutonic: nobly resolute.
Adelard.

Abernethy Scottish Gaelic: the
mouth of the Nethy River.

Abi Turkish: an elder brother.

Abiel Hebrew: God is the father.

Abijah Hebrew: the Lord is my
father.

Abir Hebrew: strong.

Abisha Hebrew: God's gift.

Abner Hebrew: the father of light. A
biblical name.
Avner.

Abraham Hebrew: the father of
many; a biblical figure.
Abram, Abramo (Italian), Abran
(Spanish), Aperahama (Maori),
Avram (Greek), Avrom (Hebrew),
Avron (Hebrew), Ebrahim (Arabic),
Ibrahim (Arabic).
Diminutives: Abe, Abie, Bram.

Abram/Abran *See* Abraham.

Absalom Hebrew: the father of peace;
a son of David in the Bible. *See also*
Axel.
Absolom, Absolon.

Ace Latin: unity.

Acelin French: noble.

Achilles A handsome figure in Greek
mythology.
Achille (French), Achilleo (Italian).

Ackerley Old English: a dweller in the meadow.

Ackley Old English: a dweller in the oak-tree meadow.

Acton Old English: from the settlement with oak trees.

Adair Scottish Gaelic: from the oak tree near the ford.

Adam Hebrew: a man of the red earth. According to the Bible, the first man.
Adama, Adamh, Adamo (Italian), Adan (Italian, Spanish), Adao (Portuguese), Adda (Welsh), Adem (Turkish), Adhamh (Irish, Scottish), Arama (Maori).

Adamson The son of Adam. Adamsen.

Adan *See* Adam and Aidan.

Adao *See* Adam.

Adar Hebrew: fiery.

Adda Welsh form of Adam.

Addison Old English: the son of Adam.
Addis, Addisyn, Addyson, Adison, Adisyn, Adyson.

Adel Teutonic: noble.

Adelard *See* Abelard.

Adelpho Greek: a brother.

Adem *See* Adam.

Aden Arabic: a Red Sea gulf and port. *See also* Aidan.
Aaden, Aadyn, Adyn.

Adhamh *See* Adam.

Adin Hebrew: sensual.

Adir Hebrew: noble, majestic.

Adison/Adisyn *See* Addison.

Adlai Hebrew: my witness. A biblical name.

Adler Teutonic: an eagle. A man of keen perception.

Adnan Arabic: the settler.

Adney Old English: a dweller on the island.

Adolph Teutonic: a noble wolf.
Adolf (German), Adolfo (Italian), Adolphe (French), Adolphus (Swedish).
Diminutives: Dolf, Dolph.

Adon Hebrew: the Lord.

Adonis Greek: in mythology, the handsome youth loved by Venus.

Adrian Latin: the dark one, or a man from the sea, as in the Adriatic.
Adriaan, Adriano (Italian, Spanish), Adrie, Adrien (French), Arje (Dutch), Arjen (Dutch), Hadrian.

Adriel Hebrew: from God's congregation.
Adrial.

Adrien French form of Adrian.

Adyn *See* Aden.

Adyson *See* Addison.

Aedan *See* Aidan.

Aeneas Greek: the praised one.
Eneas, Inia (Maori).

Aengus *See* Angus.

Aeolus Greek: in mythology, the ruler of the winds.

Aeron Welsh: an unusual boy's name.

Aesh *See* Ash.

Afi Polynesian: fire.

Afon Welsh: a river. *See also* Avon.

Afro From African. The name of a hairstyle.

Agate French: a precious stone.

Agilard Teutonic: bright.

Agosto/Agustin *See* Augustus.

Agu Nigerian: a leopard.

Ahab Hebrew: an uncle. A king of Israel in the Bible.

Aharon Hebrew form of Aaron.

Ahearn Irish Gaelic: a horse lord. *See also* Hearn.
Aherin, Ahern, Aherne.

Ahi Maori: fire.

Ahmed Arabic: most highly praised.
Ahmad, Ahmet, Amadou (French).

Ahohako Polynesian: a storm.

Ahomana Polynesian: thunder.

Ahren Teutonic: an eagle.
Ahrens.

Aidan Irish Gaelic: the little fiery one. The name of a saint. *See also* Aden.
Adan, Aden, Aedan, Aiden, Aodan (Irish Gaelic), Aydan, Ayden, Aydin, Edan, Eden.

Aikane Polynesian: friendly.

Aiken Old English: little Adam.
Aickin, Aikin.

Ailani Hawaiian: a high chief.

Ailean/Ailin *See* Alan.

Aillen A figure from Irish mythology.

Aimon French from Teutonic: a house.

Aindréas Scottish Gaelic form of Andrew.

Ainsley Old English/Scottish: a wood or clearing. Also a girl's name.
Ainslee, Ainsleigh, Ainslie.

Airlie After the Earl of Airlie, a Scottish lord.
Airlee, Airley, Airli, Airly.

Aithan/Aithen *See* Ethan.

Ajani Nigerian: the victor.

Ajax Greek: the legendary hero of the Trojan War.

Ajay Sanskrit: invincible.

Aka Hawaiian: a shadow.

Akamu Hawaiian: red earth.

Akar Turkish: flowing water.

Akbar Arabic: great.

Akihiro A well-known Japanese name.

Akil Arabic: intelligent.
Akeel.

Akim Russian form of Joachim.

Akin Nigerian: a hero.

Akira Japanese: intelligent.

Akiva Hebrew: the supplanter.

Akiyama Japanese: the autumn, or a mountain.

Akram Arabic: generous, noble.

Aksel *See* Axel.

Akuhata Maori: August.

Al A diminutive of names such as Alan, Albert and Alfred.

Aladin Arabic: a servant of Allah.
Aladdin.

Alain French form of Alan.

Alako The Romany Gypsy moon god.

Alamo A place in Texas, USA.
Alamoe, Alamoh.

Alan Irish and Scottish Gaelic: harmony, or the cheerful handsome one.
Ailean (Scottish), Ailin (Irish), Alain (French), Aland, Alawn (Welsh), Alen, Allan, Allen, Alleyne, Allon, Allyn, Alun (Welsh), Alyn, Arana (Maori, Polynesian).
Diminutives: Al, Als.

Aland Celtic: as bright as the sun. *See also* Alan.
Alland.

Alard Teutonic: a noble ruler.
Alart, Ellard.

Alaric Teutonic: the ruler of all.

Alasdair/Alasdhair/Alastair Scottish forms of Alexander.

Alawn Welsh form of Alan.

Alban Latin: fair-complexioned. A saint's name.
Alben, Albin, Albino (Italian, Spanish), Aubin (French).

Albany A poetic name for England.

Alber Teutonic: a quick mind.

Alberich Teutonic: the king of the dwarves in German legend.

Albern Old English: a noble warrior.

Albert Teutonic: noble and illustrious. The name became popular after the marriage of Queen Victoria to Prince Albert.
Adelbert, Ailbert (Scottish), Alberto (Italian), Albrecht (German), Arapata (Maori), Arapeta (Maori), Aubert (French), Elbert.
Diminutives: Al, Albie, Bert, Bertie.

Albin/Albino *See* Alban.

Albion Latin: white. An archaic name for England.

Alcott Old English: from the stone cottage.

Alden Old English: an old wise friend.
Aldin, Aldwin, Aldwyn, Elden, Eldin.

Alder Old English: the alder tree.

Alderney One of the Channel Islands.

Aldous Teutonic: old, wise or great.
Aldis, Aldo (Italian), Aldus.

Aldred Old English: a great counsellor.
Eldred.

Aldrich Old English: an old, wise ruler.
Aldric, Audric (French), Eldric, Eldrich.

Aldridge *See* Eldridge.

Aldwin/Aldwyn *See* Alden and Alvin.

Alec/Aleck/Aleczander *See* Alexander.

Aled Welsh: a son.

Alejandro *See* Alexander.

Alekos/Aleks/Aleksandr *See* Alexander.

Alemana Hawaiian: a warrior.

Alen *See* Alan.

Aleph Hebrew: the first letter of the alphabet, similar to the Greek alpha.
Alef.

Aleron Latin: an eagle.

Alessandro/Alessio Italian forms of Alexander.

Alex/Alexas *See* Alexander.

Alexander Greek: the protector and helper of mankind. *See also* Sanders and Sasha.
Alasdair (Scottish), Alasdhair (Scottish), Alastair (Scottish), Aleczander, Alejandro (Spanish), Alekos (Greek), Aleksandr (Russian), Alessandro (Italian), Alessio (Italian), Alexanda, Alexandr (Russian), Alexandre (French), Alexas, Alexei (Russian), Alexi, Alexio (Portuguese), Alexis (Greek), Alexius, Alexsandar, Alexsander, Alika (Polynesian), Alistair (Scottish), Alister, Allister (Scottish), Alsandair (Irish Gaelic), Alyxander, Alyxsander, Araketenara

(Maori), Elek (Hungarian).
Diminutives: Alec, Aleck, Alek, Aleks, Alex, Alik, Alix, Alleck, Alyk, Alyks, Alyx, Alyxs, Lex, Sacha (French), Sandie, Sandor (Hungarian), Sandy, Sascha (German), Sasha (Russian), Santo (Cornish), Xahn, Xan, Xander, Zahn, Zan, Zander.

Alexavier A combination of Alexander and Xavier.

Alexei/Alexi/Alexio/Alexis/ Alexsander *See* Alexander.

Alf/Alfie *See* Alfred.

Alfons/Alfonso *See* Alphonso.

Alford Old English: from the old ford.

Alfred Old English: a wise counsellor. King Alfred the Great ruled England from AD 871–899.
Ailfrid (Irish), Alfredo (Italian, Spanish), Alfreds, Alifeleti (Tongan), Arapeti (Maori).
Diminutives: Al, Alf, Alfie, Fred, Freddie, Freddy.

Alger Old English: a noble spearman.

Algernon French: with whiskers, bearded.
Diminutives: Al, Algie, Algy.

Ali Arabic: exalted, or noble.

Alifeleti Tongan form of Alfred.

Alika Polynesian form of Alex.

Alipate Polynesian: bright.

Alison Old English: the son of a nobleman. More commonly a girl's name.
Allison.

Alistair/Alister *See* Alexander.

Allan/Allen/Alleyne *See* Alan.

Alland *See* Aland.

Allard Old English: sacred, brave.

Allighiero Italian: a noble spear. Allegri.

Allister *See* Alexander.

Allon/Allyn *See* Alan.

Almo Old English: noble and famous.

Almon Hebrew: forsaken.

Alonso/Alonzo *See* Alphonso.

Aloysius An archaic form of Louis. Alois, Aloisia (Italian), Aloys.
Diminutive: Lewie.

Alphonso Teutonic: noble and ready. Alfons (German), Alfonso (Italian, Spanish, Swedish), Alonso (Spanish), Alonzo, Alphonse (French), Alphonsus (Irish).
Diminutives: Fonz, Fonzie, Lon, Lonnie.

Alric *See* Ulrich.

Alroy Irish Gaelic: a red-headed boy.

Alsandair Irish Gaelic form of Alexander.

Alston Old English: from the old place.
Alton.

Altair Arabic: a bird.

Altman Teutonic: an old wise man.

Alun A Welsh form of Alan.

Alvah Hebrew: the exalted one. Alva.

Alvin Teutonic: a noble friend. Aldwin, Aldwyn, Alvan, Alwan, Alwin, Alwyn, Aylwin, Elvin.

Alvis Old Norse: all wise. Alvise, Elvis.

Alwan/Alwin/Alwyn *See* Alvin.

Alyk/Alyks/Alyxander/Alyxs *See* Alexander.

Alyn *See* Alan.

A – Boys

Amadeus Latin: a lover of God.
Amadeo (Italian), Amado (Spanish).

Amadou French form of Ahmed.

Amal Arabic: hope. Hebrew: work or labour.
Amahl.

Amama Polynesian: open-mouthed.

Aman Indonesian: secure and safe.

Amana Hawaiian: a warrior.

Amaro Portuguese: dark, like a Moor.

Amat Indonesian: the observer.

Ambar Sanskrit: the sky.

Ambert Teutonic: a bright, shining light.

Ambler Old English: a stable-keeper.

Ambrose Greek: immortal. The name of a saint.
Ambroise (French), Ambros (Irish), Emrys (Welsh).

Ameer See Amir.

Amery See Amory.

Amida Japanese: the name of the Buddha of pure light.

Amiel Hebrew: the Lord of my people.

Amin Arabic/Hebrew: honest and trustworthy.

Amir Arabic: princely.
Ameer.

Amiri Maori: the east wind.

Amirov Hebrew: my people are great.

Ammon Ancient Egyptian: hidden. The name of a god.

Amoho Maori form of Amos and Moses.

Amoka Hawaiian form of Amos.

Amokura Maori: a red-tailed bird.

Amon Hebrew: trustworthy.

Amory Teutonic: divine, or a famous ruler.
Amery.

Amos Hebrew: the bearer of burdens. An Old Testament prophet.
Amoho (Maori), Amoka (Hawaiian).

Amrit Sanskrit: the immortal one.

Amsden Old English: from the valley of Ambrose.

Amund Scandinavian: divine protection.

Anakin A character in the *Star Wars* movie series, also known as Darth Vader.

Anakoni Hawaiian: valuable.

Analu Hawaiian: manly.

Anand Sanskrit: joyful.

Anaru Maori and Polynesian form of Andrew.

Anastasius Greek: resurrection, one who shall rise again.
Anastase (French).

Anatole Greek: from the east.
Anatol, Anatolie, Anatolio (Italian, Spanish), Anatoly (Russian).

Ancel Teutonic: godlike. *See also* Ansel.
Ancelin, Ancelot.

Anders Scandinavian form of Andrew.

Anderson The son of Andrew.
Andersen.

Andie/Andy See Andrew.

Andis Greek: of strong desire.

Andon Slavic form of Anthony.

Andras/André/Andreas/Andres See Andrew.

158

Andrew Greek: strong and manly. St Andrew is the patron saint of Scotland and Russia.
Aindréas (Scottish), Anaru (Maori, Polynesian), Anders (Scandinavian), Andrae, Andras (Hungarian), André (French), Andrea (Italian), Andreas (Dutch, German, Welsh), Andres (Spanish), Andretti, Andreus, Andrey, Andries, Andris (Latvian), Ani (Maori), Ondray, Ondré.
Diminutives: Andie, Andy, Drew (Scottish).

Androcles Greek: glory. A figure from Roman legend.

Aneurin Welsh: truly golden.
Diminutive: Nye.

Angelo Italian: an angel or saintly messenger.
Ange (French), Angel, Angelico, Angelino (Spanish), Angell, Angelos (Greek), Angelus, Aniello (Italian).

Angus Scottish Gaelic: of unique strength, outstanding. A former Scottish county.
Aengus, Angas, Aonghas, Aonghus, Enos (Irish Gaelic).
Diminutives: Gus, Gussy.

Angwyn Welsh: very handsome.

Ani Maori form of Andrew.

Aniello Italian form of Angelo.

Anil Sanskrit: of the wind.

Anlon Celtic: a great champion.

Annan Celtic: from the stream.

Anno Hebrew: grace. The masculine form of Anne.

Anntoin Irish form of Anthony.

Anoke Native American: an actor.
Anoki.

Ansari Arabic: a helper.

Anscom Old English: a dweller in the secret valley.
Anscomb.

Ansel Old French: a nobleman's follower. Also a diminutive of Anselm.
Ancel, Ansell.

Anselm Teutonic: a divine helmet. The name of a saint.
Anselme (French), Anselmo (Spanish).
Diminutive: Ansel.

Ansley Old English: from the hermitage clearing.

Anson Old English: the son of Anne or Agnes.

Anstice Greek: the resurrected one.
Anstiss.

Anthony Latin: praiseworthy, of inestimable worth.
Andon (Slavic), Anntoin (Irish), Antal (Hungarian), Anthany, Anthonie, Antoine (French), Anton (German), Antoni (Polish), Antonio (Italian, Spanish), Antony, Antoun, Antoune, Antun (Croatian), Atonio (Maori, Samoan).
Diminutives: Ant, Anto, Toney, Toni, Tonie, Tony.

Antoine/Anton/Antoni/Antonio/ Antony *See* Anthony.

Anu The king of the gods in Babylonian mythology.

Anwar Arabic: the bright one.

Anwell Celtic: beloved or dear.

Anyon Celtic: an anvil.

Anzac A patriotic name. From the World War I Australian and New Zealand Army Corps.
Anzack, Anzak.

Aodan *See* Aidan.

Aonghas *See* Angus.

Apache A Native American tribe.

Aperahama Maori form of Abraham.

Apollo Greek: a beautiful youth. The god of music, poetry and healing in Greek mythology.

Aquila Greek: like an eagle. The name of a constellation.
Aquilino (Italian).

Ara Armenian: kingly. Latin: an altar.

Arailt *See* Harold.

Araketenara Maori form of Alexander.

Arama Maori form of Adam.

Aran Hebrew: active, nimble. Thai: a forest.

Arana Maori and Polynesian form of Alan.

Arapata/Arapeta Maori forms of Albert.

Arapeti Maori form of Alfred.

Arawa Maori: a shark.

Arcas A figure in Greek mythology who became the constellation of Ursa Minor, the little bear.

Archard Teutonic: sacred and powerful.

Archer Old English: a bowman.

Archibald Teutonic: noble and bold. *Diminutives*: Arch, Archee, Archey, Archie, Archy.

Archie *See* Archibald.

Ardal Irish Gaelic: a brave warrior.
Ardall, Ardel, Ardell, Ardghal, Ardil, Ardill.

Ardan Celtic: a name from the Arthurian legends.

Arden Old English: a dwelling place.

Latin: ardent and sincere.
Ardin.

Ardley Old English: from the meadow of the home-lover.

Ardolph Old English: the wolf (a wanderer) who longs for home.

Arel *See* Ariel.

Aren Danish: the ruler of the eagles.

Arend Dutch form of Arnold.

Ares Greek: the god of war. Also a constellation and the root of the name Aries, a zodiac sign.
Arian, Arien, Aries, Arius.

Argus Greek: watchful.
Argos.

Argyll Scottish Gaelic: from the land of the Gaels. A Scottish county.
Argyle, Argylle.

Ari Hebrew: a lion. Also a diminutive of Aaron and Aristotle.
Arie.

Arian Welsh: silver.
Aryan.

Aric Old English: a sacred ruler.

Ariel Hebrew: a lion of God.
Arel.

Aries *See* Ares.

Ariki Polynesian: a chief.

Arion A figure from Greek mythology.

Aristedes Greek: descended from the aristocracy.
Aristede (Italian), Aristeo, Aristo.

Aristotle Greek: a thinker. A famous Greek philosopher.
Diminutives: Ari, Arie.

Aritz Basque: an oak tree.
Ariz.

Arizona A USA state.

Arje/Arjen Dutch forms of Adrian.

Arjun Sanskrit: the white one.
Arjuna.

Arkwright Old English: a carpenter.

Arlen Irish Gaelic: a pledge.
Arlan, Arlin.

Arley Old English: from the hare or stag meadow.
Arlee, Arleigh, Arlie, Harlee, Harleigh, Harley, Harlie, Harly, Hartlee, Hartleigh, Hartley, Hartlie.

Arlo Old English: from the protected town or hill.
Arloe, Arlow, Arlowe.

Armand French form of Herman.

Armature From Latin: a protective covering, like armour.
Armatura.

Armen Armenian: a man from Armenia.

Armin/Armond *See* Herman.

Armon Hebrew: a castle.

Armour Old French: protective covering.
Armeur, Armor, Armore, Armoure, Armure.

Armstrong Old English: a strong-armed warrior.

Arnald/Arnaud *See* Arnold.

Arnall Teutonic: a gracious eagle.

Arne Dutch form of Arnold.

Arnett French: a little eagle.
Arnatt, Arnott.

Arnold Teutonic: as strong as an eagle. A name introduced to England by the Normans.
Arend (Dutch), Arnald, Arnaldo (Spanish), Arnaud (French), Arne (Dutch), Arnel, Arneld, Arnoldo (Italian).
Diminutives: Arne, Arni (Icelandic), Arnie.

Aron/Arone/Aronne *See* Aaron.

Aroon Thai: of the dawn.

Arran The name of a Scottish island.
See also Aaron.
Arron, Arryn.

Arsen Greek: virile.
Arsène (French), Arseni (Greek), Arsenio (Italian), Arsenios, Arsenius.

Art/Artair/Artie *See* Arthur.

Artan Turkish: a lion.

Artek Polish form of Arthur.

Arthur Celtic: strong as a bear, or strong as a rock. A legendary king of Britain.
Artair (Scottish), Artek (Polish), Arthek (Cornish) Arthes (Welsh), Arthuur, Arthyr, Artur (Irish), Arturo (Italian, Spanish), Artus (French).
Diminutives: Art, Artie.

Arthyen Cornish: born of a bear.
Arthien (Welsh).

Arun Sanskrit: the dawn.

Arundel Old English: he who dwells with the eagles.

Arvad Hebrew: the wanderer.

Arval Latin: from the cultivated land.

Arve Scandinavian: an heir.

Arvin Teutonic: a friend of the people.
Arvid.

Aryan *See* Arian.

Asa Hebrew: the healer, a physician. A biblical name.

Ascher *See* Asher.

Ascot Old English: one who lives in the east cottage.
Ascott.

Asera Hawaiian: lucky.

Ash Middle English: a type of tree. Also a diminutive of name such as Asher and Ashley.
Aesh, Asch, Asche, Ashe, Ashen.

Ashburn Old English: from the brook by the ash tree.

Ashby Old English: a farm by the ash tree.
Ashbeigh, Ashbey.

Ashden Old English: from the hill of the ash trees.
Ashenden.
Diminutive: Ash.

Asher Hebrew: happy, fortunate. A biblical name.
Ascher.
Diminutives: Ash, Ashe.

Ashford Old English: one who lives at the ford by the ash tree.
Ashforde.

Ashley Old English: from the ash-tree meadow.
Ashleigh, Ashlie.
Diminutives: Ash, Ashe.

Ashlin Old English: a dweller by the ash tree pool.
Ashlen.

Ashok Sanskrit: without sadness.

Ashraf Arabic: honourable.

Ashton Old English: one who lives at the ash-tree farm.
Ashten, Ashtin, Ashtyn.

Ashur Hebrew: black.

Ashwin Hindi: a star; the Hindi name for the month of October. Old English: a spear comrade or protector.
Ashvin, Ashwyn, Asvin, Aswin.

Asim Arabic: the protector.
Aseem.

Askel Norse: a divine cauldron.

Aslak Norse: divine sport.

Aslan Turkish: a lion.

Aspen Old English: the aspen tree, a type of poplar.
Aspenn, Aspin, Aspyn.

Astley Old English: from the eastern wood or clearing.
Astlee, Astley, Astlie, Astly.

Aston Old English: from the eastern place.

Astron A modern name, derived from the Greek word astro, meaning a star.
Astro.

Asvin/Aswin *See* Ashwin.

Aswad Arabic: black.

Atalik Hungarian: like his father.

Atarah Hebrew: a crown. Also a girl's name.
Atara.

Atea A god of the sky in Polynesian mythology.

Athelstan Old English: a noble stone. The name of an early English king.

Atherton Old English: one who lives at the spring farm.
Athderden, Atherdon, Atherten.

Athol Scottish Gaelic: new Ireland. A placename.
Atholl.

Athos Greek: an alternative name for Zeus, the ruler of the heavens.

Atiu Polynesian: the eldest.

Atlas Greek: a demigod who supported the sky on his shoulders.

Atley Old English: from the meadow.

Atonio Maori and Samoan form of Anthony.

Attila The warlike king of the Huns.

Atwater Old English: one who lives by the water.

Atwell Old English: a dweller by the spring.

Atworth Old English: from the farm.

Auberon Teutonic: noble.
Oberon.

Aubert See Albert.

Aubin See Alban.

Aubrey Teutonic: the golden-haired ruler of the elves.
Aubrie, Aubry.

Auburn Middle English: golden-brown or reddish-brown.

Auden An English surname, best known through the poet W H Auden.

Audric See Aldrich.

August A 'month name'. Also a form of Augustus.

Augustine Latin: belonging to Augustus. *See also* Austin.
Augusten, Augustijn (Dutch), Augustin, Austin, Awstin (Welsh).
Diminutive: Stijn (Dutch).

Augustus Latin: venerable, the exalted one. The name of the first great Roman emperor.
Agosto (Italian), Aguistin (Irish), Agustin (Spanish), August (German), Auguste (French).
Diminutives: Augie, Gus, Gussy.

Aurelius Latin: the golden one.
Aurel, Aurele (French), Aurelian, Aurelien, Aurelio (Italian), Auryn (Welsh).

Auska/Auskah/Auskar See Oscar.

Austell The name of a Cornish saint and a placename.

Austin A modern form of Augustine.
Austen, Austyn, Awstin (Welsh), Osten, Ostin, Ostyn.

Avalon A legendary island, believed to be the place where King Arthur is buried. Also a girl's name.
Avilion, Avilon.

Avan Hebrew: proud.

Avatar Sanskrit: an incarnation.
Avitar.

Avel Greek/Russian: breath.

Avenall Old French: a dweller in the oat field.
Avenel, Avenell.

Averell Old English: the slayer of the boar.
Averel, Averil, Averill, Everild.

Avery Old English: the ruler of the elves. Also a girl's name.
Averey, Averi, Averie.

Avi Hebrew: from Av, the fifth lunar month of the Hebrew calendar, corresponding to the zodiac sign of Leo.
Avie.

Avilion/Avilon See Avalon.

Aviv Hebrew: of the springtime.

Avner *See* Abner.

Avon The name of an English county, and rivers in England and New Zealand.
Afon, Aven, Avonn.

Avram/Avrom/Avron *See* Abraham.

Awstin Welsh form of Augustine and Austin.

Axel Teutonic from Hebrew: the father of peace. A form of Absalom.
Aksel (Norwegian), Axell, Axl, Axle.

Axton Old English: the stone of the sword-wielder.

Aydan/Ayden *See* Aidan.

Aydin Turkish: the enlightened one. Also a form of Aidan.

Ayer Old French: an heir.
Ayers, Ayre, Ayres, Ayrten, Ayrton.

Aylmer Old English: noble and famous.

Aylward Old English: an awe-inspiring guardian.

Aylwin *See* Alvin.

Ayton Middle English: the town on the Eye Water, a Scottish river.
Ayten.

Azar The angel of November.

Azariah Hebrew: he whom the Lord helps.
Azarias.

Azi Nigerian: a youth.

Azim Arabic: grand.

Aziz Arabic: the powerful one.
Azizah (Malaysian).

Azriel Hebrew: an angel of the Lord.

Azul Spanish: blue.

Azzan Hebrew: very strong.

B

Babar Turkish: a lion.

Bacchus Greek: the Roman god of wine.

Baden A modern name of uncertain meaning.
Badin, Badon, Badyn, Bayden, Baydin, Baydon, Baydyn.

Badge Middle English: an emblem or token.
Badg, Badj, Badje.

Bae Korean: inspiration.

Baez Welsh: a boar.

Bahadur A popular Malaysian name.

Bailey Old French: a bailiff or official. Also a modern girl's name.
Baileigh, Bailen, Bailley, Baillie, Bailly, Baily, Baylen, Bayley, Bayly.

Bailly The name of a crater on the moon. *See also* Bailey.
Bailley.

Baird Scottish Gaelic: a bard or minstrel.
Bairde, Bard, Barde.

Bakari Swahili: promising.

Balan One of the knights of King Arthur's legendary Round Table.

Baldric Teutonic: a bold or princely ruler.

Baldwin Teutonic: a brave friend or protector.
Baudouin (French).

Balfour Scottish Gaelic: from the village by the pasture.

Ballantyne Scottish Gaelic: possibly meaning a god of fire.

Ballantine, Ballentine, Ballentyne.

Ballard Teutonic: strong, bold.

Balthasar Greek: the Lord protects the king. One of the three wise men in the Bible.
Baldassare (Italian), Balthazar, Belshazzar (Hebrew).

Bamboo A subtropical plant.
Bambu.

Bancroft Old English: from the bean field.

Bandit A robber or outlaw.
Bandito (Italian).

Banjo A musical instrument.
Banjoe, Banjow, Banjowe.

Barak Hebrew: a flash of lightning.
Barack.

Barclay Old English: from the birch-tree wood or meadow.
Berkeley, Berkly.

Bard/Barde *See* Baird.

Barden Old English: from the valley of barley.
Bardon.

Barend Dutch: a strong bear.

Barley Middle English: a grain.
Barlee, Barleigh, Barli, Barlie, Barly.

Barlow Old English: from the barley hill.

Barnabas Hebrew: a son of consolation. A name from the Bible.
Barnaba, Barnabe, Barnabé (French), Barnaby, Barnebas.
Diminutives: Barney, Barnie, Barny.

Barnard *See* Bernard.

Barnet Old English: from the place cleared by burning.
Barnett.

Barney/Barnie/Barny Diminutives of Barnabas.

Barnum Old English: a stone house.

Baron Old French: a nobleman.
Barron.

Barrett Old French: possibly meaning a bonnet-maker.
Barat, Baret, Barett, Barrat, Barret.

Barrington Old English: the place of the warrior, or the warrior's followers.
Barington.
Diminutives: Barri, Barrie, Barry.

Barry Irish Gaelic: like a spear. Also a diminutive of several names.
Barrey, Barri, Barrie.
Diminutives: Baz, Bazza.

Bart A diminutive of Bartholomew and Barton.

Bartholomew Hebrew: a son of the furrows; a farmer. A biblical name.
Bartek (Polish), Bartolo (Italian), Bartolomeo (Italian).
Diminutives: Bart, Bartlett, Bartel, Bartle (Irish).

Barton Old English: from the barley fields.
Diminutive: Bart.

Bartram/Bartrand *See* Bertram.

Baruch Hebrew: blessed.

Barwick *See* Berwick.

Bashir Arabic: a good omen.

Basil Greek: royal, kingly. Also a 'herb name'. *See also* Vasily.
Basile (French), Basilio (Spanish), Bazel (Dutch), Vasily (Russian).
Diminutives: Bas, Baz.

Basim Arabic: the smiling one.

Bastian/Bastien *See* Sebastian.

Baudouin *See* Baldwin.

Baxter Old English: a baker.

Bay Vietnamese: born on a Saturday. Also a herb and a reddish-brown colour.

Bayard Old French: with reddish-brown hair.

Bayden/Baydin/Baydon/Baydyn *See* Baden.

Baylen/Bayley/Bayly *See* Bailey.

Baz *See* Barry and Basil.

Bazel *See* Basil.

Beade *See* Bede.

Beagan Irish Gaelic: the little one.

Beale Old French: the beautiful one. Beal.

Bear Middle English: an 'animal name'.

Bearnard Gaelic form of Bernard.

Beathan Scottish Gaelic form of Benjamin.

Beattie Irish Gaelic: the provider.

Beau French: handsome. *See also* Beaudel, Beaumont and Beauregard. Beauh, Bo, Boh, Bohe, Bow, Bowe.

Beaudel A modern form of Beau. Beaudell, Beaudelle.

Beaumont Old French: a beautiful hill or mountain. *Diminutives*: Beau, Bo.

Beauregard Old French: a beautiful view or expression. *Diminutives*: Beau, Bo.

Beavan/Beaven *See* Bevan.

Beaver Middle English: an 'animal name'. Bever.

Beavis *See* Bevis.

Becán Irish Gaelic: a little one.

Beck Old English: a brook or small stream. Becke, Bek, Bekk, Bekke.

Becket Old English: from the small stream. Beckett.

Beckham Old Norse: the stream by the meadow. The surname of a famous soccer player. Beckenham, Bekham.

Bede Old English: a prayer. Beade, Beda (Welsh).

Bedrich *See* Frederick.

Bek/Bekk/Bekke *See* Beck.

Bekham *See* Beckham.

Bela Hungarian: the white one.

Bellamy Old French: a handsome friend.

Belshazzar *See* Balthasar.

Ben Hebrew: the son of. Also a diminutive of names such as Benedict and Benjamin.

Benaud From French: after the legendary cricketer Richie Benaud.

Bendek/Bendick *See* Benedict.

Benedict Latin: blessed. Bendek (Hungarian), Bendick, Bendix, Benedetto (Italian), Benedick, Benedikt (Dutch, German), Benen (Irish), Benet, Benito (Spanish), Bennet, Benneit (Scottish Gaelic), Bennett, Benoit (French). *Diminutives*: Ben, Bendix, Benn, Bennie, Benny.

Benito *See* Benedict.

Benjamin Hebrew: a son of the south, or the son of the right hand. A brother of Joseph in the Bible. Beathan (Scottish Gaelic),

Beniamino (Italian), Benjamen, Benja, Benjah, Benjan, Benjen, Benjimen, Benjo, Binjamen, Binjamin, Binyamin (Jewish). *Diminutives*: Ben, Benji, Benjie, Benjy, Benn, Bennie, Benny, Peni (Polynesian, Tongan).

Benn/Bennet/Bennett/Bennie *See* Benedict and Benjamin.

Benoit French form of Benedict.

Benson Old English: the son of Benedict or Benjamin. Bensen, Bensyn.

Bentley Old English: from the bent-grass clearing or meadow.

Benton Old English: from the bent-grass farm.

Beppe Italian diminutive of Joseph.

Berg Teutonic: a mountain.

Bergen A Norwegian port.

Berger Teutonic: from the mountains.

Berkeley/Berkly *See* Barclay.

Bernard Teutonic: as brave as a bear. *See also* Björn. Barnard, Bearnard (Gaelic), Bernardo (Italian, Spanish), Bernhard (German), Burnard. *Diminutives*: Bern, Bernie, Berny.

Berrick *See* Berwick.

Bershawn Modern American: a form of Shawn. Bershaun, Bershaune, Bershawne.

Bert/Bertie Diminutives of Albert, Bertram, Herbert, Robert and other names. *See also* Burt.

Bertram Teutonic: a bright raven. Bartram, Bartrand, Bertran, Bertrand. *Diminutives*: Bert, Bertie.

Berwick Old English: from the barley farm. Barwick, Berrick.

Berwyn Welsh: fair-haired, or a bright friend. Also a girl's name. Berwin.

Bevan Welsh: from ap Evan, meaning the son of Evan. *See* John. Beavan, Beaven, Beven, Bevin.

Bever *See* Beaver.

Beverly Old English: from the stream of the beaver. More commonly a female name.

Bevin *See* Bevan.

Bevis French: after the city of Beauvais, meaning a beautiful outlook or view. Beavis, Bevys.

Bharat Sanskrit: being maintained. The Hindu god of fire.

Bhima Sanskrit: the mighty one.

Bill/Billy Diminutives of William.

Bing Old English: from the hollow. Also a diminutive of Bingham and Bingley. Byng.

Bingham Old English: from the homestead in the hollow. Byngham. *Diminutives*: Bing, Byng.

Bingley Old English: a clearing with a hollow. Binglee, Bingleigh. *Diminutive*: Bing.

Binh Vietnamese: the peaceful one. Bin.

Binjamen/Binjamin/Binyamin *See* Benjamin.

Birch Old English: a 'tree name'.

Björn Old Norse: brave, like a bear. *See also* Bernard.
Bjarne (Norwegian).

Blade Old English: glory, prosperity.
Blaid, Blaide, Blayd, Blayde.

Blaike *See* Blake.

Blaine Irish Gaelic: thin. Also a girl's name.
Blain, Blane, Blayne.

Blainey/Blainie *See* Blaney.

Blair Scottish Gaelic: from the plain.
Also a girl's name.
Blaire.

Blaise Latin: one who lisps or stammers. The name of a saint.
Blaize, Blaze.

Blake Old English: pale or fair-haired.
Blaike, Blayke.

Blakeley Old English: from the black meadow.

Blane *See* Blaine.

Blaney Irish Gaelic: the place of the creeks.
Blainey, Blainie, Blanee, Blanie.

Blaxland Old English: from the black land.

Blaxton Old English: a black stone.

Blayd/Blayde *See* Blade.

Blayke *See* Blake.

Blayne *See* Blaine.

Blaze Old English: a bright fire or flame. Also a form of Blaise.
Blaize, Blayz, Blayze, Blayzey.

Bledig Welsh: like a wolf.

Bligh *See* Blythe.

Blue Middle English from Old French: a modern 'colour name'.

Bleu (French), Blu.

Blythe Old English: cheerful, gentle.
Bligh, Blyth.

Bo Chinese: precious. Old Norse: a householder. *See also* Beau.
Boh, Bohe.

Boadey/Boadie *See* Bodie.

Boaz Hebrew: swift and strong. The husband of Ruth in the Bible.
Boas, Boaze.

Bob/Bobbie/Bobby *See* Robert.

Bodi Hungarian: God protects the king. *See also* Bodie.
Bodhi.

Bodie A modern name, sometimes given to girls.
Boadey, Boadi, Boadie, Boady, Bode, Boden, Bodey, Bodhi, Bodi, Bowdey, Bowdi, Bowdie.

Bodil Scandinavian: the commander.

Bodo Teutonic: a leader.

Bogart Old French/Teutonic: a strong bow.

Bogdan Slavic: a gift from God.
Bohdan.

Boh/Bohe *See* Bo and Beau.

Bolan Old English: the place of tree trunks or planks.
Bolam.

Bolt Middle English: to run or dash, or part of a lock.
Bolte.

Bolton Old English: of the manor farm.

Bon French: good. Also a diminutive of names beginning with Bon.
Bonn.

Bonamy French: a good friend.

Bonar Old French: kind and gentle.

Bond Old English/Old Norse: a peasant farmer.

Bonner Old French: gracious, gentle. Bonnar.

Booth Old Norse: a hut or shelter. Boothe.

Borden Old English: from the valley of the boar.

Borg Scandinavian: from the castle.

Boris Russian/Slavic: a warrior.

Bosley Old English: a grove of trees.

Boston Old English: possibly meaning the stone of Botulf. The name of a city in the USA. Bosten, Bostyn.

Bosworth Old English: from the boar enclosure.

Boulder Middle English: a large rock.

Bourke See Burke.

Bow Middle English: a device to shoot arrows. Also a form of Beau. Bowe.

Bowdey/Bowdi/Bowdie See Bodie.

Bowen Welsh: the son of Owen.

Bowie Scottish Gaelic: golden-haired.

Boyce Old French: from the wood or forest.

Boyd Scottish Gaelic: yellow-haired. Boyde.

Bracken Middle English: a type of fern. Brackin, Brackyn, Braken, Brakin, Brakyn.

Brad A diminutive of Bradley and similar names.

Braden Old English: from the wide valley. Bradan, Bradon, Braedan, Braeden, Braedon, Braedyn, Braidan, Braiden, Braidyn, Braydan, Brayden, Braydon.

Bradford Old English: from the broad ford.

Bradley Old English: from the broad meadow. Bradlee, Bradleigh, Bradly. *Diminutive*: Brad.

Bradwell Old English: from the broad stream.

Bradwen English/Welsh: broad and fair. Bradwenn, Bradwyn, Bradwynn.

Brady Irish Gaelic. From an old surname. Also a modern girl's name. Bradee, Bradey, Bradie.

Brae Cornish/Gaelic: a hill. Bray, Braye, Brea.

Braidan/Braiden/Braidyn See Braden.

Braith Middle English: the broad one. Braithe, Brayth, Braythe.

Braken/Brakin/Brakyn See Bracken.

Braksten/Brakston/Brakstyn See Braxton.

Bram See Abraham.

Bramley Old English: from the field overgrown with broom. Bramlee, Bramleigh, Bramlie, Bramly.

Bran Celtic: a raven. Brann.

Branagh Irish Gaelic: a Welshman. Brana, Branah, Branna, Brannah, Brannagh.

Brandan See Brandon.

Brander Old Norse: a fiery sword.

Brando After the legendary actor

CELEBRITIES' KIDS' NAMES – BOYS

Celebrities' kids sometimes have very strange names. It all started back in the 1960s and 1970s – consider David Bowie's son Zowie, Mia Farrow's boy Satchel and Frank Zappa's Dweezil. More recent unusual names include Ever, Moroccan and Sparrow, and Angelina Jolie and Brad Pitt's Pax Thien. Here are many more examples of boys' names (*see* page 147 for girls' names).

Aleph	Natalie Portman	Levon Green	Uma Thurman
Amadeus	Boris Becker	Liam	Tori Spelling
Arlo	Toni Collette	Louis Bardo	Sandra Bullock
Atlas	Anne Heche	Luca Cruz	Hilary Duff
Aurelius	Elle MacPherson	Maddox	Angeline Jolie
Axel	Will Ferrell	Mason Dash	Kourtney Kardashian
Bear Blu	Alicia Silverstone	Max	Christina Aguilera
Beckett	Stella McCartney	Milan	Shakira
Bingham	Kate Hudson	Miller	Stella McCartney
Bronx Mowgli	Ashlee Simpson	Milo	Liv Tyler
Brooklyn	David Beckham	Moroccan	Mariah Carey
Buddy Bear	Jamie Oliver	Moses	Gwyneth Paltrow
Charles	Jodie Foster	Nayib	Gloria Estefan
Chester	Tom Hanks	Nelson	Celine Dion
Christian	Princess Mary	Otis	Tobey Maguire
Damian	Liz Hurley	Preston	Brett Lee
Dashiell	Cate Blanchett	Quinlin	Ben Stiller
Enzo	Patricia Arquette	Rafferty	Jude Law
Ever Imre	Alanis Morrisette	Rocco	Madonna
Exton Elias	Robert Downey Jr	Ryder	Kate Hudson
Flynn	Miranda Kerr	Seven Sirius	Erykah Badu
Holden	Mira Sorvino	Sindri Eldon	Björk
Hopper	Sean Penn	Sparrow	Nicole Richie
Jackson	Charlize Theron	Tennessee	Reese Witherspoon
Jaden	Andre Agassi	Tennyson	Russell Crowe
Jagger	Lindsay Davenport	Trey	Will Smith
Johan	Heidi Klum	Truman	Tom Hanks
Kingston	Gwen Stefani	Weston	Nicholas Cage
Knox Léon	Angelina Jolie	Winston	Billie Piper
Lennon	Liam Gallagher	Zachary	Elton John
Leo	Penelope Cruz	Zuma	Gwen Stefani

Marlon Brando.
Brandoe, Brandow, Brandowe.

Brandon Old English: from the gorse-covered hill.
Brandan, Brandyn, Branton.

Brannan From an Irish Gaelic surname, possibly Branagh.
Brannen, Brannon.

Braxton A modern name of uncertain meaning.
Braksten, Brakston, Brakstyn, Braxten, Braxtyn.

Bray/Braye *See* Brae.

Braydan/Brayden *See* Braden.

Brayson The son of Bray.
Braysen.

Brayth/Braythe *See* Braith.

Brazil A South American country.
Brasil.

Brea *See* Brae.

Breck Manx Gaelic: dappled or speckled.
Brek.

Brecon Welsh: the name of a group of mountains.
Breckon, Brekon.

Breeze From Spanish: a light wind; someone who is carefree.
Breese, Breez.

Brendan Irish Gaelic: a prince.
Breandan (Irish), Brenden, Brendin, Brendon, Brennan.

Brendle A modern form of Brent.
Brendall, Brendel, Brendell.

Brenin Welsh: a king.
Brennin, Brennon, Brenon.

Brenleigh/Brenley/Brenly *See* Brinley.

Brennan *See* Brendan.

Brent Celtic/Old English: from the steep hill.
Brenton.

Breok Cornish/Welsh: the name of an early saint.
Bryok.

Breton Old English: the place of the Briton. Also a native of Brittany, a region of France.
Bretton.

Brett Old English: a Breton, a native of Brittany.
Bret.

Brewster Middle English: a brewer.

Brian Celtic: noble and virtuous. A famous 10th-century Irish king.
Briand, Briant, Brien, Bryan, Bryant.

Brice Celtic: the speckled, or freckled, one. Also a girl's name.
Bryce, Brychan (Welsh) Bryz, Bryze.

Briden/Bridon/Bridyn *See* Bryden.

Brien *See* Brian.

Brigham Old English: from the homestead by the bridge.

Brinley Old Norse: burning wood.
Brenleigh, Brenley, Brenly, Brinleigh, Brinly.

Brisen/Brison/Brisyn *See* Bryson.

Bristol Old English: the site of a fort. A British city.
Bristole, Bristoll.

Brock Old English: a badger.
Broc, Brok.

Broderick Welsh: the son of Roderick.
Broderic.

Brodie Irish Gaelic: a ditch. Also a girl's name.
Brodey, Brody.

Brogan Irish Gaelic: a surname of

uncertain meaning.
Brogain, Brogann.

Bromley Old English: from the place where broom grows.

Bron A diminutive of names such as Bronson and Bronx.

Brone Celtic: one who is sorrowful.

Bronson Old English: son of the brown-haired one.
Bronsen, Bronsyn.

Bronx A region of New York City.
Bronks.

Brook Old English: at the brook or stream. Also a girl's name.
Brooke, Brooks.

Brooklyn A New York suburb; the name of one of David Beckham's sons.
Brooklin.

Brosnan Possibly Irish Gaelic. The name of a well-known actor (Pierce Brosnan).
Brosnahan, Brosnen.

Broughton Old English: from the town on a hill.

Bruce Old French: from a surname and possibly a French placename.
Diminutives: Brucie, Brucey.

Bruno Teutonic: brown.
Bruin (Dutch), Brun, Brunet (French), Brunon (Polish).

Bruton Old English: from a place in Somerset.

Bryan/Bryant *See* Brian.

Bryce/Brychan *See* Brice.

Bryden A popular modern name, possibly from an English placename.
Bridan, Briden, Bridon, Bridyn, Brydan, Bryden, Brydon, Brydyn.

Brylie *See* GIRLS.

Bryn Welsh: a hill. Also a modern girl's name.
Brynn.

Brynmor Welsh: a large hill.

Bryok *See* Breok.

Bryson Middle English: the son of Brice or Bryce.
Brisen, Brison, Brisyn, Bryscen, Bryscon, Brysen, Brysyn.

Bryz/Bryze *See* Brice.

Buchan Scottish Gaelic: a placename.

Buchanan Scottish Gaelic: possibly meaning the canon's house.

Buck Old English: a male deer.

Buckley Old English: from the meadow of the buck deer.

Bud American: originally a short form of buddy (friend).
Budd, Buddy.

Buddha Sanskrit: one who is wise or enlightened.
Buddhika.

Budi Indonesian: the wise one.

Budock Cornish: a placename and the name of a saint.
Budoc.

Burchard Teutonic: a strong protector.
Burgrard, Burkhard (German), Burkhart.

Burdon Old English: a dweller at the hill fort.
Burden.

Burgess Old French from Teutonic: the citizen of a town.

Burke Old English: from the fort or hill.
Bourke.

Burkhard/Burkhart *See* Burchard.

Burl Old English: a cup bearer or wine server.

Burley Old English: from the fort or castle meadow.
Burleigh.

Burnaby Old Norse: the warrior's estate.

Burnard *See* Bernard.

Burnell Old French: the little brown-haired one.

Burnet Old French: the brown one. Also a 'plant name'.
Burnett.

Burt A short form of Burton. Also a variation of Bert.

Burton Old English: from the fortified farm or town.
Burtan, Burten.
Diminutive: Burt.

Busby Old Norse: from the farm in the thicket.
Buzby.

Buster Generally a nickname.

Butler Old French: the head servant.

Button Old French: a button-maker.
Butten.

Buzz Generally an American nickname.
Buz, Buzze.

Byford Old English: a dweller by the ford.

Byng/Byngham *See* Bing and Bingham.

Byrne Irish: a descendant of the bear or raven.
Byrn.

Byron Old English: from the byres or cattle sheds. Originally a surname.
Byram, Byran, Byrom.

C

Cadan An old Cornish and Welsh name.
Cadann.

Cadby Old Norse: the warrior's settlement.

Cade A modern name, possibly from Cadell or Caden.
Caed, Caede, Caid, Caide, Cayd, Cayde, Kade, Kaid, Kaide, Kayd, Kayde.

Cadell Welsh: the battle spirit.
Cadel.

Caden A popular modern name of uncertain origin.
Caeden, Caiden, Caidyn, Cayden, Caydyn, Kaden, Kaeden, Kaiden, Kaidyn, Kayden, Kaydyn.

Caderyn Welsh: a king of battle.

Cadman Celtic: a man of battle.

Cadmus Greek: a man from the east. A mythological figure.

Cadog Welsh: warlike. A saint's name.
Cadoc, Cadok.

Cadogan Old Welsh: honour in battle.

Caed/Caeden *See* Cade and Caden.

Caedmon Celtic: a wise warrior. The first English poet.

Caelan/Caelen/Caelyn *See* Kalan.

Caelum Latin: a chisel; the name of a southern constellation. *See also* Callum.
Caelem, Caellum.

Caerleon *See* Carlyon.

Caernarfon/Caernarvon *See*

Carnarvon.

Caerwyn Welsh: a holy fort.

Caesar Latin: a famous Roman emperor.
Césaire (French), César (French), Cesare (Italian), Kesar (Russian).

Cahil Turkish: young and inexperienced.

Cahn *See* Khan.

Cai Welsh form of Kay.

Caid/Caide *See* Cade.

Caiden/Caidyn *See* Caden.

Cailean *See* Colin.

Cain Hebrew: possessed. In the Bible, the son of Adam and Eve who murdered his brother Abel. Old French: a battlefield. *See also* Cane. Caine.

Cairo From Arabic: the capital of Egypt.

Cal *See* Calvert and Calvin.

Calan/Calen/Calyn *See* Callan and Kalan.

Calder Old English: from the rocky river.

Cale Probably derived from Caley, an Irish Gaelic name meaning slender. Cail, Caile.

Caleb Hebrew: the devoted one. A biblical name.
Caled, Cayleb, Kaleb, Kayleb.

Calem *See* Callum.

Caley Irish Gaelic: slender. Also a girl's name. *See also* Calum. Calie, Kaley, Kalie.

Callaghan Irish Gaelic: the warlike one. *See also* Callan.
Callahan, Kallaghan, Kallahan.

Callan A popular modern name, probably from Callaghan.
Calan, Callen, Callin, Callun, Callyn, Kallan, Kallen, Kallin, Kallun, Kallyn.

Callum Scottish Gaelic form of Columba. *See also* Coleman.
Caelem, Caelum, Caellum, Calem, Callem, Calum.
Diminutives: Caley, Cally.

Calvert Old English: a calf herder. Calverd.
Diminutive: Cal.

Calvin Latin: the little bald one.
Calvino (Italian, Spanish), Calvyn, Kalvin, Kalvyn.
Diminutives: Cal, Kal.

Cam/Camm Diminutives of Cameron, Campbell and similar names.

Cambell *See* Campbell.

Camden Gaelic: from the winding valley.

Cameron Scottish Gaelic: a crooked nose; from a Scottish surname. Also a modern girl's name.
Cameren, Camren, Camron, Camryn, Kameren, Kameron, Kamren, Kamron, Kamryn.
Diminutives: Cam, Camm, Kam.

Camille French: from a Roman family name. The masculine form of Camilla.
Camillo (Italian), Camillus, Kamil (Czech).

Campbell Scottish Gaelic: a crooked mouth. One of the great Scottish Highland clans.
Cambell.
Diminutives: Cam, Camm.

Camren/Camron/Camryn *See* Cameron.

Canaan Hebrew: a biblical region.
Canan, Canen, Kanaan, Kanan,
Kanen.

Cane Manx Gaelic: an old surname.
Cain, Caine.

Canice Irish Gaelic: handsome. The
name of several early saints.

Cannon From French: a large gun.
Canon.

Canute *See* Knut.

Caradoc Celtic/Welsh: beloved or
amiable.
Caradog.

Carden Irish Gaelic: from the black
fortress.
Cardin.

Cardew Cornish/Welsh: the black
fort.
Carew.

Carel *See* Charles.

Carey Celtic: from the river. Cornish:
the loved one. Irish: the name of a
castle.
Carie, Cary.

Carl *See* Charles.

Carleon *See* Carlyon.

Carlin Cornish: from the fort by
the pool. Irish Gaelic: the little
champion.
Carling, Carlyn.

Carlisle Old English: the place of the
fort. A town in north-west England.
Carlile, Carlyle.

Carlo/Carlos *See* Charles.

Carlton Old English: from the
settlement of the free peasants.
Carleton, Charleton, Charlton.

Carlyle *See* Carlisle.

Carlyon Cornish: from the slate
earthworks.
Caerleon, Carleon.

Carmelo Hebrew: from the garden.
After Mount Carmel in the Holy
Land.
Carmello, Carmine (Italian).

Carmichael From the fort of Michael.
Karmichael.

Carmine *See* Carmelo.

Carnaby An English placename.
Carnabee, Carnabie.

Carnarvon From Celtic: a town in
Wales.
Caernarfon (Welsh), Caernarvon
(Welsh).

Carne Cornish: a pile of rocks.
Carn.

Carnelian A 'gemstone name'.
Cornelian.

Carney Celtic: a warrior.
Carnie, Carny.

Carr Old Norse: from the marshland.
See also Carson.

Carrick Irish Gaelic: from the rocky
cliff or cape.

Carroll Irish Gaelic: a fierce warrior.
Caryl.

Carson Old English: the son of the
marsh dweller. *See also* Carr.
Carsen, Carrsen, Carrson.

Carsten *See* Christian.

Carter Old English: a cart driver or
maker.

Carvell Old French: the marshy
estate, or the estate of the spearman.
Carvel (Manx Gaelic).

Carver Old English: a carver or

sculptor.

Carwyn Welsh: blessed love.

Cary *See* Carey.

Caryl *See* Carroll.

Casey Irish Gaelic: the vigilant one.
Casee, Casie, Kacey, Kacie, Kasey,
Kaycee, Kaycie.

Cash A predominantly Irish surname.
Cashe, Cassh, Casshe.

Cashel Irish: a bulwark; also a
placename.

Casimir Old Slavic: the great
destroyer. The name of several Polish
kings and a saint.
Casimiro (Spanish), Kasimir
(German), Kazimir (Czech).

Caspar Persian: the treasurer. One
of the three wise men in the New
Testament. *See also* Gaspar and
Jasper.
Caspa, Caspah, Casper, Kaspa,
Kaspah, Kaspar (German), Kasper
(Polish).
Diminutive: Cass.

Cassh/Casshe *See* Cash.

Cassian *See* Cassius.

Cassidy Irish Gaelic: the clever or
ingenious one.
Kassidy.

Cassius Latin: hollow, empty.
Cassian.

Cathal Irish Gaelic: a battle ruler.
Catheld, Kathel.

Cathan Irish Gaelic: of the battle. *See
also* Kane.

Cathmor Irish Gaelic: a great warrior.

Cato Latin: the wise one.
Caton (French).

Cavan Irish Gaelic: the handsome

one. An Irish county.
Kavan.

Caxton After the 15th-century writer
and printer William Caxton.
Caxten, Caxtin, Caxtyn.

Cayd/Cayde *See* Cade.

Cayden/Caydyn *See* Caden.

Cayleb *See* Caleb.

Cecil Latin: the blind one, or the
sixth.
Cecilio, Cecilius, Cecyl.
Diminutives: Cec, Cece.

Cedar Middle English: a coniferous
tree.
Cedarr, Ceder, Cederr.

Cedric Probably invented in the
early 1800s by Sir Walter Scott for a
character in *Ivanhoe*.

Celt *See* Kelt.

Celtee/Celtey/Celtie/Celty *See*
Keltie.

Celten/Celton *See* Kelton.

Cemal *See* Kamal.

Census From Latin: an official count
and survey of citizens or inhabitants.
Censuss.

César/Cesare *See* Caesar.

Chace *See* Chase.

Chad Old English: a 7th-century
saint. Also a diminutive of
Chadwick, and the name of an
African country.
Chadd.

Chadwick Old English: the town of
the warrior.
Diminutives: Chad, Chadd.

Chahaya Indonesian: light.

Chaim *See* Hyam.

Challis Old French: a ladder or stairs.

Chamba Sherpa/Tibetan: the loved one.

Chan A Chinese clan name.

Chance/Chancey *See* Chauncey.

Chand Sanskrit: the moon.

Chandan Sanskrit: of the sandalwood tree.

Chander *See* Chandra.

Chandler Old French: the candle-maker.

Chandra Sanskrit: a shining moon.
Chander, Chandran.

Chaney Old French: an oak grove.
Cheney, Cheyney.

Chang Chinese: free.

Channing Old French: a canon.

Chaplin Middle English: a priest or chaplain.
Chaplain, Chapling.

Chapman Old English: a merchant or trader.

Charles Teutonic: a free man. A popular name since the time of the Holy Roman Emperor Charlemagne (AD 742–814), and the name of many kings.
Carel (Dutch), Carl (German), Carlo (Italian), Carlos (Portuguese, Spanish), Charleston, Hare (Maori), Karel (Czech, Dutch), Karl (German, Scandinavian), Karol (Polish), Károly (Hungarian), Siarl (Welsh), Tiare (Maori).
Diminutives: Charlee, Charley, Charli, Charlie, Chas, Chaz, Chico, Chuck, Chuckie.

Charleton/Charlton *See* Carlton.

Charon Greek: in mythology, the

ferryman of the River Styx in the Underworld. Also a satellite of the planet Pluto.

Chas *See* Charles.

Chase Old French: the hunter.
Chace, Chayce, Chayse.

Chau Vietnamese: a pearl.

Chaucer Old French: a bootmaker.

Chauncey Old French: a church official or chancellor.
Chance, Chancey, Chauncy.

Chaz A diminutive of Charles.

Che Spanish diminutive of Joseph.
Chay.

Cheiron *See* Chiron.

Chen Chinese: great or vast.

Cheney *See* Chaney.

Cherokee Native American: the name of a tribe.

Chester Latin: a Roman site or camp, the name of an English city.
Cheston.
Diminutive: Chet.

Chet Thai: a brother. Also a diminutive of Chester and Chetwin.

Chetwin Old English: from the cottage on the winding path.
Chetwyn.
Diminutive: Chet.

Cheung Chinese: good luck.

Chevy French: from chevalier, meaning a knight.
Chevey, Chevi, Chevie.

Chewang Sherpa/Tibetan: life and power.

Cheyenne Native American: a tribe and a city in the USA.

Cheyney *See* Chaney.

Chico *See* Charles and Francis.

Chiko Japanese: like an arrow.

Chile A 'country name'.

Chilli From a Native American word, meaning spicy.
Chili, Chilie, Chillie.

Chilton Old English: from the children's farm.

Chin Korean: the precious one.

Chino Spanish: the name of a fabric.

Chiron Greek: a wise teacher. A symbol of the zodiac sign Sagittarius.
Cheiron, Kiron, Kyron.

Chivan A Cambodian name of uncertain meaning.

Chivas Scottish Gaelic: a narrow place. The name of a famous whisky.
Schivas.

Chrétien *See* Christian.

Chris A diminutive of names such as Christian and Christopher.

Christian Latin: a follower of Christ; a Christian. *See also* Christopher.
Carsten (German), Chrétien (French), Christiaan, Christien, Christen, Christer (Danish, Swedish), Chrystopher, Cristan, Cristen, Cristian, Cristiano (Italian), Karsten (German), Kiritowha (Maori), Kristen (Danish), Kristian (Swedish), Kristinn (Icelandic).
Diminutives: Chris, Christie, Christy, Chrys, Cris, Kit, Kris.

Christie/Christy Irish and Scottish diminutives of Christian and Christopher.

Christmas Old English: born at Christmas.

Christopher Greek: bearing Christ. The patron saint of travellers. *See also* Christian.
Christof, Christoff, Christoffe, Christoffel, Christoph (German), Christophe (French), Christos (Greek), Cristóbal (Spanish), Cristof, Cristoff, Cristoffe, Cristoforo (Italian), Cristopher, Kester (Scottish), Kristof (Slavic), Kristoff, Kristoffer (Scandinavian), Krystof (Czech).
Diminutives: Chris, Christie, Christy, Cris, Cristo (Spanish), Kit, Kitto (Cornish), Kittow (Cornish), Kris, Kristo (Finnish), Krys, Risto (Finnish), Topher.

Christos Greek form of Christopher.

Chrys/Chrystopher *See* Christopher.

Chrysander Greek: a golden man.

Chuck/Chuckie *See* Charles.

Chung Chinese: the wise one.

Chungda Sherpa/Tibetan: the youngest.

Churchill Old English: from the church on the hill.

Cian *See* Kean.

Ciarán *See* Kieran.

Cicero Latin: a famous Roman statesman and orator.
Ciceron.

Ciprian/Cipriano/Ciprien *See* Cyprian.

Ciro *See* Cyrus.

Cisco Spanish diminutive of Francisco.
Cisko.

Clae/Claeton *See* Clayton.

Clancy Irish Gaelic: a red or ruddy warrior.

Clancee, Clancey, Clanci, Clancie.

Clarence Latin: the illustrious one.
Diminutive: Clarrie.

Clarey *See* GIRLS.

Clark Old French: a cleric or scholar.
See also Cleary.
Clarke.

Clarrie *See* Clarence.

Claude Latin: the lame one.
Claud, Claudio (Italian, Spanish),
Claudius (German), Klaud.

Claus *See* Nicholas.

Clay Old English: from the clay. Also
a diminutive of Clayton.
Claye.

Clayton Old English: from the
settlement in the clay.
Claeten, Claeton, Clayten, Klaeten,
Klaeton, Klayten, Klayton.
Diminutives: Clae, Clay, Klae, Klay.

Cleary Irish Gaelic: a clerk or scholar.
See also Clark.
Clery.

Cleave Middle English: to cut or split
apart.
Cleaver, Cleve, Kleave, Kleaver,
Kleve.

Cleavon American: a contemporary
name.
Clevon, Kleavon, Klevon.

Cledwyn Welsh: rough but blessed.

Clein *See* Klein.

Clement Latin: merciful, mild.
Clemence, Clément (French),
Clemens, Clements, Clemon,
Klemens (German), Kliment
(Russian).
Diminutives: Clem, Clemmie.

Cleon Greek: the famous one.

Kleon.

Clery *See* Cleary.

Cleve *See* Cleave, Cleveland and
Clive.

Cleveland Old English: from the
hilly place, or the place of cliffs. An
English and US placename.
Diminutive: Cleve.

Cliff A diminutive of Clifford and
Clifton.
Cliffe, Clift.

Clifford Old English: from the ford
by the cliff or slope.
Cliff, Cliffe.

Clifton Old English: from the
settlement on the cliff.
Cliff, Cliffe.

Cline *See* Klein.

Clinton Old English: from the place
on the headland.
Diminutive: Clint.

Clive Old English: from the cliff.
Cleve, Clyve.

Clooney Irish Gaelic: from the
meadow.
Cloony, Cluney, Cluny.

Clovis Teutonic: a famous warrior.

Clunes Scottish Gaelic: a resting
place, or meadow.
Clunies.

Cluney/Cluny *See* Clooney.

Clyde Scottish: the name of a river.

Clyve *See* Clive.

Coan/Coen *See* Cohen.

Cobden Old English: from the hill
with a knob.

Cobee/Cobey/Cobie/Coby *See* Kobe.

Cody Old English: a pillow or

cushion. Also a girl's name.
Codey, Codi, Kodi, Kodie, Kody.

Cohen Hebrew: a priest.
Coan, Coen, Cohan, Cohn, Koen, Kohan, Kohen.

Colan *See* Colin.

Colbert Teutonic: a bright seafarer.

Colby Old Norse: from the dark country.
Coleby.

Cole Old English/Teutonic: dark and swarthy. Also a diminutive of Nicholas.
Kole.

Coleman Latin: like a dove. Teutonic: dark. *See also* Callum and Columba.
Collman, Colman, Colomen (Welsh).

Colin Greek: the victory of the people. Originally a diminutive of Nicholas.
Cailean (Scottish Gaelic), Colan, Collin.

Collen Welsh: a hazel tree.

Collin *See* Colin.

Colm *See* Columba.

Colman *See* Coleman.

Colomen Welsh form of Coleman and Columba.

Colt Old English: a young horse.
Colte, Kolt, Kolte.

Colton Old English: from the dark town.

Columba Latin: dove-like. A 6th-century Irish saint and also a southern constellation. *See also* Callum and Coleman.
Colm (Irish Gaelic), Colomen (Welsh), Colum (Irish Gaelic), Columb.

Coman Arabic: noble.

Compton Old English: from the farm in the valley.

Con A diminutive of names such as Connor and Conrad.

Conall Celtic: as strong as a wolf.
Conal, Connall, Connell.

Conan Irish Gaelic: wise and intelligent. The name of a saint.
Conant, Connan, Conyn (Welsh), Cynan, Konan, Kynan.

Condor Spanish: a bird of the Americas.

Conlan Irish Gaelic: the hero.
Conlin, Conlon.

Conn Irish Gaelic: a chief. Also a diminutive of Connor.

Connall/Connell *See* Conall.

Connaught Irish Gaelic: brave and wise.
Connacht.

Connery Irish Gaelic: a surname of uncertain meaning.

Connolly Irish Gaelic: brave or wise.
Conolly.

Connor Irish Gaelic: a strong will.
Connah, Connaugh, Conner, Conor.
Diminutives: Con, Conn.

Conrad Teutonic: a bold counsellor.
Conrade (French), Corrado (Italian), Konrad (German, Polish).
Diminutives: Con, Curt, Kurt (German).

Conroy Irish Gaelic: wise.

Constantine Latin: steadfast.
Constant, Constantin, Constantino (Spanish), Costanzo (Italian), Konstantin (German, Russian, Scandinavian), Konstantyn (Polish),

Kostas (Greek).
Diminutives: Con, Kostya (Russian).

Conway Irish: a yellow hound.
Welsh: holy water.
Conwy.

Conyn Welsh form of Conan.

Cooper Middle English: a barrel or tub maker.
Coopa, Coopah, Kooper, Kupa, Kupah.

Copeland Old English: from the bought land.
Copland, Coupland.

Copper Old English: a reddish-brown metal.
Copor (Welsh).

Corbett Old French: a raven.
Corbet, Corbin.

Cordell Old French: a rope-maker.
Cordel.

Corentyn The name of a Breton saint.

Corey Celtic/Gaelic: dweller in the hollow. Also a girl's name.
Coree, Cori, Corie, Cory, Koree, Korey, Kory.

Corin Cornish: from the corner.
Latin: a Roman deity; possibly meaning a spear.
Coren, Coryn, Quirino (Italian).

Corley Old English: from the wood of the herons.
Corleigh.

Cormac Irish Gaelic: the lad of the chariot.
Cormack, Cormag (Scottish Gaelic), Cormick.

Cornelian *See* Carnelian.

Cornelius Latin: a horn.

Corneille (French), Cornel (Romanian), Cornelis (Dutch), Cornell, Cornelle, Kornel (Czech, Polish).
Diminutives: Kees (Dutch), Niels.

Corrado *See* Conrad.

Corrigan Irish Gaelic: a little spear, or a spear carrier.
Corigan, Corigen, Corrigen.

Cortez Spanish: the conqueror of Mexico.
Cortes.

Corwin Old French: a friend of the heart.
Corwen, Corwyn.

Cory *See* Corey.

Corydon Greek: a lark.

Coryn *See* Corin.

Cosmo Greek: perfect order and harmony, as in the cosmos.
Cosimo (Italian), Cosmos, Kosmo, Kosmos.

Costanzo Italian form of Constantine.

Costello An Irish surname with Norman (French) origins.
Costelloe.

Cotton Middle English: a type of fabric. Also a girl's name.
Coton.

Coupland *See* Copeland.

Court Old French: a manor or castle.
Courte.

Courtland Old English: from the court land.

Courtney Old French: the short-nosed one, or from a placename. Also a modern girl's name.
Courtenay, Courtnay.

Craig Scottish Gaelic: a rock or crag.
Craige, Craigh, Craigie.

Crandon Old English: from the hill of the cranes.

Cranley Old English: from the meadow of the cranes.

Cranog Welsh: a heron.

Crantock Cornish: a placename and the name of a saint.
Carantoc, Crantoc.

Crawford Old English: from the ford with the crows.

Creed Middle English from Latin: one who believes.
Crede, Creedan, Creeden.

Crepin/Crespin *See* Crispin.

Crest Middle English: the top of something, or a heraldic device.
Creste, Krest, Kreste.

Crevan Irish Gaelic: a fox.

Crewe Old English: stepping stones or a ford. An English placename.
Crew, Crue.

Cris/Cristen/Cristian/Cristiano *See* Christian and Christopher.

Crisiant Welsh: a crystal.

Crispin Latin: the curly-haired one. St Crispin was a 3rd-century martyr.
Crepin, Crespin, Crispen, Crispian, Crispus, Krispen, Krispin.

**Cristo/Cristoff/Cristoforo/
Cristopher** *See* Christopher.

Cromwell Old English: from the winding stream.

Cronan Irish Gaelic: swarthy.

Crosby Old Norse: from the village with the cross.
Crosbey, Crosbie.

Cruise A modern name, probably inspired by the actor Tom Cruise.
Cruis, Cruiz, Cruize, Cruz, Cruze, Kruis, Kruise, Kruiz, Kruize, Kruze.

Cruz Spanish: a cross (as in the crucifixion). *See also* Cruise.

Cuba A Caribbean country.

Cubert Cornish: a Celtic saint and a placename.

Cullen Old French: from the colony.
Cullan, Cullin.

Culley Gaelic: from the forest. Also a girl's name.
Cullee, Culli, Cullie, Cully.

Cupid Latin: desire, passion. The Roman god of love, the son of Venus.

Curio Something that is of a rare or curious nature.

Curnow *See* Kernow.

Curran Irish Gaelic: an old family name.
Curren.

Curt A diminutive of Conrad and Curtis.

Curtis Old French: the courteous one.
Curtiss, Kurtis, Kurtiss.
Diminutives: Curt, Kurt.

Curtleigh A combination of Curt and Leigh (a meadow or clearing).
Curtlee, Curtlie, Curtly, Kurtlee, Kurtleigh, Kurtlie, Kurtly.

Cuthbert Old English: famous and bright.

Cy A diminutive of names such as Cyprian and Cyrus.
Cye.

Cynan *See* Conan.

Cynfor Welsh: a great chief.

Cynric Old English: of kingly lineage.

Cypress From Latin: an evergreen tree.

Cyprian Latin: a man from the island of Cyprus.
Ciprian, Cipriano, Ciprien, Cyprien (French), Sibran (Breton).
Diminutive: Cy.

Cyrano Greek: a man from Cyrene, an ancient Greek colony in North Africa.

Cyril Greek: lordly. The name of several early saints.
Cyrill, Cyrille (French), Kirill (Russian).

Cyro *See* Cyrus.

Cyrus Persian: the name of the founder of the Persian empire.
Ciro (Italian), Cyro, Syrus.
Diminutive: Cy.

D

Daan/Daaniel *See* Daniel.

Dabert French: bright action.

Dacey Gaelic: the southerner.
Dacie, Dacy.

Dade A modern, probably made-up, name.
Daed, Daede, Daid, Daide.

Daemon *See* Damon.

Daen/Daene *See* Dane and Dean.

Dafad Welsh: a sheep or ram.

Dafydd Welsh form of David. *See also* Dewi.

Dag Old Norse: the day.

Dagan Hebrew: grain, or the earth.
Dagon.

Dai Welsh: a diminutive of David and Dewi.

Daibhidh Irish and Scottish form of David.

Dail/Daile *See* Dale.

Daimon *See* Damon.

Dain/Daine *See* Dane and Dean.

Dakota Native American: a friend; the name of two states of the USA.
Dakotah.

Dalbert Old English: from the shining valley.

Dale Old English/Teutonic: a valley dweller. Also a girl's name.
Dail, Daile.

Daley Irish Gaelic: a counsellor.
Daly.

Dallas Celtic: skilled, or from the field of water. A city in Texas.
Dallis.

Dallen A modern name, possibly a variation of Allen (*see* Alan).
Dallan, Dallin, Dallyn.

Dalton Old English: from the farm in the valley.

Dalziel Scottish Gaelic: from the little field.

Damian/Damien *See* Damon.

Damodar Sanskrit: tied with a rope around the belly.

Damon Greek: tame, domesticated; or a true friend.
Daemon, Daimon, Daman, Damen, Damian, Damiano (Italian), Damien, Damion, Damyon, Dayman, Daymon, Demian, Demyan (Russian), Dyfan (Welsh).

Dan *See* Daniel.

Dana Old English: from Denmark. *See also* Dane.

Danbey/Danby *See* Denby.

Dane A man from Denmark. *See also* Dean.
Daen, Daene, Dain, Daine, Dayn, Dayne.

Daneel/Danell *See* Daniel.

Danek *See* Daniel.

Danger Middle English: risk or peril.

Dani/Danial *See* Daniel.

Daniel Hebrew: God is my judge. An Old Testament prophet.
Daaniel, Danail (Bulgarian), Daneel (Dutch), Danell, Dani (Jewish), Danial, Daniale, Daniall, Daniele (Italian), Daniell, Danijel (Slavic), Danil (Russian), Dannel (Swiss), Dannell, Danniel, Danya (Russian), Danyal, Danyall, Danyel, Danyell, Danyle, Danylle, Raniera (Maori), Taniel (Armenian).
Diminutives: Daan, Dan, Danek (Czech), Dannie, Danny.

Danion *See* Danyon.

Dannie/Danny *See* Daniel.

Dante Italian: enduring, steadfast. *See also* Durant.

Danu *See* Dhanu.

Danyal/Danyel/Danyle *See* Daniel.

Danyon A name made popular by the swimmer Danyon Loader, possibly a form of Daniel.
Danion, Danyan, Danyen.

Dara Cambodian: a star. Irish Gaelic: a son of oak.

Darby Irish Gaelic: free from envy (*see also* Dermot). Middle English: the deer settlement.
Derby.

Darcy Old French: a placename and a Norman family name.
Darcey, D'Arcy, Darcey, Darcie, Darsey, Darsy.

Dare *See* Darius.

Darell *See* Darrell.

Daren Nigerian: born at night. *See also* Darren.

Darien Greek: wealthy. Spanish: a placename.
Darian.

Darius Greek: wealthy. The name of several ancient Persian kings.
Dare, Dario.

Dark Middle English: without light.
Darke.

Darnell French: from the hidden place.
Darnall, Darnel.

Darragh Irish Gaelic: wealthy.
Darra, Darrah, Darrach.

Darrell Old French: the dear one.
Darell, Darrel, Darryl, Daryl, Derrell, Derryl, Deryl.

Darren Possibly a form of Dorian.
Daren, Darin, Darrin.

Darrick *See* Derek.

Darryl *See* Darrell.

Darsey/Darsy *See* Darcy.

Darshan Sanskrit: an audience with a sage or guru. The name implies a seeker of knowledge.

Darth From Darth Vader, a character in the *Star Wars* movie series.

Darton Old English: from the deer forest or estate.

Darwin Old English: a beloved friend.
Darwyn, Derwin, Derwyn.

Dashiell After Dashiell Hammett, US novelist and author of *The Maltese Falcon*. Made popular by actress Cate Blanchett's son.
Dashiel.
Diminutives: Dash, Dashe.

Dave/Davey/Davie Diminutives of David.

Daved/Daveth *See* David.

Daven Old Norse: two rivers.
Davin, Davyn.

Davenport Old English: from the town on the River Dane; a UK placename.

David Hebrew: the beloved, the adored one. The famous Israelite king of the Bible and also the patron saint of Wales. *See also* Davidson, Dawes and Dewi.
Dafydd (Welsh), Daibhidh (Irish, Scottish), Daved, Daveth (Cornish), Davi (Portuguese), Davide (French), Davyd, Davydde, Davyyd, Dawud (Arabic), Devi (Breton), Dewi (Welsh), Dewy (Cornish), Dowd (Middle English), Rawiri (Maori), Taavi (Finnish), Tevita (Tongan).
Diminutives: Dai (Welsh), Dave, Davee, Davey, Davie, Davy, Rewi (Maori), Taffy (Welsh), Tavi (Jewish).

Davidson The son of David.
Davis, Davison.

Davin Scandinavian: the bright one from Finland.

Davis/Davison *See* Davidson.

Davy/Davyd/Davyyd *See* David.

Dawa Sherpa/Tibetan: born on a Monday. Also a girl's name.

Dawes Old English: the son of Dawe or David.
Dawkin, Dawkins, Dawsey, Dawson.

Dawud *See* David.

Dax An English surname; the meaning is unknown.

Dayman/Daymon *See* Damon.

Dayn/Dayne *See* Dane.

Dayron A modern name of uncertain meaning.

Deacon Middle English: an officer of the church.
Deacan, Deakin, Dekan, Dekon.
Diminutives: Deak, Deek.

Dean Latin: a religious official. Old English: from the valley.
Daen, Dain, Dane, Deane, Dein, Dene, Dino (Italian).

Declan Irish Gaelic: a 5th-century bishop.
Decklan, Declyn, Deklan, Deklyn.

Dedric/Dedrick *See* Derek.

Deek *See* Deacon.

Deepak Sanskrit: like a lamp or light.
Dipak.

Dein *See* Dean.

Dekan/Dekon *See* Deacon.

Deklan/Deklyn *See* Declan.

Del A diminutive of Derek and names beginning with Del.

Delaney Gaelic: the challenger's descendant.
Delainey, Delainy, Delany.
Diminutive: Del.

Delano Old French: from the forest of nut trees.

Delbert Old English: bright as day.

Dell From the dell or hollow. Also a diminutive of names such as Wendell.

Delling Old Norse: the shining one.

Delmar Latin: from the sea.
Delmer, Delmor, Delmore.

Delon A French surname.

Delroy Old French: the son or servant of the king.

Delwyn Old English: a friend from the valley.
Delwin.

DeMarcus American: of Marcus. A modern name (*see* Mark).
Demarcus, Demarkus, DeMarkus.

Demas Greek: popular.

Demetrius Greek: belonging to Demeter, the Earth Mother and goddess of fertility.
Demetri, Demetrio (Italian, Spanish), Demetrios (Greek), Dimitri, Dmitri (Russian).

Demian *See* Damon.

Demos Greek: of the people.

Dempsey Irish Gaelic: the proud one.

Dempster Old English: the judge.

Demyan Russian form of Damon.

Denby Old Norse: from the Dane's settlement.
Danbey, Danby, Denbeigh, Denbey, Denbigh.

Dene *See* Dean.

Denham Old English: a homestead in the valley.
Denholm.

Denim A fabric, from de Nîmes, meaning of Nîmes (the French town where the material originated).
Denym.

Denis *See* Dennis.

Deniz Turkish: of the sea.

Denley Old English: from the meadow in the valley.

Denmark A 'country name'.

Dennis Greek: a lover of wine. A modern form of Dionysus, the god of wine and drama. *See also* Dennison and Tennyson.
Denis, Denize, Denys, Deon, Dion, Dione, Dionisio (Italian), Dionysus (German).
Diminutives: Den, Dennie, Denny.

Dennison Old English: the son of Dennis. *See also* Tennyson.

Densiel/Densil *See* Denzil.

Denton Old English: from the farm or town in the valley.

Denver Old English: from the edge of the valley. A surname and a US placename.
Denvah.

Denym *See* Denim.

Denys *See* Dennis.

Denzil Cornish: from a placename meaning a high stronghold.
Densiel, Densil, Denzel, Denzell, Denziel, Denzill.

Deon *See* Dennis.

Derby *See* Darby.

DeReese American: of Reese. A modern name (*see* Rhys).
DeReece, DeRees, DeRhys, DeRhyse.

Derek Teutonic: a ruler of the people. *See also* Theodoric.
Darrick, Dedric, Dedrick (German), Derick, Derik, Derk, Derrek,

Derrick, Diederik (Danish), Dietrich (German), Dirk (Dutch, Flemish), Dirke, Dyrke.
Diminutives: Del, Derry.

Derk/Derrek *See* Derek.

Dermot Irish Gaelic: without envy. *See also* Darby.
Dermid, Dermott, Diarmad (Scottish Gaelic), Diarmid, Diarmit.

Derrell/Derryl/Deryl *See* Darrell.

Derren From an old Welsh name. Also a girl's name.
Derrin, Derryn, Deryn.

Derrick Cornish: from the oak grove. *See also* Derek.

Derry Cornish: of the oak trees. Irish Gaelic: red-headed; the name of an Irish county. *See also* Derek.
Derrey, Derri, Derrie.

Derryn *See* Derren.

Derward Old English: the deer-keeper.

Derwen Welsh: an oak tree.
Derwenn, Derwin, Derwinn, Derwyn, Derwynn.

Derwent Welsh: the name of rivers in England and Tasmania.

Derwin/Derwyn *See* Darwin and Derwen.

Derwood *See* Durward.

Des Diminutive of Desmond.

Desi Diminutive of Desiderius.

Desiderius Latin: the desired one.
Desiderio (Italian, Spanish), Didier (French).
Diminutive: Desi.

Desmond Irish Gaelic: a man from South Munster, an Irish province.
Desmonde, Desmun, Desmunde.
Diminutives: Des, Desy.

Deuce Old French: two (as in a duo).

Dev Sanskrit: godlike.

Devdan Sanskrit: the gift of the gods.

Deverell Celtic: from the riverbank.

Devereux From Old French: originally a Norman surname.
Deveraux.

Devi *See* David.

Devin Celtic: a poet.
Devyn.

Devlin Irish Gaelic: fierce bravery.
Devlen, Devlyn.

Devon English: a south-western English county.
Devan, Deven.

Devonte African-American: possibly a form of Devon.

Devron A modern name, possibly a form of Devon.
Devran, Devren.

Devyn *See* Devin.

Dewayne *See* Duane.

Dewi Welsh form of David. *See also* Dafydd.
Dewey, Dewy (Cornish).
Diminutive: Dai.

De Witt Flemish: the blond or fair one. *See also* Dwight.
Dewitt.

Dexter Latin: right-handed, dextrous.
Diminutive: Dex.

Dhani Hindi/Nepali: wealthy.

Dhanu Sanskrit: a bow, one of the symbols of the zodiac sign of Sagittarius.
Dhanus, Danu.

Dharma Sanskrit: religion, or the religious one. Also a girl's name.

Dhillan/Dhillon/Dhylan/Dhylon
See Dylan.

Dhondup Sherpa/Tibetan: one who accomplishes.

Diablo Spanish: a devil.

Diamond Old English: a shining protector.

Dian Indonesian: a candle.

Diarmad/Diarmid/Diarmit *See* Dermot.

Dick/Dickie/Dicky *See* Richard.

Dickson Old English: the son of Richard (Dick).
Dixon.

Didier *See* Desiderius.

Diederik Danish form of Derek.

Diego Spanish form of James. *See also* Santiago.

Diesel After Rudolf Diesel, the German engineer who invented the diesel engine.
Diezel.

Dieter Old German: of a warrior race.

Dietrich *See* Derek.

Digby Old Norse: from the settlement by the dyke.

Diggory Cornish from Old French: lost or strayed.
Digory.

Dilan/Dillan/Dillon *See* Dylan.

Dime A US silver coin.
Dyme.

Dimitri/Dmitri *See* Demetrius.

Dinesh Sanskrit: the lord of the day.

Dinh Vietnamese: the summit of the mountain.

Dino *See* Dean.

Dinsdale Welsh: born on Sunday.

Dion/Dione/Dionysus *See* Dennis.

Dipak *See* Deepak.

Dirk/Dirke *See* Derek.

Dix Latin: ten, or the tenth.
Dixie.

Dixon *See* Dickson.

Dizzy After the legendary jazz musician Dizzy Gillespie.
Dizzey, Dizzie.

Django An unusual name, after the jazz musician Django Reinhardt.

Djimon A West African name.

Dobie Probably a nickname; after American soul singer Dobie Gray.
Dobee, Dobey, Dobi, Doby.

Dobry Polish: good.

Dodd Teutonic: of the people.

Dolan Irish Gaelic: black-haired.

Dolf/Dolph *See* Adolf and Rudolph.

Dom A diminutive of Dominic.

Dominic Latin: belonging to the Lord. St Dominic founded an important order of monks.
Domenic, Domenick, Domenico (Italian), Domenik, Domingo (Spanish), Dominick, Dominik (Czech, Polish), Dominique (French).
Diminutives: Dom, Nic, Nick, Nickie, Nicky.

Don A diminutive of Donald and other Don names.

Donahue Irish Gaelic: a warrior dressed in brown.
Donaghue, Donoghue, Donohue.

Donal/Donall Irish forms of Donald.

Donald Scottish Gaelic: the ruler of the world. *See also* Donnelly.

Donal (Irish), Donall (Irish), Donalt, Donell, Donnell.
Diminutives: Don, Donnie, Donny.

Donato Latin: a gift, given by God.
Donat (Polish), Donatello (Italian), Donatien (French), Donatus.

Donegal Irish Gaelic: the name of a county.

Donell/Donnell *See* Donald.

Donn Irish Gaelic: the dark one.
Donne.

Donnelly Gaelic: the dark brave one.
Donnel, Donnell.

Donnie/Donny Diminutives of Donald and other Don names.

Donoghue/Donohue *See* Donahue.

Donovan Irish Gaelic: dark brown.
A name made popular by the 1960s folk singer Donovan.
Donavan, Donaven, Donoven.
Diminutives: Don, Donnie, Donny.

Dooley Irish Gaelic: a dark hero.

Doone Irish Gaelic: a placename.
Doon.

Dorado Spanish: the golden one. The name of a southern constellation.

Doran Irish Gaelic: a wanderer or stranger. *See also* Doron.

Dorian Greek: A man belonging to the Dorian tribe (one of the ancient Greek tribes). Probably invented by Oscar Wilde for the main character of his 1890s novel *The Portrait of Dorian Gray*.

Dorjee Sherpa/Tibetan: a thunderbolt.
Dorjé.

Doron Greek: a gift. A modern Jewish name.
Doran, Dorran.

Dorsey Irish Gaelic: the place of the gateways.
Dorsee, Dorsie, Dorsy.

Dory French: golden-haired.

Doug/Dougie/Duggie *See* Douglas.

Dougal Gaelic: a dark stranger.
Dougall, Doyle, Dugal, Dugald.

Douglas Scottish Gaelic: from the dark stream.
Douglass, Duglass.
Diminutives: Doug, Dougie, Duggie.

Dov Hebrew: a bear.

Dover Old English: of the waters. A coastal town in Kent, England.

Dow Irish Gaelic: black-haired.

Dowd Middle English form of David.

Doyle *See* Dougal.

Draco Greek: a dragon. A constellation in the northern sky.
Dracoe, Draconis, Drako, Drakoe.

Dragan Slavic: the dear one.

Draig Welsh: a dragon.

Drake Old English: a dragon.

Draven A modern name of uncertain meaning.
Drayven, Drayvyn, Dreaven, Dreayven, Dreayvyn.

Drax Old English: possibly from the word drag.
Draxx.

Dre Probably a short form of André.
Drae, Drai, Drey.

Dreaven/Dreayven/Dreayvyn *See* Draven.

Drew Scottish diminutive of Andrew.
See also Druce.
Dru, Drue.

Driscoll Irish: the interpreter.

Driscol, Driscolle, Driskol, Driskoll, Driskolle.

Driver Old English: one who drives.
Dryver.

Drostan/Drystan *See* Tristram.

Dru/Drue *See* Drew.

Druce Celtic: the son of Drew.

Druid A priest in ancient Celtic religions.
Druide.

Drury Old French: the dear one, a sweetheart.

Dryden Old English: from the dry valley.

Dryver *See* Driver.

Duane Irish Gaelic: a little dark one. A popular name in the USA.
Dewayne, Du'aine, Dwaine, Dwane, Dwayne.

Duarte Portuguese form of Edward.

Duca Italian: a duke or nobleman.
Duka.

Dudley English: a town in the UK, and the name of an aristocratic family.
Dudleigh, Dudly.
Diminutives: Dud, Duddy.

Duff Scottish Gaelic: dark-haired, or of a dark complexion.

Duffel A type of coat or bag.
Duffle.

Duffy Gaelic: a man of peace.
Duffey, Duffie.

Dugal/Dugald *See* Dougal.

Dugan Gaelic: dark-skinned.

Duglass *See* Douglas.

Duka *See* Duca.

Duke Old French: a leader. Also a

diminutive of Marmaduke.

Duman Turkish: smoke or mist.

Dunbar Gaelic: a dark branch.

Duncan Scottish Gaelic: a dark warrior.
Diminutive: Dunc.

Dundee A Scottish city.

Dunedin A South Island city.

Dunham Celtic: a dark man.

Dunley Old English: from the meadow on the hill.

Dunmore Scottish Gaelic: from the fortress on the hill.

Dunstan Old English: from the dark stone or hill. The name of a saint.

Dupree Old French: of the price or prize (du prix).

Durack An Irish surname.
Durak.

Duran/Durand *See* Durant.

Durant Latin: enduring, steadfast. *See also* Dante.
Duran, Durand, Durante.

Durban A city in South Africa.
Durbin, Durbyn.

Durham Old English: a hilly peninsula. An English city and county.

Durward Old English: the gatekeeper.
Derwood, Durwood.

Durwin Old English: a dear friend.
Durwyn.

Durwood *See* Durward.

Dusan Czech: the soul, the spirit.

Dustin Old Norse: Thor's stone, or valiant.
Dustan, Dusten, Dustyn.

Duval French: from the valley.

SHAKESPEAREAN NAMES

These names are from William Shakespeare's plays – from tragedies such as *Hamlet* to comedies like *A Midsummer Night's Dream* and *Much Ado About Nothing*.

Girls

Adriana	Julia		
Aemilia	Juliet		
Alice	Juno		
Anne	Katherine		
Ariel	Lavinia		
Audrey	Luciana		
Beatrice	Lucretia		
Bianca	Margaret		
Cassandra	Maria		
Celia	Mariana		
Charmian	Marina		
Cleopatra	Meg		
Constance	Miranda		
Cordelia	Nan		
Cressida	Nell		
Diana	Nerissa		
Dionyza	Octavia		
Dorcas	Olivia		
Eleanor	Ophelia		
Elinor	Patience		
Elizabeth	Perdita		
Emilia	Phebe		
Francisca	Portia		
Helen	Regan		
Helena	Rosalind		
Hermia	Silvia		
Hermione	Tamora		
Hero	Timandra		
Imogen	Titania		
Iris	Ursula		
Isabella	Valeria		
Jaquenetta	Viola		
Jessica	Violenta		

Boys

Aaron	Lorenzo
Adam	Macbeth
Alexander	Marcus
Alexas	Matthew
Angelo	Montague
Angus	Nathaniel
Antonio	Nicholas
Arthur	Oberon
Benedict	Oliver
Charles	Orlando
Chiron	Othello
Christopher	Owen
Cleon	Paris
Conrade	Pedro
Corin	Pierce
Curtis	Prospero
Dion	Ralph
Duncan	Richard
Edward	Robin
Fabian	Romeo
Fenton	Ross
George	Sebastian
Griffith	Shadow
Hamlet	Silvius
Henry	Simon
Hugh	Tarquin
Jack	Taurus
John	Thomas
Laurence	Timon
Lear	Titus
Lennox	Toby
Leonardo	Valentine
Lewis	William

Duvall, Duvalle.

Dwaine/Dwane/Dwayne *See* Duane.

Dweezil A name made up by musician Frank Zappa for his son.

Dwight Teutonic: fair or blond. *See also* De Witt.

Dyami Native American: an eagle.

Dyfan Welsh form of Damon.

Dylan Welsh: a man from the sea. Also a girl's name.
Dhilan, Dhillan, Dhillon, Dhilon, Dhylan, Dhylon, Dilan, Dillan, Dillon, Dilon, Dyllan, Dyllon, Dylon.

Dyme *See* Dime.

Dyre Scandinavian: a dear one.

Dyrke *See* Derek.

Dyson Old English: the son of Dye (from Dionysus).
Dysen.

Dzong Tibetan: a fortress.

E

Eachan Scottish Gaelic: a brown horse.
Eachann.

Eadgar *See* Edgar.

Eamonn Irish Gaelic form of Edmund.
Eammon, Eamon.

Ean *See* Ian.

Eanraig Scottish Gaelic form of Henry.

Earl Old English: a nobleman.
Earle, Erle, Errol, Erroll.

Earnest *See* Ernest.

Earvin *See* Irving.

Easton Old English: a place that faces east.
Easten, Eastyn.

Eathan/Eathen *See* Ethan.

Eaton Old English: from the estate by the river.
Eton.

Ebenezer Hebrew: the rock of help. A placename mentioned in the Bible.
Ebanezer.
Diminutives: Eban, Eban.

Eberhard Teutonic: as brave as a wild boar. *See also* Everard.
Eberhart.

Ebrahim Arabic form of Abraham.

Ed/Eddie/Eddy Diminutives of names such as Edgar, Edmund, Edward and Edwin.

Edan *See* Aidan.

Edbert Old English: prosperous and bright.

Edega Hawaiian: wealthy.

Eden Hebrew: the place of pleasure (as in the Garden of Eden). Irish Gaelic: fiery (*see also* Aidan). Old English: a bear cub.
Edenn.

Edgar Old English: a prosperous spearman.
Eadgar, Edgard (French), Edgardo (Italian, Spanish).
Diminutives: Ed, Eddie, Eddy.

Edison Old English: the son of Edgar, Edmund or Edward.
Edinson, Edson, Edyson.

Edlin Old English: a prosperous friend.

Edmund Old English: a prosperous protector. *See also* Eamonn. Eamonn (Irish Gaelic), Edmond (Dutch, French), Edmonde, Edmondo (Italian), Edmundo (Spanish), Eumann (Scottish Gaelic). *Diminutives*: Ed, Eddie, Eddy.

Edoardo/Édouard *See* Edward.

Edolf Old English: a prosperous wolf.

Edom Hebrew: red.

Edric Old English: a prosperous ruler. Edrick, Edris.

Edryd Welsh: a storyteller. Edred, Edrydd.

Edsel *See* Etzel.

Edson/Edyson *See* Edison.

Edwada Hawaiian form of Edward.

Edward Old English: a rich guardian. Duarte (Portuguese), Edoardo (Italian), Édouard (French), Edu, Eduard (Czech, German), Eduardo (Spanish), Eduward, Eduwerd, Edvard (Russian, Scandinavian), Edwada (Hawaiian), Edwerd, Eetu (Finnish), Eideard (Scottish Gaelic), Eruera (Maori). *Diminutives*: Ed, Eddi, Eddie, Eddy, Eddye, Ned, Neddie, Neddy, Ted, Teddie, Teddy.

Edwin Old English: a prosperous friend. Edwinn, Edwyn, Edwynn. *Diminutives*: Ed, Eddie, Eddy.

Eetu Finnish form of Edward.

Effie/Effy Diminutives of Ephraim.

Efrain/Efram/Efrem *See* Ephraim.

Efydd Welsh: bronze or brass. Efyd.

Egan Irish Gaelic: the little fiery one.

Iagan (Scottish).

Egbert Old English: a bright sword.

Egon Teutonic: the point of a sword.

Egor Russian form of George.

Egypt An unusual 'country name'.

Ehren Teutonic: honourable.

Ehud Hebrew: the sympathetic one.

Eian *See* Ian.

Eideard *See* Edward.

Einar Old Norse: a lone warrior. Inar.

Einstein After Albert Einstein, the famous German physicist.

Eirik *See* Eric.

Eitan *See* Ethan.

Eivind Norwegian: a happy warrior.

Eladio Latin: a man from Greece.

Elan Hebrew: a tree. Native American: the friendly one.

Eland Old English: from the island.

Elbert *See* Albert.

Elden/Eldin *See* Alden.

Eldene A modern American name.

Eldon Old English: from the hill. Elden, Eldyn.

Eldred *See* Aldred.

Eldric/Eldrich *See* Aldrich.

Eldridge Old English: from the alder-tree ridge. Aldridge, Eldredge.

Eldur Icelandic: like fire.

Eldyn *See* Eldon.

Eleazar/Elezar *See* Lazarus.

Eleias Welsh form of Elijah.

Elek Hungarian form of Alexis (*see* Alexander).

Eleu Hawaiian: alert and lively

Elfed Welsh: autumn.
Elfedd.

Elgar Old English: a noble spear.

Eli Hebrew: the highest. A biblical name. Also a diminutive of names such as Elias, Elijah and Elisha.
Elie, Eligh, Elih, Ely.

Elia/Elias *See* Elijah.

Eliel Finnish form of Elisha.

Elijah Hebrew: the Lord is God. An Israelite prophet in the Bible. *See also* Elliott, Ellis and Ellison.
Eleias (Welsh), Elia, Eliah, Elias, Elihu, Eliyahu (Jewish), Ellia, Elliah, Eriha (Maori), Ilie (Romanian), Ilya (Russian).
Diminutives: Eli, Ely.

Eliot/Eliott *See* Elliott.

Elis/Eliss *See* Ellis.

Eliseo *See* Elisha.

Elisha Hebrew: God is my salvation. The successor of Elijah in the Bible.
Eliel (Finnish), Eliseo (Italian, Spanish).
Diminutives: Eli, Ely.

Elkan Hebrew: possessed by God.
Elkanah.

Ellar Scottish Gaelic: a butler or steward.

Ellard *See* Alard.

Ellery Cornish: a swan. Teutonic: from the elder tree. Also a form of Hilary.
Ellerey, Ellerie.

Elliah/Elliah *See* Elijah.

Elliott From Old French: a form of Elias. *See* Elijah.
Eliot, Eliota (Samoan), Eliott, Eliotte, Elliot, Elliotte.

Ellis From Greek: a form of Elias. *See* Elijah.
Elis, Eliss, Elliss.

Ellison From Greek: the son of Ellis or Elias. *See* Elijah.

Elmer Old English: noble and famous.
Elmar.

Elmo Italian from Teutonic: a protector. The name of a saint.

Elmore Old English: from the riverbank with elm trees.

Elner Teutonic: famous.

Eloy Latin: to choose. A Spanish name.

Elroy From French: the king. *See also* Leroy.

Elsdon Old English: from the noble one's valley.
Elsden.

Elston Old English: from the noble one's farm.

Elton Old English: from the old settlement or estate.

Elvin *See* Alvin.

Elvis *See* Alvis.

Elvy Old English: an elfin warrior.

Elward Old English: a noble guardian.

Elwin Old English: a friend of the elves.
Elwyn.

Elwood Old English: the ruler of the elves.

Ely *See* Eli, Elijah and Elisha.

Emerson The son of Emery.
Emmerson.

Emery Teutonic: an industrious ruler.

Emeric, Emmery, Emory, Emrey, Imre (Hungarian).

Emil Teutonic: industrious. The masculine form of Emily.
Émile (French), Émilien (French), Emilio (Italian, Spanish), Emlen, Emlyn (Welsh).

Emlen/Emlyn *See* Emil.

Emmanuel Hebrew: God is with us.
Emanuel (Scandinavian), Emanuele (Italian), Immanuel (German), Manoel (Portuguese), Manuel (Spanish).
Diminutives: Mannie, Manny.

Emmerson *See* Emerson.

Emmery *See* Emery.

Emmet Old English: little Emma.
Emmett, Emmit.

Emre Turkish form of Henry.

Emrey *See* Emery.

Emrys Welsh form of Ambrose.

Emyr Welsh: honour.

Enda Irish Gaelic: bird-like.

Endymion Greek: a beautiful youth in mythology.
Endimion.

Eneas *See* Aeneas.

Eneki Hawaiian: eager.

Engelbert Teutonic: a bright Angle (a Germanic people).
Englebert, Inglebert.

Ennio Italian: favoured by God.

Ennis Celtic: from the island. *See also* Innes.
Enis, Ennys, Enys.

Ennor Cornish: from the boundary.

Enoch Hebrew: experienced, or consecrated. A biblical name.

Enos Hebrew: mankind. A character in the Bible. Also an Irish form of Angus.

Enrico/Enrique *See* Henry.

Enys *See* Ennis.

Enzo Italian diminutive of Lorenzo and other names.

Eoghan Irish Gaelic: from the yew tree.

Eoin Gaelic form of John and Owen.

Eon Greek: an age or lifetime.

Epeha Maori: of the Ephesians.

Ephraim Hebrew: fruitful. One of the sons of Joseph in the Bible.
Efrain (Spanish), Efram, Efrem, Ephrem, Yefrem (Russian).
Diminutives: Effie, Effy.

Equinox Middle English: the time of equality between day and night.

Eran Hebrew: watchful.

Erasmus Greek: worthy of love.
Diminutives: Ras, Rasmus.

Erastus Greek: the loving one.
Diminutive: Rastus.

Ercole *See* Hercules.

Erebus Greek: the mythological god of darkness.

Erhard Teutonic: strong and honourable.
Erhart.

Eric Old Norse: an all-powerful ruler.
Eirik (Norwegian), Erich (German), Erick, Erik (Swedish), Eriks (Russian), Erix.
Diminutives: Ric, Rick.

Eriha Maori form of Elijah.

Erik/Eriks *See* Eric.

Erin Irish Gaelic: from Ireland. More

commonly a girl's name.

Erith Old English: from the gravelly landing place. An English placename.

Erix *See* Eric.

Erland Old Norse: a foreigner, a stranger.

Erle *See* Earl.

Ermanno *See* Herman.

Ernest Teutonic: the serious, earnest one.
Earnest, Ernesto (Italian, Spanish), Ernst (German).
Diminutives: Ern, Ernie, Erny.

Ernst German form of Ernest.

Eron/Erron *See* Aaron.

Eros Greek: the god of love.

Errol Scottish: from an old family name. *See also* Earl.
Erroll.

Erskine Scottish Gaelic: from the heights.

Eruera Maori form of Edward.

Ervin *See* Irving.

Erwin *See* Irwin.

Eryx Greek: a mythological figure.

Esau Hebrew: the hairy one. The son of Isaac and brother of Jacob in the Bible.

Esbern Old Norse: a divine bear. A Danish name.
Esben, Esbjörn (Swedish).

Eseia Welsh form of Isaiah.

Esidor *See* Isidore.

Esmond Old English: the gracious or handsome protector.
Esmonde, Esmund.

Esra *See* Ezra.

Essex Old English: the Saxons from the east. An English county.

Este Italian: from the east.
Estes.

Estéban Spanish form of Stephen.

Etana Hawaiian: strong.

Etera Maori form of Ezra.

Ethan Hebrew: steadfast, or long-lived. A biblical name.
Aithan, Aithen, Eathan, Eathen, Eitan (Jewish), Etan, Ethen.

Ethelred Teutonic: a noble counsellor.

Étienne French form of Stephen.

Eton *See* Eaton.

Ettore *See* Hector.

Etu Native American: of the sun.

Etzel Teutonic: the noble one.
Edsel.

Euan *See* Ewan.

Eugene Greek: the noble or well-born one.
Eugen (German), Eugène (French), Eugenio (Italian, Spanish), Yevgeni (Russian).
Diminutive: Gene.

Eumann *See* Edmund.

Eunan Irish Gaelic: a saint.

Eurwyn Welsh: fair and golden.

Eusebio Greek: pious, respectful.
Eusebius.

Eustace Greek: fruitful, or steadfast.
Eustice, Eustis.

Evan Welsh: well-born. *See also* Bevan, Ieuan, John and Owen.
Evann, Evarn, Evin, Evyn.

Evander Greek: a good man. A mythological character.
Diminutive: Vander.

Evangelos Greek: the evangelist.

Eveleigh *See* Everley.

Evelyn English: from an old surname. Primarily a girl's name.
Evelin.

Ever *See* GIRLS.

Everard Old English: as strong or brave as a boar. *See also* Eberhard. Evered, Everet, Everett, Evert (German), Evrard (French).

Everest The world's highest mountain.

Everild *See* Averell.

Everley Old English: from the place of the wild boar.
Eveleigh.

Everton Old English: the town of the wild boar.
Everten, Evertyn.

Evin/Evyn *See* Evan.

Ewald Teutonic: he who rules by the law.

Ewan Scottish Gaelic: possibly meaning born of the yew tree.
Euan, Ewen, Ewin, Uan.

Ewart Old English: an ewe herder.
Ewert.

Ewing Old English: a friend of the law.

Exavier *See* Xavier.

Exodus *See* GIRLS.

Exton Old English: from the ox farm.
Exten, Extyn.

Eyre Teutonic: an eagle's nest.

Ezekiel Hebrew: God strengthens, or the strength of God. One of the books of the Bible.
Ezequiel (Spanish).

Diminutives: Eze, Ezy, Zeik, Zeke.

Ezera Hawaiian form of Ezra.

Ezio Latin: like an eagle.

Ezra Hebrew: the helper. A prophet in the Bible.
Esra, Etera (Maori), Ezera (Hawaiian), Ezrah, Ezri.

F

Faber *See* Fabron.

Fabian Latin: a bean grower.
Fabiano (Italian), Fabien (French), Fabio (Italian, Portuguese, Spanish), Fabius.

Fabio/Fabius *See* Fabian.

Fabrice Latin: a craftsman.
Fabricio (Spanish), Fabricus, Fabrizio (Italian).

Fabron French: a little blacksmith.
Faber.

Fadil Arabic: the generous or distinguished one.

Fáelán Irish Gaelic: a little wolf
Faolán.

Fagan Gaelic: the little fiery one.
Fagin.

Fain/Faine *See* Fane.

Fairfax Old English: the one with beautiful hair.

Fairley Old English: a clearing in the woods. Also a girl's name.
Fairleigh, Fairlie, Fairly.

Faisal Arabic: a wise judge.
Faysal.

Falcon Old French: a bird of prey.
Falkon.

Falconer *See* Falkner.

Fale Samoan: a house.

Falk Yiddish: the falcon.

Falkner Old French: a falconer, or falcon handler.
Falconer, Faulkner.

Fallon Irish: a leader. Also a girl's name.
Fallan, Fallyn.

Fane Old English: eager or glad.
Fain, Faine.

Faolán *See* Fáelán.

Farand Teutonic: attractive, pleasant.
Farant, Farrand.

Farid Arabic: unique or unrivalled.
Fareed.

Faris The angel of the night.
Fares, Farres, Farris.

Farley Old English: from the fern clearing.
Farleigh.

Farman Old Norse: a traveller or hawker.

Farnell Old English: from the hill of ferns.
Farnall, Farnill.

Farnley Old English: from the fern meadow.
Fernleigh, Fernley.

Farook Arabic: one who can distinguish right from wrong.
Farooq, Farouk, Faruq.

Farquhar Scottish Gaelic: the dear one.

Farrand *See* Farand.

Farrell Celtic: the valorous one.
Farrel.

Farres/Farris *See* Faris and Ferris.

Faruq *See* Farook.

Faulkner *See* Falkner.

Faust Latin: the fortunate one.
Fausto (Italian).

Favian Latin: understanding.

Faysal *See* Faisal.

Feargal/Fearghal *See* Fergal.

Fearghas/Feargus *See* Fergus.

Fedele *See* Fidel.

Federico *See* Frederick.

Feenix/Fenix *See* Phoenix.

**Felice/Feliciano/Felicien/Felicio/
Feliks** *See* Felix.

Felipe *See* Philip.

Felix Latin: fortunate, lucky.
Felice (Italian), Feliciano (Italian, Spanish), Felicien, Felicio, Feliks (Polish), Felise, Felixe, Felixx, Felixxe, Felizio.

Felton Old English: from the farm in the field.

Fenlon Irish: son of the fair one.

Fenn Old English: a marsh or fen.

Fenton Old English: from the marshlands.

Fenwick Old English: from the farm in the marshland.

Feodore *See* Theodore.

Ferdinand Teutonic: prepared for the journey; an adventurer or traveller.
Ferdinando (Italian), Ferdynand, Fernán (Spanish), Fernand (French), Fernando (Spanish), Hernando (Spanish).
Diminutives: Ferd, Ferdie, Fez (Spanish).

Fergal Irish Gaelic: a man of valour.
See also Friel.

Feargal, Fearghal, Fergall.

Fergus Gaelic: the chosen man, or a man of vigour. *See also* Ferguson.
Fearghas (Gaelic), Feargus.
Diminutive: Fergie.

Ferguson Gaelic: the son of Fergus.

Fermin *See* Firmin.

Fernán/Fernand/Fernando *See* Ferdinand.

Fernleigh/Fernley *See* Farnley.

Feroz Arabic: victorious and successful.
Feroze, Firoz, Firoze.

Ferrand Old French: a grey-haired man.

Ferrer Old French: the blacksmith.
Ferrar.

Ferris Gaelic: a rock. A form of Peter.
Farris.

Festus Latin: steadfast.

Fetu Samoan: a star. The god of the night sky.

Fez Spanish diminutive of Fernando. Also a type of hat.
Fezz, Fezze.

Fiachra Irish Gaelic: a raven.
Fiacre.

Fiberte *See* Filbert.

Fidel Latin: faithful.
Fedele (Italian), Fidele, Fidelio, Fidelis.

Fielding Old English: a field dweller.
Field, Fielder.

Fife Scottish: a man from the region of Fife.
Fyfe.

Figaro Latin: daring, cunning.

Filbert Teutonic: very bright.

Fiberte, Filiberto (Italian), Philbert.

Filep Hungarian form of Philip.

Filib/Filip/Filippo *See* Philip.

Fin A diminutive of Fingal, Finlay and similar names.
Finn.

Finan *See* Finian.

Finbar Irish Gaelic: fair-headed.

Findlay/Findley *See* Finlay.

Fineas *See* Phineas.

Fingal Scottish Gaelic: the fair stranger.
Fingall.
Diminutives: Fin, Finn.

Finian Irish Gaelic: fair or white. The name of a saint.
Finan, Finean, Fineen, Finnian.

Finlay Scottish Gaelic: the fair warrior.
Findlay, Findley, Finley, Finnlay, Finnley.
Diminutives: Fin, Finn.

Finn Irish Gaelic: the white or fair one. Old Norse: a man from Finland. Also a diminutive of names such as Fingal and Finlay.
Fin, Fionn, Fyn, Fynn.

Finnegan Irish Gaelic: fair.
Finnigan.

Finnlay/Finnley *See* Finlay.

Fintan Irish Gaelic: the name of several Irish saints.

Fionn *See* Finn.

Firdos Arabic: paradise.
Firdaus.

Fire From Greek: heat, energy and passion.
Fyre.

Firmin Latin: steadfast and firm.
Fermin (Basque), Firman.

Firoz *See* Feroz.

Firth Old English: of the woodland.
Firthe, Frith.

Fitch Old French: a lance or spear.

Fitz Old French: a son. Also a
diminutive of names such as
Fitzgerald.

Fitzgerald Old French: the son of
Gerald.

Fitzhugh Old French: the son of
Hugh.

Fitzjames Old French: the son of
James.

Fitzpatrick Old French: the son of
Patrick.

Fitzroy Old French: the son of the king.

Fiyero A character in the musical
Wicked.

Flae/Flai/Flaie *See* Flay.

Flame Middle English: something
that burns or blazes.
Flaime, Flaym, Flayme.

Flanagan *See* Flannan.

Flanders Old French: the submerged
land. A region of north-west Europe.
Flannders.

Flannan Irish Gaelic: ruddy, or red-
haired.
Flann, Flanagan.

Flannery Irish Gaelic: the red one.
Flanary, Flanery, Flannary, Flanner.

Flavian Latin: golden-haired.
Flavien (French), Flavio (Italian),
Flavius.

Flax Middle English: a 'plant name'.
Flaxen.

Flay Middle English: to strip or
criticise.
Flae, Flai, Flaie, Flaye.

Flaym/Flayme *See* Flame.

Fleming Old French: a man from
Flanders.
Flemming.

Fletcher Old French: an arrow maker.
Diminutive: Fletch.

Flex From Latin: to bend.
Fleks, Flexx.

Flin/Flinn *See* Flynn.

Flinders After Matthew Flinders, the
renowned 19th-century navigator
and explorer.

Flint Old English: a hard stone.
Flindt, Flynt.

Florian Latin: a flower, blooming.
The masculine form of Flora.
Florean, Florent (French), Floro
(Spanish).

Floyd *See* Lloyd.

Flynn Irish Gaelic: the red-haired
one.
Flin, Flinn, Flyn, Phlyn, Phlynn.

Flynt *See* Flint.

Folant Welsh form of Valentine.

Fontaine French form of Fountain.

Fonz/Fonzie *See* Alphonso.

Forbes Scottish Gaelic: a placename.

Ford Old English: from the ford or
river crossing.
Forde.

Forester Old French: a forester or
gamekeeper.
Forrester.

Forrest Old French: a forest dweller.
Forest.

Forster *See* Foster.

Fortescue Old French: a strong shield.

Fortunato Latin: the fortunate one. Fortune.

Foster Old English: a foster parent. Old French: a shearer. Forster.

Fountain Old French: a spring or fountain. Fontaine (French), Fontayne, Founten, Fountin, Fountyn.

Fox Middle English: an 'animal name'. Foxe, Foxx.

Frain/Fraine *See* Frayne.

Franc/Francesco *See* Francis.

Francis Latin: from France, or a free man. Franc (Slavic), Francesco (Italian), Francilo (Spanish), Francisco (Spanish), Franco (Italian), François (French), Frans (Scandinavian), Franz (German), Werahiko (Maori). *Diminutives*: Chico, Cisco (Spanish), France, Frank, Frankie, Paco (Spanish), Pancho (Spanish).

Franco/François *See* Francis.

Frank Teutonic: a member of the tribe of the Franks. Also a diminutive of Francis and Franklin.

Franklin Old French: a free citizen. Franklen, Franklyn. *Diminutive*: Frank.

Frans/Franz *See* Francis.

Frase/Fraze *See* Phrase.

Fraser Old French: a strawberry, or from a Norman family name. Frasier, Frazer, Frazier.

Fray *See* Frey.

Frayne Old English: a stranger. Old French: an ash tree. Frain, Fraine, Freyne.

Frazer/Frazier *See* Fraser.

Fred/Freddie/Freddy Diminutives of Alfred, Frederick and Wilfred.

Frederick Teutonic: a peaceful ruler. Bedrich (Czech), Federico (Italian, Spanish), Frederic, Frédéric (French), Frederik (Danish), Fredric, Fredrick, Fredrik (Swedish), Friedrich (German). *Diminutives*: Fred, Freddie, Freddy, Fritz (German).

Freeman Old English: a freeborn man.

Freitag German form of Friday.

Fremont Teutonic: the noble protector.

Frey Old Norse: the god of weather and fertility, and the patron of seafarers. Fray, Freyr.

Freyne *See* Frayne.

Friday A 'day name', from an Old Norse word – literally the day of Freya, the Norse equivalent of the Roman goddess Venus. Freitag (German).

Friedrich German form of Frederick.

Friel A form of Fergal, meaning a man of valour. Friele, Friels.

Frith *See* Firth.

Fritz *See* Frederick.

Frixo An unusual modern name.

Fudo Japanese: the god of fire and wisdom.

Fuego Spanish: fire.

Fuller Old English: a fuller, or cloth-thickener.

Fulton Old English: from the muddy place.

Furnell Old French: a furnace.
Furneaux.

Furze Middle English: gorse.
Furse, Fursey, Furzey, Furzy.

Fyfe *See* Fife.

Fyn/Fynn *See* Finn.

Fyodor *See* Theodore.

Fyre *See* Fire.

G

Gabe/Gabi/Gabie *See* Gabriel.

Gable French: little Gabriel.

Gabor Hungarian form of Gabriel.

Gabriel Hebrew: a man of God. One of the archangels in the Bible.
Gabor (Hungarian), Gabriele (Italian), Gabriello (Italian), Gavril (Russian).
Diminutives: Gab, Gabbie, Gabe, Gabi, Gabie.

Gaddiel Hebrew: God is my fortune.
Gadi, Gadiel.

Gael French form of Gale.

Gaelan/Gaelen *See* Galen.

Gage Old French: a pledge.

Gaile *See* Gale.

Gair Irish Gaelic: short.

Gaius Latin: to rejoice.

Galahad From a placename in the Bible. One of King Arthur's knights.

Gale Old French: gay, lively. More commonly a girl's name. *See also* Gaylord.
Gael (French), Gaile, Gayle.

Galen Greek: the calm one, or the helper.
Gaelan, Gaelen, Galan, Galeno (Spanish).

Galileo A man from Galilee. Also after the famous Italian scientist and astronomer.

Gallagher Irish Gaelic: the foreign helper.

Gallard *See* Gaylord.

Galloway Gaelic: a stranger or foreigner.
Galway.

Galor *See* Gaylord.

Galton Old English: from the rented estate or farm.

Galvin Irish Gaelic: the bright one.
Galvan, Galven, Galvyn.

Galway *See* Galloway.

Gamaliel Hebrew: the recompense of God. A biblical name.

Gamel Scandinavian: the old one.

Gan Chinese: adventurous.

Gandolf Teutonic: the progress of the wolf.
Gandolph.

Ganesh Sanskrit: the lord of the hosts. The elephant-headed Hindu god of wisdom.
Ganesa.

Gannon Irish Gaelic: the little blond or fair one.

Ganymede Greek: a mythological youth.

Gara Irish Gaelic: a mastiff.

Gardiner Old French: one who tends the garden.
Gardener, Gardner, Garner.

Garek *See* Garrick.

Gareth Welsh: gentle, or an old man.
Garath, Garreth, Geraint (Welsh), Gerens (Cornish), Geronte (French).
Diminutive: Gary.

Garett *See* Garrett.

Garey *See* Gary.

Garfield Old English: from the triangular field.
Diminutive: Gary.

Garie *See* Gary.

Garisen/Garison *See* Garrison.

Garland Old French: a wreath or garland.

Garman Old English: the spearman.

Garmond Old English: a spear protector.
Garmon.

Garner *See* Gardiner.

Garnet Old French: dark red, from the colour of pomegranates. Also a 'gemstone name'.
Garnett.

Garran Possibly a form of Gary.
Garren, Garrin.

Garrett From Old French: a spear warrior. *See also* Gerald and Gerard.
Garett, Garret, Garritt.
Diminutive: Gary.

Garrick Old English: a spear ruler.
Garek.

Garrie/Garry *See* Gary.

Garrison Middle English: a fortified place.
Garisen, Garison, Garrisen.

Garth Old Norse: from the garden or enclosure.

Garton Old Norse: a dweller at the fenced farm.

Garuda Indonesian: the messenger of the gods, similar to the Greek god Hermes and the Roman god Mercury.

Garvan *See* Garvin.

Garvey Gaelic: from the rough place.
Garvie.

Garvin Teutonic: a spear friend.
Garvan, Garwin.

Garwin *See* Garvin.

Garwood Old English: from the fir trees.

Gary English/Teutonic: a spearman. Also a diminutive of Gareth, Garfield and Garrett.
Garey, Garie, Garrey, Garrie, Garry.
Diminutives: Gaz, Gazza.

Gaspar Persian: the master of the treasure. *See also* Caspar and Jasper.
Gaspard (French), Gasparo (Italian).

Gaston French: a man from the province of Gascony.

Gatsby From F Scott Fitzgerald's classic novel *The Great Gatsby*.
Gatsbey, Gatsbi, Gatsbie.

Gautama Sanskrit: the original name of the Buddha.
Gotama.

Gautier *See* Walter.

Gavin Celtic: probably derived from Gawain.
Gavain, Gavaine, Gavan, Gaven, Gawen (Cornish).

Gavril *See* Gabriel.

Gawain Celtic: a battle hawk. One of

King Arthur's knights. *See also* Gavin.

Gawen Cornish form of Gavin.

Gayle *See* Gale.

Gaylord Old French: gay and lively, or a dandy. *See also* Gale.
Gallard, Galor, Gayler, Gaylor.

Gaz/Gazza *See* Gary.

Gearalt/Gearoid Irish forms of Gerald.

Geary Old English: changeable.
Gearey.

Gedeon *See* Gideon.

Geir/Geire *See* Gere.

Gemini Greek: a twin. The name of a zodiac sign and a constellation.
Geminie, Geminio, Geminius, Geminus.

Gene A diminutive of Eugene.

Genesis Middle English from Greek: the beginning or origin.

Geoffrey Teutonic: divinely peaceful; derived from Godfrey. *See also* Jefferson.
Geffrey, Geffroy (Old French), Geoffroy, Jeffery, Jeffrey, Jeffri, Jeffrie, Jeffry, Jefri, Jefrie, Joffre, Joffrey, Sieffre (Welsh).
Diminutives: Geof, Geoff, Jeff, Jeffra (Cornish).

Geordan *See* Jordan.

Geordie A diminutive of George and Jordan.
Geordi.

George Greek: a farmer. St George is the patron saint of England. *See also* Juri.
Egor (Russian), Georg (German), Georges (French), Georgi (Russian), Georgios (Greek), Giorgio (Italian),
Goran (Swedish), Hori (Polynesian), Igor (Russian), Jerzy (Polish), Jiri (Czech), Joji (Japanese), Jorge (Portuguese, Spanish), Jorgen (Danish, Swedish), Joris (Dutch), Jory (Cornish), Jurgen (German), Juri, Juris (Latvian), Jurrien (Dutch), Keoki (Hawaiian), Siôr (Welsh), Yiorgos (Greek), Yorick (Old English), Yuri (Russian).
Diminutives: Geordie, Georgie, Gino (Italian).

Geraint Welsh form of Gareth.

Gerald From Old French: a spear warrior. *See also* Garrett and Gerard.
Gearalt (Irish), Gearoid (Irish Gaelic), Geraldo (Spanish), Gerallt (Welsh), Geraud (French), Gerhold (German), Gerrald, Giraldo (Italian), Jerald, Jerold.
Diminutives: Gerri, Gerry, Jerrie, Jerry.

Gerard From Old French: a spear warrior, or brave spearman. *See also* Garrett and Gerald.
Gerardo (Italian, Spanish), Gerhardt (German), Gerrard, Gerrit (Dutch), Gert (Dutch), Jerrard.
Diminutives: Gerri, Gerry, Jerrie, Jerry.

Gere A modern name, possibly inspired by actor Richard Gere.
Geir, Geire.

Gerens/Geronte *See* Gareth.

Gerhardt *See* Gerard.

Germain Latin: a brother. A male version of Germaine.
Germaine, Germayne, Jermain, Jermaine.

German *See* Jarman.

Gerome/Geronimo *See* Jerome.

Gerrald *See* Gerald.

Gerrard/Gerrit *See* Gerard.

Gerri/Gerry *See* Gerald and Gerard.

Gershom Hebrew: in exile, a stranger.
Gershon.

Gert Dutch form of Gerard.

Gervase Teutonic: a spear servant.
Gervais (French), Gervaise, Gervis,
Jarvis, Jervaise, Jervis.

Gerwyn Welsh: fair love.

Gethin Welsh: dark-skinned.
Gethen, Gethyn.

Ghassan Arabic: in the prime of
youth.

Gi Korean: the brave one.

Giacobbe Italian form of Jacob.

Giacomo Italian form of James.

Gianni Italian form of John.

Gib/Gibb *See* Gilbert.

Gibson Old English: the son of
Gilbert.

Gideon Hebrew: the mighty warrior.
A biblical name.
Gedeon.

Gifford Teutonic: a gift.

Gig Probably a nickname.
Gigg.

Gil A diminutive of names such as
Gilbert.

Gilbert Teutonic: a bright or famous
pledge. *See also* Gibson and Gillet.
Gilberto (Italian, Portuguese,
Spanish), Gilburt, Guilbert (French).
Diminutives: Bert, Gib, Gibb, Gil,
Gill.

Gilby Norse: a pledge.
Gilbey.

Gilchrist Gaelic: the servant of Christ.

Gilead Hebrew: an Old Testament
placename.

Giles From Greek: a kid, or young
goat.
Gil (Spanish), Gilles (French), Gillis
(Danish, Dutch), Gyles, Gylles, Jiles,
Jyles, Jylles.

Gilford Old English: by the ford.
Guildford.

Gilles/Gillis *See* Giles.

Gillespie Scottish Gaelic: the bishop's
servant.
Gillespey.

Gillet French: little Gilbert.

Gilmer Scottish Gaelic: a servant of
the Virgin Mary.
Gilmore, Gilmour.

Gilroy Gaelic: a son of the red-haired
man.

Gino Italian. A diminutive of names
such as Giorgio and Luigi.

Giordan/Giordano *See* Jordan.

Giorgio Italian form of George.

Giovanni Italian form of John.

Giraldo *See* Gerald.

Girvan Gaelic: the rough little one.
Girven, Girvin.

Giulio *See* Julius.

Giuseppe Italian form of Joseph.

Gladstone Old English: a bright rock.

Gladwin Old English: a bright or
kind friend.

Glanville Old French: from the estate
of oak trees.

Glen Cornish/Gaelic/Welsh: from the
valley or glen.
Glenn, Glyn, Glynn.

Glendon Gaelic: from the fortress in

the glen.
Glenden.

Glover Old English: a glove-maker.

Glyn/Glynn *See* Glen.

Goddard Old English: divinely brave or strong.

Godfrey Teutonic: divinely peaceful. *See also* Geoffrey.
Godfried (Dutch), Gottfried (German).

Godwin Old English: a divine or good friend.
Goodwin.

Golding Old English: the son of the golden one.

Goldwin Old English: a golden friend.
Goldwinn, Goldwyn. Goldwynn.

Goliath Hebrew: revealing.

Gomer Hebrew: complete. Old English: good and famous.

Gomez Spanish: a man.

Gonzales Spanish: a wolf.
Gonzalo.

Goodwin *See* Godwin.

Gopal Sanskrit: the cowherd.

Goran Swedish form of George.

Gordon Scottish Gaelic: a placename, probably meaning from the great hill.
Gordan, Gorden, Gordyn.
Diminutives: Gordie, Gordy.

Gore Old English: from the triangular plot of ground.

Gorman Teutonic: blue-eyed.

Goronwy Welsh: a figure from Celtic mythology.

Gorran Cornish: a hero.

Goron, Gorron.

Gorwel Welsh: the horizon.

Gotama *See* Gautama.

Goth Middle English: a member of an early Teutonic race.
Gothe.

Gottfried *See* Godfrey.

Gough Welsh: red-haired.

Govinda Sanskrit: a cowherd.
Govind.

Gower Celtic: pure.

Graciano *See* Gratian.

Grady Irish Gaelic: illustrious, noble.
Gradie.

Graeme *See* Graham.

Graham Old English: from the gravelly place or homestead. A common Scottish surname.
Graem, Graeme, Grahame.

Grandville *See* Granville.

Granger Old English: a farmer.
Grainger, Grange.

Granite An igneous rock.

Grant Old French: the large or tall one.
Grante, Grantleigh, Grantley.

Grantham Old English: from the big meadow.

Grantleigh/Grantley *See* Grant.

Granville Old French: from the big town.
Grandville, Granvil.

Gratian Latin: pleasing, or thankful.
Graciano (Spanish), Gratien, Graziano (Italian).

Gray/Graye *See* Grey.

Grayson Old English: the son of the bailiff.

Greyson.

Graziano *See* Gratian.

Green A 'colour name'.
Greene.

Greer *See* GIRLS.

Greg/Gregg *See* Gregory.

Gregan A surname; meaning unknown.

Gregory Greek: vigilant, watchful. The name of several early saints and popes.
Grégoire (French), Gregor (Scottish), Gregorio (Italian, Spanish), Greig (Scottish), Grigor (Welsh), Griogair (Scottish Gaelic), Kerekori (Maori).
Diminutives: Greg, Gregg.

Greig *See* Gregory.

Grenfell/Grenville *See* Greville.

Gresham Old English: from the grazing land.

Greville Old French: from a placename in Normandy.
Grenfell, Grenville, Grevill.

Grey Old English: the grey-haired one.
Gray, Graye, Greye.

Greyson *See* Grayson.

Grier *See* GIRLS.

Griff/Griffin *See* Griffith and Gryffyn.

Griffith Welsh: a powerful lord. *See also* Gryffyn.
Gryffith.
Diminutive: Griff.

Grigor/Griogair *See* Gregory.

Griswold Teutonic: from the grey forest.

Grosvenor Old French: a great huntsman.
Grovener, Grovenor.

Grover Old English: from the grove of trees.

Gryffith *See* Griffith.

Gryffyn Cornish/Welsh: little Griffith. Also a girl's name.
Griffin, Griffyn, Gryffin.
Diminutives: Griff, Gryff.

Guglielmo Italian form of William.

Guido Italian form of Guy.

Guilbert *See* Gilbert.

Guildford *See* Gilford.

Guilhelm/Guillaume/Guillermo *See* William.

Guilherme Portuguese form of William.

Guin *See* Gwyn.

Gully A small valley or ditch.

Gunnar *See* Gunther.

Gunnel The upper part of a boat or ship.
Gunnell.

Gunner A soldier; one who works with a gun.

Gunther Teutonic: a bold warrior. Generally a German name.
Gunnar (Scandinavian), Gunter.

Guntur Indonesian: thunder.

Gurion Hebrew: of lion-like strength, or the place of God.

Guru Sanskrit: a teacher or holy man.

Gus/Gussy Diminutives of names such as Angus, Augustus and Gustav.

Gustav Old Norse: the staff of the Goths.
Gustaf (Swedish), Gustave (French), Gustavo (Italian), Gustavus.

Diminutives: Gus, Gussy.

Guthrie Scottish Gaelic: from the windy place.
Guthrey, Guthry.

Guy Teutonic: the wide one, or from the wood.
Guido (Italian), Guye, Guyon, Gye, Veit (Dutch), Wye.
Diminutive: Wyatt.

Guyten/Guyton *See* Gyton.

Gwener The Welsh name for Friday and the planet Venus.

Gwilym Welsh form of William.
Guillym.

Gwinear Cornish/Welsh: the name of a saint.

Gwydion Welsh: the god of the sky and magic in Celtic mythology.

Gwyn Welsh: white, fair, or blessed.
Guin, Gwinn, Gwynn, Gwynne.

Gwynfor Welsh: from the fair place.

Gyalpo Sherpa/Tibetan: the supreme ruler.

Gye *See* Guy.

Gyles *See* Giles.

Gyton From the place of Guy.
Guyten, Guyton, Gyeten, Gyeton, Gyten.

H

Haarlem *See* Harlem.

Habib Arabic: the beloved one.

Hadad Arabic: the virile one.
Haddad.

Haddon Old English: from the heathery hill.

Hadden.

Hadi Arabic: a guide or leader.

Hadley Old English: from the heathery field. Also a girl's name.
Hadlee, Hadleigh.

Hadrian *See* Adrian.

Hadwin Old English: a friend in battle.

Haemish *See* Hamish.

Hafiz Arabic: the guardian.

Hagen Irish Gaelic: little Hugh. *See also* Hakon.
Hagan, Haggan.

Hagley Old English: from the hawthorn-wood clearing.

Hague *See* Haig.

Hahona Maori form of Jason.

Hai Vietnamese: of the sea.

Haig Old English/Teutonic: from the enclosure or paddock.
Hague, Haige, Haigh.

Haile After Haile Selassie, a former emperor of Ethiopia.

Hailey *See* Hayley.

Haimish *See* Hamish.

Haimon/Haimond *See* Hammond.

Haines Old English: from the fenced area.

Haiz/Haize *See* Haze.

Hakan *See* Hakon.

Hakaraia Maori form of Zachary.

Hakim Arabic: wise and judicious.
Hakeem.

Hakon Old Norse: of noble birth.
Hagen (Danish), Hakan (Swedish).

Hal A diminutive of Harold, Harry and Henry.

Halbert Old English: a brilliant hero.

Halden Old English: half Danish.
Haldan, Haldane, Haldin.

Haldor Old Norse: rock of Thor (the Norse god of thunder).
Halldor.

Hale Old English: the dweller in the nook.

Haley Irish Gaelic: ingenious. *See also* Hayley.

Halford Old English: from the ford in the nook.

Hali Greek: from the sea.

Halifax Old English: from the holy field. A city in northern England.

Halim Arabic: gentle.

Hall Old English: from the manor house or hall.

Hallam Old Norse: the dweller at the rocks.

Halldor *See* Haldor.

Hallstein/Hallsten *See* Halsten.

Halse Old English: from the neck of land.
Halsey.

Halstead Old English: the stronghold.
Halsted.

Halsten Old Norse: a rock.
Hallstein, Hallsten.

Halvard Old Norse: the defender of the rock.
Halvar, Halvor.

Hamal Arabic: as gentle as a lamb. A star in the constellation of Aries.

Hamar Old Norse: ingenious.

Hamelin/Hamelyn *See* Hamlin.

Hami Maori form of Sam. *See* Samson and Samuel.

Hamid Arabic: the thankful one.
Hameed.

Hamilton Old English: from the crooked hill.

Hamish Scottish form of James.
Haemish, Haimish, Haymish, Heymish.

Hamlet Old English: from the enclosed land. A famous Shakespearean play.

Hamlin Teutonic: from the small home.
Hamelin, Hamelyn, Hamlen, Hamlyn.

Hammer Middle English: a hammer-maker.
Hammor.

Hammond From Old French: of the home.
Haimon, Haimond, Hammonde, Hamon, Hamond, Hamonde.

Hamon Greek: the faithful one.

Hampton Old English: from the river meadow.

Hamuera Maori form of Samuel.

Han Vietnamese: the ocean.

Hanan Hebrew: the gracious gift of God.

Handel Teutonic: little Hans (*see* John). A famous German composer.

Hanford Old English: from the rocky ford.

Hani Arabic: the contented one.

Hank/Hanke Diminutives of Henry and John.

Hanley Old English: from the high clearing.
Hanleigh, Henleigh, Henley.

Hannes *See* John.

Hannibal Phoenician: the famous general of Carthage (northern Africa) who crossed the Alps and invaded Italy.

Hannon An English surname, probably derived from John.
Hannan.

Hannu Finnish form of John.

Hans Sanskrit: a swan. Also a German form of John.

Hansard Old French: a cutlass- or dagger-maker.
Hannsard.

Hansel A diminutive of Hans. *See* John.

Hansi *See* John.

Hanson Old English/Teutonic: son of Hans.
Hansen.

Hao Chinese: good.

Hapu Polynesian: the name of a tribe.

Haral/Harald *See* Harold.

Haram Hebrew: a mountaineer.

Harbert *See* Herbert.

Harcourt Old English: the dweller at the falconer's cottage.

Harden Old English: from the valley of the hare.

Harding Old English: a brave warrior.

Hardwin Old English: a brave friend.
Hardwyn, Harwin.

Hardy Teutonic: bold, daring.
Hardey, Hardie.

Hare Maori form of Charles.

Harford Old English: the ford of the stag.
Hartford, Hertford.

Hargreave Old English: from the hare grove.
Hargrave, Hargreaves.

Hari Sanskrit: he who removes evil.

Harlan Old English: from the rocky land. Generally an American name.
Harland, Harlen, Harlin, Harlon, Harlyn.
Diminutive: Lanny.

Harlee/Harleigh/Harley/Harly *See* Arley.

Harlem A region of New York City. Haarlem (Dutch).

Harlow Old English: from the fortified hill.
Harlo, Harloe, Harlowe.

Harlyn *See* Harlan.

Harman/Harmon *See* Herman.

Harold Old Norse: army power, or the ruler of the army.
Arailt (Scottish Gaelic), Haral, Harald (Scandinavian), Harrold, Herold.
Diminutive: Hal.

Haroun/Harun Arabic forms of Aaron.

Harper Old English: a harp player or maker.

Harri *See* Harry.

Harris Old English: the son of Harry (Henry).
Harries, Harrisen, Harrison.

Harry A diminutive of Henry.
Harrey, Harri (Welsh), Harrie.

Hartlee/Hartleigh/Hartley *See* Arley.

Hartman Teutonic: the strong man.
Hartmann.

Hartwell Old English: from the stag ford.

Hartwin Teutonic: a brave friend.

Hartwood Old English: from the forest of stags.

Haruko Japanese: the firstborn.

Harvard A famous university in the USA.

Harvey Breton: battle-worthy. Harvie, Hervé (French), Hervey. *Diminutives*: Harv, Harve.

Harwin *See* Hardwin.

Harwood Old English: from the wood of the hares.

Hasani *See* Hussain.

Hasim Arabic: the decisive one.

Haslett Old English: from the hazel-tree wood. Haslet, Haslitt, Hazlett, Hazlitt.

Hassan Arabic: handsome and good. Hasan.

Hastings An English town.

Hauk/Hauke *See* Hawk.

Hauora Maori: lively.

Havelock Old Norse: sea sport. Havelocke, Havlock.

Haven Old English: a place of refuge. Havyn.

Havika Hawaiian: beloved.

Hawk Middle English: a bird of prey. Hauk, Hauke, Hawke.

Hawley Old English: from the hedged meadow.

Hayden Old English: from the heathery hill. Also a modern girl's name. Haydan, Haydn, Haydon, Haydyn, Heydan, Heyden, Heydon, Heydyn.

Haydn Teutonic: the heathen. A famous Austrian composer. *See also* Hayden.

Haydyn.

Hayes Old English: from the hedged area. Hayz, Hayze.

Hayley Old English: a high clearing or meadow. More commonly a girl's name. Hailey, Haley, Haylie.

Haymish *See* Hamish.

Hayward *See* Howard.

Haywood Old English: from the fenced wood. Heywood.

Hayz/Hayze *See* Hayes.

Hazan Turkish: the autumn. Hazen.

Haze A type of mist. Haiz, Haize, Hayz, Hayze.

Hazem Arabic: firm or strong. Hazim.

Hazlett/Hazlitt *See* Haslett.

Headley *See* Hedley.

Healy Irish Gaelic: possibly meaning a descendant. Healey.

Hearn Gaelic: the lord of the horses. *See also* Ahearn. Hearne, Hern, Herne.

Hearst *See* Hurst.

Heath Old English: the heathland dweller. Heathe.

Heathcliff From the cliffland heath. The hero of Emily Brontë's *Wuthering Heights*. Heathcliffe.

Heathcote Old English: from the cottage on a heath.

ASTRONOMY AND 'STAR NAMES'

These mostly rather unusual names are derived from planets and their associated gods and goddesses, stars, the sky and heavens, and other aspects of astronomy.

Girls

Altair	Mahina
Andromeda	Malara
Ariesca	Marcella
Arundhati	Martina
Asta	Mercuria
Astaire	Monday
Astral	Narada
Astrea	Nebula
Ata Marama	Neptunia
Atarau	Noelani
Auristela	Olympia
Aurora	Phoebe
Caloris	Plutia
Carina	Rehua
Carmé	Rhiannon
Celeste	Riana
Danika	Satarah
Diana	Saturday
Elara	Selena
Eleanor	Seren
Estelle	Sitara
Esther	Solana
Galaxy	Soraya
Helena	Starla
Hera	Stella
Juno	Sunday
Kala	Tara
Kaniva	Tarika
Kira	Urania
Kona	Ursa
Kopu	Vela
Lona	Venus
Lyra	Xingxing

Boys

Alako	Mark
Aland	Merak
Aquila	Mercury
Arcas	Namgyal
Aries	Neptune
Ashwin	Nirvan
Astron	Orion
Bailly	Pavo
Caelum	Phoenix
Chandra	Pinon
Charon	Pluto
Columba	Polaris
Cosmo	Ra
Dara	Rakaunui
Dorado	Ravi
Draco	Rehua
Hamal	Rigel
Hoku	Rinjin
Indra	Samson
Indus	Saturn
Jacey	Seren
Jericho	Shavar
Jove	Sirius
Jumala	Sol
Jupiter	Sorin
Kahoku	Star
Kala	Sterling
Kalani	Surya
Kami	Te Ra
Karma	Umbriel
Lynx	Whetu
Marama	Zeus
Marcus	Zodiac

Heathfield Old English: from the heather field.

Hebert *See* Herbert.

Hector Greek: to hold fast. A Trojan hero in classical mythology.
Ettore (Italian), Heitor (Portuguese).

Heddwyn Welsh: blessed peace.

Hedley Old English: a clearing in the heather.
Headley.

Heikki Finnish form of Henry.

Heilyn Welsh: a steward.

Heinrich German form of Henry.

Heinz Diminutive of Heinrich. *See* Henry.

Heiron *See* Heron.

Heitor *See* Hector.

Helios Greek: a sun god.
Heli, Helio, Helius.

Helmut Teutonic: a courageous protector.
Helmuth.

Hema A figure in Polynesian mythology.

Heman Hebrew: faithful.

Hemant Hindi: winter.

Hemi Maori form of James.

Henare Maori form of Henry.

Henderson Old English from Teutonic: the son of Henry.

Hendon Old English: from the high place.

Hendra Cornish: from the old farm.
Hendry.

Hendrick/Hendrik/Henerik *See* Henry.

Hendrix After Jimi Hendrix, legendary 1960s rock musician.

Hendricks, Hendryx.

Hendry A form of Henry. *See also* Hendra.
Hendree, Hendrey, Hendri, Hendrie.

Hendy Old English: the courteous one.

Henleigh/Henley *See* Hanley.

Hennessey Irish Gaelic: a descendant of Angus.
Hennesey, Hennessy, Hennesy.

Henning *See* Henry.

Henri/Henrik/Henrique *See* Henry.

Henry Teutonic: the ruler of the home or estate. The name of eight English kings. *See also* Harrison, Harry, Henderson, Hendry and Parry.
Eanraig (Scottish Gaelic), Emre (Turkish), Enrico (Italian), Enrique (Portuguese, Spanish), Heikki (Finnish), Heinrich (German), Henare (Maori), Hendrick, Hendrik (Dutch, Scandinavian), Hendry, Henerik (Danish), Henri (French), Henrik (Hungarian, Scandinavian), Henrique (Portuguese), Henryk (Polish), Hinrik (Icelandic), Indrek (Estonian).
Diminutives: Hal, Hank, Hanke, Harry, Heinz (German), Henna (Cornish), Henning (Danish).

Herakles *See* Hercules.

Herbert Teutonic: a bright warrior.
Harbert (Dutch), Hebert, Heribert (German).
Diminutives: Bert, Bertie, Herb, Herbie.

Hercules Greek: the glory of Hera. The exceptionally strong mythological hero.

Ercole (Italian), Herakles (Greek), Hercule (French).

Heremaia Maori form of Jeremiah (*see* Jeremy).

Herewini Maori form of Selwyn.

Herman Teutonic: a man of the army. Armand (French), Armin, Armond, Ermanno (Italian), Harman, Harmon, Hermann (German), Hermon.

Hermes Greek: the messenger of the gods.

Hermon *See* Herman.

Hern/Herne *See* Hearn.

Hernando *See* Ferdinand.

Herod A name from the Bible, probably of Greek origin. Herrod.

Herold *See* Harold.

Heron Middle English: a water bird. Heiron, Herron.

Herrick Old Norse: the army ruler. Herrik.

Hershel Jewish: a deer. Herschel, Hersh, Heshel, Hirsh.

Herst *See* Hurst.

Hertford *See* Harford.

Hervé/Hervey *See* Harvey.

Herwin Teutonic: a battle companion.

Heshel *See* Hershel.

Hesketh Old Norse: from the horseracing track.

Heston Old English: the place in the brushwood. Hesten.

Heugh/Hew/Hewie *See* Hugh.

Hewett Teutonic: little Hugh.

Hewat, Hewet, Hewitt, Hewlett, Hewlitt.

Hewston *See* Houston.

Heydan/Heyden/Heydon *See* Hayden.

Heymish *See* Hamish.

Heyward *See* Howard.

Heywood *See* Haywood.

Hiatt *See* Hyatt.

Hickson The son of Hick (a form of Dick, a diminutive of Richard). Hicksen, Hixen, Hixon.

Hieronymus German form of Jerome.

Hilary Latin: cheerful. More commonly a girl's name. Ellery, Hilaire (French), Hillary, Hillery, Ilar (Welsh), Ilario (Italian).

Hildebrand Teutonic: a battle sword.

Hillel Hebrew: the praised one. A biblical name.

Hilton Old English: from the farm on the hill. Hylton.

Hinrik Icelandic form of Henry.

Hinton Old English: from the high place or farm.

Hippolyte Greek: he who frees the horses.

Hiram Hebrew: exalted. A name from the Bible. Hyram.

Hiroshi Japanese: generous.

Hirsh *See* Hershel.

Hirst *See* Hurst.

Hiwa Hawaiian: jet-black, or choice.

Ho Chinese/Korean: goodness.

Hoani Maori form of Johnny (*see* John).

Hobart *See* Hubert.

Hobie A small sailing catamaran (Hobie Cat).
Hobee, Hobey, Hobi, Hoby.

Hobson The son of Hobb. An archaic diminutive of Robert (bright fame).
Hobbes, Hobbins, Hobbs, Hobsen.

Hoera Maori form of Joel.

Hogan Irish Gaelic: a youth.

Hohepa Maori form of Joseph.

Hohua Maori form of Joshua.

Hoku Hawaiian: a star.

Holbrook Old English: from the brook in the valley.
Holbeck.

Holden Old English: from the deep valley.

Holger Old Norse: spear-like.

Holiday Old English: a holy or religious day.
Holliday.

Holland Old English: from the enclosed or sacred ground. A 'country name'.
Holand, Hollan.

Hollis Old English: from the grove of holly trees.

Holman Old English: a dweller in the hollow.

Holmes Old English: from the island in the river.

Holt Old English: a dweller in the wood.

Homer The name of a Greek poet, possibly meaning a pledge.

Hona Maori form of Jonah.

Hone Maori form of John.

Hopkin Welsh: the son of Robert.
Hopkins, Hopkyn, Hopkyns.

Hopper Old English: a dancer or leaper.

Horace Latin: from a Roman family name.
Horatio, Horatius, Orazio (Italian).

Hori Polynesian form of George.

Horomona Maori form of Solomon.

Horst German: from the wood or wooded hill.

Horton Old English: from the grey or muddy place.
Horten.

Hosea Hebrew: salvation. *See also* Joshua.

Hotoroa Polynesian: a figure from legend.
Hoturoa.

Houghton *See* Hutton.

Houston Old English: from the place of Hugh. A city in Texas.
Hewston, Houstoun, Huston.

Howard Teutonic: the brave one, or the chief guardian.
Hayward, Heyward, Howerd.
Diminutives: Howey, Howie.

Howe Old Norse: a hillock or burial mound.

Howell Cornish/Welsh: the eminent one. *See also* Powell.
Howel, Hywel, Hywell.

Hsin Chinese: after an ancient dynasty.

Hu Chinese: a tiger. Also a Welsh form of Hugh.

Huarahi Maori: a track or road.

Huatare Maori: the name of a famous chief.

Hubert Teutonic: a brilliant mind.
See also Hugh.
Hobart, Huppert (German).
Diminutives: Huey, Hughie.

Huckleberry A North American plant. The hero of Mark Twain's novel *Adventures of Huckleberry Finn*.
Huckelberry.
Diminutive: Huck.

Hudson Old English: the son of Hugh.

Huey A diminutive of Hubert and Hugh.

Hugh Teutonic: heart and mind.
See also Hagen, Hewett, Hubert, Hudson and Hugo.
Heugh, Hew, Hu (Welsh), Hughes, Hugo (Dutch, German), Hugues (French), Huw (Welsh), Ugo (Italian).
Diminutives: Hewey, Hewie (Scottish), Huey, Hughie.

Hugo A form of Hugh.
Hugoe, Hugow, Hugowe.

Humbert Teutonic: a famous warrior.
Humberto, Umberto (Italian).

Hume Old English: from the river island.

Humphrey Teutonic: the protector of the peace.
Humfrey, Humfry, Humphry.

Hunt/Hunte *See* Hunter.

Hunter Old English: the huntsman.
Hunt, Huntah, Hunte, Hunts, Huntz, Huntze.

Huntley Old English: from the hunter's meadow.
Huntleigh, Huntlie, Huntly.

Huon A type of tree.

Huppert *See* Hubert.

Hura Maori form of Judah.

Huriu Maori form of Julius.

Hurley Gaelic: the sea tide. Old English: a clearing in the woods.
Hurleigh, Hurlie, Hurly.

Hurricane From Spanish: a violent storm.

Hurst Old English: a dweller in the wood.
Hearst, Herst, Hirst.

Hussain Arabic: the handsome little one.
Hasani, Husain, Husani (Swahili), Husayn, Hussein.

Huston *See* Houston.

Hutton Old English: from the farm on the hill.
Houghton.

Huw A Welsh form of Hugh.

Huxley Old English: the inhospitable place.

Hyam Hebrew: life.
Chaim, Hyman.
Diminutives: Hy, Hymie.

Hyatt Old English: a high gate.
Hiatt.

Hyde Old English: a hide (an old measurement) of land.

Hylton *See* Hilton.

Hyman *See* Hyam.

Hyram *See* Hiram.

Hythe Old English: a landing place.
Hyth.

Hywel/Hywell *See* Howell.

I

Iagan *See* Egan.

Iago Spanish and Welsh form of James. *See also* Santiago.

Ian From Hebrew: God is gracious. A Scottish form of John.
Ean, Eian, Iaian (Gaelic), Iain (Gaelic).

Iau The Welsh name for Jupiter.

Ibrahim *See* Abraham.

Ibsen Teutonic: the son of the archer.
Ibson, Ibsyn.

Icarus Greek: a legendary figure.

Ichabod Hebrew: the glory has departed.

Icon Latin from Greek: a picture or image.
Ikon.

Iden Old English: prosperous.

Idris Arabic: a good man. Welsh: a fiery, impulsive lord.

Idwal Welsh: the lord of the wall or rampart.

Iestin/Iestyn Welsh forms of Justin.

Ieuan Welsh form of John. *See also* Evan and Owen.
Iefan, Ifan, Ioan, Iwan.

Ifor Welsh: a traditional name of uncertain meaning.

Ignatius Latin: ardent, fiery.
Ignace (French), Ignacio (Spanish), Ignacius, Ignate, Ignatz (German), Ignazio (Italian), Inigo.
Diminutives: Iggie, Iggy, Nacio (Spanish).

Igor Scandinavian: a hero. Also a Russian form of George.

Ihaka Maori form of Isaac.

Ihakara Polynesian: the name of a great chief.

Ihi Maori: power.

Ihorangi Polynesian: rain.

Ijaz Arabic: a miracle.

Ikale Polynesian: an eagle.

Ike/Ikey/Ikie *See* Isaac.

Ikon *See* Icon.

Ilar/Ilario *See* Hilary.

Ilfryn An unusual Welsh name.

Ilie Romanian form of Elijah.

Ilya Russian form of Elijah.

Imam Arabic: a religious leader.

Imants Latvian: the name of a national hero.

Immanuel *See* Emmanuel.

Imran Arabic: the exalted one.
Imraan.

Imre *See* Emery.

Inar *See* Einar.

Indiana *See* GIRLS.

Indra Sanskrit: the god of the atmosphere and sky.

Indrek Estonian form of Henry.

Indus A major Asian river; also a southern constellation.

Ingemar Old Norse: a famous son.
Ingmar.

Inger Norse: from the son's army.

Inglebert *See* Engelbert.

Ingo Teutonic: the masculine form of Inge (*see* Ingrid).

Ingram Teutonic: the raven.

Inia Maori form of Aeneas.

Inigo *See* Ignatius.

Innes Celtic/Gaelic: an island in the river, or from the island. *See also* Ennis.
Iniss, Inness, Innis.

Innocent Latin: harmless, innocent. The name of several saints and popes. Innocenzo (Italian), Innokenti (Russian), Inocencio (Spanish).

Ioan *See* Ieuan.

Ioane Samoan form of John.

Ioannes Greek form of John.

Iolo/Iolyn *See* Iorweth.

Ion Romanian form of John.

Iorweth Welsh: a handsome lord.
Diminutives: Iolo, Iolyn.

Ira Hebrew: watchful, vigilant. A biblical name.

Irawaru Polynesian: a figure from legend.

Ireland Old English: the land of the Irish.

Irirangi Maori: a spirit voice.

Irving A Scottish placename.
Earvin, Ervin, Irvin, Irvine.

Irwin Old English: from the words boar and friend.
Erwin.

Isa Sanskrit: a lord. *See also* Isaac and Isaiah.

Isaac Hebrew: laughter, the laughing one. The son of Abraham in the Bible.
Ihaka (Maori), Isaak (German), Isacco (Italian), Isak (Swedish), Isaki, Issac, Itzaak, Itzik (Jewish), Izaac, Izaak (Dutch), Izac, Izzac, Yitzaak, Yitzak.

Diminutives: Ike, Ikey, Ikie, Isa, Isi, Izi.

Isador/Isadore *See* Isidore.

Isaiah Hebrew: God is salvation, or God is my helper. One of the prophets in the Bible.
Eseia (Welsh), Isaia, Isaya, Isayah.
Diminutive: Isa.

Isak/Isaki *See* Isaac.

Ishmael Hebrew: The Lord will hear. The first son of Abraham in the Bible
Ismael, Ismail.

Isidore Greek: the gift of Isis (an Egyptian goddess).
Esidor, Isador, Isadore, Isidor (German), Isidoro (Italian).
Diminutives: Isi, Issy, Izzy.

Ismael/Ismail *See* Ishmael.

Isra Arabic: one of the journeys of Muhammad. Thai: freedom.

Israel Hebrew: the Lord's soldier.
Isreal, Isriel, Izrael, Izreal, Izriel.
Diminutives: Isi, Issy, Izzi, Izzie, Izzy.

István Hungarian form of Stephen.

Itzaak/Itzik *See* Isaac.

Iva *See* Ivar.

Ivan Slavic form of John.
Ivann, Ivon.
Diminutives: Ivo, Van, Vanya.

Ivar Old Norse: a battle archer.
Iva, Iver, Ivor.

Ivaylo A Slavic name that possibly means a wolf.
Ivailo.

Ives Old English: the little archer. The name of a saint.
Ivo (German), Yves (French).

Ivo *See* Ivan and Ives.

Ivon *See* Ivan.

Ivor *See* Ivar.

Iwan *See* Ieuan.

Ix Mayan: a jaguar.

Izaac/Izaak/Izi/Izzac *See* Isaac.

Izrael/Izreal/Izriel *See* Israel.

Izumi Japanese: a placename.

Izzi/Izzie/Izzy Diminutives of Isidore and Israel.

J

Jaak *See* Jack.

Jabari Swahili: the brave or powerful one.
Jabar, Jabbar.

Jabez Hebrew: sorrowful.

Jabir Arabic: the comforter.

Jac/Jacca *See* Jack.

Jace *See* Jason.

Jaceb *See* Jacob.

Jacek Polish: a lily. A male form of Hyacinth.

Jacey A modern name, probably from Jacob or Jason. Also a Native American name meaning the moon.
Jace, Jacee, Jaci, Jacie, Jacy.

Jack A diminutive of John.
Jaak, Jac, Jacca (Cornish), Jak, Jakka, Jax, Jaxx, Jock (Scottish).
Diminutives: Jackie, Jacky, Jaki, Jakki.

Jackson Old English: the son of Jack.
Jacksen, Jacksten, Jackston, Jacksyn, Jakson, Jaxen, Jaxon, Jaxson, Jaxxen, Jaxxon, Jaxxyn, Jaxyn.

Jacob Hebrew: the supplanter; one who takes the place of another. A biblical name. *See also* Jake and James.
Giacobbe (Italian), Jaceb, Jaco (Portuguese), Jacobi, Jacobo (Spanish), Jacopo (Italian), Jacques (French), Jaicob, Jaikob, Jakko, Jakob (Dutch, German, Scandinavian), Jakub (Czech, Polish), Jayceb, Jaycob, Jaykeb, Jaykob, Yakov (Hebrew, Russian).
Diminutives: Jaike, Jake, Jay, Jeb.

Jacques French form of Jacob and James.

Jacy *See* Jacey.

Jadan/Jadem/Jaden *See* Jayden.

Jade *See* GIRLS.

Jadon Hebrew: one who is thankful. An Old Testament name.

Jae *See* Jay.

Jaedan/Jaedon/Jaedyn *See* Jayden.

Jael Hebrew: to ascend. Also a girl's name.

Jaemes/Jaemz *See* James.

Jagan An unusual modern name. Jagen.

Jagdish Sanskrit: the ruler of the world.

Jagger Middle English: a carter or hawker.
Jaggar, Jaggard.

Jago Cornish form of James.

Jahan Sanskrit: the world.

Jai/Jaie *See* Jay.

Jaicob/Jaike/Jaikob *See* Jacob.

Jaiden/Jaidon/Jaidyn *See* Jayden.

Jaik/Jaike/Jaiki *See* Jake.

Jaiman/Jaimen/Jaimon *See* Jamen.

Jaime/Jaimes *See* James.

Jairus Hebrew: a figure from the Bible.

Jaithan A modern name, derived from Jai.
Jaitham.

Jak/Jakka/Jakki *See* Jack.

Jake A diminutive of Jacob.
Jaik, Jaike, Jaiki, Jaki, Jaque, Jaques, Jay, Jayk, Jayke.

Jakko/Jakob/Jakub *See* Jacob.

Jalan/Jalen/Jalin/Jalyn *See* Jaylen.

Jalil Arabic: majestic.
Jaleel.

Jalon A modern name, probably derived from Jay.
Jalan, Jalen, Jalyn.

Jamal Arabic: the handsome one.
Jamaal, Jamil.

Jambo Swahili: a greeting; literally hello.

Jamen A popular modern name, probably derived from James or Jay.
Jaiman, Jaimen, Jaimin, Jaimon, Jaman, Jamin, Jamon, Jayman, Jaymen, Jaymin, Jaymon.

James Hebrew: the supplanter; a form of Jacob. *See also* Jamieson and Seamus.
Diego (Spanish), Giacomo (Italian), Hamish (Scottish), Hemi (Maori), Iago (Spanish, Welsh), Jacques (French), Jaemes, Jaemz, Jago (Cornish), Jaime (Spanish), Jaimes, Jamez, Jaume (Catalan), Jaymes, Jaymez, Jhames, Kimo (Hawaiian), Seamus (Irish), Semisi (Tongan), Shamus (Irish), Yago (Spanish).
Diminutives: Jamesey, Jamie, Jamiee, Jamo, Jay, Jayme, Jaymie, Jem, Jhim, Jhimmy, Jhimy, Jhyimy, Jim, Jimi, Jimmi, Jimmie, Jimmy.

Jamie/Jamiee Diminutives of James.

Jamieson Old English: the son of James. Also a modern girl's name.
Jameson, Jamison.

Jamil *See* Jamal.

Jan Slavic and Scandinavian form of John.
Janek, Janko.

Jangal Hindi: a forest. *See also* Jungle.

Janos *See* John.

Jansen/Janson *See* Jensen.

Janus Latin: the Roman god of doors and gates (beginnings and endings). The month of January is derived from this name.

Japhet Hebrew: youthful. A son of Noah in the Bible.
Japheth, Yaphet.

Jaque/Jaques *See* Jake.

Jardine Old French: a garden.
Jardene.

Jared Hebrew: a descendant of Adam in the Bible.
Jarad, Jarid, Jarod, Jarrad, Jarred, Jarrid, Jarrod, Jarryd, Jaryd, Jered, Jerod, Jerrad, Jerred, Jerrod, Yered (Hebrew).

Jaret *See* Jarratt.

Jarl Scandinavian: an earl or chieftain.
Jaral, Jarle.

Jarlath Irish Gaelic: a leader or prince.

Jarman Celtic: a man from Germany.
German, Jerman, Jermyn.

Jarod *See* Jared.

Jaron Hebrew: to sing.

Jaroslav Slavic: the glory of spring. A

popular Czech name.

Jarrad/Jarred/Jarrod *See* Jared.

Jarrah Aboriginal: a type of eucalyptus tree.
Jarra.

Jarratt Teutonic: a spearman.
Jaret, Jarrett.

Jarvis *See* Gervase.

Jaryd *See* Jared.

Jason Greek: the healer. The mythological hero who retrieved the Golden Fleece.
Hahona (Maori), Jasen, Jasin, Jasun, Jaycen, Jaycin, Jaysen, Jaysin, Jayson, Jaysun.
Diminutives: Jace, Jase, Jayce.

Jasper Persian: the treasurer. A 'gemstone name'. *See also* Caspar and Gaspar.
Jaspa, Jaspah, Jaspar, Jazpar, Jazper, Jesper (Danish).

Jaume Catalan form of James.

Jav *See* Javan and Javed.

Java An Indonesian island.

Javan Hebrew: of the clay. An Old Testament name. Hindi: the young one.
Javen.
Diminutive: Jav.

Javed Persian: eternal. A popular Muslim name.
Diminutive: Jav.

Javier *See* Xavier.

Jax/Jaxx Modern forms of Jack.

Jaxon/Jaxson/Jaxxen/Jaxyn *See* Jackson.

Jay Old English: a bird. Sanskrit: victory. Also a diminutive of Jacob, Jake, James and many names

beginning with J.
Jae, Jai, Jaie, Jaye, Jhae, Jhai, Jhaye.

Jayce/Jaycen/Jaycin *See* Jason.

Jayceb/Jaycob *See* Jacob.

Jayden English: a modern name, derived from Jai or Jay.
Jadan, Jadem, Jaden, Jaedan, Jaeden, Jaedin, Jaedon, Jaedyn, Jaidan, Jaiden, Jaidin, Jaidon, Jaidyn, Jaydan, Jaydem, Jaydin, Jaydn, Jaydon, Jaydyn.

Jaygen Possibly a form of Jayden.
Jaygan.

Jayk/Jayke *See* Jake.

Jaykeb/Jaykob *See* Jacob.

Jaylen A modern American name.
Jalan, Jalen, Jalin, Jalyn, Jaylan, Jaylin, Jaylyn.

Jayme/Jaymes/Jaymez/Jaymie *See* James.

Jaymen/Jaymin/Jaymon *See* Jamen.

Jaysen/Jayson *See* Jason.

Jazpar/Jazper *See* Jasper.

Jazz A musical genre. Also a girl's name.
Jaz, Jazze.

Jean French form of John.

Jeb A diminutive of Jacob.

Jedediah Hebrew: beloved of God. A biblical name.
Jediah, Jedidiah.
Diminutives: Jed, Jedd.

Jeden Polish: number one.

Jedward A combination of Jed and Edward.
Jeddward, Jeddwarde, Jedwarde.

Jeff/Jeffery/Jeffra/Jeffrey *See* Geoffrey.

Jefferson Old English: the son of

Jeffrey (*see* Geoffrey).
Jeffers, Jeffson.

Jefri/Jefrie *See* Geoffrey.

Jehosophat Hebrew: the Lord judges.

Jelani Swahili: mighty.

Jelle Dutch diminutive of William.

Jem A diminutive of James and Jeremy.

Jen Chinese: able.

Jenkin A diminutive of John.
Jenk, Jenking, Jenkings, Jenkins, Jenkinson, Jenkison, Jenks, Jenkyn, Jenkyns.

Jenner An English surname, possibly meaning an architect.

Jens *See* John.

Jensen Scandinavian: the son of John (God is gracious).
Jansen, Janson, Jenson, Jentzen.

Jerald/Jerold *See* Gerald.

Jered *See* Jared.

Jereme/Jeremie *See* Jeremy and Jerome.

Jeremy Hebrew: appointed by God; from the biblical name Jeremiah. *See also* Jerome.
Heremaia (Maori), Jereme, Jeremiah, Jeremias (Dutch, German, Spanish), Jeremie, Jorma (Finnish).
Diminutives: Jem, Jerrie, Jerry.

Jericho Arabic: probably meaning the city of the moon.
Jeriko, Jerricho, Jerriko.

Jermain/Jermaine *See* Germain.

Jerman *See* Jarman.

Jermyn Cornish: a saint's name. *See also* Jarman.

Jerod *See* Jared.

Jeroen Dutch form of Jerome.

Jerome Greek: a sacred or holy name. *See also* Jeremy.
Gerome, Geronimo (Italian), Hieronymus (German), Jereme, Jeremie (French), Jeroen (Dutch), Jeronimo (Spanish), Jerrome.
Diminutive: Jerry.

Jeronimo *See* Jerome.

Jerrad/Jerred *See* Jared.

Jerrard *See* Gerard.

Jerricho/Jerriko *See* Jericho.

Jerrie/Jerry Diminutives of Gerald, Gerard, Jeremy and Jerome.

Jerrod *See* Jared.

Jersey One of the Channel Islands, off the coast of France.
Jersee, Jersie, Jerzey, Jerzy.

Jervase/Jervis *See* Gervase.

Jerzy Polish form of George. *See also* Jersey.

Jesper *See* Jasper.

Jesse Hebrew: God's gift. Also a girl's name.
Jessie, Jessy, Jezzee.
Diminutive: Jess.

Jesús Hebrew: the saviour, or God is salvation. A variation of Joshua, and primarily a Spanish and Portuguese name.

Jet Latin: a black decorative material.
Jett, Jette, Jhet, Jhett, Jhette.

Jethro Hebrew: excellence. A biblical name.
Jethroe.

Jevan/Jevon Welsh forms of John.

Jezzee *See* Jesse.

Jhae/Jhai/Jhaye *See* Jay.

Jhames *See* James.

Jhet/Jhett/Jhette *See* Jet.

Jhim/Jhimmy/Jhyimy Modern diminutives of James.

Jhon *See* John.

Jigme Sherpa/Tibetan: one who does not fear.

Jiles *See* Giles.

Jim/Jimi/Jimmie/Jimmy Diminutives of James.

Jimeoin A well-known Irish comedian. Possibly a combination of Jim and Owen.
Jimoein, Jimowen, Jymeoin, Jymoein, Jymowen.

Jimoh Swahili: born on a Friday.

Jin Chinese: golden.

Jiri Czech form of George.

Jitender Sanskrit: the powerful conqueror.
Jitendra, Jitinder.

Jo *See* Joseph.

Joab Hebrew: praise the Lord.

Joachim Hebrew: established by God. The name of a king of Judah in the Bible.
Akim (Russian), Joaquim (Portuguese), Joaquin (Spanish), Jochim (German).

Joah Hebrew: a biblical name, possibly meaning a brother.

Joal/Joall *See* Joel.

Joaquim/Joaquin *See* Joachim.

Job Hebrew: the persecuted one. A name that is associated with patience.
Jobe, Jobi, Jobie.

Jocelin Latin: the merry one. More commonly a girl's name.

Jocelyn, Joscelin.
Diminutive: Joss.

Jochim *See* Joachim.

Jock Scottish form of Jack. *See* John.

Jodi/Jody *See* Joseph.

Joe/Joey Diminutives of Joseph.

Joel Hebrew: the Lord is God. A name from the Bible.
Joal, Joall, Joell, Hoera (Maori), Yoel.

Joesef/Joesph *See* Joseph.

Joffre/Joffrey *See* Geoffrey.

Joh/Johan/Johann/Johannes *See* John.

Johar Hindi: a jewel.

John Hebrew: God is gracious. The name of many saints. *See also* Ian, Jack, Jan, Jenkin, Jonathan, Jonty, Owen, Sean, Shane and Zane. Bevan (Welsh), Eoin (Gaelic), Evan (Welsh), Gianni (Italian), Giovanni (Italian), Hannes, Hannu (Finnish), Hans (German), Hone (Maori), Ieuan (Welsh), Ioane (Samoan), Ioannes (Greek), Ion (Basque, Romanian), Ivan (Russian, Slavic), Jan (Czech, Dutch, Polish, Scandinavian), Janos (Hungarian), Jean (French), Jens (Danish, Norwegian), Jevan (Welsh), Jevon (Welsh), Jhon, Johan (Scandinavian), Johann (German), Johannes (Dutch, German), Jon (Swedish), Jone (Polynesian), Jonty, Jovan (Slavic), Jowan (Cornish), Juan (Spanish), Juhani (Finnish), Sean (Irish), Shane (Irish), Shaughn (Irish), Shaun (Irish), Shawn (Irish), Siôn (Welsh), Sione (Tongan), Yann (Breton), Yannis (Greek), Zane.
Diminutives: Handel (German),

Hank, Hanke (German), Hansel (German), Hansi (German), Hoani (Maori), Jack, Jackie, Jacky, Jock, Joh, Johnnie, Johnno, Johnny, Nino (Italian), Vanya (Russian), Yannick (Breton), Yianni (Greek).

Johnas *See* Jonas.

Johnathan/Johnathon *See* Jonathan.

Johnhenry A combination of John and Henry (ruler of the home or estate).
John-Henry.

Johnnie/Johnny *See* John and Jonathan.

Johnson English: the son of John. *See also* Jones.
Johnston, Jonson.

Joji Japanese form of George.

Jojo African: born on a Monday.

Jolyon *See* Julian.

Jon A diminutive of Jonathan. *See also* John.

Jonah Hebrew: a dove; a man of peace.
Hona (Maori), Johnas, Jona, Jonas, Yona (Russian), Yonah, Younus (Arabic).

Jonas *See* Jonah.

Jonathan Hebrew: God has given, or a gift of the Lord. The friend of David in the Bible. *See also* John.
Johnathan, Johnathon, Jonathon, Yonatan (Hebrew).
Diminutives: Johnny, Jon, Jonnie, Jonno, Jonny, Yoni (Hebrew).

Jone Polynesian form of John.

Jones The son of John. *See also* Johnson.

Jonnie/Jonno/Jonny Diminutives of Jonathan.

Jonty A form of John.
Jonte, Jontee, Jontey, Jonti, Jontie.

Joop *See* Joseph.

Joost *See* Justin.

Jora Hebrew: the autumn.
Jorah.

Joram Hebrew: the Lord is exalted.
Yoram.
Diminutives: Jori, Jorie, Jory.

Jordan Hebrew: flowing down, as in the River Jordan. Also a girl's name.
Geordan, Giordan, Giordano (Italian), Jordaan (Dutch), Jordayn, Jordayne, Jorden, Jordin, Jordon, Jordyn, Jourdain (French), Jourdan, Yordan (Bulgarian).
Diminutives: Geordi, Geordie, Jordi, Jordie, Jordy, Jori, Jorie, Jouri, Jourie, Jud, Judd.

Jorge/Jorgen *See* George.

Jori/Jorie Diminutives of Joram and Jordan.

Joris Dutch form of George.

Jorma *See* Jeremy.

Jory Cornish form of George. Also a diminutive of Joram.

Joscelin *See* Jocelin.

José/Josef *See* Joseph.

Joseph Hebrew: God shall add.
Giuseppe (Italian), Hohepa (Maori), Joesef, Joesph, José (Spanish), Josef (Czech, Dutch, German, Scandinavian), Josif, Józef (Polish), Jozeph, Jozif, József (Hungarian), Osip (Russian), Yosef (Hebrew), Yusuf (Arabic).
Diminutives: Beppe (Italian), Che (Spanish), Jo, Jodi, Jody, Joe, Joey, Joop (Dutch), Jose, Joze, Pepe (Spanish).

Joshua Hebrew: God is salvation. The biblical figure who led the Israelites to the Promised Land. *See also* Hosea and Jesús.
Hohua (Maori), Joshuah, Jozua (Dutch), Yeshua (Hebrew).
Diminutives: Josh, Joshi, Joshie, Joshy.

Josiah Hebrew: God heals. A biblical name.
Josaia, Josia, Josias.

Josif *See* Joseph.

Joss Chinese: fate. Also a diminutive of Jocelin.
Josse.

Jourdain/Jourdan/Jouri/Jourie *See* Jordan.

Journey Middle English: a voyage.
Jurney.

Jovan A Slavic form of John.

Jove Another name for the Roman god Jupiter, lord of the heavens, rain and the thunderbolt.
Jovi, Jovo (Welsh).

Jovi A form of Jove but also the name of a rock singer (Jon Bon Jovi).
Jovie.

Jowan *See* John.

Joze/Józef/Jozif/József *See* Joseph.

Jozua Dutch form of Joshua.

Juan Spanish form of John.
Diminutive: Juanito.

Jud/Judd *See* Jordan and Judah.

Judah Hebrew: the praised one. A son of Jacob in the Bible.
Hura (Maori), Juda (Arabic), Judas, Judd, Yehuda (Jewish).
Diminutive: Jude.

Jude *See* Judah.

Judson The son of Jud or Judd.
Juddsen, Juddson, Judsen.

Juhani Finnish form of John.

Juke A Creole word meaning wicked. Best known as part of the term jukebox.

Jules *See* Julian and Julius.

Julian English form of Julius. Suitable for a child born in July.
Jolyon, Julien (French), Julion, Julyan.
Diminutive: Jules.

Julius Latin: a Roman family name, possibly meaning youthful; born in July. *See also* Julian.
Giulio (Italian), Huriu (Maori), Julai (Swahili), Jules (French), Julian, Julio (Spanish).
Diminutive: Yul.

Jumah Swahili: born on a Friday.
Juma.

Jumala The supreme god in Finnish mythology; the equivalent of Jupiter.

Jun Chinese: the truth, or handsome. Japanese: truthful. Nepali: moonlight.

Jungle From the Hindi word for a forest (*see* Jangal).

Junius Latin: born in June.
Junio (Spanish).

Jupiter Latin: a planet and the Roman god of the heavens, rain and the thunderbolt. Also known as Jove, and the equivalent of the Greek god Zeus.
Iau (Welsh), Jupitor, Jupyter.

Jurgen German form of George.

Juri A form of George.
Jurie, Juriel (Spanish), Juris.

Jurney *See* Journey.

Jurrien Dutch form of George.

Justin Latin: fair and just.
Iestin (Welsh), Iestyn (Welsh), Joost (Dutch), Juste (French), Justen, Justinian, Justino, Justis, Justo (Portuguese), Justus, Justyn, Yestin (Welsh).

Jyles/Jylles *See* Giles.

Jymeoin/Jymowen *See* Jimeoin.

Jyotis Sanskrit: light.

K

Kaamran *See* Kamran.

Kacey/Kacie *See* Casey.

Kade *See* Cade.

Kaden/Kaeden *See* Caden.

Kadir Arabic: powerful.
Kadar, Kedar, Qadir.

Kadish Aramaic: the holy one.

Kaelan/Kaelen/Kaelyn *See* Kalan.

Kafka The surname of a famous Czech author (Franz Kakfa), possibly meaning a bird.

Kaha Maori: strong.

Kahai The god of lightning in Hawaiian mythology.

Kahika Maori: a white pine.

Kahil Polynesian: the young one.

Kahlan/Kahlen/Kahlyn *See* Kalan.

Kahn *See* Khan.

Kahnay/Kahne *See* Kane.

Kaho Polynesian: an arrow.

Kahoku Hawaiian: a star.

Kahua Polynesian: the sea.

Kahukura Maori: a rainbow.

Kahurangi Maori: sky-blue.

Kai Danish: the earth. Hawaiian: of the sea. *See also* Ky.
Kaie, Kaii, Kaiis, Kaj.

Kaid/Kaide *See* Cade.

Kaiden/Kaidyn *See* Caden.

Kailash A sacred mountain in Tibet.

Kaimana Hawaiian: like a diamond.

Kain/Kaine *See* Kane.

Kainoa A Hawaiian name of uncertain meaning.

Kaipo Hawaiian: a sweetheart.

Kaj *See* Kai.

Kaka Maori: a native New Zealand parrot.

Kakariki Maori: green, or a lizard.

Kal *See* Calvin.

Kala Hawaiian: the sun. Sanskrit: black. Also the Javanese god of the ocean.

Kalahari A desert in southern Africa.

Kalan A popular modern name, probably from an Irish Gaelic word.
Caelan, Caelen, Caelyn, Calan, Calen, Calyn, Kaelan, Kaelen, Kaelyn, Kahlan, Kahlen, Kahlyn, Kalen, Kalin, Kalyn, Kaylan, Kaylen, Kaylin, Khalan, Khalen, Khalyn.

Kalani Hawaiian: of the heavens.

Kalden Sherpa/Tibetan: of the golden age.
Kaldon.

Kale Hawaiian: strong and manly.

Kaleb *See* Caleb.

Kalevi An unusual Finnish name.

Kaley/Kalie *See* Caley.

Kalid *See* Khalid.

Kalil *See* Khalil.

Kalis A modern name of uncertain origin.
Kallis, Kelis, Kellis.

Kallaghan/Kallahan *See* Callaghan.

Kallan/Kallen/Kallin/Kallyn *See* Callan.

Kalm A form of calm, meaning peaceful and quiet.

Kalon Greek: handsome.

Kalvin/Kalvyn *See* Calvin.

Kama Thai: the golden one.

Kamal Arabic: perfect. The name of the Baha'i month that encompasses 1–19 August, so suitable for a Leo baby.
Cemal, Kamahl, Kamil, Kemal.

Kamar *See* Qamar.

Kameren/Kameron *See* Cameron.

Kami Hindi: loving. Japanese: heavenly.

Kamil *See* Camille and Kamal.

Kamran Persian: prosperous.
Kaamran, Kamuran (Turkish).

Kamren/Kamron/Kamryn *See* Cameron.

Kana Hawaiian: the name of a demigod.

Kanaan/Kanan/Kanen *See* Canaan.

Kanaloa Hawaiian: the god of the deep ocean.

Kane Irish Gaelic: warlike. *See also* Cathan.
Kain, Kaine, Kayn, Kayne, Khain, Khaine, Khane, Khayn, Khayne.

Kane Hawaiian: the god of artistic beauty.
Kahnay, Kahne, Kanye.

Kaniel Arabic: spear-like. Hebrew: a reed.

Kano Japanese: the god of the waters.

Kanuha Hawaiian: the sulky one.

Kanye *See* Kane.

Kapena Hawaiian: a captain.

Kapono Hawaiian: righteousness.

Kapua Maori: a cloud.

Kapura Maori: fire.

Kara Maori: an old man.

Karan Sanskrit: a warrior.

Karel/Karl *See* Charles.

Karim Arabic: noble and generous.
Kareem.

Karma Sanskrit: fate or destiny. Sherpa/Tibetan: a star. Also a girl's name.
Karmah.

Karmichael *See* Carmichael.

Karo Maori: a New Zealand tree.

Karol/Károly *See* Charles.

Karsten *See* Christian.

Kasen Basque: a helmet.

Kasey *See* Casey.

Kasim *See* Qasim.

Kasimir *See* Casimir.

Kason Burmese: the month of April/May, corresponding to Taurus.

Kaspa/Kaspah/Kaspar/Kasper *See* Caspar.

Kassidy *See* Cassidy.

Kathel *See* Cathal.

Kauariki A Polynesian name of uncertain meaning.

Kauri Polynesian: a New Zealand tree.

Kavan *See* Cavan.

Kawa Japanese: a river.

Kawau Maori: a figure from legend.

Kay Welsh: rejoiced in. An Arthurian knight.
Cai (Welsh), Kaye.

Kaycee/Kaycie *See* Casey.

Kayd/Kayde *See* Cade.

Kayden/Kaydyn *See* Caden.

Kaylan/Kaylen/Kaylin *See* Kalan.

Kayleb *See* Caleb.

Kayn/Kayne *See* Kane.

Kazimir *See* Casimir.

Kealii Hawaiian: a chief.

Kean Irish Gaelic: ancient. *See also* Keane.
Cian, Kian.

Keane Old English: handsome and bold.
Kean, Keen, Keene.

Keanu Hawaiian: a sea breeze.
Keaneau.

Kearney Irish Gaelic: victorious.
Kearny.

Keaton Old English: the town of the outhouse.
Keaten.

Kedar *See* Kadir.

Kedjo Ghanaian: born on a Monday.

Keefe Irish Gaelic: handsome, noble.
Keef.

Keefer *See* Kiefer.

Keegan Irish Gaelic: fiery, determined.

Keel Middle English: part of a ship's hull.
Keele, Kiel, Kiele.

Keelan *See* Kelan.

Keeley *See* GIRLS.

Kee-Lin Chinese: a little dragon.
Keelin, Keelyn.

Keen/Keene *See* Keane.

Keenan Irish Gaelic: little, ancient.

Keeran *See* Kieran.

Kees Dutch diminutive of Cornelius.

Kei Hawaiian: dignified or glorious.

Keifer/Keiffer *See* Kiefer.

Keiki Hawaiian: a boy or son.

Kiel/Kiele *See* Keel.

Keir Celtic: dark. Scottish: probably from the surname Kerr.
Kier.

Keiran/Keirnan *See* Kieran and Kiernan.

Keisuke An unusual name from Japan.

Keith Celtic: from the forest.
Keigh, Keithe.

Kekipi Hawaiian: a rebel.

Kekoa Hawaiian: the brave one.

Kekona Hawaiian: a second (as in time).

Kelan Irish Gaelic: slender.
Keelan.

Kelby Old German: from the farm by the spring or ridge.
Kelbeigh, Kelbi, Kelbie, Kellbeigh, Kellbi, Kellbie, Kellby.

Kelis/Kellis *See* Kalis.

Kell Old Norse: from the well or spring.

Kellbie/Kellby *See* Kelby.

Keller Irish Gaelic: a little companion.

Kelly Irish Gaelic: a warrior. Also a girl's name.

Kelley.

Kelsey Old Norse: a dweller on the island or by the water.
Kelsee, Kelsi, Kelsie, Kelsy.

Kelso A Scottish town.

Kelt Greek: a Celtic person.
Celt.

Keltie From Latin: a Celtic person.
Celtee, Celtey, Celti, Celtie, Celty, Keltee, Keltey, Kelti, Kelty.

Kelton Old English: from the calf farm.
Celten, Celton, Kelten.

Kelvin The name of a Scottish river.
Kellvin, Kellvyn, Kelvyn.

Kem Gypsy: the sun.

Kemal *See* Kamal.

Kembell/Kemble *See* Kimball.

Kemp Old English: a warrior or champion.

Ken Japanese: clear water. Also a diminutive of Kenneth.

Kenan A legendary Cornish king.

Kendall English: from the bright valley.
Kendal, Kendel, Kendell.

Kendel/Kendell *See* Kendall.

Kendrick Celtic: a hill. Old English: royal power.

Kenedy *See* Kennedy.

Kenelm Old English: a brave helmet; a protector. The name of a saint.

Keneth *See* Kenneth.

Kenley Old English: from the royal meadow.

Kenn Celtic/Welsh: as clear as bright water.

Kennard Old English: bold and hardy.

Kennedy Irish Gaelic: an ugly head, or a helmeted chief.
Kenedy.

Kenneth Scottish Gaelic: handsome and fair, or born of fire.
Keneth, Kennet, Kennith, Kennyth.
Diminutives: Ken, Kenny, Kent.

Kennett An English river and placename.
Kennet.

Kenny A diminutive of Kenneth.

Kenrick Old English: a bold ruler.

Kent Celtic: bright, white. An English county, and a diminutive of Kenneth.

Kenta Japanese: healthy.

Kenton Old English: from the royal manor or estate.

Kenver Cornish: a great chief.

Kenward Old English: a bold guardian, or a brave soldier.
Kenway.

Kenway *See* Kenward.

Kenwyn Cornish/Welsh: a splendid chief; the name of a saint. Also a girl's name.
Kenwyn, Kenwynn.

Kenya An African country.

Kenyon Irish Gaelic: white- or fair-haired.

Kenzie *See* GIRLS.

Keoki Hawaiian form of George.

Keoni Polynesian: the righteous one.

Kerby *See* Kirby.

Kerekori Maori form of Gregory.

Kereru Maori: a wood pigeon.

Kereteki Polynesian: a mythological figure.

Kerey English Gypsy: homeward bound.
Keri, Kerie.

Kermit Manx Gaelic/Irish Gaelic: a free man.

Kern Irish Gaelic: the little dark one.

Kernick Cornish: from the little corner.

Kernow Cornish: from Cornwall.
Curnow.

Kerr Irish Gaelic: dark.

Kerrin See Kieran.

Kerry Irish Gaelic: the dark one. Also the name of an Irish county and a girl's name.
Kerrey, Kerri, Kerrie.

Kersen Indonesian: a cherry.

Kerwin Irish Gaelic: the little black-haired one.
Kerwan, Kerwen, Kerwyn, Kirwin.

Kesar Russian form of Caesar.

Kester Scottish form of Christopher.

Kestrel Middle English: a small falcon.
Kestrell, Kestryl, Kestryll.

Kevan/Keven See Kevin.

Keverne Cornish: the name of a saint and a placename.
Kevern.

Kevin Irish Gaelic: beloved.
Kevan, Keven, Kevon, Kevyn.
Diminutive: Kev.

Keyt/Keyte See Kite.

Khain/Khaine/Khane See Kane.

Khalan/Khalen/Khalyn See Kalan.

Khalid Arabic: eternal.
Kalid.

Khalif Arabic: successor.

Khalifa, Khalipha.

Khalil Arabic: a friend.
Kalil.

Khan Arabic: a prince or king.
Cahn, Kahn, Khanh.

Khayn/Khayne See Kane.

Khi/Khie See Ky.

Khian See Kyan.

Khobee/Khobie/Khoby See Kobe.

Khyan See Kyan.

Ki/Kie See Ky.

Kian See Kean and Kyan.

Kiefer Irish Gaelic: pleasure, enjoyment.
Keefer, Keifer, Keiffer, Kief, Kieffer.

Kiel/Kiele See Keel.

Kier See Keir.

Kieran Irish Gaelic: dark, black.
Ciarán (Irish), Keeran, Keiran, Kerrin, Kieren, Kyran (Irish).

Kiernan Irish Gaelic: a form of Tiernan, meaning a lord.
Keirnan.

Killarney Irish Gaelic: the church of sloes. An Irish county.

Killian Irish Gaelic: the little warlike one.
Kilian.

Kilpatrick Gaelic: from the church of St Patrick.

Kim Rudyard Kipling's hero in the novel of the same name. Vietnamese: the golden one. *See also* Kimball and Kimberley.

Kimball Celtic: a warrior chief.
Kembell, Kemble, Kimble.
Diminutive: Kim.

Kimberley Old English: from the

meadow. More commonly a girl's name.
Kimberly.
Diminutive: Kim.

Kimble *See* Kimball.

Kimi Finnish: the name of a well-known racing car driver (Kimi Raikkonen).

Kimo Hawaiian form of James.

Kin Japanese: golden.

Kindred Affinity, as in a kindred spirit.

King English: a ruler, a sovereign.
Kinge, Kingi (Maori).

Kingsley Old English: from the king's wood or meadow.
Kingslee, Kingsleigh, Kingslie, Kinsley.

Kingston Old English: from the king's farm.
Kingsten.

Kinnard Irish Gaelic: from the high hill.

Kinsey Old English: a victorious king or prince.

Kinsley *See* Kingsley.

Kio A modern name of uncertain meaning.
Kioh.

Kipling After Rudyard Kipling, a famous English novelist.
Diminutives: Kip, Kipp.

Kipp English: the dweller on the pointed hill. *See also* Kipling.
Kip.

Kippax Middle English: the town in the ash trees.

Kiran Sanskrit: a ray of light.

Kirby *See* GIRLS.

Kirill *See* Cyril.

Kirin Japanese: a mythological unicorn.

Kiritowha Maori form of Christopher.

Kirk Old Norse: a dweller by the church. Also a diminutive of names such as Kirkland.
Kirke.

Kirkland Old Norse: the church land.
Diminutives: Kirk, Kirke.

Kirkley Old English: from the church meadow.

Kirkwood Old English: from the church wood.

Kiron *See* Chiron.

Kirwin *See* Kerwin.

Kit A diminutive of Christian and Christopher.
Kitt.

Kite Middle English: a type of hawk.
Keyt, Keyte, Kyte.

Kito Swahili: a jewel.

Kitto Cornish diminutive of Christopher.
Kittoe, Kittow.

Kiva Hebrew: protected.

Kiwi Maori: a native New Zealand bird.

Kiyoshi Japanese: the quiet one.

Kjell Scandinavian: from an Old Norse word meaning a kettle or helmet.
Kjeld.

Klaas/Klaes/Klaus *See* Nicholas.

Klae/Klaeton/Klayten/Klayton *See* Clayton.

Klaud *See* Claude.

Kleave/Kleaver/Kleve *See* Cleave.

Kleavon/Klevon *See* Cleavon.

Klein Dutch and German: small, the little one.
Clein, Cline, Kline.

Klemens/Kliment *See* Clement.

Kleon *See* Cleon.

Knight Old English: a mounted soldier.
Knights.

Knox Irish Gaelic: from the hillock.

Knut Old Norse: a knot. The name of several Danish kings.
Canute, Knud, Knute.

Koa Hawaiian: brave, fearless.

Kobe A popular modern name, particularly in the USA. Probably derived from Jacob (the supplanter).
Cobe, Cobee, Cobey, Cobi, Cobie, Coby, Khobee, Khobi, Khobie, Khoby, Kobee, Kobey, Kobi, Kobie, Koby.

Kodi/Kodie/Kody *See* Cody.

Koen *See* Cohen.

Kofi Ghanaian: born on a Friday.

Kohan/Kohen *See* Cohen.

Kole *See* Cole.

Kolt/Kolte *See* Colt.

Kolya A Russian diminutive of Nikolai (*see* Nicholas).

Kona Hawaiian: the south.

Konan *See* Conan.

Konrad German and Polish form of Conrad.

Konstantin/Konstantyn *See* Constantine.

Kooper *See* Cooper.

Koray Turkish: the ember moon.

Koree/Korey/Kory *See* Corey.

Kornel *See* Cornelius.

Kosmo/Kosmos *See* Cosmo.

Kostas Greek form of Constantine.

Kostya *See* Constantine.

Kressley A modern American name, probably inspired by Carson Kressley of the *Queer Eye* TV series.
Kreslee, Kresleigh, Kresley, Kresslee, Kressleigh.

Krest/Kreste *See* Crest.

Krikor An unusual Turkish name.

Kris *See* Christian and Christopher.

Krishna Sanskrit: dark or black. An important Hindu god.

Krispen/Krispin *See* Crispin.

Kristen/Kristian/Kristinn *See* Christian.

Kristo/Kristof/Kristoffer/Krystof *See* Christopher.

Kruise/Kruize/Kruze *See* Cruise.

Krys A diminutive of Christopher.

Kukuwai Maori: swampy.

Kulapo Tongan: possibly meaning a fish.

Kumar Sanskrit: a boy, a son.

Kumera Sanskrit: a god of war.

Kupa/Kupah *See* Cooper.

Kupe Polynesian: an heroic explorer.

Kura Polynesian: red.

Kurt *See* Conrad and Curtis.

Kurtis/Kurtiss *See* Curtis.

Kurtlee/Kurtleigh/Kurtly *See* Curtleigh.

NEW ZEALAND SPORTSPEOPLE

Women		Men	
Adine	Wilson	Arthur	Lydiard
Allison	Roe	Ben	Fouhy
Anna	Rowberry	Blyth	Tait
Anne	Audain	Bob	Charles
Annelise	Coberger	Carlos	Spencer
Barbara	Kendall	Chris	Cairns
Beatrice	Faumuina	Christian	Cullen
Bernice	Mene	Colin	Meads
Caroline	Meyer (Evers–Swindell)	Dan	Carter
Casey	Williams	Daniel	Vettori
Donna	Wilkins	Danyon	Loader
Emily	Naylor	David	Tua
Erin	Baker	Dean	Barker
Eve	Rimmer	Edmund	Hillary
Georgina	Earl (Evers-Swindell)	Eric	Murray
Irene	van Dyk	George	Nepia
Jo	Aleh	Graham	Henry
Jodi	Te Huna	Hamish	Bond
Julie	Seymour	Ivan	Mauger
Kate	McIlroy	Jonah	Lomu
Kayla	Sharland	Mahé	Drysdale
Linda	Jones	Mark	Todd
Lisa	Carrington	Martin	Crowe
Lois	Muir	Matthew	Ridge
Lorraine	Moller	Michael	Campbell
Marise	Chamberlain	Murray	Halberg
Melissa	Moon	Pero	Cameron
Neroli	Fairhall	Peter	Blake
Olivia	Powrie	Possum	Bourne
Penny	Whiting	Richard	Hadlee
Rebecca	Perrott	Richie	McCaw
Rita	Fatialofa	Russell	Coutts
Sandra	Edge	Scott	Dixon
Sarah	Ulmer	Sean	Fitzpatrick
Sarah	Walker	Sonny Bill	Williams
Susan	Devoy	Stacey	Jones
Temepara	George	Stephen	Fleming
Valerie	Adams (Vili)	Tana	Umaga
Waimarama	Taumaunu	Wynton	Rufer
Yvette	Williams	Zinzan	Brooke

Kuruk Native American: a bear.

Kwain/Kwaine *See* Quain.

Kwame Ghanaian: born on a Saturday.

Kwan Korean: strong.

Kwayd/Kwayde/Kweyd/Kweyde *See* Quade.

Ky A popular modern name, probably an abbreviation of Kyle. *See also* Kai.
Khi, Khie, Ki, Kie, Kya, Kyah, Kye, Kygh.

Kyal/Kyel *See* Kyle.

Kyan A modern name, probably from Kian (*see* Kean), or a variation of Ky.
Khian, Khyan, Kian.

Kyden A modern name derived from Ky.
Kyeden, Kyedon, Kydon.

Kyffen A modern name, possibly from Kevin.
Kyfen, Kyff.

Kyle Scottish Gaelic: from the narrow strait. A Scottish region.
Kyal, Kyall, Kyel, Kyell, Kylan, Kylen.

Kyloe Old English: from the cows' meadow.
Kylow, Kylowe.

Kynan *See* Conan.

Kyne Old English: royal.

Kyran *See* Kieran.

Kyrie Greek: from kyrios (O Lord).

Kyron *See* Chiron.

Kyson A modern 'Ky combination name' literally the son of Ky.
Kyesen, Kyeson, Kysen.

Kyte *See* Kite.

L

Laban Hebrew: white.

Labhras Irish Gaelic form of Laurence.

Lachlan Scottish Gaelic: from the land of the lochs.
Lachlane, Lachlann, Lachlin, Lachlyn, Lauchlan, Lauchlann, Laughlan, Laughlin, Lochlainn (Irish Gaelic), Lochlan (Irish Gaelic), Lockelan, Lockelin, Lockelyn, Locklan, Locklin, Locklyn, Loclan, Loclyn, Loughlin.
Diminutives: Lachie, Lachy, Lochie, Lochtie, Lockey, Lockie, Locky.

Ladd English: a page or attendant.

Ladislav Slavic: a glorious ruler, or glorious power. *See also* Vladislav.
Ladislas (Polish), Ladislaus (Polish), Ladislo (Italian), Laszlo (Hungarian).

Lael Hebrew: belonging to God.
Lale.

Laertes Greek: a legendary figure.

Lafayette French: faith.

Laibrook Old English: the path by the brook.

Laidley Old English: from the water meadow.

Laike *See* Lake.

Laiken/Laikin *See* Laykin.

Laine *See* Lane.

Laing *See* Lang.

Laird Scottish Gaelic: a landowner, the lord of the manor.
Lairde.

Lajos Hungarian form of Louis.

Lake Old English: the original meaning was a stream rather than a pool or pond.
Laike, Layke.

Laken/Lakin *See* Laykin.

Laki Hawaiian and Samoan form of Lucky.

Lakshman Sanskrit: auspicious.
Laxman.

Lal Sanskrit: the beloved one.

Lalama Hawaiian: clever and daring.

Lale *See* Lael.

Lamar Teutonic: famous around the land.
Lamarr, Lemar.

Lambert Teutonic: from the bright or famous land.
Lamberto (Italian), Lammert, Landbert.

Lamech Hebrew: strong or powerful.

Lamont French: the mount. Old Norse: a lawyer.
Lamond, Lammond, Lammont.

Lance Old French: a lance-bearer. *See also* Lancelot.
Launce.

Lancelot Old English/Old French: a spear or lance attendant. The most famous of King Arthur's knights.
Launcelot.
Diminutive: Lance.

Landbert *See* Lambert.

Landers Old French: a launderer.
Lander, Landor.
Diminutive: Lanny.

Landon Old English: from the long hill.
Langdon, Langston.

Landor *See* Landers.

Lane Old English: from the narrow road.
Laine, Layne.

Lang Teutonic: a tall man.
Laing, Lainge, Lange.

Langdon/Langston *See* Landon.

Langford Old English: from the long ford.

Langi Polynesian: heaven.

Langley Old English: from the long meadow.

Langston Old English: the farm of the tall man.

Langworth Old English: from the long enclosure.

Lani Polynesian: the sky. Also a girl's name.

Lann Celtic: a sword.

Lanny *See* Harlan and Landers.

Lanyon Cornish: a cold pool or lake.

Laris Latin: cheerful.

Lark A songbird.
Larke.

Larrie/Larry *See* Laurence.

Lars Scandinavian form of Laurence.

Larson Scandinavian: the son of Lars.

Lascelles Old French: the hermitage or cell.

Laser A light-emitting device.
Lazer.

LaShawn American: a variation of Shawn (*see* Sean).
LaShaughan, LaShaun, LaShaune.

Lasse Finnish form of Laurence.

Laszlo Hungarian form of Ladislav.

Latham Old Norse: from the barn.

Latif Arabic: kind and gentle.

Lateef.

Latimer Old French: an interpreter or teacher.

Lauchlan/Laughlan/Laughlin *See* Lachlan.

Laughton *See* Lawton.

Launce *See* Lance.

Launcelot *See* Lancelot.

Laurans/Lauras *See* Laurence.

Laurence Latin: from the laurel tree, or crowned with laurels. *See also* Lawson.
Labhras (Irish Gaelic), Lars (Scandinavian), Lasse (Finnish), Laurans, Lauras (Lithuanian), Laurens (Dutch), Laurent (French), Lauri (Finnish), Lavrenti (Russian), Lawrance, Lawren, Lawrence, Loren, Lorencio (Spanish), Lorenz (German), Lorenzo (Italian), Lorin, Lorne.
Diminutives: Enzo (Italian), Larrie, Larry, Laurie, Lawrie, Laz, Lenz (German), Lon, Lonnie.

Lauri/Laurie *See* Laurence.

Lavrenti Russian form of Laurence.

Lawford Old English: from the ford by the hill.

Lawler Irish Gaelic: the mumbler, the soft-spoken one.

Lawley Old English: from the meadow on the hill.

Lawn From Old French: grass-covered land.
Lawne.

Lawrance/Lawren/Lawrence/Lawrie *See* Laurence.

Lawson Old English: the son of Lawrence or Laurence.

Lawton Old English: from the town on the hill.
Laughton.

Laxman *See* Lakshman.

Layke *See* Lake.

Laykin Old English: from the little field or meadow.
Laiken, Laikin, Laken, Lakin, Leghken, Leghkin, Leykin.

Layland *See* Leland and Leyland.

Layne *See* Lane.

Layten/Layton *See* Leighton.

Laz Diminutive of Laurence.

Lazarus Hebrew: God is my help. The man who Jesus raised from the dead in the Bible.
Eleazar (Hebrew), Elezar (Hebrew), Lazar (Hungarian), Lazare (French), Lazrus, Lazzaro (Italian).

Lazer *See* Laser.

Leaf Middle English: a 'plant name'. *See also* Leif.
Leafe.

Leal Old English: loyal and true.

Leam/Leeam *See* Liam.

Leander Greek: the lion man. A hero in Greek legend. *See also* Leo, Leonard and Lionel.
Léandre (French), Leandro (Italian, Spanish), Leandros (Greek).

Lear Teutonic: joyful, or from the sea. A Shakespearean character.
Llyr (Welsh).

Lebron American: a name popularised by basketball player Lebron James.
LeBron, Lebronn, LeBronn, Lebronne, LeBronne.

Lech Polish: the legendary founder of

Poland.

Ledger Teutonic: probably from the surname St Leger.
Leger.

Lee Old English: a meadow or clearing.
Leigh.

Leeroi/Leeroy/Lee-Roy *See* Leroy.

Leeston *See* GIRLS.

Leeuwin Dutch: a lioness.

Leevi/Leevie *See* Levi.

Leger *See* Ledger.

Leghken/Leghkin *See* Laykin.

Lei Chinese: thunder.

Leicester *See* Lester.

Leif Old Norse: beloved; or a descendant, an heir.
Leaf, Leiv (Norwegian), Lief, Liev.

Leigh *See* Lee.

Leighton Old English: the dweller at the farm by the meadow. Also a modern girl's name.
Layten, Layton, Leighten, Leyton Lleyton.

Leiham/Leihem *See* Liam.

Leith Scottish Gaelic: a broad river. A Scottish placename.
Leithe.

Leiv Norwegian form of Leif.

Leka A popular Albanian name.

Leland Old English: from the meadow-land.
Layland.

Lemar *See* Lamar.

Lemuel Hebrew: devoted to God. The first name of Gulliver, the hero of Jonathan Swift's *Gulliver's Travels*, and also a biblical name.

Len/Lennie/Lenny Diminutives of names such as Lennox and Leonard.

Lenard/Lennard/Lennart *See* Leonard.

Lennon Irish Gaelic: a little cape or cloak.
Lenan, Lennan, Lenon.

Lennor English Gypsy: the springtime.

Lennox Scottish Gaelic: a Scottish district and a surname.
Diminutives: Len, Lennie, Lenny.

Lenz A diminutive of Laurence.

Leo Latin: a lion, lion-hearted. *See also* Leander, Leonard, Leopold and Lionel.
Leoh, Leon, Léon (French), Léonce (French), Leoncio (Spanish), Leone (Italian), Leontes, Leonti (Russian), Leonzio (Italian), Leos (Czech), Lev (Russian), Levin, Lio, Lioh.

Leon/Léon *See* Leo.

Leonard Teutonic: as brave as a lion. *See also* Leander, Leo and Lionel.
Lenard, Lennard, Lennart (Scandinavian), Léonard (French), Leonardo (Italian, Portuguese, Spanish), Leonerd, Leonhard (German), Leonid (Russian), Levon (Armenian).
Diminutives: Len, Lennie, Lenny.

Leonardo *See* Leonard.

Léonce/Leoncio/Leone/Leontes *See* Leo.

Leonid/Leonti Russian forms of Leo and Leonard.

Leopard Middle English from Greek: a wild cat.
Lepard, Leppard.

Leopold Teutonic: brave for the people, patriotic.

Léopold (French), Leopoldo (Italian, Spanish).
Diminutive: Leo.

Leor *See* Lior.

Leos Czech form of Leo.

Leroy French: the king. A popular name in the USA. *See also* Elroy.
Leeroi, Lee-Roi, Leeroy, Lee-Roy, Leroi, Le-Roi, Le-Roy.

Leslie Scottish Gaelic: from an ancient surname.
Leslee, Lesleigh, Lesley.
Diminutive: Les.

Lester Old English: from the placename Leicester, meaning a Roman site or fort.
Leicester.

Leuca/Leuka *See* Luke.

Lev/Levin *See* Leo.

Leverett Old French: a young hare.

Leverton Old English: from the farm of the rushes.

Levi Hebrew: united.
Leevi, Leevie, Levey, Levie, Levy.

Levon Armenian form of Leonard.

Lew/Lewes/Lewey/Lewy *See* Lewis, Llewellyn and Louis.

Lewie A diminutive of Aloysius, Lewis and Louis.

Lewis A variation of Louis. Also an Anglicised form of the Welsh name Llewellyn.
Lewes, Lewys, Ludovic (Scottish).
Diminutives: Lew, Lewey, Lewie, Lewy, Louie.

Lex A diminutive of Alexander.

Leykin *See* Laykin.

Leyland Old English: from the fallow land.

Layland.

Leyman *See* Lyman.

Leyton *See* Leighton.

Lhakpa Sherpa/Tibetan: born on a Wednesday.

Lhawang Sherpa/Tibetan: the powerful one.

Li Chinese: strength.

Lial/Liall *See* Lyle.

Liam Irish Gaelic: a short form of Uilleam (William).
Leam, Leeam, Leiham, Leihem, Liamh, Lian, Liham, Lyam.

Liang Chinese: excellence.

Lief/Liev *See* Leif.

Liel/Liell *See* Lyle.

Liko Hawaiian: a bud.

Lim A popular Korean name.

Limerick A county in Ireland. Also a type of humorous verse.

Lin Burmese: bright.

Lincoln Old English: the settlement at the lake or pool. An English city.
Linken, Linkin, Linkyn.
Diminutives: Linc, Link.

Lind/Lindan/Linden/Lindon *See* Lyndon.

Lindberg Teutonic: the hill of the lime trees.

Lindell Old English: from the valley of lime trees.
Lyndell.

Lindley Old English: from the lime-tree meadow.

Lindsay Scottish: from an old surname.
Lindesay, Lindsey.

Linford Old English: from the

lime-tree ford.
Lynford.

Link Middle English: a bond or connection. Also a diminutive of Lincoln.
Linke, Lynk, Lynke.

Linken/Linkin/Linkyn *See* Lincoln.

Linley Old English: from the field of flax. Also a girl's name.
Lynleigh.

Linton Old English: from the flax farm or enclosure.
Linten, Lynten, Lynton.

Linus Greek: flaxen-haired.
Lynas, Lynus.

Linx/Linxe *See* Lynx.

Lio/Lioh Modern forms of Leo.

Lionel Old French: a young lion. *See also* Leander, Leo and Leonard.
Lionell, Lyonel, Lyonell.

Lior Hebrew: my light.
Leor.

Lisle French form of Lyle.

Liston An English placename.
Listen, Listyn.

Litton Old English: from the place on the river.
Lytton.

Livingston Old English: a dear friend's place.
Livingstone.

Llewellyn Welsh: lion-like, a leader or ruler. *See also* Lewis.
Lewis, Llewellen.
Diminutives: Lew (Cornish), Llew, Lyn, Lynn.

Lleyton *See* Leighton.

Lloyd Welsh: grey-haired.
Floyd, Loyd.

Lluís A Spanish form of Louis.

Llyr Welsh form of Lear.

Lobsang Sherpa/Tibetan: the kind-hearted one.

Loch Scottish Gaelic: a lake. *See also* Lachlan.
Diminutive: Lochie.

Lochinvar Scottish Gaelic: the hilltop loch or lake.
Lockinvar.

Lochlainn/Lochlan Irish Gaelic forms of Lachlan.

Lochtie A diminutive of Lachlan.

Locke Old English: from the stronghold.

Lockelin/Lockie/Locklin *See* Lachlan.

Lockinvar *See* Lochinvar.

Locksley *See* Loxley.

Lockwood Old English: from the enclosed wood.

Lockyer Old English: a locksmith.
Lockyear.

Loclan/Loclyn *See* Lachlan.

Lodge Old French: a hut or cottage.

Lodovico/Loic *See* Louis.

Logan Scottish Gaelic: a little hollow.
Logen, Logyn.

Lok Chinese: happiness.

Loman Irish Gaelic: enlightened. The name of several Irish saints.

Lomax An English surname, meaning the retreat by the pool.
Lomas.

Lombard Latin: long-bearded.

Lon/Lonnie Diminutives of Alphonso and Laurence.

London The capital of England.
Londen, Londin, Londyn.

Long Chinese: a dragon.

Lopeti Tongan form of Robert.

Lorant Hungarian form of Roland.

Lorcan Irish Gaelic: a fierce little one.

Loren/Lorencio/Lorenz/Lorenzo *See* Laurence.

Lorimer Old French: a spur-maker. Lorimar, Lorrimer.

Lorin *See* Laurence.

Loring Teutonic: a man from Lorraine, a former French province.

Lorne A Scottish placename. *See also* Laurence. Lorn.

Lorrimer *See* Lorimer.

Lote A Fijian name, well known due to rugby player Lote Tuqiri. Loti.

Lothair/Lothaire/Lothar/Lothario *See* Luther.

Lou/Louie *See* Lewis and Louis.

Louca/Loucah/Louk/Louka *See* Luke.

Loudon A Scottish placename, possibly meaning a low valley. Loudan, Louden.

Loughlin *See* Lachlan.

Louis Teutonic: a famous warrior. The name of sixteen French kings. *See also* Aloysius and Lewis. Lajos (Hungarian), Lewis, Lluís (Spanish), Lodovico (Italian), Loic (French), Ludi (Swiss), Ludovic (Scottish), Ludvig (Scandinavian), Ludvik (Czech), Ludwig (German), Ludwik (Polish), Luigi (Italian), Luis (Portuguese, Spanish), Luiz (Portuguese), Luthais (Scottish Gaelic).

Diminutives: Gino (Italian), Lewie, Lewey, Lewy, Lou, Louie, Ludo (Dutch, Scottish Gaelic).

Lovel/Lovell *See* Lowell.

Lowell Old French: a little wolf. Lovel, Lovell, Lowel.

Loxley Old English: the place of a lock of hair. Locksley.

Loxton Old English: the town of a lock of hair. Loxten.

Loyal Old French: true, faithful. Loyale.

Loyd *See* Lloyd.

Luc/Luca/Lucais *See* Luke.

Lucan *See* Lucian.

Lucas *See* Luke.

Lucian Latin: light. *See also* Luke. Lucan (Irish), Luciano (Italian, Portuguese, Spanish), Lucias, Lucien (French), Lucio (Italian, Spanish), Lucius, Lukan, Luzio (Italian). *Diminutives*: Luce, Lukey.

Lucio/Lucius *See* Lucian.

Luckner *See* Lukener.

Lucky Middle English: fortunate. Laki (Hawaiian, Samoan), Luckee, Luckey, Lucki, Luckie.

Lucretius Latin: gain. An early Roman poet.

Ludi Swiss form of Louis.

Ludlow Old English: from the prince's hill.

Ludo Dutch and Scottish Gaelic diminutives of Louis. Italian: light or brightness.

Ludovic *See* Lewis and Louis.

Ludvig/Ludvik/Ludwig/Ludwik *See* Louis.

Luger German: a type of gun. Lugar.

Lugh Irish Gaelic: a sun god. Luw.

Luigi/Luis/Luiz *See* Louis.

Luk/Luka/Lukah/Lukas *See* Luke.

Lukan *See* Lucian and Luke.

Luke Greek: a man from Lucania. One of Christ's apostles, the author of the third book of the New Testament. *See also* Lucian. Leuca, Leuka, Louca, Loucah, Louk, Louka, Loukah, Louke, Luc (French, Welsh), Luca (Italian), Lucah, Lucais (Scottish), Lucas, Luk (Cornish), Luka (Russian), Lukah, Lukan, Lukas (German, Swedish), Lukasz (Polish), Ruka (Maori). *Diminutive*: Lukey.

Lukener A form of Luke. Luckner.

Lund *See* Lunt.

Lundy French: born on Monday. Also an island off the coast of England. Lundi (French).

Lunt Old Norse: from the sacred wood. Lund.

Lute Middle English: a stringed musical instrument.

Luthais Scottish Gaelic form of Louis.

Luther Old French: a lute player. Teutonic: a famous warrior. Lothair, Lothaire, Lothar (German), Lothario (Italian).

Luw *See* Lugh.

Lux Latin: light.

Luzio *See* Lucian.

Lyal/Lyall/Lyell *See* Lyle.

Lyam *See* Liam.

Lyle Old French: from the island. Lial, Liall, Liel, Liell, Lisle (French), Lyal, Lyall, Lyel, Lyell.

Lyman Old English: a man from the meadow or valley. Leyman.

Lyn/Lynn Diminutives of the Welsh name Llewellyn.

Lynas/Lynus *See* Linus.

Lyndell *See* Lindell.

Lyndon Old English: from the hill of the lime trees. Lind, Lindan, Linden, Lindon, Lyndan, Lynden.

Lynford *See* Linford.

Lynk/Lynke *See* Link.

Lynleigh *See* Linley.

Lynten/Lynton *See* Linton.

Lynx From Greek: a North American wild cat. The name of a constellation. Linx, Linxe, Lynxe.

Lyonel *See* Lionel.

Lysander Greek: the liberator.

Lytton *See* Litton.

M

Maaka Maori form of Mark.

Maardi *See* Mardi.

Maarten Dutch form of Martin.

Mabon Welsh: a son.

Mac Scottish: the son of. A diminutive of names beginning with Mac.

Mack.

Macarius Latin: blessed.
Macharios, Makarios (Greek).

Macarthur Scottish Gaelic: the son of Arthur.
McArthur.

Macauley Irish and Scottish Gaelic: the son of Olaf.
McAulay, McAuley.

Macbeth A Scottish name, best known from the Shakespearean play of the same name.
McBeth.

McCartney Scottish Gaelic: the son of Arthur.
Macartney, McArtney.

Macdonald Scottish Gaelic: the son of Donald.

Mace Middle English: a 'spice name'.

McEwan Scottish Gaelic: the son of Ewan.
McEwen, McEwing.

Macey Old English: little Matthew. Also a girl's name.
Macy.

McGregor Scottish Gaelic: the son of Gregor or Gregory.
MacGregor.

McGuire See Maguire.

Macho Spanish: manly or virile.

McIntosh Scottish Gaelic: son of the chieftain.
MacIntosh, Mackintosh.

Mack See Mac.

Mackay Gaelic: son of the fiery one.
Magee, McKay.

MacKenna See GIRLS.

Mackenzie Scottish Gaelic: the son of the handsome one.

MacKensie, MacKenzie, McKenzie.

Macks See Max.

McLaren Scottish Gaelic: the son of Laurence.
Maclaren.

Maclean Scottish Gaelic: the son or follower of St John.
Maclaine, MacLaine, Maclayne, McLaine, McLane, McLean.

McMahon Irish Gaelic: son of the bear.
MacMahon.

Macquarie Scottish Gaelic: the son of Godfrey.
McQuarie.

McTavish Scottish Gaelic: the son of Thomas; a twin. See also Tavish.
MacTavish.

Macy See Macey.

Maddix/Maddoc/Maddox See Madoc.

Madison See GIRLS.

Madoc Old Welsh: fortunate. The name of a saint.
Maddix, Maddoc, Maddock, Maddox, Madog, Madok (Cornish), Maedoc, Maidoc.

Madron Latin: a nobleman. A Cornish placename and the name of a saint.

Maehe Maori form of March.

Maesen/Maeson See Mason.

Maex See Max.

Magdi See Majid.

Magee See Mackay.

Magnus Latin: the great one. Generally a Scandinavian name.
Maghnus (Irish Gaelic), Magnuss, Mànas (Scottish Gaelic), Manus (Irish), Mogens (Danish).

Maguire A common Irish surname. McGuire.

Magus Greek: a magician or priest.

Mahé French: the main island of the Seychelles.

Mahela An unusual name from Sri Lanka.

Mahendra Sanskrit: the great god Indra (the god of the sky). Mahindra, Mohinder.

Mahesh Sanskrit: a great ruler.

Mahir Hebrew: industrious.

Mahmood Arabic: praiseworthy. *See also* Muhammad. Mahmud.

Mahomet/Mahommed *See* Muhammad.

Mahon Irish: a bear.

Mahsen/Mahson *See* Mason.

Mahsood *See* Masud.

Maidoc *See* Madoc.

Maik/Maikel Dutch forms of Mike and Michael.

Maine The name of a state of the USA. Main, Mayn, Mayne.

Maisen/Maison *See* Mason.

Maitland Old French: from the meadow land.

Majid Arabic: the illustrious one. Magdi, Majeed, Majdi, Majeed.

Major Middle English: greater, larger or superior. Majors.

Maka Maori: a South Island chief. Also a form of Mark. Makah.

Makaha Hawaiian: fierce.

Makai Hawaiian: towards the sea.

Makani Hawaiian: the wind.

Makarios *See* Macarius.

Makis Greek form of Michael.

Mako A type of shark.

Makoa Maori/Polynesian: either a form of Maaka (Mark), or from Maka.

Maks/Maksim/Makswell *See* Max, Maximilian and Maxwell.

Makya Native American: the eagle hunter.

Mal Diminutive of Malcolm, Malden and other names.

Malachi Hebrew: the messenger of the Lord. A prophet in the Bible. Malachai, Malachy.

Malcolm Scottish Gaelic: a follower of St Columba, known as the dove. Malcom.
Diminutive: Mal.

Malden Old English: from the hill with a monument. Maldon.
Diminutive: Mal.

Malik Arabic: the master or king.

Malin Old English: a little warrior.

Malise Scottish Gaelic: the servant of Jesus.

Mallory Old French: unlucky. Also a girl's name. Malorey, Malorie, Malory.

Malo French: the name of a saint. Hawaiian: the winner.

Malone Irish Gaelic: a devotee of St John.

Malvern Old Welsh: the bare hill.

Mamo Hawaiian: yellow.

Manaia Maori: a seahorse.

Mànas *See* Magnus.

Manchu Chinese: pure.

Mandel Jewish: a little man.
Teutonic: an almond.

Manfield Old English: from the
communal field.

Manfred Teutonic: a man of peace.
Manfredo (Italian), Manfrid,
Manfried (German).

Mani Sanskrit: a jewel.

Manley Middle English: brave and
manly.
Manly.

Mannie/Manny *See* Emmanuel.

Manning Old English: the man.

Mannix Irish Gaelic: a little monk.

Manoel *See* Emmanuel.

Mansa African: a king.

Mansell An English surname,
possibly meaning a person from
Le Mans, France.
Mansel.

Manson Literally the son of a man.
Mansan, Mansen.

Mansoor Arabic: victorious.
Mansur.

Manu Maori/Polynesian/Samoan: a
bird, or the man of the birds.

Manuel *See* Emmanuel.

Manus *See* Magnus.

Manzo Japanese: the third son.

Marama Maori: the moon.
Polynesian: radiant. Also a girl's
name.

Marc/Marcel/Marcello *See* Mark.

Marco/Marcos/Marcus *See* Mark.

Marconi Italian: after the wireless
telegraph inventor Guglielmo
Marconi.

Mardi French: Tuesday, after Mars,
the Roman god of war.
Maardi, Mardy, Martedi (Italian),
Martes (Spanish).

Marek *See* Mark.

Maren Basque: from the sea. *See also*
Marion.
Maran.

Marian *See* Marion and Marius.

Marino Latin: of the sea. Masculine
form of Marina.
Marin (Slavic).

Mario *See* Marius.

Marion Old French from Latin: little
Mary. Most often a girl's name.
Maren, Marian, Marien.

Marius Latin: virile; the warlike one.
See also Mark, Mars and Martin.
Marian (Polish), Mariano (Italian,
Spanish), Mario (Italian, Spanish),
Mariusz (Polish).

Marjan Swahili: coral.

Mark Latin: relating to Mars, the
god of war. One of the four New
Testament envangelists. *See also*
Marius, Mars and Martin.
Maaka (Maori), Maka (Maori), Marc
(French, Welsh), Marcel (French),
Marcell (German), Marcellin
(French), Marcellino (Italian),
Marcello (Italian), Marcellus
(French), Marcelo (Portuguese),
Marco (Italian, Spanish), Marcos
(Portuguese), Marcus, Marek (Czech,
Polish), Marke, Markku (Finnish),
Marko (Slavic), Markos (Greek),
Markus (German).

Markku/Marko/Markos/Markus *See*
Mark.

Marland Old English: from the lake land.

Marlen *See* Marlon.

Marley Old English: from the pleasant meadow.
Marlee, Marleigh, Marli, Marlie, Marly.

Marlin The name of a fish. *See also* Marlon.

Marlon Old French: a little hawk. Also a modern girl's name.
Marlen, Marlin.

Marlow Old English: from the lake or pond.
Marlowe.

Marmaduke Irish: the servant of Madoc.
Diminutive: Duke.

Marmion French: the tiny one.

Maron Greek: a character from Greek mythology. *See also* Marron.

Maroo *See* Maru.

Maroon From French: a 'colour name'.
Maroun.

Marquis French: a nobleman.
Marques, Marquest, Marquist.

Marriott A diminutive of Mary (a bitterly wanted child).
Marriot.

Marron French: brown, or a chestnut. Spanish: brown.
Maron.

Mars Latin: the Roman god of war (the equivalent of the Greek god Ares) and the ruler of the zodiac sign of Aries. *See also* Marius, Mark and Martin.
Marse, Marz, Marze, Mawrth (Welsh).

Marsden Old English: from the valley boundary.

Marsena Persian: dignified.

Marsh Old English: from the marshy land.

Marshall Teutonic: a horse-keeper, or a steward.
Marshal, Marshel, Marshell.

Marston Old English: the place by the marsh.

Martedi/Martes *See* Mardi.

Martin Latin: of Mars, the Roman god of war. *See also* Marius and Mark.
Maarten (Dutch), Mártan (Irish Gaelic), Marten, Martijn (Dutch), Martino (Italian), Marton (Hungarian), Martyn, Merten (German), Morten (Danish).
Diminutives: Mart, Martie, Marty.

Marty/Martyn *See* Martin.

Martyr Someone with strong convictions.

Maru Polynesian: the god of war.
Maroo.

Marv/Marvin/Marvyn *See* Mervyn.

Marz/Marze *See* Mars.

Masa Japanese: good.

Mascot Something that brings good luck.
Mascott, Mascotte.

Mason Old French: a stonemason.
Maesen, Maeson, Mahsen, Mahson, Maisen, Maison, Masen, Maysen, Mayson, Mehsen, Mehson.

Massimo *See* Maximilian.

Masud Arabic: the fortunate one.
Mahsood.

Mat/Matt Diminutives of Matthew.

Mata *See* Matthew.

Matai Maori: to gaze out to sea.

Matangi Samoan: the wind.

Matareka Polynesian: the one with a smiling face.

Mateo/Mateus/Mateusz *See* Matthew.

Mathieu/Mathiu *See* Matthew.

Matiu Maori form of Matthew.

Matrix A scientific and mathematical term, meaning what gives form or origin to something.
Matriks.

Mats *See* Matthew.

Matthew Hebrew: a gift of God. One of the twelve apostles and the author of the first book of the New Testament. *See also* Macey and Madison.
Mata (Scottish Gaelic), Mateo (Spanish), Mateus (Portuguese), Mateusz (Polish), Mathew, Mathias, Mathieu (French), Mathiu, Matiu (Maori), Mats (Swedish), Mattea, Matteo (Italian), Mattew, Matthias, Matti (Finnish), Matz (German).
Diminutives: Mat, Matt, Matte (German), Matti, Mattie, Matty, Thies (Dutch), Thijs (Dutch).

Matti/Mattie/Matty/Matz *See* Matthew.

Matu Native American: a brave warrior. Polynesian: the north wind.

Maui Polynesian: a legendary hero. The name of an Hawaiian island.

Maunga Maori: a mountain.

Maurice Latin: dark-skinned, like a Moor. *See also* Morrison.
Mauri (Finnish), Mauricio (Spanish), Maurise, Maurizio (Italian), Mauro (Italian), Merrick (Welsh), Meurig (Welsh), Morice, Moritz (German), Morrell, Morris, Morriss, Morse, Muiris (Irish).
Diminutives: Maurie, Maury, Mo, Moe, Morrie, Morry.

Maverick American: a dissenter or a loner.

Mawgan Cornish: the name of a saint.

Mawnan Cornish: a placename and the name of a saint.

Mawrth Welsh form of Mars.

Mawson The surname of a famous Antarctic explorer (Sir Douglas Mawson).
Mawsen.

Max A diminutive of Maximilian and Maxwell.
Macks, Maex, Maks, Maxx, Maxxe.

Maxence A modern name, derived from Max.
Maxsence.

Maxey Old English: from the island of Magnus. *See also* Maximilian and Maxwell.

Maxim/Maxime *See* Maximilian.

Maximilian Latin: the greatest.
Maksim (Russian), Massimo (Italian), Maxim, Maxime (French), Maximilien (French), Maximo, Maximus, Maxium.
Diminutives: Maks, Max, Maxey, Maxi, Maxx, Maxy.

Maxsence *See* Maxence.

Maxwell Scottish Gaelic: from the stream of Magnus.
Makswell.
Diminutives: Maks, Max, Maxey,

Maxi, Maxx, Maxy.

Mayer *See* Meir.

Mayn/Mayne *See* Maine.

Maynard Teutonic: strong and brave.
Meinard (German).

Maysen/Mayson *See* Mason.

Mc names – *see* Mac.

Mead Old English: from the meadow.
Meade, Meades, Meads.

Meadows Old English: from the
meadow.
Meddowes, Meddows.

Medwin Old English: a friend from
the meadow.

Mehsen/Mehson *See* Mason.

Meical Welsh form of Michael.

Meinard *See* Maynard.

Meir Hebrew: one who gives light.
Mayer, Meier, Meyer, Myer.

Meirion Welsh: a traditional name of
uncertain meaning.

Meka Hawaiian: the eyes.

Mel A diminutive of names such as
Melville and Melvin.

Melburn Old English: from the
millstream.
Melbourn, Melbourne, Milbourn,
Milbourne, Milburn.

Melchior Persian: the king of the city.
One of the three wise men in the Bible.
Melchor, Melek (Jewish).

Melford Old English: from the ford
by the hill.

Melor *See* Mylor.

Melrose Old English: from the bare
moor.

Melville Old French: from the poor
settlement.

Melvil, Melvill, Melvin, Melvyn.
Diminutive: Mel.

Memphis The Ancient Egyptian
capital and a city in Tennessee, USA.
Also a girl's name.
Memphys.

Menachem Hebrew: the comforter.
Menahem, Menchem, Mendel.

Menadue Cornish: from the dark hill.

Mendel *See* Menachem.

Mentor Greek: a counsellor or
advisor. A wise old man in Greek
mythology.

Menzies Scottish: a well-known
surname.

Merak Arabic: the loin of the bear.
A star in the constellation of Ursa
Major, the Great Bear.

Mercer Old French: a merchant.

Mercury Latin: a planet and the
Roman messenger of the gods.
Mercher (Welsh), Mercurino,
Mercurio, Mercutio.

Meredith Old Welsh: a lord. Also a
girl's name.
Meredeth, Merideth, Meridith,
Meridyth.

Merfyn Welsh form of Mervyn.

Merivale Old English: a pleasant
valley.

Merle Old French: a blackbird. More
commonly a girl's name.

Merlin Old Welsh: from the fort by
the sea, or a falcon. The legendary
magician from the court of King
Arthur.
Merlyn, Myrddin (Welsh).

Merrick A Welsh form of Maurice.
Merik, Meyrick.

Merrill Old English: the son of Muriel.
Merrell, Merril, Meryll.

Merryn *See* GIRLS.

Merten *See* Martin and Merton.

Merton Old English: the place by the lake.
Merten.

Mervyn Old English: a famous friend.
Marvin, Marvyn, Merfyn (Welsh), Mervin, Merwin, Merwyn.
Diminutives: Marv, Merv.

Meryll *See* Merrill.

Metro A short form of metropolitan.
Metraux, Metroe, Metroh, Metrow.

Meurig A Welsh form of Maurice.

Meyer *See* Meir.

Meyrick *See* Merrick.

Mial/Miall *See* Myall.

Mica Latin: the name of a mineral.

Micah A Hebrew form of Michael, mentioned in the Bible.
Mika (Maori).

Michael Hebrew: like the Lord. One of the archangels in the Bible. *See also* Mitchell.
Maikel (Dutch), Makis (Greek), Meical (Welsh), Micah (Hebrew), Miceal, Michal (Polish), Micheál (Scottish Gaelic), Michel (French), Michele (Italian), Michell (Cornish), Mickel, Mickell, Miguel (Portuguese, Spanish), Mika (Finnish), Mikael (Swedish), Mikaere (Maori), Mikel (Slavic), Mikell (Scandinavian), Mikhail (Russian), Mikkel (Danish), Mikko (Finnish), Mitchell, Myall, Mychal, Mychael, Mykel, Mykell, Mykle.

Diminutives: Maik (Dutch), Mick, Micke, Mickey, Mickie, Micky, Micko, Mik, Mike, Mikey, Mikie, Mikkeli, Mischa (Russian), Mitch, Myke.

Michal/Michel/Michele/Michell *See* Michael.

Michelangelo Italian from Hebrew: Michael the angel.

Mick/Mickel/Mickey *See* Michael.

Midas Greek: a legendary figure who transformed all that he touched into gold.

Midnight The middle of the night.
Midnite.

Midwinter The middle of winter.
Midwynter.

Miguel *See* Michael.

Miharo Polynesian: a wanderer.

Mik/Mikael/Mikel/Mikhail *See* Michael.

Mika Maori form of Micah. Also the Finnish form of Michael.

Mikaere Maori form of Michael.

Mike/Mikey *See* Michael.

Miki Japanese: a tree.

Mikkel/Mikkeli/Mikko *See* Michael.

Miklós Czech form of Nicholas.

Milan Czech: the favoured or beloved one. *See also* Milos.

Milbourn/Milbourne/Milburn *See* Melburn.

Miles Latin: a soldier. Teutonic: merciful.
Milles, Myles, Mylles.
Diminutives: Milo, Mylo.

Milford Old English: from the ford by the mill. Welsh and New Zealand placenames.

Milhouse *See* Millhouse.

Millard Old English: the mill-keeper.
Millward.

Miller Old English: a grain-grinder
or miller.
Millar, Milner.

Millhouse Old English: the house of
the miller.
Milhouse.

Millward *See* Millard.

Milner *See* Miller.

Milo *See* Miles.

Milos Czech: favoured. *See also*
Milan.

Milton Old English: from the town
with a mill, or the middle farm.

Milu The Polynesian god of the
underworld.

Ming Chinese: the name of a dynasty.

Mingma Sherpa/Tibetan: born on a
Tuesday.

Minh Vietnamese: bright and clear.

Minik Greenlandic: possibly meaning
whale oil.

Minos Greek: the son of Zeus in
Greek mythology.

Miron *See* Myron.

Miroslav Slavic: great glory.

Mischa *See* Michael.

Mitch A diminutive of Michael and
Mitchell.

Mitcham Old English: from the large
homestead.

Mitchell Old English: big. Also a
form of Michael.
Mitchel, Mitchyl, Mitchyll, Mytchel,
Mytchell.

Diminutives: Mitch, Mytch.

Mitiaro Polynesian: the face of the
ocean.

Mo/Moe Diminutives of Maurice.

Moana Maori/Polynesian: the sea or
ocean.

Modred *See* Mordred.

Modris Latvian: alert.

Moffatt Scottish Gaelic: from the
long plain.
Moffat, Moffett, Moffitt.

Mogens *See* Magnus.

Mohammed *See* Muhammad.

Mohan Sanskrit: the bewitching one.

Mohandas Sanskrit: the servant of
Mohan.

Mohinder *See* Mahendra.

Moises/Moishe *See* Moses.

Mojo African-American: a magic
charm bag.
Mojoe, Mojow, Mojowe.

Moke Hawaiian form of Moses.

Mokhtar *See* Mukhtar.

Moko Polynesian: a lizard god.

Mokoiro Polynesian: a mythological
figure.

Molloy Irish Gaelic: a venerable
chieftain.

Monday *See* GIRLS.

Mondrian After Piet Mondrian, an
early-20th-century Dutch artist.
Mondriaan.

Monro/Monroe *See* Munro.

Montague Old French: from the
pointed hill.
Montagu.
Diminutives: Monte, Montey, Monty.

Montana *See* GIRLS.

Monte Italian: a mountain. *See also* Montague, Montgomery and Montmorency.
Montel (Spanish), Montes (Italian), Montez (Spanish).

Montego Spanish: mountainous.

Montey/Monty Diminutives of Montague, Montgomery and Montmorency.

Montgomery Old French: from the hill of the powerful man.
Montgomerie.
Diminutives: Monte, Montey, Monty.

Montmorency Old French: from the hill of Maurentius.
Diminutives: Monte, Montey, Monty.

Montrose Scottish Gaelic: the moor on the cape.

Moran A common Irish surname.

Morant After 'Breaker' Morant, a famous Boer War soldier.

Moray *See* Murray.

Morcum Cornish: from the valley near the sea.
Morcom, Morcomb, Morcumb.

Mordecai Babylonian or Hebrew: a biblical name.

Mordred Teutonic: brave counsel. An Arthurian knight.
Modred.

Moren A Welsh name of uncertain meaning.

Morgan Welsh: the bright sea. Also a girl's name.
Morgen, Morgwn.

Morgen German: the morning. Also a form of Morgan.

Morice/Moritz *See* Maurice.

Morland Old English: from the moors.
Moreland.

Morley Old English: from the clearing on the moor.

Morlo Welsh: a seal.

Morné An unusual South African name.

Moroccan A person from Morocco.
Morocan, Morokan, Morokkan.

Morocco An unusual 'country name'.
Moroco, Morokko.

Moroto Polynesian: the name of a god.

Morrell *See* Maurice.

Morrie/Morry *See* Maurice.

Morris/Morriss/Morse *See* Maurice.

Morrison Old English: the son of Maurice.
Morrieson, Morson.

Morrissey From Irish Gaelic: the son of Muiris (Maurice).

Mort Middle English: stumpy. Also a diminutive of Mortimer and Morton.

Morten *See* Martin and Morton.

Mortimer Old French: from the still or stagnant water.
Mortemer, Mortemor, Mortemore, Mortimor, Mortimore.
Diminutives: Mort, Morty.

Morton Old English: from the settlement on the moor.
Morten.
Diminutives: Mort, Morty.

Morven Gaelic: a Scottish region. Also a girl's name.
Morvan.

Moses Egyptian: probably meaning delivered or saved. The biblical

patriarch who led the Israelites out of Egypt.
Amoho (Maori), Moises (Portuguese), Moishe (Yiddish) Moke (Hawaiian), Mose (German), Mosese (Tongan), Moshe (Jewish), Mozes (Dutch), Musa (Arabic). *Diminutives*: Mose, Moss, Moze.

Moshe Jewish form of Moses.

Mosi Swahili: the firstborn.

Moss *See* Moses.

Mostyn Welsh: from the field of the fortress.

Mowgli The main character in Rudyard Kipling's *The Jungle Book*.

Moze/Mozes *See* Moses.

Mubarak Arabic: blessed, fortunate.

Muhammad Arabic: the praised one. *See also* Mahmood.
Mahomet, Mahommed, Mohammed, Muhammed.

Muir Scottish: the moor.

Muiris Irish form of Maurice.

Mukhtar Arabic: the chosen one. Mokhtar.

Mullion A Cornish placename. Mullian, Mullyan, Mullyon.

Mungo Scottish Gaelic: a dear friend.

Munro Irish Gaelic: from the mouth of the River Roe, in Ireland. Monro, Monroe, Munroe.

Murdoch Scottish Gaelic: a mariner. Murdo, Murdock.

Murihiku Maori: the Southland.

Murphy Irish Gaelic: a warrior of the sea.
Murphey.

Murray Scottish Gaelic: from the

land by the sea. Derived from the region of Moray.
Moray, Murrey, Murry, Mury.

Musa An Arabic form of Moses.

Mustafa Arabic: the chosen one. Mustapha.

Myall Aboriginal: wild, or an acacia tree. Also a form of Michael and a girl's name.
Mial, Miall, Myal.

Mychal/Mychael *See* Michael.

Myer *See* Meir.

Myke/Mykell/Mykle *See* Michael.

Myles/Mylles/Mylo *See* Miles.

Mylon American: a modern name.

Mylor Celtic: a Cornish placename. Melor.

Myrddin Welsh form of Merlin.

Myron Greek: fragrant. From myrrh, an aromatic shrub.
Miron.

Mytch/Mytchel/Mytchell *See* Mitchell.

N

Naaman Hebrew: pleasant.

Nabil Arabic: noble.

Nacio *See* Ignatius.

Nadal Spanish form of Natale.

Nadir Arabic: precious, rare.

Nahoa Hawaiian: bold and defiant.

Nahum Hebrew: the comforter. Naham, Nahman, Naum (Russian).

Nainoa Hawaiian: a navigator, or the protector of children.

Nairne Scottish Gaelic: from the alder tree.
Nairn.

Nait/Naite Diminutives of Nathan and Nathaniel.

Najib Arabic: the noble one.
Najeeb, Nayeeb, Nayib, Nayibe.

Nalu Hawaiian: an ocean wave.

Nam Vietnamese: from the south.

Namgyal Sherpa/Tibetan: the sky king.

Namid Native American: a dancer.

Namir Hebrew: like a leopard.

Nanda Sanskrit: joy.

Nansen Danish: the son of Nancy.

Napier A New Zealand city.

Napoleon Greek: a new city.

Narayan Sanskrit: the son of man.
Narain.

Narcissus Greek: a 'flower name'. The youth in Greek mythology who fell in love with his own reflection.
Narciso (Spanish).

Narendra Sanskrit: the mighty man.

Naresh Sanskrit: a lord or king.

Nash Old English: at the ash tree.
Nasche, Nashe.

Nasir Arabic: the helper, the supporter.
Nassar, Nasser.

Nason A variation of the popular name Mason.
Nasen, Naysen, Nayson.

Nat/Nate *See* Nathan and Nathaniel.

Natale Italian: born at Christmas. *See also* Noel.
Nadal (Spanish), Natal (Spanish), Natalino (Italian), Natalio (Italian).

Nataniel *See* Nathaniel.

Nathan A modern form of Nathaniel.
Natham, Nathel, Nathon.
Diminutives: Nait, Naite, Nat, Nate, Nayt, Nayte.

Nathaniel Hebrew: a gift of God. The name of a biblical prophet. *See also* Nathan.
Nataniel, Nathanael, Nathanial.
Diminutives: Nait, Naite, Nat, Nate, Nayt, Nayte.

Naum *See* Nahum.

Navajo Native American: the name of a tribe.
Navaho.

Nawang Sherpa/Tibetan: the possessive one.

Nayeeb/Nayib/Nayibe *See* Najib.

Naysen/Nayson *See* Nason.

Nayt/Nayte Diminutives of Nathan and Nathaniel.

Neal Irish Gaelic: the champion. *See also* Nelson and Niles.
Neale, Neall, Neil, Neild, Neile, Neill, Nial, Niall (Gaelic), Niel, Niele.

Nealson *See* Nelson.

Neave *See* GIRLS.

Neco A diminutive of Nicholas.

Ned/Neddie/Neddy *See* Edward.

Nedup Sherpa/Tibetan: he who possesses sacred things.

Nehemiah Hebrew: the consolation of the Lord.
Neemia (Polynesian), Nemiah.

Nehru Sanskrit: after Jawaharlal Nehru, a former Indian Prime Minister.

Neifion The Welsh name for Neptune.

Neil/Neild/Neill *See* Neal.

Neilsen/Neilson *See* Nelson.

Neko A diminutive of Nicholas.

Nekoda Hebrew: an Old Testament name.

Nelson English: the son of Neal or Neil. Also after the famous British admiral Lord Nelson.
Nealson, Neilsen, Neilson, Nelsen, Nilsen, Nilson.

Nemiah *See* Nehemiah.

Nemo Greek: a man from the glen.

Neo From the Greek word neos, meaning new. African: a gift.
Neoh, Nio, Nioh.

Neot The name of an English saint.

Neptune Latin: a planet and the Roman god of the sea, similar to the Greek god Poseidon.
Neifion (Welsh).

Nero Latin: dark, or black-haired.

Nestor Greek: wisdom.

Nevada Spanish: snow. A state of the USA.

Nevan Irish Gaelic: the servant of the saints.
Neven, Nevin, Nevins, Niven, Nivens.
Diminutive: Nev.

Neve *See* Neave.

Neville Old French: from the new town or settlement.
Nevel, Nevell, Nevil, Nevile.
Diminutive: Nev.

Newbold Old English: from the new building.

Newell Old English: from the new hall.
Newall.

Newlyn Celtic: the dweller at the new pool.
Newlin.

Newton Old English: from the new town or estate.

Ngaio Maori: a native New Zealand tree. More commonly a girl's name.

Ngaru Polynesian: a hero.
Ngaro.

Ngawari Maori: patient.

Nial/Niall *See* Neal.

Nic/Nicca *See* Dominic and Nicholas.

Nicander Greek: a man of victory.
Nicanor.

Nicholas Greek: the victory of the people. *See also* Colin, Nichols and Nixon.
Miklós (Czech), Nichol, Nicholaos, Nicholl, Nicholos, Nickolas, Nickollas, Niclas, Nicol (Scottish), Nicola (Italian), Nicolaas, Nicolas (Spanish), Nicolo (Italian), Nicolos, Niels (Danish), Niklas, Niklaus (Scandinavian), Nikolai (Russian), Nikolas, Nikolaus (German), Nikos (Greek), Nils (Norwegian, Swedish).
Diminutives: Claus (Dutch and German), Cole, Klaas (Dutch), Klaes (Frisian), Klaus (Danish, German), Kolya (Russian), Neco, Neko, Nic, Nicca (Cornish), Nico (Italian), Nick, Nickie, Nicky, Nik, Nique.

Nichols The son of Nicholas.
Nicholds, Nicholls, Nicholson.

Nick/Nickie/Nickolas/Niclas *See* Nicholas.

Nickel A metal and a US coin.
Nickell, Nickle.

Nickson *See* Nixon.

Nico/Nicol/Nicola/Nicolas *See*

'NOUN NAMES'

It is increasingly common to name babies after places (India, Morocco, Siena), brands (Chivas, Holden, Luger, Prada), proper nouns (Anzac, Fedora, Sistine) and 'things' in general so here is a selection of noun names. Although listed separately, many are suitable for both boys and girls.

Girls

Affinity	Jewel
Alchemy	Jubilee
Angel	Kite
Apple	Lake
Aria	Liberty
Autumn	Lotus
Bliss	Magenta
Bluebell	Mantra
Bolero	Mink
Breeze	Mirage
Calico	Mystique
Caress	Navy
Chardonnay	Orange
Charisma	Painter
Destiny	Pepper
Dove	Pine
Dusk	Poet
Echo	Rain
Eclipse	Satin
Essence	Savannah
Eternity	Scout
Fairy	Season
Fedora	Shade
Finesse	Shiraz
Flair	Sierra
Flax	Sky
Halo	Sonata
Haven	Summer
Heaven	Tamarind
Holly	Vogue
Hope	Voile
Illusion	Willow
Indigo	Zephyr

Boys

Anzac	Link
Badge	Matrix
Bandit	Maverick
Banjo	Mojo
Barley	Morocco
Blade	Nickel
Blue	Ocean
Button	Pirate
Cedar	Polo
Census	Prince
Chilli	Quest
Chivas	Radar
Danger	Reef
Dare	River
Denim	Rocket
Deuce	Rover
Diesel	Safari
Druid	Sailor
Equinox	Seal
Flame	Sequoia
Forest	Seven
Garrison	Shadow
Hawk	Spark
Haze	Speck
Heron	Squire
Holden	Storm
Holiday	Story
Icon	Teak
Journey	Teal
Juke	Tiger
Jungle	Track
Lark	Treat
Leaf	Trick

Nicholas.

Nicodemus Greek: the conqueror for the people.
Nicodeme (French).

Niel/Niele *See* Neal.

Niels *See* Cornelius and Nicholas.

Nigel Latin: dark, black-haired.
Nigell, Nygel, Nygell.

Nik/Niklas/Niklaus/Nikolai/ Nikolaus *See* Nicholas.

Nikita Russian: unconquerable.
Nika (Russian), Nikitas (Greek).

Nikos Greek form of Nicholas.

Nile A 'river name'.
Nyle.

Niles An unusual name, probably a form of Neil or Neal.
Nilles, Nyles, Nylles.

Nils *See* Nicholas.

Nilsen/Nilson *See* Nelson.

Nima Sherpa/Tibetan: born on a Sunday. Also a girl's name.

Nimrod Hebrew: valiant, or a great hunter.

Ninian Gaelic. A 5th-century saint.

Ninja A Japanese fighter or warrior.
Ninjah.

Nino Italian diminutive of Gianni and Giovanni. *See* John.

Nio/Nioh *See* Neo.

Nique A diminutive of Nicholas.

Niran Thai: eternal.

Nirvan From nirvana, the Buddhist and Hindu word for a heavenly state.
Nirvana, Nirvann.

Nishan Armenian: a sign.

Nitro From nitrogen, a gaseous element.

Nitroe, Nitrow, Nitrowe.

Niven/Nivens *See* Nevan.

Nixon Old English: the son of Nicholas.
Nickson.

Noah Hebrew: rest, comfort. A biblical figure.
Noa, Noha.

Noam Hebrew: pleasant.

Noble Latin: famous, noble.
Nobel.

Noel Old French: Christmas. *See also* Natale.
Noal, Noale, Noël, Noele, Nowell.

Noha *See* Noah.

Nolan Irish Gaelic: famous, a champion.
Noland, Nolen.

Norbert Teutonic: light or brilliance from the north.

Norbu Sherpa/Tibetan: a precious gem.

Nord German form of North.

Norden Teutonic: the north.
Nordan.

Norman Teutonic: a man from the north. *See also* Norris.
Normand.
Diminutives: Norm, Normie, Normy, Norrie.

Norris From the same root as Norman.

North Old English: from the north.
Nord (German), Northe.

Northcliff Old English: from the north cliff.
Northcliffe.

Northrop Old English: from the northern farm.

Norton Old English: from the northern farm or town.

Norville Old English: from the northern estate or farm.
Norvel, Norvil.

Norvin Old English: a friend from the north.
Norvyn, Norwin, Norwyn.

Norwell Old English: from the north spring or well.

Norwood Old English: from the northern forest.

Nouri Hungarian: light.

Novak Slavic: new.
Novac, Novack.

Nowell *See* Noel.

Nui Maori/Polynesian: many.

Nukuhia Maori: increase.

Nuncio Italian: a messenger.
Nunzio.

Nur Arabic: light. Hebrew: fire.
Nuri.

Nuren Arabic: light.

Nye *See* Aneurin.

Nygell *See* Nigel.

Nyle/Nyles/Nylles *See* Nile and Niles.

Nyoka Swahili: a snake.

O

Oak Old English: a 'plant name'.
Oake.

Oakley Middle English: from the oak-tree meadow.
Oakes, Oakleigh, Oaklie, Oakly, Okely.

Oata Polynesian: a shadow.

Obadiah Hebrew: the servant of God.
Obadias, Obediah.

Oberon A character in William Shakespeare's *A Midsummer Night's Dream. See* Auberon.

Obert Teutonic: wealthy and bright.

O'Brien Irish Gaelic: a descendant of Brian or Brien.
O'Brian.

Ocean Middle English: of the sea.
Oceanis, Oceano, Oceanus.

Octavius Latin: eight or the eighth-born.
Octave (French), Octavian, Octavio, Octavus, Ottavio (Italian).

Odell Old Norse: wealthy.

Odin Old Norse: the Scandinavian god of war.

Odion African: the firstborn twin.

Odolf Teutonic: a noble wolf.
Odulf.

O'Donnell Irish Gaelic: a descendant of Donald.
O'Donell, O'Donnel.

Odran Irish Gaelic: pale green.
Odren, Odrin.

Ogai A popular Japanese name.

Ogden Old English: from the valley of oak trees.
Ogdan, Ogdon.

Ogilvie Celtic: from the high hill.
Ogilvy.

Oglesby Old English: awe-inspiring.

Ogun African: the god of war.

Ohio Native American: a beautiful river. Also a state of the USA.

Oke Hawaiian form of Oscar.

Okely *See* Oakley.

Okko Finnish diminutive of Oscar.

Olaf Old Norse/Scandinavian: a descendant.
Olafur (Icelandic), Olav, Ole, Olin, Olof, Olov.

Oleg Russian: the name of an early prince of Kiev.

Olin *See* Olaf.

Oliver Latin: an olive tree or branch; a symbol of peace.
Olivar, Oliverio (Spanish), Oliviae, Olivier (French), Oliviero (Italian), Ollivar, Olliver, Ollivier.
Diminutives: Oli, Ollie, Olly.

Olof/Olov *See* Olaf.

Olsen A Scandinavian surname, meaning the son of Ole (*see* Olaf).
Ollsen, Ollson, Olson.

Omaka Maori: a place where a stream flows.

Omar Arabic: flourishing, long-lived.
Omer, Umar.

Onan Turkish: prosperous.

Ondray/Ondré *See* Andrew.

O'Neil Irish Gaelic: a descendant of Neil.
O'Neal, O'Neale, O'Neall, O'Neill.

Onepu Maori: sand.

Onslow Old English: the hill of the zealous one.

Ora Polynesian: life.

Oram Old English: from the enclosure by the river bank.

Oran Irish Gaelic: pale-skinned.
Oren, Orin, Orran, Orren, Orrin.

Orazio *See* Horace.

Orban *See* Urban.

Orchard Old English: a place where trees are grown.
Orcheard, Orchird.

Ordway Old English: the spear fighter.

Oregon The name of a US state.
Oregan.

Oren Hebrew: a pine tree. *See also* Oran.

Orestes Greek: a man of the mountain. A hero of Greek mythology.

Orfeo *See* Orpheus.

Orford Old English: a dweller at the ford.

Orin *See* Oran.

Orion Greek: the son of light. The name of a constellation.

Orlan Old English: from the pointed land.
Orland.

Orlando Italian form of Roland. The hero in Shakespeare's *As You Like It*.

Ormond Old English: a spearman.
Orman, Ormand.

Ornette An unusual modern American name.
Ornet, Ornett.

Oro Polynesian: the Tahitian god of war and peace. Spanish: golden.

Oroiti Polynesian: the slow-footed one.

Orpheus Greek: a name from ancient mythology.
Orfeo (Italian), Orphée (French).

Orran/Orren/Orrin *See* Oran.

Orson Old French from Latin: a little bear.

Orsino, Orso, Urson.

Orton Old English: from the farm by the river.

Orville Old French: from the golden place or town.

Orvin Old English: a spear friend. Orvon, Orvyn.

Osama *See* Usama.

Osbert Old English: divinely bright or famous.

Osborn Old English: a divine warrior. Osborne, Osbourne, Osburn.

Oscar Old English: a divine spearman. Auska, Auskah, Auskar, Oke (Hawaiian), Osca, Oscah, Oscer, Osgar (Scottish Gaelic), Oska, Oskah, Oskar (German), Oskari (Finnish), Osker. *Diminutives*: Okko (Finnish), Ossi, Ossie, Oz, Ozzie.

Oscer/Osgar *See* Oscar.

Osgood Old Norse: a pagan god.

O'Shea Irish Gaelic: a descendant of the dauntless one. O'Shay.

Osip *See* Joseph.

Oska/Oskar/Oskari/Osker *See* Oscar.

Osman Arabic: an Ottoman Turk, or a servant of God. Usman.

Osmar Old English: divinely glorious.

Osmond Old English: a divine protector. Osmonde, Osmund.

Osric Old English: a divine ruler.

Ossi/Ossie Diminutives of Oscar.

Osten/Ostin/Ostyn *See* Austin.

Oswald Old English: divinely powerful. Osvaldo (Italian, Spanish).

Oswin Old English: a friend of God, or a divine friend.

Otello/Othello Italian forms of Otto.

Otho *See* Otto.

Otis Greek: keen of hearing.

Ottavio *See* Octavius.

Otter Old Norse: a mythological figure, who was turned into an otter. Ottar.

Otto Teutonic: rich, prosperous. Otello (Italian), Othello (Italian), Otho.

Otway Teutonic: fortunate in battle. Ottway.

Ouray Native American: an arrow.

Ove A popular Scandinavian name. Uwe.

Owain/Owayne *See* Owen.

Owen Welsh: well-born. Also a Welsh form of John (*see* Evan and Ieuan). Eoin (Irish Gaelic), Owain, Owayn, Owayne, Owenn.

Oxford Old English: from the ford of the oxen. An English university city.

Oxley Old English: from the meadow of the ox. Oxlea, Oxleigh, Oxlie, Oxly.

Oxton Old English: from the ox enclosure.

Oz/Ozzie Diminutives of Oscar.

Ozias *See* Uzziah.

Ozuru Japanese: a stork, implying longevity.

P

Paaveli Finnish form of Patrick.

Paavo Finnish form of Paul.

Pablo Spanish form of Paul.

Pace Middle English: a step or rate of movement.
Paice, Payce.

Pacifico Spanish from Latin: peaceful.

Paco Native American: a gold eagle. Also a Spanish diminutive of Francis.

Paddy/Padraig/Padrig/Padruig See Patrick.

Page/Paige See GIRLS.

Paice See Pace.

Paine Old French: a countryman.
Payne.

Pakaa Hawaiian: the god of the wind.
Paka, Pakah.

Palaki Polynesian: black.

Palani Hawaiian: a free man.

Palauni Polynesian: brown.

Palmer Old English: a palm-bearing pilgrim.

Palmiro Latin: born on Palm Sunday.

Pan The Greek god of nature.

Pancho Spanish diminutive of Francis.

Pancras Greek: all-powerful. The name of a saint.

Paolo Italian form of Paul.

Paora/Paoro Maori forms of Paul.

Papa Polynesian: the earth.

Paraone Maori: brown.

Paris Greek: a character in Greek mythology. Also the capital of France.
Paride (Italian), Parris, Parrys, Parys.

Park Old English: from the park.
Parke.

Parker Old English: the park-keeper.

Parkin Old English: little Peter.

Parnell Latin: from the Greek word for a stone. The name is therefore related to Peter.
Parnel, Pernel, Pernell.

Parr Old English: a dweller by the cattle pen.

Parris/Parrys See Paris.

Parrish Old English: from the church parish.
Parish.

Parry Welsh: the son of Harry.

Parsefal/Parsifal See Percival.

Parys See Paris.

Pasang Sherpa/Tibetan: born on a Friday. Also a girl's name.

Pascal Latin: born at Easter.
Pascale, Paschal, Pascoe (Cornish), Pascual (Spanish), Paskal, Paskale, Pasquale (Italian).

Pascoe Cornish form of Pascal.

Pasquale See Pascal.

Pat A diminutive of Patrick.

Patariki Maori form of Patrick.

Paten/Paton See Payton.

Paterson The son of Pat or Patrick.
Patersen, Pattersen, Patterson, Pattisen, Pattison.

Patrick Latin: noble, well-born. The patron saint of Ireland.
Paaveli (Finnish), Padraig (Irish Gaelic), Padrig, Padruig (Scottish

Gaelic), Patariki (Maori), Patric, Patrice (French), Patrich, Patricio (Portuguese, Spanish), Patrik, Patrizio (Italian).
Diminutives: Paddy, Pat, Patsy, Patty, Ric, Rick.

Patrik/Patrizio *See* Patrick.

Patterson/Pattisen/Pattison *See* Paterson.

Patton Old English: a warrior. Patten.

Patu Polynesian: a weapon.

Paul Latin: small. *See also* Pollock. Paavo (Finnish), Pablo (Spanish), Paolo (Italian), Paora (Maori), Paoro (Maori), Paula (Tongan), Paule, Paull, Paulle, Paulo (Portuguese), Paulot (French), Pavel (Polish, Russian, Swedish), Pavlos (Greek), Pawley (Cornish), Pol (Irish, Gaelic). *Diminutives*: Paulie, Pauley.

Pavel/Pavlos *See* Paul.

Pavo Latin: a peacock. The name of a small constellation. Pavonis.

Pawley Cornish form of Paul.

Pax Latin: peace.

Paxton Old English: from the estate of the warrior.

Payce *See* Pace.

Payne *See* Paine.

Payton Old English: from the warrior's farm. Paten, Paton, Payten, Peyten, Peyton.

Peadar Irish and Scottish Gaelic form of Peter.

Pearce *See* Peter.

Pearson *See* Pierson.

Peder/Pedr/Pedro/Pedyr *See* Peter.

Pedrek/Pedrog *See* Petroc.

Pedrie *See* Petrie.

Peers *See* Piers.

Peeter *See* Peter.

Pekelo Hawaiian: a stone.

Pell Old English: a scarf.

Pelton Old English: from the farm by a pool.

Pema Sherpa/Tibetan: a lotus. Also a girl's name.

Pemba Sherpa/Tibetan: born on a Saturday.

Pembroke Celtic: from the headland. A Welsh county.

Pendragon Celtic: the head of the dragon. The name of King Arthur's father.

Peni Polynesian and Tongan form of Ben.

Penjor Sherpa/Tibetan: the wealthy one.

Penley Old English: from the enclosed meadow.

Penn Old English: an enclosure or pen.

Penrice Cornish: from the end of the ford.

Penrith Welsh: the main ford. Penryth.

Penrod Teutonic: a famous commander.

Penrose Cornish/Welsh: the end or top of the moor. Penroze.

Penwyn Welsh: the fair-haired one.

Pepe Spanish diminutive of José. *See* Joseph.

Pepin Teutonic: the petitioner, one who seeks a favour.

Per Scandinavian form of Peter.

Peran *See* Piran.

Percival Old French: to pierce the valley. One of the knights in Arthurian legend.
Parsefal, Parsifal, Perceval.
Diminutives: Perce, Percy.

Percy A Norman surname and a diminutive of Percival.

Peregrine Latin: a stranger or pilgrim. A type of falcon.
Peregrin, Peregryn.
Diminutive: Perry.

Pernel/Pernell *See* Parnell.

Pero Slavic diminutive of Petar (*see* Peter).

Perran/Perren/Perrin *See* Piran.

Perry Old English: from the pear tree. Also a diminutive of Peregrine.
Perrey, Perri, Perrie.

Perseus A hero in Greek mythology, best known for rescuing the maiden Andromeda from a sea monster.

Perth Celtic: a thornbush thicket. A Scottish city.

Pervez Persian: fortunate.

Peter Greek: a stone or rock. One of Christ's apostles. *See also* Ferris, Parkin, Parnell, Peterson, Petrie, Pierce, Piers and Pierson.
Peadar (Irish and Scottish Gaelic), Pearce, Peder (Cornish, Danish), Pedr (Welsh), Pedro (Spanish), Pedyr (Cornish), Peeter, Per (Scandinavian), Petar (Slavic), Petera (Maori), Petr (Czech), Petrie (Scottish Gaelic), Petros (Greek), Petur (Icelandic), Pierce, Piero (Italian), Pierre (French), Piers, Piet (Dutch), Pieter, Pietro (Italian), Pita

(Maori, Tongan), Pyrs (Welsh).
Diminutives: Pero (Slavic), Pete, Petey, Petya (Russian), Pierrick (Breton), Pierrot (French).

Petera A Maori form of Peter.

Peterson The son of Peter. *See also* Pierson.
Peters, Petersen.

Petr Czech form of Peter.

Petrie Scottish Gaelic form of Peter.
Pedrie, Petre, Petri, Petry.

Petroc Cornish/Welsh: the name of a Celtic saint.
Pedrek, Pedrog, Petrok.

Petros Greek form of Peter.

Petur Icelandic form of Peter.

Petya Russian diminutive of Peter.

Peverall French: a piper.
Peverel, Peverell, Peveril, Peverill.

Peyten/Peyton *See* Payton.

Pharaoh An Ancient Egyptian king.
Pharoah.

Phelan Irish Gaelic: as brave as a wolf.

Phelps Old English: the son of Philip.

Pheonix *See* Phoenix.

Philbert *See* Filbert.

Philemon Greek: loving.

Philip Greek: a lover of horses. One of the New Testament apostles. *See also* Phelps and Phillips.
Felipe (Spanish), Filep (Hungarian), Filib (Scottish Gaelic), Filip (Polish), Filippo (Italian), Philipp, Philippe (French), Phillip, Pilib (Irish Gaelic), Piripi (Maori, Tongan).
Diminutives: Phil, Phill, Phillie, Philly, Pino (Italian), Pip.

Phillips Old English: the son of
Philip.
Philips.

Philo Greek: loving.

Phineas Egyptian: the Nubian (a
dark-skinned person). Hebrew: an
oracle.
Fineas, Phinneas.

Phintso Sherpa/Tibetan: prosperity.

Phlyn *See* Flynn.

Phoenix Greek: the legendary bird
that rose again from its own ashes.
The name of a southern constellation.
Feenix, Fenix, Pheonix.

Phrase From Latin: a sequence of
words.
Frase, Fraze, Phraze.

Phunahele Hawaiian: the favourite.

Phurba Sherpa/Tibetan: born on
Thursday.

Pickford Old English: from the ford
at the peak.

Pierce A form of Peter.
Pierse, Pyrs (Welsh).

Piero/Pierre *See* Peter.

Pierpont French: a stone bridge.
Pierrepont.

Pierrick/Pierrot *See* Peter.

Piers A form of Peter.
Peers, Pierz.

Pierson English: the son of Peter. *See
also* Peterson.
Pearson.

Piet/Pieter/Pietro *See* Peter.

Piko Maori: to bend.

Pilib Irish Gaelic form of Philip.

Pilot From French: a guide or leader.
Pilote (French), Pilott, Pylot, Pylott.

Pim Dutch diminutive of William.

Pine Middle English: a coniferous
tree.
Pyne.

Pino Italian: a diminutive of names
such as Filippo (*see* Philip).

Pinon Native American: a star or a
constellation.

Pinto Spanish: piebald or mottled,
like a pinto horse.
Pintoe, Pintoh, Pintow.

Pip A diminutive of Philip.

Piper *See* GIRLS.

Pipiri Polynesian: the equivalent of
the star Castor, in the constellation
of Gemini.

Piran Cornish: a saint's name.
Peran, Perran, Perren, Perrin.

Pirate Middle English: one who
plunders at sea.
Pyrate.

Piripi Maori and Tongan form of
Philip.

Pita Maori and Tongan form of Peter.

Pitney Old English: preserving one's
island.

Pitt Old English: from the hollow.

Pius Latin: pious, devout. The name
of several popes.

Placido Latin: serene, untroubled. A
Spanish name.

Plato Greek: broad-shouldered.

Platt Old French: from the flat land
or plateau.

Pluto Greek: a planet and the god of
the underworld in Greek mythology.

Pol *See* Paul.

Polaris Latin: the North Star, part of

the constellation of Ursa Minor, the Little Bear.

Pollock Old English: little Paul.

Polo After Marco Polo, the legendary 14th-century explorer, or from a game played on horseback.

Pomare Polynesian: the name of a hero.

Pomeroy French: from the apple orchard.

Pontius Latin: the fifth.
Pons.

Porter French: the gatekeeper.

Possum An Australian marsupial. Also a term of endearment used by Dame Edna Everage.

Pouaka Maori: a box.

Poutini Polynesian: greenstone.

Powell Welsh: the son of Howell.

Powys Welsh: a man from Powys, a Welsh county.

Prakash Sanskrit: light, or famous.

Pramana Indonesian: wisdom.

Prasad Sanskrit: brightness.

Prem Sanskrit: love.

Prentice Old English: an apprentice or learner.
Prentiss.

Prescott Old English: from the priest's house.
Prescot, Prestcott.

Presley Old English: from the priest's meadow.
Preslee, Presleigh, Preslie, Presly.

Preston Old English: from the priest's farm or town.
Presten, Prestin, Prestyn.

Priam Greek: a mythological king of Troy.

Price Welsh: the son of the loving man.
Pryce, Prys, Pryse.

Prideaux Old French: near water.

Primo Latin: the firstborn son.

Prince Latin: the first in rank.
Printz, Printze, Prynce.

Prior Latin: the head of a monastery or priory.
Pryor.

Prize Middle English: a reward.
Pryze.

Probert Welsh: the son of Robert.

Proctor Latin: the administrator or manager.
Procter.

Prometheus Greek: forethought.

Prosper Latin: fortunate, prosperous. Prospero (Italian, Portuguese, Spanish, a character in Shakespeare's play *The Tempest*).

Proteus Greek: changeable.

Pryce/Pryse *See* Price.

Pryderi Welsh: to care for.

Prynce *See* Prince.

Pryor *See* Prior.

Pryze *See* Prize.

Puke Maori: a hill.

Puriri Maori: a New Zealand tree.

Purvis Old French: the purveyor, or provider.
Purves.

Pylot/Pylott *See* Pilot.

Pyne *See* Pine.

Pyrate *See* Pirate.

Pyrs Welsh form of Peter and Pierce.

Q

Qadir *See* Kadir.

Qamar Arabic: of the moon.
Kamar.

Qasim Arabic: one who shares or distributes.
Kasim.

Quade A modern name, possibly of Gaelic origin.
Kwayd, Kwayde, Kweyd, Kweyde, Quaden, Quaid, Quaide, Quayd, Quayde, Qwade, Qwaid, Qwaide.

Quaife Old French: a cap maker or seller.
Quaif.

Quaile Manx Gaelic: the son of Paul. Also a girl's name.
Quail, Quale, Quayl, Quayle.

Quain Old French: the clever one.
Kwain, Kwaine, Quaine, Quane, Quayn, Quayne.

Quant Old French: clever or crafty.
Quante.

Quarto Latin: the fourth, or fourth child.

Quartz Greek: a silicon-based mineral that comes in many varieties and colours.
Quarz.

Quemby/Quenby *See* Quimby.

Quennel French: the one who lives at the little oak tree.
Quennell, Quinnell.

Quentin Latin: the fifth, as in the fifth-born child.
Quenten, Quentin, Quenton,

Quentyn, Quinten, Quintin, Quinton, Quintyn.

Quest Middle English: a search or pursuit.
Queste.

Quetzal A Central American bird.
Quetzall, Quezal, Quezall.

Quigley Irish Gaelic: a spinning distaff.

Quill Middle English: a feather or an old-fashioned pen.
Quiele, Quil, Quille.

Quillan Irish Gaelic: a cub.

Quilliam Manx Gaelic form of William.

Quimby Old Norse: from the woman's estate.
Quemby, Quenby, Quinby.

Quincy French/Latin: from the fifth son's estate.
Quincey.

Quinlan Irish Gaelic: well-shaped, athletic.
Quinlin.

Quinn Irish Gaelic: wise and intelligent.
Quin, Quinne, Quyn, Quynn, Quynne.

Quinnane Probably a form of Quinn.
Quinan, Quinane, Quinnan.

Quinnell *See* Quennel.

Quinney Manx Gaelic: the son of the crafty one.
Quiney.

Quintin/Quinton *See* Quentin.

Quintus Latin: the fifth, as in the fifth child.

Quirce Spanish. A 4th-century martyr.

Quirino Italian form of Corin.

Quong Chinese: bright.
Quon.

Quoyle A character in the popular novel *The Shipping News*.
Quoil, Quoile, Quoyl.

Quyn/Quynn *See* Quinn.

Qwade/Qwaid/Qwaide *See* Quade.

R

Ra Polynesian: a sun god. Also the Ancient Egyptian god of the sun,whose symbols were a falcon and scarab (sacred beetle).

Rab/Rabbie Scottish diminutives of Robert.

Rabi Arabic: a breeze.

Rad Old English: a counsellor. Also a diminutive of names beginning with Rad.
Radd.

Radar A detection system that uses electromagnetic waves.
Raydar.

Radborne Old English: from the red brook or stream.
Radbourn, Radbourne, Radburn.

Radcliffe Old English: from the red cliff.

Radek *See* Radko.

Radford Old English: from the red ford.
Redford.

Radike A Fijian name of uncertain meaning.

Radko Czech: joyful.

Diminutive: Radek.

Radley Old English: from the red meadow.
Radleigh.

Radnor Old English: from the red shore. A town in Wales.

Raebon *See* Raybon.

Raex *See* Rex.

Rafael/Rafal/Raffaele/Raffaello *See* Raphael.

Rafe An alternative form and pronunciation of Ralph. *See also* Raphael.
Raif, Raife.

Rafferty Irish Gaelic: prosperous.

Rafi Arabic: the exalted one.

Rafiq Arabic: a companion, a friend.

Rafu Japanese: a net.

Raghnall *See* Ronald.

Ragnar *See* Rayner.

Rahman Arabic: merciful.
Rahim.

Raibeart Scottish Gaelic form of Robert.

Raiden The Japanese god of thunder.

Raif/Raife *See* Rafe.

Raimond/Raimondo *See* Raymond.

Raine *See* GIRLS.

Rainer/Rainier *See* Rayner.

Rainger *See* Ranger.

Raj Sanskrit: a king.
Raja, Rajah, Raju.

Rajendra Sanskrit: a mighty king.

Rajiv Sanskrit: striped.

Raka Polynesian: a wind god.
Rakah.

Rakaia Polynesian: the name of an

early convert to Christianity.

Rakaunui Maori: the full moon.

Rake Middle English: a rogue or rascal.

Raleigh Old English: from the meadow of the roe deer.
Rawley, Rawly.

Ralph Old English: the counsel of the wolf, implying a fearless adviser. *See also* Rafe, Rolf and Rudolph.
Rafe, Ralf, Ralphed, Raoul (French), Raul (Italian), Raúl (Spanish).

Ralston Old English: a dweller on Ralph's farm or estate.

Rama Sanskrit: pleasing. An alternative name for the Hindu god Vishnu.
Ram, Ramah, Raman.

Rambert Teutonic: mighty and brilliant.

Ramelan Indonesian: a prophecy.

Rameses Ancient Egyptian: born of the sun.
Ramses.

Ramiro Spanish: a great judge or adviser.

Ramón/Ramone *See* Raymond.

Ramsay Old English: an island of wild garlic.
Ramsey.

Ramsden Old English: the ram's valley.

Ranald *See* Ronald.

Rand/Randie Diminutives of Randolph.

Randal/Randall/Randell *See* Randolph.

Randolph Old English: a wolf-like shield. *See also* Rendell.
Randal, Randall, Randell, Randolf.

Diminutives: Rand, Randie, Randy, Rendell.

Randy *See* Randolph.

Ranen Hebrew: to sing with joy.

Ranger Old French: the keeper of the forest.
Rainger.

Rangi Maori/Polynesian: heaven.

Raniera Maori form of Daniel.

Raniero Italian form of Rayner.

Ranjit Sanskrit: the delighted one.

Ranjiv Sanskrit: victorious.

Rankin Old English: a little shield.

Ransford Old English: from the ford of the raven.

Ransley Old English: from the meadow of the raven.

Ransom Old English: a warrior's son.

Ranulf Old Norse: wolf-like advice.
Ranulph.

Raoul French form of Ralph.

Rapata Maori form of Robert.

Raphael Hebrew: God heals, or healed by God. One of the four archangels in the Bible.
Rafael (German, Portuguese, Spanish), Rafaele, Rafaelle, Rafal (Polish), Raffaele (Italian), Raffaello (Italian), Raphaell.
Diminutives: Raf, Rafa, Rafe, Raff.

Ras/Rasmus *See* Erasmus.

Rashid Arabic: the well-guided one; a director.
Rasheed.

Rastafarian A member of a Jamaican cult that believes in black supremacy.
Diminutive: Rasta.

Rastus *See* Erastus.

Rata Maori: friendly. Polynesian: the name of a great chief.

Rauf Arabic: the compassionate one.

Rauiti Maori: a small leaf.

Raul *See* Ralph.

Raupo Maori: a bulrush.

Raven Middle English: a 'bird name'.

Ravi Sanskrit: of the sun.

Ravid Hebrew: the wanderer.

Rawiri A Maori form of David. *See also* Rewi.

Rawley/Rawly *See* Raleigh.

Rawson Old English: the son of the little wolf.

Ray Old French: a king. *See also* Raymond, Rex and Roy.
Raye, Rey, Reye.

Raybon From French: the good king.
Raebon, Reabon, Reybon.

Rayburn Old English: from the brook of the deer.

Raydar *See* Radar.

Raymond Teutonic: a wise or mighty protector.
Raimond, Raimondo (Italian), Ramón (Spanish), Ramone, Raymon, Raymund, Réamann (Irish Gaelic), Redmond (Irish), Redmund. *Diminutive*: Ray.

Raynard *See* Reynard.

Rayner German: a wise warrior.
Ragnar (Scandinavian), Rainer (German), Rainier (French), Raniero (Italian), Raynar, Raynor, Reiner (German), Reyner.

Raynold *See* Reynold.

Razvan A Romanian name of uncertain meaning.

Reabon *See* Raybon.

Read Old English: red-haired.
Reade, Reed, Reede, Reid.

Reading Old English: son of the red-headed one.
Redding.

Reagan/Reagen *See* Regan.

Réamann Irish Gaelic form of Raymond.

Rearden/Reardon *See* Riordan.

Reave/Reaves *See* Reeve.

Rebel Latin: the rebellious one. Also a girl's name.

Red Often a diminutive but can be used as a proper name.
Redd.

Redding *See* Reading.

Redford *See* Radford.

Redman Old English: a protector, an adviser.

Redmond/Redmund *See* Raymond.

Reece/Rees *See* Rhys.

Reed/Reede *See* Read.

Reef An unusual modern name.
Reefe, Rif, Ryf, Ryfe.

Reeves Old English: a steward.
Reave, Reaves, Reeve, Reive, Reives.

Regan Irish Gaelic: the descendant of a king. Also a girl's name.
Reagan, Reagen.

Regin Old Norse: a figure from mythology.

Reginald Old English: a wise and powerful ruler. *See also* Reynold and Ronald.
Reginauld, Regnauld. *Diminutives*: Reg, Reggie.

Régis French: a ruler or king.

Regis.

Rehua Polynesian: a god of the stars.

Reid *See* Read.

Reiley/Reilly *See* Riley.

Reiner *See* Rayner.

Reinhard *See* Reynard.

Reinhold *See* Reynold.

Reis/Reise *See* Rhys.

Reive/Reives *See* Reeve.

Reks *See* Rex.

Remi/Remie *See* Rémy.

Remington Old English: from the farm of ravens.

Remo *See* Remus.

Remus Latin: fast. In legend, one of the brothers who founded Rome. Remo (Italian).

Rémy French from Latin: an oarsman, one who rows. Remi, Remie.

Renaldo *See* Ronald.

Renard/Renaud/Rennard *See* Reynard.

Renato *See* René.

Rendell A diminutive of Randolph. Rendall, Rendle, Rendoll.

René Latin: reborn. Renato (Italian, Portuguese, Spanish).

Renfred Old English: mighty but peaceful.

Renfrew Celtic: from the still river.

Renny Irish Gaelic: small but powerful. Also a girl's name. Renney, Rennie.

Renshaw Old English: from the forest of the ravens.

Reo/Reon *See* Rio.

Reuben Hebrew: behold, a son. One of Jacob's sons in the Bible. Reubin, Reuvin, Ruben, Rubens (Portuguese), Rubin, Rueben. *Diminutives*: Rube, Ruby.

Reuel Hebrew: a friend of God. Ruel.

Reuvin *See* Reuben.

Revel Old French: a rebel, or one who makes merry. Also a girl's name. Revell, Revelle, Revil, Revill, Reville.

Revere Latin: to regard with respect.

Rewi Maori form of Dave. *See* David and Rawiri.

Rex Latin: a king. *See also* Ray and Roy. Raex, Reks, Rexim, Rexx, Rexxe.

Rexford From Latin: the ford of the king.

Rey *See* Ray and Reynard.

Reybon *See* Raybon.

Reynard Teutonic: brave, or a fox. Raynard, Reinhard (German), Renard, Renaud (French), Rennard. *Diminutive*: Rey.

Reyner *See* Rayner.

Reynold Old English: a wise and powerful ruler. *See also* Reginald and Ronald. Raynold, Reinhold (German), Reynaud (French).

Rez Hungarian: red-haired, or like copper.

Rhauri *See* Rory.

Rhett Possibly a form of Rhys, but most likely invented by Margaret Mitchell for her character Rhett Butler in *Gone with the Wind*.

Rhian/Rhien *See* Ryan.

Rhisiart *See* Richard.

Rhobert Welsh form of Robert.

Rhodes Greek: the place of roses. The name of an Aegean island.

Rhodri Welsh: the ruler of the wheel.

Rhori/Rhorie/Rhory *See* Rory.

Rhudd Welsh: red.
Rhud, Rud, Rudd.

Rhun Welsh: grand.

Rhyan/Rhyen *See* Ryan.

Rhyden *See* Ryden.

Rhydwyn Welsh: a dweller by the white ford.

Rhylee/Rhylie/Rhly *See* Riley.

Rhyll The name of a Welsh town.
Rhyl, Ryl, Ryll.

Rhys Welsh: ardent.
Reece, Rees, Reese, Reis, Reise, Rheece, Rhees, Rheese, Rhyce, Rhyse.

Rian *See* Ryan.

Ric A diminutive of Eric, Patrick and Richard.

Ricardo/Riccardo *See* Richard.

Richard Teutonic: brave and strong. The name of three English kings. *See also* Rix.
Rhisiart (Welsh), Ricard, Ricardo (Spanish), Riccardo (Italian), Richerd, Rickert, Rikard (Scandinavian).
Diminutives: Dick, Dickie, Dicky, Ric, Rich, Richie, Rick, Rickie, Ricky, Rico (Spanish), Rik, Ritchie.

Richman Old English: a powerful protector.
Richmond.

Rick/Rickie/Ricky Diminutives of Eric, Patrick and Richard.

Ricker Old English: a powerful army.

Rickert *See* Richard.

Ricks/Rickson *See* Rix.

Rico Spanish: prosperous. *See also* Richard.

Rider Old English: a horseman or knight.
Ryder.

Ridge Old English: a ridge or long hill.
Rydge.

Ridgeway Old English: from the ridge road.

Ridgley Old English: from the meadow's ridge.

Ridley Old English: from the cleared wood.
Ridlee, Ridleigh, Ridlie, Ridly.

Rif *See* Reef.

Rigby Old English: the valley of the ruler.

Rigel The brightest star in the constellation of Orion, marking the figure's left foot.

Rigg Old English: from the ridge.

Rik/Rikard *See* Richard.

Riki Maori: small.

Riley Irish Gaelic: valiant. Old English: a rye meadow. Also a modern girl's name.
Reiley, Reilly, Rhylee, Rhyley, Rhylie, Rhly, Rylee, Ryley, Ryly.

Rinaldo Italian form of Ronald.

Rinchen *See* Rinzen.

Ring Old English: a ring.

Ringo Japanese: an apple. Old

English: a bell-ringer.

Rinjin Japanese: the god of the oceans, similar to the Roman god Neptune.
Rinjen.

Rinky A modern Japanese name.

Rinzen Sherpa/Tibetan: the holder of intellect. Also a girl's name.
Rinchen.

Rio Spanish: a river.
Reo, Reon, Rion.

Riordan Irish Gaelic: a royal poet.
Rearden, Reardon.

Ripley Old English: from the meadow of the shouter or loud one.
Diminutive: Rip.

Risley Old English: from the brushwood meadow.

Risto Finnish diminutive of Christopher.

Riston Old English: from the brushwood farm.

Ritchie *See* Richard.

Ritter Teutonic: a knight.

Rive French: a riverbank.

River From Old French: a river or waterway.
Rivers, Ryver, Ryvers.

Rix Old English: the son of Richard.
Ricks, Rickson, Rixon.

Roald Old Norse: a famous ruler. A Norwegian form of Ronald.

Roam Middle English: to wander or ramble.
Roame.

Roan *See* Rowan.

Roarke Irish Gaelic: a famed ruler.
Rorke, Rourke, Ruark.

Rob/Robbie/Robby Diminutives of Robert.

Robben/Robbin/Robbyn *See* Robin.

Robert Teutonic: famous, or bright fame. *See also* Hobson, Hopkin, Probert, Robertson, Robin and Robinson.
Lopeti (Tongan), Raibeart (Scottish Gaelic), Rapata (Maori), Rhobert (Welsh), Robbert, Roberto (Italian, Spanish), Ropata (Maori), Rupert (German).
Diminutives: Bert, Bob, Bobbie, Bobby, Rab (Scottish), Rabbie (Scottish), Rob, Robbie, Robby, Robin, Robyn.

Robertson The son of Robert.

Robin Originally a diminutive of Robert.
Robben, Robbin, Robbyn, Roben, Robyn.

Robinson English: the son of Robert or Robin.
Robis, Robison, Robson.

Roc/Roca *See* Rock.

Rocco Teutonic: to rest.
Rocko, Rocky, Roco, Rokko, Roko.

Rochester Old English: a rocky fortress, or camp on the rocks.

Rock Old English: from the rock.
Roc, Roca (Spanish), Roche (French), Rocke, Roque (Portuguese, Spanish).

Rocket From French: a firework or missile.
Rockett, Roquet (French), Roquett.

Rockley Old English: from the rocky meadow.

Rocko/Roco *See* Rocco.

Rockwell Old English: from the rocky well or spring.

Rocky *See* Rocco.

Rod/Roddie/Roddy *See* Roderick and Rodney.

Rodda A Cornish surname.

Roden Old English: from the valley of the reeds.
Rodan, Rodden.

Roderick Teutonic: a renowned ruler. *See also* Broderick.
Roderic, Roderich (German), Rodrick, Rodrigo (Italian, Spanish), Rodrigue (French), Rurik (Russian, Scandinavian).
Diminutives: Rick, Ricky, Rod, Roddie, Roddy.

Rodger *See* Roger.

Rodman Teutonic: a famous hero.

Rodney English: from an old surname.
Rodnie, Rodny.
Diminutives: Rod, Roddie, Roddy.

Rodolf/Rodolfo/Rodolphe *See* Rudolph.

Rodrick *See* Roderick.

Rodrigo/Rodrigue *See* Roderick.

Rodwell Old English: from the Christian's well.

Roe *See* Rowe.

Roel/Roell *See* Rowell.

Roeland *See* Roland.

Rogan Irish Gaelic: the red-haired one.
Rogen.

Roger Teutonic: a famous spearman or warrior.
Rodger, Rogerio (Spanish), Rogero, Rüdiger (German), Ruggiero (Italian), Rutger (Dutch).
Diminutives: Rodge, Rog.

Rohan Sanskrit: ascending. *See also* Rowan.

Roi/Roie *See* Roy.

Rokko/Roko *See* Rocco.

Roland Teutonic: from the famed land.
Lorant (Hungarian), Orlando (Italian), Roeland (Dutch), Rolan, Rolando, Rolant (Welsh), Roldan (Spanish), Rowland.
Diminutives: Roley, Rollo.

Roldan Spanish form of Roland.

Rolf Teutonic: the famous wolf. *See also* Ralph and Rudolph.
Rolfe, Rolph.

Roller One who rolls.

Rollo *See* Roland.

Rolph *See* Rolf.

Roly *See* Rowley.

Roman Latin: a citizen of Rome.
Romain (French), Romane, Romano (Italian), Rome.

Romeo Latin: a pilgrim to Rome. A famous Shakespearean character.

Romney Welsh: a curving river. A placename from Kent, England.

Romolo *See* Romulus.

Romulus Latin: one of the legendary brothers who founded Rome.
Romolo.

Ron A diminutive of Ronald and other names beginning with Ron.

Ronald Old English: a wise and powerful ruler. *See also* Reginald, Reynold and Ronson.
Raghnall (Irish), Ranald, Renaldo (Spanish), Rinaldo (Italian), Roald (Norwegian), Ronaldo (Portuguese).
Diminutives: Ron, Ronnie, Ronny.

Ronan Irish Gaelic: a little seal (the animal).
Ronin.

Rondell American: probably a form of Ron.
Rondel, Rondelle.

Rongo Maori/Polynesian: the god of rain and fertility.

Roni Hebrew: my joy.

Ronit Hebrew: a song. Irish Gaelic: prosperity.

Ronnie/Ronny Diminutives of Ronald and other Ron names.

Ronson Old English: the son of Ronald.

Rooney Irish Gaelic: red-haired.

Ropata Maori form of Robert.

Roper Old English: a rope-maker.

Roque *See* Rock.

Roquet/Roquett *See* Rocket.

Rorke *See* Roarke.

Rory Irish Gaelic: the red king.
Rhauri, Rhaurie, Rhori, Rhorie, Rhory, Roree, Rorey, Rori, Rorie, Ruairi, Ruari, Ruaridh.

Roscoe Old Norse: from the deer forest.
Rosco.

Roshan Persian: splendid; one who emanates light. Also a girl's name.

Roslin Old French: the small red-haired one.
Rosselin, Rosslyn.

Rosmer Danish: from the sea.

Ross Scottish Gaelic: from the headland or peninsula.
Rosse.

Rosselin/Rosslyn *See* Roslin.

Rostam A figure from Persian legend.

Roswald Teutonic: a mighty horse.
Roswell.

Rothwell Old Norse: from the red well or spring.

Rourke *See* Roarke.

Rouse *See* Rowse.

Routledge *See* Rutledge.

Rove Middle English: to wander.

Rover Old English: a roofer, or one who roves.

Rowan Irish Gaelic: little red-haired one.
Roan, Rohan, Rowen.

Rowe Old English: either a hedgerow or the rough one.
Roe, Row, Wroe.

Rowell Old English: from the deer spring.
Roel, Roell, Rowel.

Rowland *See* Roland.

Rowley Old English: from the rough meadow.
Roly, Rowleigh, Rowly.

Rowse Cornish: from the heathland.
Rouse.

Rowson Old English: the son of the red-haired man.
Rowsan.

Roxbury Old English: from the rock fortress.
Roxburgh.
Diminutive: Rox.

Roy Old French: a king. Scottish Gaelic: the red one. Also a diminutive of Royce, Royston and similar names. *See also* Ray and Rex.
Roi (French), Roie, Roye.

Royal Middle English: one who is

king-like.
Royale, Royall, Royalle.

Royce Old English: the son of the king.
Royse.
Diminutive: Roy.

Roydon Old English: from the hill
of rye.
Royden.

Royns *See* Ryence.

Royston Old English: a placename.
Roysten.
Diminutive: Roy.

Rua Maori: a lake.

Ruairi/Ruari/Ruaridh *See* Rory.

Ruanaku Polynesian: a legendary
figure.

Ruark *See* Roarke.

Ruben/Rubens/Rubin/Ruby *See*
Reuben.

Rud/Rudd *See* Rhudd.

Rudi/Rudy *See* Rudolph.

Rüdiger German form of Roger.

Rudolph Teutonic: a famous wolf.
See also Ralph and Rolf.
Rodolf (Dutch, German), Rodolfo
(Italian, Spanish), Rodolphe
(French), Rudolf (Scandinavian,
Slavic).
Diminutives: Dolf, Dolph, Rudi,
Rudy, Ruud (Dutch).

Rudyard Old English: from the red
enclosure.

Rueben *See* Reuben.

Ruel *See* Reuel.

Rufford Old English: from the rough
ford.

Rufus Latin: red-haired.

Ruggiero Italian form of Roger.

Ruka Maori form of Luke.

Rumford Old English: from the wide
ford.

Rune Old Norse: secret lore.

Rupe Polynesian: the brother of
Maui, a legendary hero.

Rupert *See* Robert.

Rurik Russian and Scandinavian
form of Roderick.
Ruric.

Ruru Maori: a New Zealand owl.

Rush Old English: a marshy plant.
Rusch, Rusche, Rushe.

Rushdi Arabic: one who follows the
right path.
Rushdie.

Rushford Old English: from the ford
with rushes.

Ruskin Teutonic: the small red-haired
one.

Ruslan Turkish: like a lion.

Russ Diminutive of Russell.

Russell Old French: one with red hair.
Russel.
Diminutives: Russ, Rusty.

Russet Middle English: a reddish-
brown colour.
Russett.

Ruston Old English: the farm in the
brushwood.
Rustan, Rusten, Rustin, Rustyn.

Rutger *See* Roger.

Rutherford Old English: from the
cattle ford.

Rutland Old Norse: from the stump
land.

Rutledge Old English: from the red
pool.

UNISEX NAMES

Unisex naming is increasingly popular and the following list reveals many possibilities for names to suit both sexes (some meanings will therefore be found in the Boys' section, others in the Girls').

Addison	Darcy	Lani	Rhys
Aidan	Delaney	Leeston	Riley
Ainslie	Derryn	Leith	Ripley
Archer	Dexter	Leroy	Ronan
Ariel	Dion	Lorne	Rory
Ashleigh	Doone	Luca	Roshan
Aspen	Drew	Lyle	Rowan
Aubrey	Dylan	MacKenna	Ryan
Avery	Eden	Mackenzie	Sage
Bailey	Emerson	Mallory	Sasha
Blaine	Erin	Marley	Shannon
Blair	Felix	Marlon	Shay
Blake	Finlay	Maxwell	Shelby
Blaze	Garnet	Memphis	Sheldon
Bodie	Greer	Merlin	Sheridan
Brady	Gryffyn	Moana	Sidney
Brice	Hadley	Montana	Skylar
Brodie	Harley	Morgan	Slaney
Brooklyn	Harper	Murphy	Sloan
Caley	Harris	Myall	Sonam
Carey	Hayden	Myron	Sorrel
Carson	Indiana	Nevada	Spencer
Casey	Jarrah	Ngaio	Sweeney
Cassidy	Jay	Nima	Tashi
Charlie	Jazz	Noa	Tate
Chase	Jesse	Paige	Tennessee
Claude	Jet	Parker	Tobie
Cody	Jordan	Perry	Trevena
Corey	Judah	Peyton	Trilby
Corin	Jude	Phoenix	Tully
Cotton	Karma	Piper	Tulsa
Culley	Keeley	Quentin	Tyler
Curtis	Kelsey	Quincy	Tyson
Dacey	Kendall	Rebel	Whitney
Dakota	Kenwyn	Regan	Winter
Daley	Kirby	Rémy	Zen
Dallas	Krishna	Renny	Zenith
Darby	Kyle	Rex	Zola

Routledge.

Rutley Old English: from the stump meadow.

Ruud Dutch diminutive of Rudolph.

Ry/Rye Diminutives of names such as Rylan and Ryman.

Ryan Irish Gaelic: a little king.
Rhian, Rhien, Rhyan, Rhyen, Rian, Riann, Ryann, Ryen, Ryenn, Ryhan, Ryhen, Ryon.

Rycroft Old English: from the rye field.

Ryden Old English: from the place of rye.
Rhyden.

Ryder *See* Rider.

Rydge *See* Ridge.

Ryen/Ryenn *See* Ryan.

Ryence Celtic: a Welsh king in Arthurian legend.
Royns, Ryens, Ryons.

Ryf/Ryfe *See* Reef.

Ryhan/Ryhen *See* Ryan.

Ryker A modern name, meaning unknown.

Ryl/Ryll *See* Rhyll.

Rylan Old English: from the rye land.
Ryland, Rylen, Rylon.
Diminutives: Ry, Rye.

Ryle Old English: from the hill of rye.

Rylee/Ryley *See* Riley.

Ryman Old English: a rye seller.
Diminutives: Ry, Rye.

Ryon *See* Ryan.

Ryton Old English: from the rye farm.

Ryver/Ryvers *See* River.

S

Saban *See* Saben.

Sabastain/Sabastian/Sabastyan *See* Sebastian.

Saben Latin: a Sabine man (from central Italy).
Saban, Sabian, Sabin, Sabino.

Saber *See* Sabre.

Sabian/Sabin/Sabino *See* Saben.

Sabir Arabic: the patient one.

Sabre French: sword-like.
Saber.

Sacha *See* Alexander and Sasha.

Sachel/Sachell *See* Satchel.

Sacheverell Old French: a leap of the young goat.

Sachin Hindi: pure existence. The name of a famous Indian cricketer (Sachin Tendulkar).

Sachio Japanese: fortunate.

Sadik Arabic: truthful, or faithful.
Sadiki, Sadiq.

Sadorn/Sadwyn The Cornish and Welsh names for Saturn.

Saeth Welsh: an arrow.

Safari Swahili: an adventurous expedition. Also a girl's name.
Safarie, Saffari, Saffarri.

Safford Old English: from the willow ford.

Sage Old French: wise. Also the name of a herb.
Saige, Sayge.

Sailor Middle English: one who sails.
Sailer, Sayler, Saylor.

Saimoni Polynesian form of Simon.

Sakari Finnish form of Zachary.

Sakda Thai: power.

Sakima Native American: a king.

Sal A diminutive of Salvador and similar names.

Salah Arabic: good, righteous. Saladin, Saleh.

Salim Arabic: safe, secure. Salama, Saleem, Selim.

Salisbury Old English: the fort by the willow pool.

Salman/Salomo/Salomon *See* Solomon.

Salter Old English: a salt seller.

Salton Old English: from the place in the willows.

Salvador Spanish from Latin: a saviour. Salvarie, Salvator (Polish), Salvatore (Italian), Salvidor, Salvitore. *Diminutive*: Sal.

Sam Korean: an achievement. Also a diminutive of Samson and Samuel.

Sami Arabic: the elevated one.

Sammie/Sammuel/Sammy *See* Samson and Samuel.

Samson Hebrew: of the sun, or a strong man. A biblical name. Sampson, Sansom, Sanson, Sansone (Italian). *Diminutives*: Hami (Maori), Sam, Sammie, Sammy.

Samuel Hebrew: asked of God; a name from the Bible. *See also* Saul. Hamuera (Maori), Sammual, Sammuel, Samual, Samuale, Samuele, Samuil (Russian), Samuile, Shmuel (Hebrew).

Diminutives: Hami (Maori), Sam, Samm, Samme, Sammie, Sammy.

Sanborn Old English: from the sandy brook.

Sancho Spanish: truthful and sincere.

Sanders Old English: the son of Alexander. Sander, Sanderson, Saunders, Saunderson.

Sandie/Sandy *See* Alexander.

Sandon Old English: from the sandy hill. Sanden, Santon.

Sandor Hungarian diminutive of Alexander.

Sanford Old English: from the sandy ford. Sandford.

Sanjay Sanskrit: triumphant.

Sanjiv Hindi: long-lived, or a good man. Sanjeev.

Sankara Sanskrit: auspicious.

Sansom/Sanson/Sansone *See* Samson.

Santiago Spanish: of St James. *See* Iago. Diego.

Santo Italian and Spanish form of Santos. Also the Cornish diminutive of Alexander.

Santon *See* Sandon.

Santos Spanish: of the saints. *See also* Toussaint. Santo (Italian, Spanish), Sanzio (Italian).

Santoso Indonesian: peaceful.

Sanzio *See* Santos.

Sargent Old French: a military officer.
Sargant, Sarjant, Sergeant, Sergent.

Sargon Persian: the sun prince.

Sarkis Armenian: a protector.

Sasha A Russian diminutive of Alexander.
Sacha (French), Sasa (Russian), Sascha (German), Sasho (Slavic), Zascha, Zasha.

Satchel Middle English: a bag, often used for carrying books.
Sachel, Sachell, Satchell.

Saturday *See* GIRLS.

Saturn From Latin: the Roman god of agriculture. Also a planet name.
Sadorn (Cornish), Sadwyn (Welsh), Saturne, Saturni, Saturnin, Saturno.

Saul Hebrew: asked for, or prayed for. A name from the Bible. *See also* Samuel.
Saule, Sawyl (Welsh).

Saunders/Saunderson *See* Sanders.

Savan Hindi: the moon.

Saviero *See* Xavier.

Saville Old French: from the willow estate.
Savile, Savill.

Saviour Middle English: one who rescues or saves. *See also* Salvador.
Savior.

Sawyer Old English: a sawer of wood.

Sawyl Welsh form of Saul.

Saxby Old Norse: from the farm of the short sword.

Saxon Old English: of the Saxons, or people of the sword.
Saxen, Saxin, Saxyn.

Saxton Old English: from the farm of the Saxon.
Saxten.

Sayed Arabic: the lord, the master.
Sayid, Seyed.

Sayer Celtic: a carpenter.
Sayers, Sayre.

Sayge *See* Sage.

Sayler/Saylor *See* Sailor.

Schain/Schaine/Scheine *See* Shane.

Schivas *See* Chivas.

Schylar/Schyler/Schylor *See* Skylar.

Scipio Latin: a staff or walking stick.

Scott Old English: from Scotland.
Scot, Scotte.
Diminutives: Scottie, Scotty.

Scout Middle English: one who observes and reports.
Scoute, Scoutt, Scoutte, Scowt, Scowte.

Scully Irish Gaelic: a herald or town crier.
Sculley, Scullie.

Seabert Old English: sea glorious.
Sebert.

Seaborne Old English: the sea warrior.
Seaborn, Seabourne.

Seabrook Old English: from a brook by the sea.

Seager *See* Seger.

Seal Middle English: a hall, or a marine animal.
Seale, Seel, Seele, Sele.

Sealey Old English: blessed.
Sealy, Seeley, Seely.

Seamus Irish Gaelic form of James.
Seamas, Shamus, Shaymus.

Sean Irish Gaelic form of John. *See*

also Shane.
Shaan, Shaughan, Shaun, Shaune, Shawn, Shawne, Siôn (Welsh).

Seanan *See* Senan.

Searle Teutonic: an armed warrior.
Searl, Serle.

Seaton Old English: a place by the sea.
Seton.

Seb The Ancient Egyptian god of the earth. Also a diminutive of Sebastian.

Sebastian Latin: a man from Sebasta. A 3rd-century saint.
Sabastain, Sabastian, Sabastyan, Sebastain, Sebastiano (Italian), Sébastien (French), Sebastyan, Sebastyen, Sevastian (Russian).
Diminutives: Bastian, Bastien, Seb, Sebi.

Sebedeus Welsh form of Zebediah.

Secundus Latin: the second child.

Sedgewick Old English: from the farm in the rushes.

Sedgley Old English: from the warrior's meadow.

Seel/Seele *See* Seal.

Seeley/Seely *See* Sealey.

Sefton Old English: the dweller at the place in the rushes.

Seger Old English: the sea warrior.
Seager, Segar.

Seith/Seithe *See* Seth.

Selby Old Norse: from the willow farm. Also a girl's name.
Selbee, Selbeigh, Selbey, Selbie.

Seldon Old English: from the house on the hill.
Selden.

Sele *See* Seal.

Selevan Cornish form of Solomon.

Selig *See* Zelig.

Selim *See* Salim.

Selwyn Latin: of the woods.
Herewini (Maori), Selwin, Selwinn, Selwynn.

Selyf Welsh form of Solomon.

Semi Latin: half.
Semie, Semih.

Semisi Tongan form of James.

Semyon Russian form of Simon.

Senan Irish Gaelic: old, or wise. The name of a saint.
Seanan, Sinan.

Senior Middle English: one who is older or of higher rank.

Sennett Old English: bold in victory.
Sinnett, Sinnott.

Septimus Latin: the seventh son.

Sequoia Native American: a large coniferous tree. Also a girl's name.
Sequoya.

Serafino Italian from Hebrew: ardent. The masculine form of Seraphina.

Serdar *See* Sirdar.

Seren Welsh: a star.
Serren.

Serge/Sergei *See* Sergius.

Sergeant/Sergent *See* Sargent.

Sergius Latin: a Roman family name.
Serge (French), Sergei (Russian), Sergio (Italian).

Serle *See* Searle.

Sesto *See* Sextus.

Seth Hebrew: a biblical name meaning the appointed one. One of the sons of Adam and Eve. Sanskrit: a bridge. Also the Ancient Egyptian

god of darkness.
Seith, Seithe, Set, Sethe.

Setiawan Indonesian: faithful.

Seton *See* Seaton.

Sevastian *See* Sebastian.

Seven Middle English: an unusual 'number name'. Also a girl's name.

Severn The name of a British river.

Seville A Spanish city.

Seward Old English: a sea defender.

Sexton Old French: a church official.

Sextus Latin: the sixth son.
Sesto (Italian).

Seyed *See* Sayed.

Seymour Old French: from a placename.
Seymore.

Shaan *See* Sean.

Shade Middle English: comparative darkness. Also a girl's name.
Shady, Shadye, Shayde.

Shadow Middle English: a shaded area. A character in one of Shakespeare's plays.

Shadwell Old English: from the shady stream.

Shae *See* Shay and Shea.

Shafiq Arabic: compassionate.

Shah Persian: a king.

Shahar Jewish: the dawn.

Shahin Persian: an eagle or falcon.
Shaheen.

Shaka Zulu: the founder.

Shakil Arabic: handsome.
Shakeel, Shaquil, Shaquille.

Shakir Arabic: the grateful one.
Shakur.

Shale Old English: a type of rock.
Shayle.

Shalom Hebrew: peace. *See also* Solomon.

Shamir Hebrew: as hard as flint.

Shamus *See* Seamus.

Shanahan Irish Gaelic: the wise one.

Shandy Old English: boisterous.

Shane A form of Sean. *See also* John.
Schain, Schaine, Schein, Scheine, Shayn, Shayne, Sheyn, Sheyne.

Shani Hebrew: red.

Shankar Sanskrit: he who gives happiness.

Shanley Irish Gaelic: a venerable hero.

Shannon Irish: the name of a river in Ireland. Also a girl's name.
Shannan, Shannen, Shannyn, Shanon, Shanyn.

Shaquil/Shaquille *See* Shakil.

Sharif Arabic: the honourable one.

Sharma Sanskrit: giving protection.

Sharrod A modern name, possibly a form of Jarrod.
Shared, Sharod, Sharred.

Shashi Sanskrit: like a moonbeam.

Shaughan/Shaun/Shaune/Shawn *See* Sean.

Shaugnessy Irish Gaelic: a common surname.
Shaugnessey, Shaunessey, Shawnessey, Shawnessy.

Shavar Hebrew: a comet.

Shaw Old English: from the grove of trees.

Shay Tibetan: crystal. *See also* Shea.
Shae, Shaye.

Shayde *See* Shade.

Shayden A combination of Shane and Hayden.
Shaydon, Shaydyn.

Shayle *See* Shale.

Shaymus *See* Seamus.

Shayn/Shayne *See* Shane.

Shea Irish Gaelic: the stately one.
Shae, Shay.

Sheehan Irish Gaelic: peaceful.

Sheffield Old English: from the crooked field, or the sheep field.

Shelby Old English: the dweller at the ledge estate.
Shelbee, Shelbey, Shelbie.

Sheldon Old English: from the steep valley.
Sheldan, Shelden.

Shelley Old English: from the wood, or the meadow's edge. More commonly a girl's name.
Shelly.

Shelton Old English: from the place on the ledge.

Shen Chinese: a deep thinker.

Sheng *See* Shing.

Sher Sanskrit: a lion.

Sherborne Old English: a clear stream.
Sherborn, Sherbourn, Sherbourne, Sherburn.

Sheridan Irish Gaelic: the wild one.
Sheriden, Sheridon, Sheridyn.

Sherlock Old English: fair-haired.
Sherlocke.

Sherman Old English: a wool-cutter.

Sherwin Old English: a swift runner.
Sherwyn, Sherwynd.

Sherwood Old English: from the bright forest.

Sheyn/Sheyne *See* Shane.

Shiloh Hebrew: a place of rest. A biblical placename.
Shilo, Shylo, Shyloh.

Shima Japanese: an island dweller.

Shimon *See* Simon.

Shinden Japanese: a temple.

Shine Middle English: a glow, or to excel.
Shyne.

Shing Chinese: a victory.
Sheng.

Shipley Old English: from the sheep pasture.

Shipton Old English: the dweller at the sheep farm.

Shiro Japanese: the fourth son.

Shiva Sanskrit: benign. An important Hindu god.
Shiv, Shivendra, Shivesh, Siva.

Shlomo *See* Solomon.

Shmuel *See* Samuel.

Sholto Scottish Gaelic: a sower of seed.

Shomari Swahili: forceful.

Shylo/Shyloh *See* Shiloh.

Shyne *See* Shine.

Siarl Welsh form of Charles.

Sibran Breton form of Cyprian.

Siddartha Sanskrit: one who has accomplished his goal. A name of the Buddha.

Sidell Old English: from the broad valley.
Siddal, Siddall, Siddel.

Sidney Old English: from the

riverside meadow. Old French: from St Denis.
Sidnee, Sidny, Sydnee, Sydnei, Sydney.
Diminutives: Sid, Syd.

Sieffre Welsh form of Geoffrey.

Siegbert Teutonic: a famous victory.
Diminutives: Siggy, Sigi.

Siegfried Teutonic: peace after victory.
Siegfrid, Sigfrid, Sigfried.
Diminutives: Siggy, Sigi.

Siemen *See* Simon.

Siggy/Sigi Diminutives of names such as Siegbert and Siegfried.

Sigmund Teutonic: a victorious protector.
Siegmund, Sigismund, Sigmond, Zigmond, Zigmund.

Sigurd Old Norse: a victorious guardian.

Siimon *See* Simon.

Silas/Silus *See* Silvanus.

Silvanus Latin: from the forest. *See also* Silvester.
Silas, Silus, Silva, Silvan, Silvano (Italian), Silvino (Portuguese), Silvio (Italian), Silvius, Sylvain (French), Sylvan, Sylvano.
Diminutive: Sly.

Silvester Latin: of the woods. *See also* Silvanus.
Silvestre (Spanish), Silvestro (Italian), Sylvester.
Diminutive: Sly.

Silvino/Silvio/Silvius *See* Silvanus.

Sim/Sime *See* Simon.

Simba Swahili: a lion.

Simeon The biblical form of Simon.

Simon Hebrew: the listener. *See also* Simpson.
Saimoni (Polynesian), Semyon (Russian), Shimon (Jewish), Siemen (Dutch), Siimon, Sim (Scottish Gaelic), Simeon, Simond, Simone (Italian), Siomon (Irish Gaelic), Symin, Symon, Szymon (Polish), Ximen (Spanish), Ximenes (Spanish), Ximens (Spanish), Ximun (Basque).
Diminutives: Sim (Scottish Gaelic), Sime (Slavic), Sims, Sym, Syms.

Simpson The son of Simon.
Simson.

Sinan *See* Senan.

Sinbad Teutonic: a sparkling prince.

Sinclair French: from St Clair.

Sindri Icelandic: a figure in Norse legend.

Singh Sanskrit: a lion.
Singa, Singha (Indonesian).

Sinnett/Sinnott *See* Sennett.

Siomon Irish Gaelic form of Simon.

Sion Hebrew: one who is praised. Also a Welsh form of John and Sean (Siôn).
Syon.

Sione Tongan form of John.

Siôr Welsh form of George.

Sirdar Nepali: a leader or guide.
Serdar.

Sirius Greek: hot or scorching. The brightest star in the sky, also known as the Dog Star.

Sisay An Ethiopian name of uncertain meaning.

Siva *See* Shiva.

Skeeter Old English: the fast one, or a swift (the bird).

Skeet.

Skelly Irish Gaelic: a storyteller.

Skelton Old English: from the place on the ledge.

Skene Scottish Gaelic: a bush.

Skipper Dutch: a ship's captain.
Diminutives: Skip, Skipp.

Skylar Dutch: a scholar or schoolmaster. Also a girl's name.
Schylar, Schyler, Schylor, Skyler, Skylor.

Slade Old English: from the valley.

Slader/Slaiter *See* Slater.

Slaney Irish Gaelic: a placename, meaning a river.
Slany.

Slate Middle English: a fine-grained rock.
Slayte.

Slater Middle English: one who works with slates.
Slader, Slaiter, Slaitor, Slator, Slatter, Slayter, Slaytor.

Slaven/Slavin *See* Slevin.

Slevin Irish Gaelic: the mountain climber.
Slaven, Slavin.

Sloan Irish Gaelic: a warrior.
Sloane.

Sly Diminutive of Silvanus and Silvester.

Smedley Old English: from the level meadow.
Smedly.

Smith Old English: a blacksmith.
Smithe, Smyth, Smythe.

Snare Middle English: a snare or trap.

Snowden Old English: from the snowy hill.
Snowdon.

Soames Old English: the homestead on the lake.
Soame.

Sobek The Ancient Egyptian crocodile god who was associated with the sun.

Socrates An ancient Greek philosopher.

Sohrab Persian: illustrious.

Sol Latin: the sun. Also a diminutive of Solomon.
Soll.

Solomon Hebrew: wise and peaceful. A son of David in the Bible. *See also* Shalom.
Horomona (Maori), Salman, Salomo (German), Salomon (Spanish), Selevan (Cornish), Selyf (Welsh), Shlomo (Jewish), Solamh (Gaelic), Solamon, Soloman, Suleiman (Arabic), Zalman (Yiddish), Zalmen, Zelman.
Diminutives: Sol, Solli, Solly, Zolli, Zolly.

Solon Greek: the wise one.

Somerby *See* Somerset.

Somerled Old Norse: the summer traveller. A Scottish name.

Somerset Old English: from the summer farm or settlement. An English county.
Somerby.

Somerton Old English: from the summer town.
Sommerton.

Somerville Old English: from the summery hill.
Somervell, Sommerville.

Sonam Sherpa/Tibetan: the fortunate one. Also a girl's name.

Sonny A son or young boy.
Sonney, Sonni, Sonnie.

Sophocles Greek. A classical dramatist.

Sorel/Sorell *See* Sorrel.

Soren Danish from Latin: the stern one.
Sorin, Sorren, Sorrin.

Sorin Romanian: of the sun. *See also* Soren.

Sorrel Old French: bitter. A 'plant name'.
Sorel, Sorell, Sorrell.

Soul A modern name, meaning the soul or spirit.
Soule.

Southwell Old English: from the southern spring.

Sparke Old Norse: the lively one.
Spark.

Sparrow Old English: a 'bird name'.
Sparo, Sparow, Sparowe, Sparro, Sparrowe.

Speck Middle English: the small or little one.
Specke, Spek.

Spencer Old French: a dispenser of provisions.
Spence, Spense, Spenser.

Spike Old English: a nail, or an ear of grain. Generally a nickname.
Spyke.

Spiridon Greek: of the soul or spirit.
Spiro, Spyro.

Sprig Middle English: a twig or small branch.
Sprigg, Sprigge.

Squire Old French: a knight's attendant.

Stack Old Norse: a haystacker.
Stac, Stak, Stakk.

Stacy *See* GIRLS.

Staffan Swedish form of Stephen.

Stafford Old English: from the ford by the landing place.
Staffard.

Stak/Stakk *See* Stack.

Stamford *See* Stanford.

Stan A diminutive of Stanley and other names starting with Stan.

Stanbury Old English: from the stone fort.

Standen Old English: a dweller in the stony valley.

Standish Old English: from the rocky pasture.

Stanfield Old English: from the stony field.
Standfield, Stansfield.

Stanford Old English: a dweller at the rocky ford.
Stamford.

Stanhope Old English: from the stony valley.

Stanislaus Slavic: a glorious ruler.
Stanislas, Stanislav (Czech, Russian).

Stanley Old English: from the stony meadow.
Stanleigh, Stanly.
Diminutive: Stan.

Stanton Old English: from the rocky farm or estate.
Stanten, Stenton.

Stanwick Old English: from the rocky village.

Star Old English: a star.
Starr.

Starbuck Old Norse: the stream in the sedges.

Stavros Greek form of Stephen.

Stearn/Stearne *See* Sterne.

Stedman Old English: a farmer. Steadman.

Steele Old English: like steel. Steel.

Stefan/Stefano/Stefanos/Steffan/ Steffen *See* Stephen.

Sten Swedish: a stone. Steen (Danish), Stein (German, Norwegian), Steiner (Norwegian).

Stenton *See* Stanton.

Stepan *See* Stephen.

Stephen Greek: a crown or garland. *See also* Stevenson and Stinson. Estéban (Spanish), Étienne (French), István (Hungarian), Staffan (Swedish), Stavros (Greek), Steaphan (Scottish Gaelic), Stefan (German, Polish, Russian, Scandinavian), Stefano (Italian), Stefanos (Greek), Steffan (Welsh), Steffen, Stepan (Czech, Russian), Stephan (German), Stéphane (French), Stephano, Stephanus, Stevan, Steven, Stevin, Stiofan (Irish Gaelic), Tepene (Maori), Tipene (Maori). *Diminutives*: Steev, Steeve, Steve, Stevey, Stevie.

Stephenson *See* Stevenson.

Sterling Old English: a little star, or a starling. Stirling.

Sterne Old English: austere, stern. Stearn, Stearne, Stern.

Stert *See* Sturt.

Stevan *See* Stephen.

Steve/Steven/Stevie *See* Stephen.

Stevenson The son of Stephen. Stephenson.

Stewart Old English: a steward, or keeper of a household. Steward, Stuart. *Diminutives*: Stew, Stewie, Stewy, Stu.

Stig Old Norse: the wanderer. Stieg.

Stijn Dutch diminutive of Augustijn (*see* Augustine).

Stiles *See* Styles.

Stinson Old English: the son of Stephen, or the son of stone. Stimson.

Stiofan Irish Gaelic form of Stephen.

Stirling *See* Sterling.

Stockard An English surname.

Stockley Old English: a clearing with tree stumps.

Stockton Old English: from the place near the tree trunk.

Stoddard Old English: the horse-keeper. Stoddart, Stoddert.

Stoke Old English: from the settlement. Stokes.

Storey Old Norse: the large one. *See also* Story. Storee, Stori, Storie, Story.

Storm Old English: a tempest. Storme.

Storr Old Norse: a great man.

Story Middle English: a tale or narrative.

Stover Old English: one who tends the stove. Stovin.

Stowe Old English: from the religious site.
Stow.

Strahan Scottish Gaelic: a little valley.
Strachan, Straughan, Straun, Strawn.

Stratford Old English: from the ford on a Roman road. An English city.

Stratton Old English: from the place on a Roman road.

Stroud Old English: the overgrown marshland.

Stu/Stuart See Stewart.

Sturt Old English: from the promontory.
Stert.

Styles Old English: from the stile.
Stiles.

Styx Greek: an underworld river in classical mythology.

Sudi Swahili: luck.

Suffield Old English: a dweller in the southern field.

Sukarno A popular Indonesian name.

Suleiman Arabic form of Solomon.

Sullivan Irish Gaelic: the black-eyed one.
Sullavan, Sullaven, Sulliven.

Sultan Arabic: a king or ruler. *See also* Zoltan.

Sulwyn Welsh: the fair sun.

Suman Sanskrit: cheerful and wise.

Sumner Old French: the one who summons.

Sun Chinese: bending, or decreasing. Nepali: gold or golden.

Sunday See GIRLS.

Suran The name of a town in Iran.

Suresh Sanskrit: the ruler of the gods.

Surya Sanskrit: the sun.

Sutcliffe Old English: from the south cliff.
Sutcliff.

Sutherland Old Norse: from the southern land.

Sutton Old English: the dweller at the southern farm or town.

Sven Old Norse: a youth.
Svein (Norwegian), Svend (Danish).

Swain Old English: a swineherd. Old Norse: youthful.
Swaine, Swayn, Swayne.

Swami Sanskrit: a religious teacher.

Sweeney Irish Gaelic: the little hero.
Sweeny.

Swindon Old English: from the hill of the pigs. An English city.

Swinford Old English: the pig ford.

Swithin Old English: strong. An English saint.
Swithun.

Sycamore Greek: a 'tree name'.

Syd/Sydnee/Sydney See Sidney.

Sydenham Old English: from the wide river meadow.

Sykes Old English: at the stream or gully.

Sylvain/Sylvan See Silvanus.

Sylvester See Silvester.

Sym/Symin/Symon/Syms See Simon.

Syon See Sion.

Syrus See Cyrus.

Szymon Polish form of Simon.

T

Taavi Finnish form of David.

Tabor Persian: a drum or drummer.
Taber.
Diminutives: Tab, Tabb.

Tad Irish Gaelic: a poet or philosopher. *See also* Teague and Thaddeus.
Tadgh, Tadhg.

Tadd/Taddeo/Tadeo *See* Thaddeus.

Taden A modern name, probably from Jaden.
Tadan, Taedan, Taeden, Taidan, Taiden, Taydan, Tayden.

Tadeusz Polish form of Thaddeus.

Tadzi Native American: the moon.

Taelan/Taelen *See* Talan.

Tafari African: the awesome one.

Taffy Welsh diminutive of David.

Taggart Gaelic: a priest.

Taha Polynesian: one, or the firstborn.

Tahi Hawaiian: a mythological figure.

Tahir Arabic: pure and virtuous.

Tahn *See* Tan.

Tahu A Polynesian name of uncertain meaning.

Tai Polynesian: the ocean. Vietnamese: the talented one. *See also* Tye.
Taie.

Taiaha Maori: a long club.

Taidan/Taiden *See* Taden.

Tailer/Tailor *See* Taylor.

Tait/Taite *See* Tate.

Taj Hindi: the crowned one.
Tahj, Taji.

Taka Japanese: a hawk

Takawai Maori: a gourd or calabash.

Takoda Native American: the friend of all.

Talan An old Breton and Cornish name, possibly from the word forehead.
Taelan, Taelen, Taland, Talen, Tallan, Talland, Tallen, Taylan, Taylen.

Talbot Old French: from the valley.
Talbott.

Talfryn Welsh: from the top of the hill.

Taliesin Welsh: a radiant brow.

Tallan/Talland/Tallen *See* Talan.

Tallis Persian: wise, learned.
Talis, Tallys, Talys.

Talor *See* Taylor.

Tam Vietnamese: the heart. *See also* Thomas.

Tama Polynesian: a boy or son.

Tamaiti Maori: a son.

Tamas *See* Thomas.

Tamati Maori form of Thomas.

Tame Maori form of Tommy.

Tamir Hebrew: tall.

Tan Vietnamese: fresh. Welsh: fire.
Tahn.

Tana Maori form of Turner.

Tancred Teutonic: a thoughtful adviser.

Tane Maori/Polynesian: a man.

Tanekaha Polynesian: a pine tree.

Tane Mahuta Maori: the god of the forest.

Tangaroa Maori/Polynesian: of the sea.

Tango The Tibetan name for January. Also a dance.

Tangohia Maori: to take hold of.

Tangwyn Welsh: peace.

Tani Japanese: from the valley.

Taniel Armenian form of Daniel.

Tanner Old English: a tanner or leather worker.

Tanzil Arabic: a revelation.
Tanzeel.

Tapanui Maori: a New Zealand town.

Tara Sanskrit: the shining one.

Taran Sanskrit: heaven. Welsh: thunder.
Taranu, Taren, Tarin, Tarran, Tarren, Tarrin.

Tariq Arabic: the night visitor.
Tarek, Tarik.

Tarkin/Tarkyn *See* Tarquin.

Tarn Old Norse: a mountain pool.

Taro Japanese: the firstborn son.

Tarquin Latin: the name of two early Roman kings.
Tarkin, Tarkyn, Tarquinn.

Tarran/Tarren/Tarrin *See* Taran.

Tarrant Old English: from the name of a river.
Tarrent, Terrant, Terrent.

Tarun Sanskrit: young, tender.

Tashi Sherpa/Tibetan: prosperity. Also a girl's name.

Tasman After Abel Tasman, the Dutch explorer who 'discovered' Tasmania.
Tazman.

Tate Old Norse: jolly, cheerful. *See also* Tatum.
Tait, Taite, Tayt, Tayte.

Tatum Old English: from Tate's homestead.
Diminutive: Tate.

Taurean A suitable name for a boy born under the zodiac sign of Taurus.
Taure, Tauri, Taurian, Taurinos, Taurinus, Tauros, Taurus.

Tavi Jewish diminutive of David.

Tavish Scottish Gaelic: a twin. A form of Thomas.
Tavis.

Tawhaki The Maori god of thunder and lightning.
Tawaki.

Tawhero Polynesian: a tree.

Tawhiri Polynesian: a tempest.

Tawhirimatea Maori: the god of the winds.

Taydan/Tayden *See* Taden.

Taye A modern American name.
Tay.

Taylan/Taylen *See* Talan.

Taylor Old French: a tailor.
Tailer, Tailor, Talor, Tayler, Taylour.

Tayt/Tayte *See* Tate.

Taz Persian: a shot of liquor, or a goblet.
Tazz.

Tazman *See* Tasman.

Teague Irish Gaelic: a poet or philosopher. *See also* Tad.
Teage, Teigue, Tighe.

Teak A 'tree name'.
Teake.

Teal English: a waterbird.

Teale.

Team Middle English: a group of people.
Teame, Teem, Teme

Tean Cornish: a placename, from the Isles of Scilly.
Tehan.

Te Aroha Polynesian: the man of the long string.

Tecwyn Welsh: white, fair.

Ted/Teddie/Teddy *See* Edward, Theobald and Theodore.

Tedrich *See* Theodoric.

Teejae/Teejai/Teejay *See* Tejay.

Teigr Welsh form of Tiger.

Teigue *See* Teague.

Teirnan/Teirnon *See* Tiernan.

Teizo A popular Japanese name.

Tejay An unusual name, from the letters T and J.
Teejae, Teejai, Teejay, Tejae, Tejai.

Tekea Polynesian: a man of the sharks.

Telford Old French: an iron-cutter.
Telfer, Telfor, Telfour.

Teme *See* Team.

Tempest Middle English: a storm.

Templar Old French: a knight.
Temple, Templer.

Temuera Maori. After the actor Temuera Morrison.

Tendai Southern African: be thankful.

Tennessee A state of the USA. Also a girl's name.
Tenessee, Tennesee.

Tennille *See* GIRLS.

Tennyson Old English: the son of Dennis.
Dennison, Tenison, Tennison, Tenyson.

Tentagel/Tentagil *See* Tintagel.

Tenzing Sherpa/Tibetan: the holder of religion.
Tenzin.

Teodor/Teodosio *See* Theodore.

Tepene A Maori form of Stephen.

Te Ra Maori: the sun.

Te Ranginui Maori: the sky father.

Terence Latin: smooth and polished.
Terencio (Spanish), Terenz (German), Terrance, Terrence, Thierry (French), Torrance.
Diminutives: Tel, Terrie, Terry.

Terran Latin: the earth.
Teran, Terra, Terrano, Terren, Terreno (Italian).

Terrant/Terrent *See* Tarrant.

Terrell Teutonic: belonging to Thor, the Norse god of thunder and lightning.
Terell, Terill, Terrel, Terril, Terrill, Terryl, Teryl.

Terrence/Terrie/Terry *See* Terence and Theodoric.

Tetsu Japanese: philosophy.

Tetsuya Japanese: the arrow of philosophy.

Tevin An African-American name of uncertain meaning, made popular through singer Tevin Campbell.
Teven, Tevenn, Tevinn, Tevvin, Tevvinn, Tevyn, Tevynn.

Tevita Tongan form of David.

Tex American: from Texas.
Texe, Texxe.

Thaddeus Greek: courageous. A
biblical name.
Taddeo (Italian), Tadeo (Spanish),
Tadeusz (Polish), Thadeus.
Diminutives: Tad, Tadd, Thad.

Thai Vietnamese: many.

Thaine *See* Thane.

Than Burmese: a million. An
auspicious number name.
Thanh (Vietnamese).

Thane Old English: a land-holding
soldier. Also a Scottish clan chieftain.
Thain, Thaine, Thayne.

Thanos Greek: noble.

Thatcher Old English: one who
thatches roofs.

Theo *See* Theobald, Theodore and
Theodoric.

Theobald Teutonic: a bold leader of
the people.
Tibald, Tibold (German), Tióbóid
(Irish Gaelic), Tybalt.
Diminutives: Ted, Teddie, Teddy,
Theo.

Theodore Greek: the gift of God.
Feodore, Fyodor (Russian), Teodor,
Teodosio (Italian, Spanish), Theodor
(German), Tudor (Welsh).
Diminutives: Ted, Teddie, Teddy,
Theo.

Theodoric Teutonic: the ruler of the
people. *See also* Derek.
Tedric, Thierry (French).
Diminutives: Terrie, Terry, Theo.

Theon Greek: godly.

Theron Greek: the hunter.

Theseus Greek: a hero of legend.

Thian Vietnamese: smooth.
Thien.

Thierry French form of Terence and
Theodoric.

Thies/Thijs Dutch diminutives of
Matthew.

Thomas Greek: a twin. One of the
twelve apostles in the Bible. *See also*
Tavish, Tom and Tomkin.
Tamas (Hungarian), Tamati (Maori),
Tavis (Scottish Gaelic), Tavish
(Scottish), Thomasz, Thomaz, Tomas
(Czech, Irish and Scottish Gaelic,
Spanish), Tomasz (Polish), Tomaz
(Slavic), Tommaso (Italian), Tomos
(Welsh).
Diminutives: Tam (Scottish), Tame
(Maori), Thom, Tom, Tommie,
Tommo, Tommy, Tos, Toss.

Thor Old Norse: the god of thunder
and lightning in Norse mythology.
See also Torvald and Tory.
Thorin, Thorr, Tor, Torben (Danish),
Tore, Tory.

Thorald Old Norse: ruling in the
manner of Thor.

Thorburn Old Norse: Thor's warrior.

Thorin *See* Thor.

Thorley *See* Thornley.

Thormund Old English: Thor's
protection.
Thormond, Thurmund.

Thorn Old English: a prickle or sharp
part of a plant.
Thorne.

Thornley Old English: from the
thorny clearing.
Thorley.

Thornton Old English: from the
place among the thorns.

Thorpe Old English: from the farm
village.

Thorp.

Thorvald *See* Torvald.

Thursday *See* GIRLS.

Thurso A Scottish placename.

Thurstan Old English: Thor's stone.
Thurston, Thurstone.

Thye *See* Tye.

Tiare A Maori form of Charles.

Tibald/Tibold *See* Theobald.

Tiberius Latin: after the River Tiber.
Tibor (Hungarian).

Tie *See* Tye.

Tien Chinese: heavenly. Vietnamese:
the first. Also a girl's name.

Tiernan Irish Gaelic: a lord. *See also*
Kiernan.
Teirnan, Teirnon, Tierney, Tiernon,
Tirnan.

Tierney Irish Gaelic: the descendant
of a lord.
Tiarney.

Tiesen/Tieson *See* Tyson.

Tiger From a Middle English word
(tigre). The name of a well-known
golfer (Tiger Woods).
Teigr (Welsh), Tiga, Tigah, Tigar,
Tigre, Tigris, Tigro, Tygar, Tyger,
Tygre.

Tighe *See* Teague.

Tiki Polynesian: one who is fetched,
as in a spirit after death.

Tilar/Tiler *See* Tyler.

Tilford Old English: from the good
man's ford.

Tim/Timmie/Timmy *See* Timothy.

Timana A Maori name of uncertain
meaning.

Timo/Timofei *See* Timothy.

Timon Greek: a reward, an honour.
Tymon.

Timor Malay: the east.

Timothy Greek: honouring God, or
honoured by God.
Timo (Dutch, Finnish), Timofei
(Russian), Timoteo (Italian,
Spanish), Timothée (French),
Timotheus, Timothi, Timothie,
Timoti (Maori), Tymothy.
Diminutives: Tim, Timmie, Timmy,
Tym.

Timoti Maori form of Timothy.

Tinan *See* Tynan.

Tino Italian. A diminutive of
Valentino.

Tintagel Celtic: a Cornish placename,
the supposed location of King
Arthur's legendary castle.
Tentagel, Tentagil, Tintagil.

Tióbóid *See* Theobald.

Tipene A Maori form of Stephen.

Tiran/Tiren *See* Tyran.

Tirnan *See* Tiernan.

Tirol *See* Tyrol.

Tisen/Tison *See* Tyson.

Titan A giant in Greek mythology. A
satellite of the planet Saturn.
Tytan.

Titian/Titiano *See* Tiziano.

Titus Latin: an old Roman name.
Tito (Italian, Portuguese, Spanish),
Titos (Greek), Tytus (Polish).

Tiziano Italian: of the Tizia people, a
Roman family.
Titian, Titiano, Titianus, Tizian.

Toa Maori: a champion.

Tobe/Tobee/Tobey *See* Tobias.

Tobias Hebrew: God is good. A biblical name.
Tobe, Tobee, Tobey, Tobi, Tobie, Toby, Tobyn, Tohbee, Tohbey, Tohbi, Tohbie, Topia (Maori).

Tobie/Toby/Tobyn *See* Tobias.

Todd Old Norse from Latin: a fox or foxhunter.
Tod.

Toft Old English: from the site of the building.

Tohbee/Tohbey/Tohbie *See* Tobias.

Tom A diminutive of Thomas.
Tam (Scottish), Tame (Maori), Thom, Tomi, Tommie, Tommo, Tommy, Toss, Twm (Welsh).

Tomas/Tomasz/Tomaz *See* Thomas.

Tomi Japanese: red. Also a diminutive of Thomas.

Tomkin Old English: little Tom or Thomas.
Tomkins, Tomkyn, Tomlin.

Tommaso/Tommie/Tommy/Tomos
See Thomas and Tom.

Tongatea Polynesian: a man from Tonga.

Tony A diminutive of Anthony.
Toney, Toni, Tonie.

Topher A diminutive of Christopher.

Topi African: an antelope.

Topia Maori form of Tobias.

Tor Celtic: a rock. *See also* Thor.

Torcall/Torkel *See* Torquil.

Tore/Torben *See* Thor.

Torey/Tori/Torie *See* Tory.

Torin Gaelic: the chief.
Torinn, Torryn, Toryn.

Tormey Irish Gaelic: a thunder spirit.

Torquil Scottish Gaelic from Old Norse: Thor's cauldron.
Torcall (Gaelic), Torkel (Swedish), Torquill.

Torr Old English: from the tower.

Torrance *See* Terence.

Torryn/Toryn *See* Torin.

Torvald Old Norse: Thor the ruler.
Thorvald, Trudeau (Old French).

Tory Irish Gaelic: a placename, meaning a tower-like rock. Old Norse: a form of Thor.
Torey, Tori, Torie.

Tos/Toss Diminutives of Thomas.

Toshiro A popular name in Japan.

Toussaint French: all the saints. *See also* Santos.

Tovi Modern Hebrew: good.

Townley Old English: from the town meadow.

Townsend Old English: from the town's end.

Tozer Old English: one who combs wool.

Trace Middle English: a mark or small quantity.
Traice, Trayce.

Track Middle English: a path or trail.
Trac, Tracke, Trak, Trakk.

Tracy Old French: from a placename. More commonly a girl's name.
Tracey.

Trae *See* Trey.

Traherne Welsh: of iron strength.
Trahern, Trehearn, Trehearnc, Treherne.

Trai Vietnamese: a pearl. *See also* Trait and Trey.

Traie *See* Trait and Trey.

Trail Middle English: a path or track.
Traile, Traill, Traille.

Trait French: a distinguishing quality
or feature. Also a form of Trey.
Trai, Traie.

Trak/Trakk *See* Track.

Tran Vietnamese: a family name.

Travis Old French: from the crossing
or crossroads.
Travers, Travice.

Trayce *See* Trace.

Traylor Old French: a hunter or
tracker. Also a girl's name.
Trayler.

Tre A form of Trey. Also the prefix
for many Cornish names such as
Trethowan and Trevena, meaning
a homestead, farm or place
(pronounced 'truh').

Treat Middle English: something that
brings pleasure.
Treate, Treet, Trete.

Trefor *See* Trevor.

Trefusis Cornish: a placename.

Trehearn/Trehearne *See* Traherne.

Treigh *See* Trey.

Trelawney Cornish: from the church
village.

Trell A modern American name.
Trel, Trelle.

Tremayne Cornish: from the place of
the stone or rock.
Tremain, Tremaine, Tremayn.

Trent English: the name of a river.
Trenton.

Tresco Cornish: a placename, one of
the Isles of Scilly.

Trete *See* Treat.

Trethowan Cornish: from the farm
by the sandhills.

Trev/Treve/Trever *See* Trevor.

Trevelyan Cornish: from the farm at
the mill.

Trevena Cornish/Welsh: a homestead
on the hill.
Treveena, Treveenah, Trevenah,
Trevenna, Trevennah, Trevina,
Trevinah.

Trevor Welsh: from the large village.
Trefor (Welsh), Treve, Trever.
Diminutive: Trev.

Trey Middle English: three, or the
third child.
Trae, Trai, Traie, Trait, Tre (Swedish),
Treigh, Treye.

Tribe Middle English: a group of
people with common customs and
traditions.
Tryb, Trybe.

Trick Middle English: a roguish
prank.
Tricke, Trik, Trikk, Trikke, Trique,
Tryk, Trykk, Trykke.

Trilby *See* GIRLS.

Trinidad Spanish: a Caribbean island.
Also a girl's name.

Trinity *See* GIRLS.

Tristan/Tristen *See* Tristram.

Tristram Celtic: the noisy one.
Drostan, Drystan, Tristain, Tristam,
Tristan, Tristen, Tristian, Tristin,
Triston, Tristrand, Tristyn, Trystan
(Cornish, Welsh).

Triton A Greek sea god who was half-
man, half-fish.
Tryton.

Trowbridge Old English: from the wooden bridge.

Troy Old French: from a placename. Also an ancient city in Asia Minor.
Troye.

Trudeau Old French form of Torvald.

Truman Old English: a trusty or faithful man.
Trueman.

Trump Old French: a trumpeter
Trumpe, Trumper.

Tryb/Trybe *See* Tribe.

Tryk/Trykk/Trykke *See* Trick.

Trystan *See* Tristram.

Tryton *See* Triton.

Tsamcho Sherpa/Tibetan: the last issue.

Tseten Sherpa/Tibetan: the defender of religion. Also a girl's name.

Tshering Sherpa/Tibetan: long life. Also a girl's name.

Tu Polynesian: the god of war.

Tua Samoan: behind.

Tuaka Maori: a legendary chief.

Tucker Old English: a cloth-worker.

Tudor Welsh form of Theodore.
Tudur, Tudyr.

Tuesday *See* GIRLS.

Tueva Polynesian: a mourner.

Tui Maori: a honeyeater.

Tulloch Irish Gaelic: a placename, meaning a little hill.
Tulla.

Tully An Irish surname.
Tullee, Tulley, Tulli, Tullie.

Tulsa A city in Oklahoma, USA. Also a girl's name.
Tulsah.

Tupac African: a warrior.
Tupak.

Turi Polynesian: a famous chief.

Turk From Turkey.
Turke.

Turner Old French: a lathe-worker.
Tana (Maori).

Turpin Old Norse: a Finnish man of Thor.

Tuscan From Tuscany, a region of Italy.

Tutapu Polynesian: a Tahitian deity.

Tuyen Vietnamese: angelic.

Twain Middle English: two. The surname of a famous author (Mark Twain).
Twaine, Twayn, Twayne.

Twm Welsh form of Tom.

Twyford Old English: from the double ford.

Tyack Cornish: a farmer.
Tyak.

Tybalt *See* Theobald.

Tycho Greek: he who hits the mark.
Tyco, Tyko.

Tye Old English: from the enclosure.
Tai, Taie, Thye, Tie, Ty, Tyh, Tyhe.

Tyesen/Tyeson *See* Tyson.

Tygar/Tyger/Tygre *See* Tiger.

Tyko *See* Tycho.

Tyler Old English: a tiler or tile-maker.
Tilar, Tiler, Tylar.

Tym/Tymothy *See* Timothy.

Tymon *See* Timon.

Tynan Gaelic: the dark one.
Tinan.

Tyne An English river. Also a girl's

name.

Tyondai A modern name, probably a form of Tye.

Tyran An unusual modern name.
Tiran, Tiren, Tyren, Tyron.

Tyrese African: a talented leader.

Tyrol After the Austrian alpine region.
Tirol.

Tyrone Irish: a county in Northern Ireland.

Tyson Old French: a firebrand. Can also be a girl's name.
Tiesen, Tieson, Tisen, Tison, Tyesen, Tyeson, Tysen.

Tytan *See* Titan.

Tytus *See* Titus.

U

Uan *See* Ewan.

Udale/Udall *See* Udell.

Udell Anglo-Saxon: from the valley of the yew trees.
Udale, Udall.

Udo German: prosperity, fortune.

Udolf Old English: a prosperous wolf.

Uenuku Maori: a rainbow.

Ugo Italian form of Hugh.

Uilleam Scottish Gaelic form of William.
Uilleag.

Ukko A god of the sky and air in Finnish mythology.

Ulan African: the firstborn twin.

Uland Teutonic: the noble land.

Ulbrecht Teutonic: noble splendour.

Ulf *See* Wolfe.

Ulfred Old English/Teutonic: peace.

Ulises/Ulisse/Ulixes *See* Ulysses.

Ulli *See* Ulrich.

Ulmer Old English: a famous wolf.
Ulmar.

Ulrich Teutonic: a ruler.
Alric (German), Ulric (Old English), Ulrick (Scandinavian), Ulrico (Italian), Ulryk (Polish).
Diminutives: Ulli, Utz (German).

Ultan Irish: an old Gaelic name.

Uluka Sanskrit: an owl.

Ulysses Greek: the angry one, wrathful. The famous wanderer of Homer's Odyssey.
Ulises (Spanish), Ulisse (Italian), Ulixes, Ulyses, Ulysse (French).

Umar *See* Omar.

Umberto *See* Humbert.

Umbriel A satellite of the planet Uranus.

Unwin Old English: the enemy.

Upravda Slavic: the upright one.

Upton Old English: from the upper farm or town.

Upwood Old English: from the forest on the hill.

Urban Latin: a city dweller. The name of several saints and popes.
Orban (Hungarian), Urbain, Urbane, Urvan (Russian).

Urgyen Sherpa/Tibetan. The name of Tibet's greatest saint.

Uri/Urie *See* Uriah and Uriel.

Uriah Hebrew: God is light. A

biblical name best known from the Charles Dickens character Uriah Heep in *David Copperfield*. *See also* Uriel.
Diminutives: Uri, Urie.

Urian *See* Urien.

Uriel Hebrew: light. *See also* Uriah. Uriele (Italian), Uriell, Urielle.
Diminutives: Uri, Urie.

Urien Welsh: of privileged birth, or born in the town.
Urian.

Ursel Latin: a bear. The masculine version of Ursula.
Urs (German), Ursell, Urshell, Ursus.

Urson *See* Orson.

Ursus *See* Ursel.

Urvan *See* Urban.

Usama Arabic: a lion.
Osama.

Usher Old French: an attendant or usher.

Ushnisha Sanskrit: a crown.

Usko Finnish: faith.

Usman *See* Osman.

Utah A state of the USA.

Uther A king of the Britons, a figure in Arthurian legend.

Utu Polynesian: to return.

Utz *See* Ulrich.

Uwe *See* Ove.

Uyeda Japanese: from the rice field.

Uzi Hebrew: my strength.

Uziel/Uzziel *See* Uzziah.

Uzziah Hebrew: the power or strength of God.
Ozias, Uziah, Uziel, Uzziel.

V

Vachel Old French: one who raises cows.

Václav Czech form of Wenceslas.

Vadim *See* Vladimir.

Vail Old English: from the valley. Vaile, Vale, Valle.

Valdemar *See* Vladimir.

Valentine Latin: strong and healthy. A 3rd-century saint.
Folant (Welsh), Valentin (Danish, French, Swedish), Valentino (Italian), Vallentin, Vallentine, Walenty (Polish).
Diminutives: Tino (Italian), Val.

Valerian Latin: strong and powerful. A 'herb name'.
Valery (French).

Vali A son of Odin in Norse mythology. He was the god of vegetation and eternal light and renowned for his strength. Tongan: paint.
Valie.

Vallis Old French: the Welshman.

Valter *See* Walter.

Valu Polynesian: the eighth child.

Vamana Sanskrit: deserving praise.

Van Dutch: from or of. Generally a prefix to a surname, but also used as a first name. Also a diminutive of Ivan and a popular Vietnamese name.

Vance Old English: a thresher.

Vander From Greek: an archer. Also a diminutive of Evander.

FAMOUS NEW ZEALANDERS

Women		Men	
Anika	Moa	Alan	Duff
Anna	Paquin	Barry	Crump
Ans	Westra	Bruno	Lawrence
Bic	Runga	Che	Fu
Brooke	Fraser	Cliff	Curtis
Carol	Hirschfeld	Colin	McCahon
Charlotte	Dawson	Dave	Dobbyn
Claire	Chitham	David	Lange
Danielle	Cormack	Don	McGlashan
Emily	Perkins	Douglas	Lilburn
Hayley	Westenra	Eric	Watson
Helen	Clark	Ernest	Rutherford
Jane	Campion	Gary	McCormick
Janet	Frame	Hugh	Sundae
Jean	Batten	Inia	Te Wiata
Joy	Cowley	Jim	Hickey
Judy	Bailey	John	Britten
Karen	Walker	John	Campbell
Kate	Sheppard	Jon	Trimmer
Kate	Sylvester	Karl	Urban
Katherine	Mansfield	Lee	Tamahori
Keisha	Castle-Hughes	Marcus	Lush
Keri	Hulme	Maurice	Gee
Kerre	McIvor	Max	Cryer
Kerry	Fox	Michael	King
Kim	Hill	Neil	Finn
Kimbra		Oliver	Driver
Kiri	Te Kanawa	Oscar	Kightley
Lana	Coc-Kroft	Paul	Holmes
Linda	Clark	Peter	Jackson
Lucy	Lawless	Pita	Sharples
Lynley	Dodd	Ralph	Hotere
Margaret	Mahy	Raybon	Kan
(Edith) Ngaio	Marsh	Richard	Pearse
Patricia	Grace	Robert	Muldoon
Rachel	Hunter	Roger	Hall
Rena	Owen	Russell	Crowe
Rima	Te Wiata	Sam	Neill
Rita	Angus	Temuera	Morrison
Sharon	O'Neill	Tim	Finn
Shona	Laing	Toss	Woollaston
Sian	Elias	Winston	Peters
Trelise	Cooper	Witi	Ihimaera

Vane *See* Venn.

Vangelis Greek: possibly from Evangelos, the evangelist.

Vanya Russian: a diminutive of Ivan. *See also* John.

Varad Hungarian: from the fortress.

Varden Old French: from the green hills.
Vardon, Verden, Verdon.

Varian Latin: the changeable one.

Varick Icelandic: a sea drifter. Teutonic: a protecting ruler.

Varley An English surname, possibly a variation of Farley (from the fern clearing).
Varlee, Varleigh, Varli, Varlie.

Vartan Armenian: a rose.

Varuna Sanskrit: the god of the night sky.

Vasco Portuguese/Spanish. The name of a 15th-century explorer (Vasco da Gama).

Vasily A form of Basil, meaning royal or kingly.
Vasil, Vasili, Vasilis (Greek), Vasilly, Vassily, Wassily.

Vasudeva Sanskrit: the father of the god Krishna.

Vaughan Welsh: small.
Vaun, Vaune.

Ved Sanskrit: knowledge.

Veit Dutch form of Guy.

Vekoslav Slavic: eternal glory.

Venn Old English: from the marsh or fen.
Vane, Ven, Venne.

Vennard An English surname.

Venton Old English: a place in a marsh or fen.
Vennten, Vennton, Venten.

Ventry The name of an Irish village.
Ventrey.

Verde Italian: green.
Verdey, Verdi, Verdie, Verdy.

Verden/Verdon *See* Varden.

Vere Latin: faithful and loyal.

Vered Hebrew: a rose.

Verge Middle English: a rim or edge.

Vergil *See* Virgil.

Verill *See* Verrell.

Verlon *See* Vernon.

Verner *See* Vernon and Warner.

Vernon Latin: spring-like.
Verlon, Vern, Verne, Verner.

Verrell French: honest.
Verill, Verrall, Verrill.

Vicente *See* Vincent.

Victor Latin: the conqueror. *See also* Vincent.
Viktor (Czech, German, Polish, Scandinavian), Vitorio, Vittore (Italian), Vittorio (Spanish). *Diminutives*: Vic, Vick.

Vidal *See* Vitale.

Vidar Old Norse: a Norse god, known for his silence and solitude.

Vidor Hungarian: cheerful.

Vidya Sanskrit: knowledge.

Viet Dutch form of Guy.

Viggo Scandinavian: a fighter.

Vijay Sanskrit: strong and victorious.

Viking Icelandic: an ancient Scandinavian warrior.

Vikram Sanskrit: valour or bravery.

Viktor *See* Victor.

Vilem/Vilhelm/Vilmos *See* William.

Viliami Tongan form of William.

Vilis Latvian form of William.

Villiers From French: from the farm or estate.
Viliers.

Vimal Sanskrit: pure.

Vincent Latin: conquering. *See also* Victor and Vinson.
Vicente (Spanish), Vincens (German), Vincente (Italian), Vincenzo (Italian), Visant (Breton), Vyncent.
Diminutives: Vin, Vince, Vinnie.

Vinson Old English: son of Vincent.

Virgil Latin: a famous Roman poet.
Vergil, Virgile (French), Virgilio (Italian, Spanish).

Virgo Latin: a virgin. A constellation and one of the zodiac signs.
Virgoe.

Visant Breton form of Vincent.

Vishnu Sanskrit: the protector. An important Hindu god.

Vitale Latin: lively. *See also* Vitus and Vivian.
Vidal, Vital, Vitali (Russian), Vitalis, Vitas, Vito.

Vito *See* Vitale.

Vitorio/Vittore/Vittorio *See* Victor.

Vitus Latin: life. A Sicilian child saint. *See also* Vitale and Vivian.

Vivian Latin: lively. *See also* Vitale and Vitus.
Vyvyan.

Vlad *See* Vladimir and Vladislav.

Vladimir Slavic: a powerful ruler. Generally a Czech or Russian name.
Vadim (Russian), Valdemar, Waldemar

(Dutch, German, Scandinavian).
Diminutive: Vlad.

Vladislav Slavic: a glorious ruler. *See also* Ladislav.
Diminutive: Vlad.

Volf Jewish form of Wolfe.

Volney Teutonic: of the people.

Vortigern Celtic: a great king.

Vulcan The Roman god of fire and metalworking, after whom volcanoes are named.
Volcan, Volkan (Turkish), Vulkan.

Vyasa Sanskrit: the arranger.

Vyncent *See* Vincent.

Vyvyan Cornish: from an old surname. Also a variation of Vivian.

W

Wade Old English: a wanderer, or from the river crossing.
Waide, Wayde.

Wagner Dutch: a wagon driver or wagon maker.
Wagoner.

Wahib Arabic: the generous one.

Waiariki Maori: hot springs.

Waihanga Maori: a builder.

Wain/Waine/Wainwright *See* Wayne.

Waitangi Maori. The signing place of the 19th-century treaty between the Maori and British.

Waite Old English: a watchman or guard.

Waitoa Maori. A New Zealand town.

Wakeman Old English: a watchman.

Wal A diminutive of Walter.

Walby Old English/Old Norse: the farm by the ancient wall.

Waldemar *See* Vladimir.

Walden Old English: from the valley in the forest.
Waldon.

Waldo Teutonic: the ruler.

Walenty *See* Valentine.

Walford Old English: from the ford over the stream.

Walid Arabic: the newborn boy.

Walker Old English: a fuller, one who thickens cloth.

Wallace Old French: a foreigner, particularly a Welshman.
Wallis, Walsh, Welch, Welsh.

Wallis *See* Wallace.

Wally/Walt Diminutives of Walter.

Walmer Old English: the pool of the Welsh.

Walmond Teutonic: the mighty protector.

Walpole Old English: from the pool by the ancient wall.

Walsh *See* Wallace.

Walter Teutonic: a mighty ruler. *See also* Watkin.
Gautier (French), Valter (Scandinavian), Walther (German), Wata (Maori), Wolter (Dutch).
Diminutives: Wal, Wally, Walt, Wat.

Walton Old English: from the farm or town of the foreigners.

Walwyn Old English: a powerful friend.
Walwin.

Wandelin *See* Wendell.

Wang Chinese: kingly.

Wangdi Sherpa/Tibetan: he who possesses power.

Warburton Old English: from the fortress town.

Ward Old English: a guard or watchman.
Warde, Warden.

Wardell Old English: from the valley of the River Wear.
Wardale.

Warfield Old English: the field by the stream.

Warley Old English: from the cattle pasture.

Warmund Old English: a loyal protector.
Warman, Warmond.

Warner Teutonic: the protecting army or warrior.
Verner (Scandinavian), Werner (German).

Warren Old English/Old French: the game park-keeper.
Warrenne.
Diminutive: Wazza.

Warrick *See* Warwick.

Warton Old English: a lookout point.

Warwick Old English: from the dairy farm at the weir.
Warrick.

Waseem *See* Wasim.

Washington Old English: from the settlement of the Wassa family.

Wasim Arabic: the handsome one.
Waseem.

Wassily *See* Vasily.

Wat/Wata *See* Walter.

Watkin Old English: the son of Walter.
Watkins, Watson.

Waverley Old English: from the village of the aspen trees.
Waverly.

Wayde *See* Wade.

Wayland Old English: from the land by the crossroads or roadway.
Waylan, Waylen, Waylon.

Wayne Old English: a cart- or wagon-maker. Actor John Wayne made this popular as a first name.
Wain, Waine, Wainwright.

Webb Old English: a weaver.
Webber, Weber, Webster.

Welby Old English/Old Norse: from the farm by the spring.

Welch/Welsh *See* Wallace.

Weldon Old English: from the hill with a spring.

Welford Old English: from the ford by the willows.

Wella Cornish diminutive of William.

Wellington Old English: from the rich man's farm.

Wells Old English: from the spring or well.
Welles.

Wen Chinese: cultured or ornamental.

Wenceslas Slavic: great glory. A 10th-century Bohemian saint.
Václav (Czech), Wenceslaus, Wenzel (Czech, German).

Wendell Teutonic: a wanderer.
Wandelin, Wendall, Wendel, Wendelin.
Diminutive: Dell.

Wendron Cornish: a placename.

Wenlock Old Welsh: from the holy monastery.

Wentworth Old English: estate of the white-haired one, or a winter estate.

Wenzel *See* Wenceslas.

Werahiko Maori form of Francis.

Werner *See* Warner.

Wes *See* Wesley.

Wesley Old English: from the west meadow. A name sometimes given in honour of the founder of the Methodist church, John Wesley.
Wesleigh, Weslie, Wesly, Wezley.
Diminutive: Wes.

Weston Old English: from the western farm or town.

Westwood Old English: from the wood to the west.

Westy One who comes from the west.
Westie.

Wetherby Old English: from the sheep farm.

Weylin Celtic: the son of the wolf.

Weymouth Old English: the mouth of the River Wey. A town in Dorset.

Wezley *See* Wesley.

Whatitiri Maori: thunder.

Whatu Maori: a pupil (as in the eye).

Wheatley Old English: from the wheat meadow.

Wheeler Old English: a wheel-maker.

Whero Maori: red.

Whetu Polynesian: a star.

Whitby Old English: the white town. A place in Yorkshire.

Whitcombe Old English: from the wide valley.
Whitcomb.

Whitfield Old English: the white field.

Whitford Old English: from the white ford.

Whitley Old English: the white meadow or clearing.

Whitman Old English: the white man.

Whitmore Old English: from the white moor.
Whitmer.

Whitney Old English: from the white island. Also a girl's name.
Whitnee, Whitnie, Whitny, Witnee, Witney, Witnie, Witny.

Whitson Old English: a white stone.
Whitsun.

Whittaker Old English: the white field.
Whitaker.

Wickham Old English: from the meadow homestead.
Wykeham.

Wil *See* William.

Wilbur Old English: the resolute one.
Wilber, Wilbert, Wilburt.

Wilcox A diminutive of William.
Wilcoxe, Wilcoxx, Wilcoxxe.

Wilder Old English: one who is wild.
Wylder.

Wiley *See* Wylie.

Wilford Old English: the ford in the willows.

Wilfred Teutonic: desirous of peace; a peacemaker.
Wilfrid, Wilfried (German).
Diminutives: Fred, Freddie, Freddy, Wilf.

Wilhelm/Wiliam *See* William.

Wilkes/Wilkie *See* William.

Will/Willie Diminutives of William.

Willard Old English: resolute and brave.
Willerd.

Willem Dutch form of William.

William Teutonic: a strong and resolute protector. Introduced to England by the Normans in the 11th century. *See also* Liam, Wilcox, Willis, Wills, Wilmer, Wilmot and Wilson.
Guglielmo (Italian), Guilhelm, Guilherme (Portuguese), Guillaume (French), Guillermo (Spanish), Gwilym (Welsh), Quilliam (Manx Gaelic), Uilleam (Scottish Gaelic), Vilem (Czech), Vilhelm (Scandinavian), Viliami (Tongan), Vilis (Latvian), Vilmos (Hungarian), Wilhelm (German), Wiliam, Wilkes, Wilkie, Willem (Dutch), Willis, Willum, Wiremu (Maori).
Diminutives: Bill, Billie, Billy, Jelle (Dutch), Liam (Irish Gaelic), Pim (Dutch), Wella (Cornish), Wil, Wilkin, Will, Willi (German), Willie, Wills, Willy, Wim (Dutch, German).

Willis The son of William.
Willison, Williss.

Willoughby Old English/Old Norse: the farm by the willows.

Wills An English surname; also a diminutive of William, Wilson and other names.

Wilmer Teutonic: famously resolute. From a similar origin to that of William.

Wilmot Teutonic: of resolute mind. Originally a diminutive of William.

Wilson Old English from Teutonic: the son of William.
Willson.

Wilton Old English: from the farm by the stream.
Diminutive: Wilt.

Wim *See* William.

Winchester Old English: a Roman site. A city in Hampshire, southern England.

Windsor Old English: from the river bank or landing place.
Winsor, Winzor.

Winford/Winforde *See* Wynford.

Wing Chinese: glory.

Winslow Old English: from a friend's hill.

Winston Old English: from a friend's estate or town.
Winstone, Wynston, Wynstone.

Winter Old English: born in the winter months.
Winters, Wynter, Wynters.

Winthrop Old English: from a friend's village.

Winton Old English: from a friend's farm.
Winten, Wynten, Wynton.

Wiremu Maori form of William.

Wistan *See* Wystan.

Witi Maori: wheat.

Witnee/Witney/Witnie *See* Whitney.

Witton Old English: a farm by the wood.

Wolfe Teutonic: wolf-like, courageous.
Ulf (Swedish), Volf (Jewish), Wolf (German).

Wolfgang Teutonic: the advancing wolf.

Wolfram Teutonic: the wolf raven.
Wulfram.

Wolter Dutch form of Walter.

Woodburn Old English: from the stream in the wood.

Woodley Old English: the meadow or clearing in the forest.

Woodrow Old English: from the row of houses in the wood.
Diminutive: Woody.

Woodward Old English: a forester, a forest guardian.

Woody Diminutive of Woodrow and similar names.

Worcester Old English: a Roman site. An English city.

Wren Old English: a tiny bird.
Wrenn.

Wright Old English: a carpenter or craftsman.

Wroe *See* Rowe.

Wulfram *See* Wolfram.

Wyatt/Wye *See* Guy.

Wyber Old English: a battle fortress.
Wybar, Wybrew.

Wyburn Old English: a battle hero.
Wyborn, Wyborne.

Wycliff Old English: from the cliff of the warrior.
Wycliffe, Wyecliff, Wyecliffe.

Wykeham *See* Wickham.

Wylder *See* Wilder.

Wylie Old English: wily or beguiling.
Wiley.

Wyman Old English: a warrior.

Wyndham Old English: from the battle protector's homestead.

Wynford Welsh: from the white ford.
Winford, Winforde, Wynforde.

Wynn Welsh: the fair or blessed one.
Wyn, Wynne.

Wynstan *See* Wystan.

Wynston *See* Winston.

Wynten/Wynton *See* Winton.

Wynter/Wynters *See* Winter.

Wystan Old English: the battle stone.
Wistan, Wynstan.

Xander A diminutive and variation of
Alexander. *See also* Zander.
Xahnder.
Diminutives: Xahn, Xan, Xand.

Xanthus Greek: golden-haired.
Xanthos, Zanthos, Zanthus.

Xavier Arabic: bright. Spanish: of the
new house.
Exavier, Javier (Portuguese, Spanish),
Saviero (Italian), Xaver (German),
Xaviero (Italian), Zavier.
Diminutives: Xavi, Zavi.

Xenophon Greek: strange voices, or
strong sounding.

Xenos Greek: a stranger.
Xeno, Xenon, Zeno, Zenon, Zenos.

Xerxes Persian: a king or ruler. The
name of a famous Persian king.

Ximen/Ximenes/Ximens Spanish
forms of Simon.

Ximun Basque form of Simon.

Xolani Southern African: peace.

Xylon Greek: from the forest.
Zylon.

Yaakov *See* Yakov.

Yael Hebrew: a wild goat. Also a girl's
name.

Yago A Spanish form of James.

Yakim Hebrew: God will establish.
Yakeem.

Yakov Hebrew and Russian form of
Jacob.
Yaakov.

Yale Old English: from the corner
of the land. Teutonic: the one who
pays.
Yail, Yaile.

Yancy Native American: the
Englishman. The word later became
Yankee.
Yance, Yancee, Yancey, Yancie.

Yang Chinese: the sun; the masculine
principle and the opposite of Yin (*see*
Yin in GIRLS).

Yann Breton form of John.
Diminutives: Yanick, Yannick.

Yannis Greek form of John.

Yaphet *See* Japhet.

Yardan Arabic: a king.
Yarden.

Yardley Old English: from the
enclosed meadow.
Yardlee, Yardleigh, Yardly.

Yasir Arabic: wealthy.
Yasar, Yaseer.

Yates Middle English: the keeper of
the gates.
Yeates, Yeats.

Yazid Arabic: ever increasing.

Yefrem *See* Ephraim.

Yehuda *See* Judah.

Yehudi Hebrew: praise to the Lord.

Yen Vietnamese: the calm or peaceful one.

Yered Hebrew form of Jared.

Yeshe Sherpa/Tibetan: wise one.

Yeshua Hebrew form of Joshua. Yeshna.

Yestin Welsh form of Justin.

Yevgeni *See* Eugene.

Yianni Greek diminutive of John.

Yigael Hebrew: God will redeem. Yigal.

Yin Chinese: silvery.

Yiorgos Greek form of George.

Yitzaak/Yitzak *See* Isaac.

Ynyr Welsh: honour.

Yo Chinese: bright. Japanese: sunshine.

Yoel *See* Joel.

Yoland From Greek: a violet.

Yona Native American: a bear. Also a Russian form of Jonah. Yonah.

Yonatan Hebrew: the original form of Jonathan. *Diminutive*: Yoni.

Yong Chinese/Korean: the brave one.

Yoram *See* Joram.

Yordan Bulgarian form of Jordan.

Yorick Old English form of George.

York Celtic: the farm of the yew tree. Old English: a boar farm. Yorke.

Yosef *See* Joseph.

Yoshi Japanese: good. Also a girl's name.

Younus Arabic form of Jonah.

Yovel Hebrew: the horn of a ram. Yoval.

Yu Chinese: like jade. Tibetan: the gemstone, turquoise.

Yuan Chinese: the original.

Yul *See* Julius.

Yule Old English: born at Christmas. Yules.

Yuma Native American: the son of a chief.

Yuri Russian form of George.

Yusuf Arabic form of Joseph. Yusef.

Yves French form of Ives.

Z

Zaac/Zaak *See* Zac.

Zabulon *See* Zebulun.

Zac A diminutive of Zachary, but increasingly used as a separate name. Zaac, Zaak, Zach, Zack, Zak, Zaki, Zakk, Zakki.

Zachary Hebrew: the Lord has remembered. *See also* Zac. Hakaraia (Maori), Sakari (Finnish), Zacarias (Spanish), Zachariah, Zacharias (German), Zachiea, Zackary, Zackery, Zakar (Russian), Zakari, Zakaria (Arabic), Zakarias (Swedish), Zakarie, Zakary, Zechariah. *Diminutives*: Zac, Zach, Zack, Zak.

Zacoda A modern made-up name,

BIBLICAL NAMES

Biblical names such as Benjamin, James, Hannah and Rebecca are always popular, so here is a large selection of placenames, personal and other names from the Bible.

Girls

Abigail	Lydia
Adah	Magdalene
Adina	Mara
Ariel	Martha
Atarah	Mary
Athalia	Michal
Bethany	Miriam
Bethel	Moriah
Beulah	Naomi
Candace	Persis
Carmel	Phoebe
Chloe	Rachel
Claudia	Rebecca
Damaris	Rhoda
Deborah	Ruth
Delilah	Salome
Dinah	Samaria
Eden	Sapphira
Elizabeth	Sarah
Esther	Sela
Eve	Seraphina
Hannah	Sharon
Jemima	Sheba
Jesse	Susannah
Joanna	Tabitha
Jordan	Talitha
Judith	Tamar
Keren	Tarah
Kerith	Thirza
Keturah	Vashti
Keziah	Zillah
Leah	Zion
Lois	Zippora

Boys

Aaron	Jonah
Abraham	Jonathan
Adam	Joseph
Alexander	Joshua
Amos	Jude
Andrew	Levi
Asher	Luke
Barnabas	Mark
Bartholomew	Matthew
Benjamin	Micah
Caleb	Michael
Canaan	Nathan
Caspar	Nekoda
Cornelius	Nicholas
Daniel	Noah
Darius	Paul
David	Peter
Eli	Philip
Ethan	Raphael
Exodus	Reuben
Ezekiel	Samuel
Ezra	Seth
Felix	Silas
Gabriel	Simeon
Gideon	Simon
Isaac	Solomon
Jacob	Stephen
Jadon	Thomas
James	Timothy
Jared	Tobias
Jericho	Zachary
Jethro	Zadok
Joel	Zebedee

based on Zac.
Zackoda, Zakoda.

Zadok Hebrew: just, righteous.
Zadoc.

Zaedan/Zaeden/Zaedon *See* Zayden.

Zafar Arabic: the triumphant one.

Zage A modern made-up name, possibly a form of Sage.
Zaige, Zayge.

Zahi Arabic: brilliant or beautiful.

Zahir Arabic: shining, radiant.
Zaheer.

Zaidan/Zaiden/Zaidon *See* Zayden.

Zain/Zaine *See* Zane.

Zak/Zakar/Zakaria/Zakary *See* Zac and Zachary.

Zaki Arabic: pure. *See also* Zac.

Zakk/Zakki *See* Zac.

Zakoda *See* Zacoda.

Zale Old English: to sell, or a salary.
Zales.

Zalman/Zalmen *See* Solomon.

Zambezi A river in southern Africa.
Zambesi.

Zamir Hebrew: a songbird.

Zan *See* Zander and Zannon.

Zander A diminutive and variation of Alexander. *See also* Xander.
Zahnder.
Diminutives: Zan, Zahn.

Zane A form of John.
Zain, Zaine, Zayn, Zayne.

Zannon A modern name, probably from Zan.
Zannan, Zannen, Zannin, Zannyn.

Zanthos/Zanthus *See* Xanthus.

Zappa Italian. The surname of a legendary 1960s–1970s musician

(Frank Zappa).
Zappah.

Zared Hebrew: an ambush.

Zareh Armenian: a legendary king.

Zascha/Zasha *See* Sasha.

Zavi/Zavier *See* Xavier.

Zayden A modern name, probably from Zavier and Jayden.
Zaedan, Zaeden, Zaedon, Zaidan, Zaiden, Zaidon, Zaydan, Zayde, Zaydon.

Zayge *See* Zage.

Zayn/Zayne *See* Zane.

Zbigniew Slavic: to get rid of anger.
A common Polish name.
Diminutives: Ziggi, Ziggy.

Zealot Latin from Greek: one who is enthusiastic.

Zeb *See* Zebadiah and Zebulun.

Zebadiah Hebrew: a gift of the Lord.
Sebedeus (Welsh), Zebadee, Zebedee, Zebediah.
Dimunitive: Zeb.

Zebulun Hebrew: exaltation, or the dwelling place. One of the sons of Leah and Jacob in the Bible.
Zabulon, Zebulon.
Diminutive: Zeb.

Zechariah *See* Zachary.

Zeco *See* Zeko.

Zedekiah Hebrew: the justice of the Lord.
Diminutive: Zed.

Zeeland A Dutch province.
Zealand.

Zeeman Dutch: a sailor or seaman.

Zeik/Zeke Diminutives of Ezekiel.

Zeki Turkish: intelligent.
Zekie.

Zeko A modern name, probably from Zeke (*see* Ezekiel).
Zeco, Zico, Ziko.

Zelig Jewish: blessed, fortunate.
Selig.

Zelman *See* Solomon.

Zelotes Greek: zealous.
Zelus.

Zen Japanese: a Buddhist sect. Also a girl's name.
Zenn, Zenne.

Zenas Greek: living.

Zenden A modern name, probably from Zen.
Zendan, Zendin, Zendon, Zendyn.

Zenith Middle English from Arabic: the highest point; the culmination.
Zenithe, Zenyth, Zenythe.

Zennor Cornish: a placename.

Zeno/Zenon/Zenos *See* Xenos.

Zephaniah Hebrew: hidden by God.
Zephan.
Diminutive: Zeph.

Zephyr *See* GIRLS.

Zero Italian: a 'number name'.

Zeroun Armenian: a sage.

Zeus Greek: the father of the gods, or living. The ruler of the heavens in ancient Greek mythology.

Zhen Chinese: precious.

Zi An unusual, and very brief, modern name.
Zhi, Zhie, Zie, Zy, Zye.

Zia Arabic: splendour.

Zico/Ziko *See* Zeko.

Zidane After the French soccer player Zinedine Zidane.
Zidaine, Zidayne.

Ziggy *See* Zbigniew.
Ziggi.

Zigmond/Zigmund *See* Sigmund.

Zinzan The name of a legendary rugby player, possibly originally from an Italian surname.

Zion A hill in Jerusalem, the site of a holy temple. Also a name for the Jewish people.
Zyon.

Zircon Persian: a mineral name.

Ziv Hebrew: full of life.
Zivan, Zivar, Ziven (Polish).

Zodiac Greek: the circle of the astrological signs.
Zodiak.

Zola *See* GIRLS.

Zolli/Zolly Diminutives of Solomon.

Zoltan Arabic: a ruler or sultan. A popular Hungarian name. *See also* Sultan.

Zoran Slavic: of the dawn.

Zordan Probably a combination of Zoran and Jordan.
Zorden, Zordin, Zordon, Zordyn.

Zoroaster Persian: a golden star.

Zowie The made-up name of singer David Bowie's son.
Zowi.

Zubin Hebrew: the exalted one.
Zuba, Zuben.

Zuma After a South African president (Jacob Zuma).
Zumah.

Zuriel Hebrew: God is my foundation.

Zy/Zye *See* Zi.

Zylon *See* Xylon.

Zyon *See* Zion.

NAMES BY ETHNIC ORIGIN

The following lists feature many thousands of names categorised by their ethnic origins or usage. Please refer to the main A–Z listings for meanings, and note that some of these names are listed under others – for example, Edvard is under Edward.

AFRICAN
General

Girls Abeo, Abina, Adeola, Akila, Aku, Alika, Ama, Amadika, Apara, Ashanti, Asmara, Awusi, Ayanna, Ayoka, Dumaka, Faithi, Jendaya, Jumoke, Kamaria, Kanika, Kenda, Kenya, Keshia, Kimana, Lula, Mandela, Mandisa, Marula, Miriamu, Oba, Seble, Shaka, Shona, Tanisha, Thandi, Yola.

Boys Agu, Ajani, Akin, Azi, Chad, Daren, Djimon, Jojo, Kalahari, Kedjo, Kenya, Kofi, Kwame, Mansa, Morné, Neo, Odion, Ogun, Shaka, Sisay, Tafari, Tendai, Topi, Tupac, Tyrese, Ulan, Xolani, Zuma.

Swahili

Girls Adia, Almasi, Barika, Dalila, Emba, Hadiya, Hasina, Ieshia, Jamila, Januari, Julai, Jumaa, Juni, Kidani, Leta, Lulu, Marini, Marjani, Masika, Nyoka, Oktoba, Ramla, Safari, Shani, Zalika, Zuri.

Boys Abasi, Husani, Jabari, Jambo, Jelani, Jimoh, Julai, Jumah, Kito, Marjan, Mosi, Nyoka, Safari, Shomari, Simba, Sudi.

AMERICAN
General

Girls Alabama, Alaska, Aloma, Beyoncé, Birdie, Chanda, Cyreta, Denver, Destiny, Dixie, Exene, Georgia, Indiana, Jolene, Kalisha, Kedra, Keisha, Kenisha, Ladonna, Lakeisha, Lakena, Laneka, Latasha, Latoya, Laverne, Louisiana, Memphis, Montana, Navana, Nevada, Philadelphia, Shenay, Suellen, Takeisha, Taleisha, Tanedra, Taneka, Tekiya, Tennessee, Tennille, Tulsa, Tupelo, Utah, Wyomia, Yetunde.

Boys Alamo, Arizona, Bershawn, Boston, Bud, Buzz, Chilli, Cleavon, DeMarcus, Denver, DeReese, Devonte, Dime, Duane, Dwayne, Eldene, Harlan, Harvard, Huckleberry, Indiana, Jaylen, Kobe, Kressley, LaShawn, Lebron, Leroy, Maine, Maverick, Memphis, Mojo, Montana, Mylon, Nevada, Nickel, Oregon, Ornette, Rondell, Taye, Tennessee, Tennille, Tevin, Tex, Trell, Tulsa, Utah.

Native American

Girls Alaqua, Aponi, Buffy, Chenoa, Cheyenne, Chu, Dakota, Dyani, Elan, Eyota, Halona, Isi, Jacey, Kai, Kiona, Koko, Magena, Neka, Nita, Nuna, Odina, Olathe, Onawa, Onida, Sequoia, Sora, Tallulah, Tenaya, Utina, Winema, Winona, Wyanet.

Boys Anoke, Apache, Cherokee, Cheyenne, Dakota, Dyami, Elan, Etu, Jacey, Kuruk, Makya, Matu, Namid, Navajo, Ohio, Ouray, Paco, Pinon, Sakima, Sequoia, Tadzi, Takoda, Yancy, Yona, Yuma.

ARABIC

Girls Abia, Abir, Adara, Adiba, Adila, Afraima, Aisha, Akila, Alima, Aliya, Almira, Alzena, Alzubra, Amala, Amani, Ambara, Amber, Amina, Amira, Anan, Asera, Atiya, Aziza, Azra, Basimah, Benazir, Bibi, Dalia, Dara, Fadila, Faiza, Farah, Farida, Fatima, Ghada, Ghazal, Habiba, Hadil, Hadiya, Hadya, Hagir, Hajar, Hala, Halima, Hana, Hanan, Hayat, Hayfa, Iman, Isra, Jala, Jamal, Jamila, Jehan, Jumah, Kabira, Kalila, Kamilah, Karima, Khalida, Latifa, Layla, Leila, Lilith, Lulu, Majida, Malak, Malika, Marya, Maryam, Maysa, Melek, Muna, Munira, Nabila, Nada, Nadira, Nawal, Noor, Oma, Qadira, Rabia, Radhia, Rafiqa, Raja, Rana, Raniya, Rashida, Rida, Rihana, Sabah, Sabira, Sabiya, Safia, Sahar, Salima, Samira, Sana, Sara, Sawsan, Shahira, Shakila, Shakira, Shamarra, Sharifa, Sultana, Tahira, Thana, Ulima, Vega, Wahiba, Wahida, Walida, Wasima, Xaviera, Yasmeen, Yasmin, Yusra, Zada, Zalika, Zara, Zarifa, Zaynab, Zenith, Zohra, Zulema.

Boys Abbas, Abdul, Abdullah, Adnan, Ahmed, Akbar, Akil, Akmal, Akram, Aladin, Ali, Altair, Amal, Amin, Amir, Ansari, Anwar, Ashraf, Asim, Aswad, Azadeh, Azim, Aziz, Bashir, Basim, Coman, Dawud, Ebrahim, Fadil, Faisal, Farid, Farook, Feroz, Firdos, Ghassan, Habib, Hadad, Hadi, Hafiz, Hakim, Halim, Hamal, Hamid, Hani, Haroun, Harun, Hasim, Hassan, Hazem, Hussain, Ibrahim, Idris, Ijaz, Imam, Imran, Isra, Iyad, Jabir, Jalil, Jamal, Juda, Kadir, Kamal, Kaniel, Karim, Khalid, Khalif, Khalil, Khan, Latif, Mahmood, Majid, Malik, Mansoor, Masud, Merak, Mubarak, Muhammad, Mukhtar, Musa, Mustafa, Nabil, Nadir, Najib, Nasir, Nuren, Nuri, Omar, Osama, Osman, Qamar, Qasim, Rabi, Rafi, Rafiq, Rahman, Rashid, Rauf, Rushdi, Sabir, Sadik, Salah, Salim, Sami, Sayed, Shafiq, Shakil, Shakir, Sharif, Suleiman, Sultan, Tahir, Tanzil, Tariq, Usama, Usman, Wahib, Wasim, Xavier, Yardan, Yasir, Yazid, Younus, Yusuf, Zafar, Zahi, Zahir, Zakaria, Zaki, Zenith, Zia, Zoltan, Zouhad.

ARMENIAN

Girls Anoush, Araxia, Arkina, Elmas, Gadar, Lucine, Perouze, Siran, Zagir.

Boys Ara, Armen, Levon, Nishan, Sarkis, Taniel, Vartan, Zareh, Zeroun.

Names by ethnic origin

ASIAN
Chinese
Girls An, Bai, Bic, Bo, Chen, Chow, Chu, Chun, Guan-yin, Heshu, Hoong, Hua, Hweiling, Jie, Jin, Jun, Lee, Li, Lian, Lien, Li-Li, Lin, Ling, Mee, Mei, Mei-Lin, Mei-Ling, Mei-Yu, Meizhen, Ming, Qing, Shuang, Shui, Tang, Tao, Tien, Tu, Ushi, Xiang, Xiaoli, Xingxing, Yi, Yin, Yu, Yue, Zhang, Ziang.

Boys Bo, Chan, Chang, Chen, Cheung, Chung, Gan, Hao, Ho, Hsin, Hu, Jen, Jin, Joss, Jun, Kee-Lin, Lei, Li, Liang, Lok, Long, Manchu, Ming, Quong, Shen, Sheng, Shing, Sun, Tien, Wang, Wen, Wing, Yang, Yin, Yo, Yong, Yu, Yuan, Zhen.

Indonesian
Girls Arti, Atika, Atin, Bali, Dewi, Indara, Kade, Lastri, Madura, Melati, Merpati, Rukmini, Sujatmi, Tuti.

Boys Aman, Amat, Budi, Chahaya, Dian, Garuda, Guntur, Java, Kersen, Pramana, Ramelan, Santoso, Setiawan, Singha, Sukarno.

Other Asian
Girls Cho, Dae, Isra, Jin, Julita, Kanya, Kyon, Mali, Noilani, Nu, Nya, Puntira, Sirikit, Song, Soo, Sumalee, Sun, Sunee, Tam, Tamarine, Tan, Thanh, Thao, Tien, Xuan, Yon, Zuan.

Boys Anh, Aran, Aroon, Azizah, Bae, Bahadur, Bay, Binh, Chau, Chet, Chin, Dara, Dinh, Gi, Hai, Han, Ho, Isra, Kama, Kason, Kim, Kwan, Lim, Lin, Minh, Nam, Niran, Sakda, Sam, Tai, Tam, Tan, Thai, Than, Thanh, Tien, Trai, Tran, Tuyen, Van, Yen, Yong.

BASQUE
Girls Alaia, Birkita, Kattalin, Maren, Satordi, Ximena.

Boys Aritz, Fermin, Ion, Kasen, Maren, Ximun.

CELTIC
General
Girls Affrica, Alma, Amena, Anwen, Arduina, Arianrhod, Armelle, Arthura, Beltane, Binnie, Boann, Briana, Bridget, Brigantia, Brice, Bryher, Carey, Cordelia, Corey, Dallas, Deirdre, Duessa, Enid, Ennis, Gryffyn, Imogen, Innes, Keitha, Keltie, Kendra, Kenna, Maura, Melora, Pixie, Rhiannon, Rowena, Sabrina, Tristanne, Ula, Vanora.

Boys Aland, Anlon, Annan, Anwell, Anyon, Ardan, Arthur, Bran, Brent,

Brian, Brice, Brone, Cadman, Caedmon, Caradoc, Carey, Carnarvon, Carney, Celt, Conall, Corey, Dallas, Deverell, Devin, Doane, Druce, Druid, Dunham, Ennis, Farrell, Gavin, Gawain, Gower, Gwydion, Havgan, Innes, Jarman, Keir, Keith, Kelt, Keltie, Kendrick, Kenn, Kent, Kimball, Lann, Newlyn, Ogilvie, Pembroke, Pendragon, Perth, Renfrew, Ryence, Sayer, Tor, Tristram, Vortigern, Weylin, York.

Breton

Girls Aamor, Aliciedik, Alodia, Harried, Joyce, Kaer, Meren, Tereza, Yannah.

Boys Corentyn, Devi, Harvey, Meren, Pierrick, Sibran, Talan, Visant, Yann, Yannick.

Cornish

Girls Berlewen, Beryan, Bronnen, Bryluen, Caja, Cara, Carey, Carleon, Carlin, Carlyon, Colenso, Delen, Demelza, Ebrel, Elowen, Emblyn, Ennor, Gweniver, Gwennap, Jaquet, Jenna, Jennifer, Kaja, Kayna, Kensa, Kenwyn, Kerensa, Kerezen, Kerra, Lamorna, Lowdy, Lowenna, Mabyn, Marya, Melloney, Melwyn, Merryn, Morenwyn, Morva, Morwenna, Nessa, Pasca, Pascoe, Penaluna, Pencast, Rosen, Rosenwyn, Rosevear, Rozen, Steren, Talwyn, Tamsin, Tean, Tegen, Trelise, Tressa, Trevena, Ula, Ursell, Verran, Vyvyan, Wenna, Wynne, Zelah, Zennor.

Boys Arthek, Arthyen, Austell, Brae, Bray, Brea, Breok, Budock, Cadan, Cardew, Carey, Carleon, Carlin, Carlyon, Carne, Corin, Crantock, Cubert, Curnow, Daveth, Denzil, Derrick, Derry, Dewy, Diggory, Ellery, Ennor, Gawen, Gerens, Glen, Gorran, Gryffyn, Gwinear, Hendra, Henna, Howell, Jacca, Jago, Jeffra, Jermyn, Jory, Jowan, Kenan, Kenver, Kenwyn, Kernick, Kernow, Kersey, Keverne, Kitto, Kittow, Lanyon, Lew, Luk, Madok, Madron, Mawgan, Mawnan, Menadue, Merryn, Michell, Morcum, Mullion, Mylor, Nicca, Pascoe, Pawley, Peder, Pedyr, Penglaze, Penrice, Penrose, Petroc, Piran, Rodda, Rowse, Sadorn, Santo, Selevan, Talan, Tean, Tintagel, Tre, Trefusis, Trelawney, Tremayne, Tresco, Trethowan, Trevelyan, Trevena, Trystan, Tyack, Vyvyan, Wella, Wendron, Zennor.

Welsh

Girls Aderyn, Aerona, Almedha, Alwin, Ambr, Anchoret, Aneira, Angharad, Angwen, Arianrhod, Arianwen, Artha, Arwen, Awsta, Aylwen, Berwyn, Bethan, Beti, Betrys, Blenn, Blodwen, Branwen, Briallen, Bronwen, Bryn, Cadi, Caillin, Carryl, Carys, Catrin, Ceinwen, Ceridwen, Cerys, Claerwen, Crisiant, Delwyn, Delyth, Derryn, Derryth, Dilys, Dylan, Ebril, Efa, Eiddwen, Eira, Eirian, Eirwen, Elen, Eleri, Eluned, Elwyn, Emrallt, Esyllt, Eurwen,

Ffion, Gaenor, Gaynor, Gladys, Glen, Glenda, Glenys, Guinevere, Gwen,
Gwendolen, Gwenllyn, Gwinau, Gwladys, Gwyn, Gwyneth, Hafwen, Heledd,
Heulwen, Isolde, Jennifer, Kenwyn, Keyna, Llawella, Llyn, Lowri, Mabli,
Mabyn, Mair, Mairwen, Mali, Marged, Megan, Meinwen, Melva, Melyn,
Melys, Meredith, Merin, Merlyn, Modlen, Morgan, Morwenna, Morwyn,
Moryn, Myfanwy, Nerys, Nesta, Olwen, Orena, Owena, Perl, Quendryth,
Rhiannon, Rhianwen, Rhonda, Rhonwen, Rhosyn, Rhys, Saffir, Seirian,
Seiriol, Seren, Sian, Siôna, Sioned, Sula, Tegan, Tegwen, Tirion, Trevena,
Valmai, Winifred, Wynne.

Boys Adda, Aeron, Afon, Alawn, Aled, Alun, Andreas, Aneurin, Angwyn,
Arian, Arthes, Arthien, Auryn, Awstin, Baez, Beda, Berwyn, Bevan, Bledig,
Bowen, Bradwen, Brecon, Brenin, Breok, Broderick, Brychan, Bryn, Brynmor,
Cadan, Cadell, Caderyn, Cadog, Cadogan, Caernarvon, Caerwyn, Cai,
Caradoc, Cardew, Carwyn, Cledwyn, Collen, Colomen, Conway, Conyn,
Copor, Cranog, Crisiant, Cynfor, Dafad, Dafydd, Dai, Derren, Derwen,
Derwent, Dewi, Dinsdale, Draig, Dyfan, Dylan, Edryd, Efydd, Eleias, Elfed,
Emlyn, Emrys, Emyr, Eseia, Eurwyn, Evan, Folant, Gareth, Geraint, Gerallt,
Gerwyn, Gethin, Glen, Goronwy, Gorwel, Gough, Griffith, Grigor, Gryffyn,
Gwener, Gwilym, Gwinear, Gwydion, Gwyn, Gwynfor, Harri, Heddwyn,
Heilyn, Hopkin, Howell, Hu, Huw, Hywel, Iago, Iau, Idris, Idwal, Iestin,
Iestyn, Ieuan, Ifan, Ifor, Ilar, Ilfryn, Ioan, Iorweth, Jevan, Jevon, Jovo, Kay,
Kenn, Kenwyn, Llewellyn, Lloyd, Llyr, Luc, Lyn, Mabon, Madoc, Malvern,
Marc, Mawrth, Meical, Meirion, Mercher, Meredith, Merfyn, Merin, Merlin,
Merrick, Meurig, Moren, Morgan, Morlo, Mostyn, Myrddin, Neifion, Nye,
Owain, Owen, Parry, Pedr, Penrith, Penrose, Penwyn, Petroc, Powell, Powys,
Price, Probert, Pryderi, Pyrs, Rhisiart, Rhobert, Rhodri, Rhudd, Rhun,
Rhydwyn, Rhyll, Rhys, Rolant, Romney, Ryence, Sadwyn, Saeth, Sawyl,
Sebedeus, Selyf, Seren, Siarl, Sieffre, Siôn, Siôr, Steffan, Sulwyn, Taffy, Talfryn,
Taliesin, Tan, Tangwyn, Taran, Tecwyn, Teigr, Traherne, Tomos, Trefor,
Trevena, Trevor, Trystan, Tudor, Twm, Urien, Vaughan, Wenlock, Wynford,
Wynn, Yestin, Ynyr.

DUTCH

Girls Alletta, Anneka, Anneke, Ans, Antje, Bendikta, Brandy, Cato,
Cornelietta, Dorothea, Doutzan, Doutzen, Elf, Francina, Geerta, Gisela,
Gratia, Hendrika, Janneke, Johanna, Juli, Jutte, Katrien, Katrine, Lene,
Margriet, Marieke, Mariet, Marleis, Marlies, Marlika, Marloes, Mechteld,
Mechtilda, Meike, Mieke, Miep, Mies, Miesje, Oktober, Saskia, Schuyler,
Skylar, Sofie.

Boys Andreas, Arend, Arje, Arjen, Arne, Augustijn, Barend, Bazel, Benedikt,
Bruin, Carel, Claus, Cornelis, Daneel, Dirk, Edmond, Gerrit, Gert, Gillis,
Godfried, Haarlem, Harbert, Hendrik, Hugo, Izaak, Jakob, Jan, Jelle,

Jeremias, Jeroen, Johannes, Joop, Joost, Jordaan, Joris, Josef, Jozua, Jurrien, Karel, Kees, Klaas, Klein, Laurens, Leeuwin, Ludo, Maarten, Maik, Maikel, Martijn, Mondrian, Mozes, Piet, Pim, Rodolf, Roeland, Rutger, Ruud, Schuyler, Siemen, Skipper, Skylar, Stijn, Tasman, Thies, Thijs, Timo, Van, Veit, Waldemar, Wagner, Willem, Wim, Wolter, Zeeland, Zeeman.

FINNISH/ESTONIAN

Girls Aili, Aino, Anu, Eila, Ilma, Inari, Inkeri, Kaisa, Kylli, Leea, Maarit, Marja, Marketta, Meri, Miia, Orvokki, Piltti, Piritta, Puna, Rikka, Sirkka, Tapania, Venla.

Boys Eetu, Eliel, Hannu, Heikki, Indrek, Jorma, Juhani, Jumala, Kalevi, Kimi, Kristo, Lasse, Lauri, Markku, Matti, Mauri, Mika, Mikko, Okko, Oskari, Paaveli, Paavo, Risto, Sakari, Taavi, Tero, Timo, Ukko, Usko.

FRENCH

Girls Adèle, Adrienne, Agathe, Agnies, Aimée, Alette, Alexandrine, Alize, Alsace, Amandine, Ambre, Amélie, Amorette, Amour, Anastasie, Ancelin, Andrée, Ange, Angelique, Annetta, Anselme, Antoinette, Aravane, Arette, Armynel, Athalie, Athène, Audrée, Auguste, Aurélie, Aurore, Aveline, Avril, Azura, Barbe, Belle, Benoite, Berthe, Bijou, Blanche, Bleu, Brigitte, Brunetta, Calais, Calandre, Calanthe, Camille, Candide, Caresse, Carole, Cartier, Cassandre, Cécile, Céline, Cerise, Chamonix, Chanel, Chantal, Chardonnay, Cher, Chic, Chiffon, Chimene, Christelle, Ciel, Claire, Claudette, Clothilde, Colette, Colombe, Cordélie, Cosette, Cyrille, Danette, Délice, Denise, Desirée, Dior, Dominique, Doré, Dorothée, Douce, Edwige, Elbertine, Eleonore, Elise, Elle, Emeraude, Émilie, Esmé, Esprit, Estée, Estelle, Étienette, Étoile, Eudocie, Eugénie, Fabienne, Fanchon, Félicité, Fernande, Finesse, Flavie, Fleur, Flore, Fontaine, Francine, Françoise, Fréderique, Gazelle, Genevieve, Georgette, Germaine, Ghislaine, Gigi, Gisèle, Hélène, Henriette, Hilaire, Honore, Huguette, Irène, Isabeau, Jacinthe, Jeanne, Jehanne, Jeudi, Jeune, Joelle, Jolie, Josée, Juillet, Juliette, Laure, Léonne, Liliane, Lionelle, Lisette, Lourdes, Luce, Lucienne, Lydie, Lys, Madelon, Manon, Marcelle, Margot, Marianne, Marie, Marielle, Marine, Marjolaine, Martine, Mathilde, Matisse, Mélisande, Micheline, Mietta, Mignon, Mireille, Monet, Monique, Moreau, Mystique, Nadine, Nanette, Nanon, Narcisse, Nathalie, Nicolette, Ninon, Nouvelle, Octavie, Odette, Odile, Olympe, Ophélie, Oriane, Pascale, Patrice, Paulette, Perette, Régine, Réjeanne, Rémy, Renée, Rochelle, Rosette, Rosine, Rouge, Sabine, Sacha, Sara, Sebastienne, Seraphine, Sévérine, Simonette, Solange, Stéphanie, Suzette, Sybille, Tatienne, Terezon, Tifaine, Toinette, Trisette, Vedette, Véronique, Vevette, Victorine, Violette, Virginie, Voile, Xavière, Yolande, Yseult, Yvette, Yvonne, Zélie, Zenobie, Zola.

Names by ethnic origin

Boys Aamadou, Abbe, Abbot, Acelin, Achille, Adolphe, Adrien, Aimé, Aimon, Alain, Alexandre, Algernon, Alphonse, Ambroise, Anastase, André, Ange, Ansel, Antoine, Armand, Arnaud, Arsène, Artus, Aubert, Aubin, Audric, Auguste, Aurele, Avent, Avril, Baptiste, Barnabé, Basile, Baudouin, Beau, Benoit, Bleu, Brunet, Camille, Caton, Césaire, Chrétien, Christophe, Clément, Conrade, Corneille, Cyprien, Cyrille, Davide, Didier, Dominique, Donatien, Duval, Edgard, Edmond, Édouard, Émile, Étienne, Eugène, Evrard, Fabien, Fabron, Fernand, Flavien, Florent, Fontaine, François, Frédéric, Gael, Gaspard, Gaston, Gautier, Georges, Geraud, Geronte, Gervais, Gilles, Grégoire, Guilbert, Guillaume, Gustave, Henri, Hercule, Hervé, Hilaire, Hugues, Ignace, Jacques, Jean, Jeremie, Jourdain, Jules, Julien, Juste, Lafayette, Lascelles, Laurent, Lazare, Léandre, Léon, Léonard, Léopold, Lionel, Lisle, Loic, Louis, Luc, Lucien, Lundi, Malo, Marc, Marcel, Mardi, Marion, Marquis, Mathieu, Maxime, Michel, Nicodeme, Nöel, Octave, Olivier, Orphée, Paris, Patrice, Paulot, Philippe, Pierre, Pierrot, Rainier, Raoul, Régis, Rémy, Renaud, Rodolphe, Rodrigue, Roi, Romain, Roquet, Sacha, Sébastien, Serge, Stéphane, Sylvain, Thierry, Timothée, Toussaint, Trudeau, Ulysse, Valentin, Valery, Virgile, Yves, Zidane, Zola.

GAELIC

General

Girls Alauda, Armorel, Cailin, Cairine, Catriona, Ceilidh, Corey, Corlette, Culley, Dacey, Danu, Delaney, Edana, Fenella, Fiona, Flanna, Glen, Innes, Maidie, Mairead, Malise, Malvina, Morven, Muirne, Muriel, Quaile, Sorcha.

Boys Abboid, Adhahm, Alan, Bearnard, Blaine, Brae, Breck, Camden, Cane, Carvel, Christie, Christy, Corey, Corlett, Culley, Dacey, Daibhidh, Dalgleish, Delaney, Dhugald, Donnelly, Dougal, Duffy, Dugan, Dunbar, Eoin, Fagan, Fergus, Ferguson, Ferris, Galloway, Galway, Garvey, Gilchrist, Gilroy, Girvan, Glen, Glendon, Hearn, Hurley, Iaian, Iain, Innes, Kermit, Kilpatrick, Macauley, Mackay, Morven, Niall, Ninian, Peadar, Quade, Quaile, Quilliam, Quinney, Ruadh, Solamh, Taggart, Tomas, Torcall, Torin, Tynan.

Irish

Girls Aidan, Aideen, Aigneis, Ailis, Aine, Aingeal, Aiofe, Aiveen, Alana, Allsun, Ashling, Athea, Augusteen, Aurnia, Avoca, Aylice, Bairbre, Berneen, Bevin, Biddy, Blaine, Blinnie, Boann, Brady, Breda, Brenda, Brenna, Bríd, Bridget, Bridie, Briege, Brighid, Brodie, Brona, Bryna, Cait, Caitlin, Caitrin, Caley, Caoimhe, Cara, Caragh, Carden, Carey, Carleen, Carlin, Casey, Cassidy, Ceara, Ciara, Clancy, Clare, Clodagh, Colleen, Crida, Crístíona, Cushla, Dairine, Daley, Darby, Deirdre, Dervla, Donla, Doone, Duana, Dymphna, Eden, Eibhlin, Eileen, Eilis, Eily, Eister, Eithne, Emer, Ena, Enda, Erin,

Etain, Evaleen, Fallon, Fennagh, Fidelma, Fina, Fiona, Grainne, Grania, Ierne, Illona, Ireland, Ita, Kathleen, Kayley, Keeley, Kelly, Kennedy, Kerry, Keverne, Kiana, Kiara, Kiera, Kyna, Léan, Luiseach, MacKenna, Maeve, Maire, Mairin, Maureen, Moira, Mona, Muirenn, Muiriol, Murphy, Myrna, Neala, Nevan, Niamh, Nola, Nuala, Onóra, Oonagh, Orla, Orna, Queenan, Quinn, Quishla, Raghnailt, Regan, Renny, Riley, Riona, Róisín, Ronan, Rory, Rosaleen, Rosheen, Rowan, Ryan, Sabia, Saoirse, Saraid, Shane, Shannah, Shannon, Sheila, Shelagh, Sheridan, Shevaun, Síle, Sinéad, Siobhán, Slaney, Sloan, Sweeney, Talulla, Tara, Teague, Tierney, Treasa, Tullia, Tully, Tynan, Úna, Vevila, Yootha.

Boys Adhamh, Aguistin, Ahearn, Aidan, Ailfrid, Ailin, Aillen, Alphonsus, Alroy, Alsandair, Ambros, Anntoin, Aodan, Ardal, Arlen, Artur, Barry, Bartle, Beagan, Beattie, Bécan, Benen, Blaney, Brady, Branagh, Branduff, Breandan, Brendan, Brian, Brodie, Brogan, Brosnan, Byrne, Caley, Callaghan, Canice, Carden, Carey, Carlin, Carrick, Carroll, Casey, Cash, Cashel, Cassidy, Cathal, Cathan, Cathmor, Cavan, Cian, Ciarán, Clancy, Cleary, Clooney, Colm, Colum, Columba, Conan, Conlan, Conn, Connaught, Connery, Connolly, Connor, Conroy, Conway, Cormac, Corrigan, Costello, Crevan, Cronan, Curran, Daley, Dara, Darby, Darragh, Declan, Dempsey, Dermot, Derry, Desmond, Devlin, Dolan, Donahue, Donal, Donegal, Donn, Donovan, Dooley, Doone, Doran, Dorsey, Dow, Driscoll, Duane, Durack, Eamonn, Eden, Egan, Enda, Enos, Eoghan, Eoin, Erin, Eunan, Fáelán, Fallon, Fenlon, Fergal, Fiachra, Finbar, Finian, Finn, Finnegan, Fintan, Fionn, Flanagan, Flannan, Flannery, Flynn, Gair, Gallagher, Galvin, Gannon, Gara, Gearalt, Gearoid, Grady, Hagen, Haley, Healy, Hennessey, Hogan, Jarlath, Jimeoin, Kalan, Kane, Kean, Kearney, Keefe, Keegan, Keeley, Keenan, Kelan, Keller, Kelly, Kennedy, Kenyon, Kern, Kerr, Kerrigan, Kerry, Kerwin, Kevin, Kian, Kiefer, Kieran, Kiernan, Killarney, Killian, Kinnard, Knox, Kyran, Labhras, Lawler, Lennon, Liam, Limerick, Lochlainn, Lochlan, Loman, Lorcan, Lucan, Lugh, McKenna, McMahon, Maghnus, Mahon, Malone, Mannix, Manus, Mártan, Molloy, Moran, Muiris, Munro, Murphy, Neal, Nevin, Nolan, O'Brien, O'Donnell, Odran, O'Neil, Oran, O'Shea, Ossian, Padraig, Patrick, Phelan, Pilib, Pol, Quigley, Quillan, Quinlan, Quinn, Rafferty, Raghnall, Réamann, Redmond, Regan, Renny, Riley, Riordan, Roarke, Rogan, Ronan, Ronit, Rooney, Rory, Rowan, Ryan, Scully, Seamus, Sean, Senan, Shanahan, Shane, Shanley, Shannon, Shaugnessy, Shaun, Shawn, Shea, Sheehan, Sheridan, Siomon, Skelly, Slaney, Slevin, Sloan, Stiofan, Sullivan, Sweeney, Tad, Tadgh, Teague, Tiernan, Tierney, Tiobóid, Tormey, Tory, Tulloch, Tully, Tyrone, Ultan, Ventry.

Scottish

Girls Adair, Aileen, Ailsa, Ainsley, Aisleen, Alexina, Annella, Barabal, Bearnas,

Beitris, Blair, Bonnie, Cairistìona, Caledonia, Cameron, Donalda, Edmé, Euna, Finlay, Fiona, Greer, Grier, Grizel, Hughina, Iona, Isbel, Iseabail, Isla, Kerrera, Kirstie, Kyla, Kyle, Leith, Lesley, Lilias, Lindsey, Lorna, Lorne, Mackenzie, Mackinley, Maclean, Maisie, Morag, Moray, Morven, Muireall, Nairne, Neilina, Nora, Norma, Raghnaid, Rona, Senga, Seònaid, Sheena, Shona, Sìleas, Siubhan, Siùsan, Skye, Vaila, Zena.

Boys Abernethy, Adair, Adhamh, Ailbert, Ailean, Aindréas, Ainsley, Airlie, Alasdair, Alasdhair, Alastair, Allister, Andrew, Angus, Arailt, Argyll, Arran, Artair, Athol, Baird, Balfour, Ballantyne, Beathan, Benneit, Blair, Bowie, Boyd, Buchan, Buchanan, Cailean, Callum, Cameron, Campbell, Chivas, Clunes, Clyde, Cormag, Craig, Dalziel, Diarmad, Donald, Douglas, Drew, Duff, Duncan, Dundee, Dunmore, Eachan, Eanraig, Eideard, Ellar, Errol, Erskine, Euan, Eumann, Ewan, Farquhar, Fife, Filib, Fingal, Finlay, Forbes, Gillespie, Gilmer, Gordon, Graeme, Gregor, Greig, Griogair, Guthrie, Hamish, Hewie, Iagan, Ian, Irving, Jock, Keir, Kelso, Kelvin, Kenneth, Kester, Kyle, Lachlan, Laird, Leith, Lennox, Leslie, Lindsay, Loch, Lochinvar, Logan, Lorne, Loudon, Lucais, Ludo, Ludovic, Luthais, Mac, Macarthur, Macbeth, McCartney, Macdonald, McEwan, MacGregor, McIntosh, Mack, Mackenzie, McLaren, Maclean, Macquarie, McTavish, Malcolm, Malise, Mànas, Mata, Maxwell, Menzies, Micheál, Moffatt, Montrose, Moray, Morven, Muir, Mungo, Murdoch, Murray, Nairne, Nicol, Osgar, Padruig, Perth, Petrie, Rab, Raibeart, Ross, Roy, Scott, Sholto, Sim, Skene, Somerled, Steaphan, Strahan, Tam, Tavis, Tavish, Thane, Thurso, Torquil, Uilleam.

GERMAN/TEUTONIC

Girls Ada, Adelheid, Adriane, Agathe, Agnethe, Alda, Alena, Amalie, Anke, Anneliese, Annerl, Antonie, Arilda, Arnika, Auguste, Axelle, Bärbel, Beatrix, Benedikta, Berta, Brigitte, Bruna, Brunhilde, Cacelie, Dorothea, Edeline, Eleonore, Elfriede, Elke, Eloise, Elrica, Else, Erika, Erma, Felicie, Franziska, Freide, Frieda, Friederike, Fritzi, Gabriele, Gerde, Gerlinde, Gertrud, Gisela, Gratia, Greta, Gretchen, Griselda, Hanne, Hannelore, Hansine, Hedwig, Heidi, Helene, Helma, Helmine, Henrike, Hermine, Hilde, Hildegard, Idette, Ilse, Irma, Johanna, Julianna, Jutta, Karlotte, Karoline, Katherina, Katja, Katrien, Katrine, Klara, Klarissa, Konstanze, Kristel, Leisel, Lene, Leni, Liese, Liesl, Lila, Lilie, Lora, Lore, Lorelei, Luana, Luise, Lulu, Luzie, Madlena, Magda, Margaretha, Margret, Mariane, Marla, Marlene, Marthe, Matilda, Meike, Minna, Mitzi, Monika, Nixie, Philippine, Raine, Rebekka, Renate, Romy, Ruperta, Rut, Sara, Sascha, Sibylle, Silke, Steffi, Stephanine, Susanne, Tabea, Tanja, Theresia, Uda, Ulrike, Uschi, Ute, Vala, Valda, Veronike, Viktoria, Wanda, Wilhelmine, Yetta, Zerlina, Zommer.

Boys Adolf, Alberich, Albrecht, Alfons, Alric, Andreas, Anselm, Anton, Aronne, August, Axel, Benedikt, Bernhard, Bruno, Burkhard, Carl, Carsten,

Christoph, Claudius, Claus, Dedrick, Dieter, Dietrich, Dionysus, Dolf, Eduard, Egon, Engelbert, Erich, Ernst, Eugen, Evert, Franz, Freitag, Friedrich, Fritz, Georg, Gerhardt, Gerhold, Gottfried, Gunther, Handel, Hanke, Hans, Hansel, Hansi, Heinrich, Heinz, Helmut, Heribert, Hermann, Hieronymus, Horst, Hugo, Huppert, Ibsen, Ignatz, Immanuel, Isaak, Isidor, Ivo, Jakob, Jeremias, Jochim, Johann, Johannes, Josef, Jurgen, Karl, Karsten, Kasimir, Kaspar, Klaus, Klein, Klemens, Konrad, Konstantin, Kurt, Lenz, Leonhard, Leopold, Lorenz, Lothar, Ludwig, Lukas, Manfried, Marcell, Markus, Matte, Matz, Meinard, Merten, Morgen, Moritz, Mose, Nikolaus, Oskar, Otto, Rafael, Rainer, Reiner, Reinhard, Reinhold, Rocco, Roderich, Rodolf, Roland, Rolf, Rüdiger, Rupert, Salomo, Sascha, Schwarz, Siegfried, Stefan, Stein, Terenz, Theodor, Tibold, Udo, Ulli, Ulrich, Urs, Utz, Viktor, Vincens, Waldemar, Waldo, Walther, Wenzel, Werner, Wilfried, Wilhelm, Willi, Wim, Wolf, Wolfgang, Xaver, Zacharias.

GREEK

Girls Acantha, Achilla, Adara, Adelpha, Adonia, Aegea, Agapé, Aglaia, Alastrina, Alatea, Alcina, Aldara, Aleka, Alethea, Aleydis, Aliki, Alpha, Althea, Altheda, Aludra, Alysia, Alyssa, Amara, Amaranth, Amaryllis, Aminta, Andrea, Andromeda, Angeliki, Annys, Anteia, Antigone, Anusia, Aphrodite, Apollonia, Ara, Arachne, Araminta, Arcadia, Areta, Ariadne, Arista, Artemis, Arva, Aspasia, Astrea, Atalanta, Athanasia, Athena, Attica, Aura, Basilia, Calandra, Calantha, Calista, Callidora, Callisto, Caloris, Calypso, Canace, Candia, Carmé, Cassandra, Castalia, Charis, Charisma, Chloe, Chloris, Chrysilla, Cleantha, Clio, Clymene, Cosima, Cynara, Cynthia, Dacia, Damaris, Danaë, Delia, Delta, Demetria, Desma, Diantha, Dido, Dione, Dora, Dyna, Dysis, Echo, Egeria, Ekaterini, Elara, Electra, Eleni, Elma, Endocia, Enora, Eranthe, Euclea, Eulalia, Euphemia, Euphrasia, Eurydice, Eustacia, Evadne, Fotini, Gaia, Galatea, Haidee, Halcyone, Hebe, Helia, Hera, Hero, Hestia, Hippolyta, Ianthe, Ileana, Iolanthe, Iphigenia, Jacinda, Jocasta, Kalika, Kalliope, Koren, Kyria, Leda, Lydia, Lyris, Lystra, Medea, Medusa, Melantha, Melina, Metis, Myra, Naida, Nike, Niki, Nymphea, Nyssa, Oceana, Pallas, Pandora, Parthenia, Penelope, Persephone, Phaedra, Philantha, Philomena, Phoebe, Psyche, Reveka, Rhea, Semele, Sofi, Stefania, Sybil, Sylph, Syna, Thea, Theophania, Theophilia, Thera, Thetis, Toula, Xanthe, Xenia, Xylia, Zafera, Zenobia, Zephyr, Zeta, Zeva, Zoë.

Boys Achilles, Adelpho, Adonis, Aeneas, Aeolus, Ajax, Alekos, Alexis, Anastasios, Andis, Androcles, Angclos, Apollo, Aquila, Arcas, Ares, Argus, Arion, Aristedes, Aristotle, Arseni, Athos, Atlas, Avel, Avram, Bacchus, Cadmus, Charon, Chiron, Christos, Chrysander, Cleon, Corydon, Cosmo, Cyrano, Damon, Darius, Demas, Demetrios, Demos, Draco, Endymion, Eneas, Eon, Erasmus, Erastus, Erebus, Eros, Eryx, Eusebio, Evander, Evangelos,

Galen, Ganymede, Georgios, Hamon, Hector, Helios, Herakles, Hermes, Hippolyte, Homer, Icarus, Ioannes, Jason, Kalon, Kosmo, Kostas, Laertes, Leandros, Linus, Lysander, Makarios, Makis, Markos, Maron, Mentor, Midas, Minos, Myron, Narcissus, Nemo, Neo, Nestor, Nicander, Nicodemus, Nikitas, Nikos, Orestes, Orion, Orpheus, Otis, Pancras, Paris, Pavlos, Perseus, Petros, Philemon, Philo, Phoenix, Plato, Pluto, Priam, Prometheus, Proteus, Sirius, Socrates, Solon, Sophocles, Spiridon, Stavros, Stefanos, Thaddeus, Thanos, Theodore, Theon, Theron, Theseus, Timon, Titan, Titos, Triton, Tycho, Ulysses, Vangelis, Vasilis, Xanthus, Xenophon, Xenos, Xylon, Yannis, Yianni, Yiorgos, Zelotes, Zenas, Zeus.

HEBREW/JEWISH/YIDDISH

Girls Abelia, Abera, Abigail, Abijah, Abra, Adah, Adalia, Adama, Adar, Adiel, Adina, Adira, Afraima, Ahuva, Aliya, Aliza, Alona, Aluma, Amana, Amaris, Amira, Amita, Anya, Aphra, Arda, Ardath, Ariella, Ariza, Arona, Asera, Asher, Ashira, Asisa, Atarah, Athalia, Atira, Avel, Avera, Aviva, Ayala, Ayla, Azaria, Azelias, Bathsheba, Batsheva, Behira, Beila, Bena, Bethany, Bethel, Bethesda, Bethia, Betulah, Beulah, Bina, Brina, Carmel, Carna, Cassia, Chava, Dara, Delilah, Devora, Dinah, Diza, Dodie, Eden, Elan, Eliora, Elula, Endora, Esara, Freyde, Gada, Galia, Galilee, Galya, Gana, Gavrila, Gilana, Golda, Hadassa, Hagar, Hannah, Hava, Haya, Hebron, Hinda, Hulda, Ilana, Inbar, Jada, Jael, Jaffa, Janna, Jarah, Jemima, Jerusha, Jezebel, Jora, Jordan, Kaila, Kelila, Keren, Kerith, Keturah, Kezia, Leah, Lemuela, Lewanna, Lilith, Livana, Madrona, Mahalia, Mahira, Malkah, Mara, Marganit, Mariamne, Mehitabel, Menorah, Menuha, Merkaba, Michal, Moriah, Naomi, Nasia, Nira, Nizana, Noa, Odelia, Ophrah, Orinda, Orna, Ozora, Rahel, Raiza, Rena, Rifka, Rivka, Ruth, Sabbathe, Sabra, Salome, Samara, Samaria, Sana, Sarina, Satarah, Sela, Semira, Shaina, Shani, Sharon, Shifra, Shiloh, Shira, Shoshana, Shulamit, Talia, Talya, Tamar, Tameka, Tarah, Thirza, Timora, Tivona, Torah, Tuvia, Uma, Varda, Yael, Yakira, Yehudit, Yona, Yovela, Zahava, Zaneta, Zara, Zelah, Zillah, Zilpah, Zion, Zippora, Ziva, Zofeya, Zulema.

Boys Abaddon, Abba, Abdiel, Abel, Abiel, Abijah, Abir, Abisha, Abner, Absalom, Adam, Adar, Adin, Adir, Adlai, Adon, Adriel, Ahab, Aharon, Akiva, Aleph, Almon, Alvah, Amal, Amiel, Amin, Amirov, Amon, Amos, Anno, Aran, Ari, Ariel, Armon, Arvad, Asa, Asher, Ashur, Atarah, Avan, Avi, Aviv, Avrom, Avron, Azariah, Azriel, Azzan, Barak, Baruch, Belshazzar, Binyamin, Boaz, Cain, Caleb, Canaan, Cohen, Dagan, Dani, Doron, Dov, Eden, Edom, Ehud, Eitan, Elan, Eleazar, Eli, Elijah, Elisha, Eliyahu, Elkan, Enoch, Enos, Eran, Esau, Ethan, Ezra, Falk, Gaddiel, Gamaliel, Gershom, Gideon, Goliath, Gomer, Gurion, Hanan, Haram, Heman, Hershel, Hillel, Hiram, Hosea, Hyam, Ichabod, Ira, Ishmael, Israel, Itzik, Jabez, Jadon, Jael, Jairus,

Japhet, Jared, Jaron, Javan, Jedediah, Jethro, Joab, Joah, Job, Joel, Jora, Joram, Jordan, Kaniel, Kiva, Laban, Lael, Lamech, Levi, Lior, Mahir, Mandel, Meir, Melek, Menachem, Micah, Moishe, Mordecai, Moshe, Naaman, Nahum, Namir, Nekoda, Nimrod, Noah, Noam, Nur, Oren, Ranen, Ravid, Reuben, Reuel, Roni, Ronit, Seth, Shahar, Shalom, Shamir, Shani, Shavar, Shiloh, Shimon, Shlomo, Shmuel, Sion, Tamir, Tavi, Tovi, Uriel, Uzi, Vered, Volf, Yael, Yakim, Yakov, Yehuda, Yehudi, Yered, Yeshua, Yigael, Yonatan, Yosef, Yovel, Zadok, Zalman, Zamir, Zared, Zebulun, Zelig, Ziv, Zion, Zubin, Zuriel.

HUNGARIAN

Girls Aniko, Aranka, Babara, Eszter, Hedviga, Ilka, Ilona, Jola, Jolan, Jolanka, Juli, Margit, Panna, Prioska, Rez, Rezia, Roskia, Terezia, Tizane, Veronika, Zigana, Zizi, Zsa Zsa.

Boys Andras, Antal, Atalik, Bela, Bendek, Bodi, Elek, Filep, Gabor, Henrik, Imre, István, Janos, József, Károly, Lajos, Laszlo, Lazar, Lorant, Marton, Nouri, Orban, Rez, Sandor, Tamas, Tibor, Varad, Vidor, Vilmos, Zoltan.

ITALIAN

Girls Adriana, Agata, Agnese, Agnola, Alba, Alessandra, Alisa, Allegra, Amadora, Amalina, Amata, Ambra, Angelina, Angiola, Aniela, Annata, Annica, Annunziata, Antonella, Arancia, Armani, Assunta, Batista, Bellino, Benedetta, Bianca, Bicetta, Brigida, Cadenza, Capri, Cara, Carezza, Carita, Carlina, Carlotta, Carmela, Carolina, Caterina, Celestina, Chiara, Cinzia, Concetta, Consolata, Cristina, Delfina, Domenica, Donatella, Dorotea, Edita, Elda, Eleganza, Elena, Eleonora, Elettra, Elisa, Elisabetta, Emilia, Enrica, Esterre, Felicita, Filippa, Fiore, Fiorella, Fiorenza, Fontana, Franca, Francesca, Gabriella, Gala, Gia, Giacinta, Giada, Gianina, Ginevra, Gioia, Giorgetta, Giovanna, Giulia, Giuseppina, Grazia, Graziella, Honorata, Ignazia, Imelda, Isabella, Jacobella, Jolanda, Lauretta, Letizia, Lia, Lidia, Lorenza, Luce, Lucia, Luciana, Luigina, Luisa, Luzia, Maddalena, Madonna, Majella, Marchesa, Margherita, Mariella, Marietta, Marta, Matilde, Mercede, Mimi, Mirella, Modesto, Natalina, Neroli, Nicla, Olimpia, Oriana, Ortense, Ottavia, Ottobra, Paola, Pasquelina, Patrizia, Pazienza, Perla, Phebe, Pia, Pietra, Quirina, Rachele, Raula, Renata, Romina, Rosa, Rosetta, Rosina, Rosmunda, Santina, Serafina, Siena, Silvana, Simonetta, Sonata, Stefania, Tathiana, Teodora, Teresina, Traviata, Trinita, Valeria, Vanni, Venezia, Verona, Vincenza, Viola, Virna, Vitalia, Vittoria, Viviana, Zita.

Boys Abramo, Achilleo, Adamo, Adan, Adolfo, Adriano, Agosto, Alberto, Albino, Aldo, Alessandro, Alessio, Alfonso, Alfredo, Allighiero, Aloisia, Amadeo, Anatolio, Andrea, Angelo, Aniello, Antonio, Aquilino, Aristede,

Arnoldo, Aronne, Arsenio, Arturo, Aurelio, Baldassare, Bartolomeo, Benedetto, Beniamino, Beppe, Bernardo, Calvino, Camillo, Candido, Carlo, Carmine, Cesare, Ciro, Claudio, Corrado, Cosimo, Costanzo, Cristiano, Cristoforo, Damiano, Daniele, Dante, Demetrio, Desiderio, Dino, Domenico, Donatello, Edgardo, Edmondo, Edoardo, Eliseo, Emanuele, Emilio, Ennio, Enrico, Enzo, Ermanno, Ernesto, Ettore, Eugenio, Fabiano, Fabio, Fabrizio, Fausto, Fedele, Federico, Feliciano, Ferdinando, Filippo, Flavio, Francesco, Franco, Gabriele, Gasparo, Gerardo, Geronimo, Gervasio, Giacobbe, Giacomo, Gianni, Gianpiero, Gilberto, Gino, Giordano, Giorgio, Giovanni, Giraldo, Giulio, Giuseppe, Graziano, Guglielmo, Guido, Gustavo, Ilario, Ignazio, Isacco, Jacopo, Ladislo, Lazzaro, Leandro, Leonardo, Leonzio, Lodovico, Lorenzo, Lothario, Luca, Luciano, Ludo, Luigi, Marcello, Marco, Mario, Martino, Massimo, Matteo, Mauro, Michelangelo, Michele, Natale, Nico, Nicola, Nino, Oliviero, Onofrio, Orazio, Orlando, Otello, Ottavio, Paolino, Paolo, Paride, Pasquale, Patrizio, Piero, Pino, Quirino, Raffaele, Raniero, Raul, Remo, Renato, Riccardo, Rinaldo, Roberto, Rodolfo, Rodrigo, Romano, Ruggiero, Salvatore, Sansone, Santo, Saviero, Sergio, Silvano, Simone, Stefano, Taddeo, Terreno, Tino, Tito, Tommaso, Ugo, Ulisse, Ulrico, Umberto, Valentino, Vincenzo, Vittore, Xaviero.

JAPANESE

Girls Aiko, Akako, Akiko, Akina, Amaya, Aneko, Anzu, Asa, Asahi, Ayame, Azami, Chika, Chizu, Cho, Dai, Emiko, Etsu, Fuki, Gen, Hama, Haruko, Hidé, Hina, Hiroko, Hoshi, Iku, Ima, Inari, Ishi, Izanami, Junko, Kagami, Kaiko, Kameko, Keiko, Kichi, Kiku, Kimiko, Kin, Kira, Kita, Kiyoko, Kohana, Koko, Kumi, Kumiko, Kuri, Kyoko, Machiko, Maeko, Mariko, Masa, Matsu, Matsuko, Megumi, Meiko, Michiko, Midori, Mika, Miki, Miko, Miya, Mura, Murasaki, Nami, Nara, Narada, Nariko, Nori, Nyoko, Ohara, Oki, Reiko, Ren, Ruri, Sachi, Sachiko, Sakura, Shima, Shina, Suki, Sumi, Suri, Suzu, Suzuki, Taka, Takara, Taki, Tama, Tamiko, Tani, Taniko, Tetsu, Toku, Tomiko, Tora, Umeko, Umiko, Yachi, Yasu, Yoko, Yori, Yoshi, Yoshiko, Yuki, Yumi, Yuri, Yuriko, Zen.

Boys Akihiro, Akira, Akiyama, Amida, Chiko, Fudo, Haruko, Hiroshi, Izumi, Joji, Jun, Kami, Kano, Kawa, Keisuke, Ken, Kenta, Kin, Kirin, Kiyoshi, Manzo, Masa, Miki, Ninja, Ogai, Ozuru, Rafu, Raiden, Ringo, Rinjin, Rinky, Sachio, Shima, Shinden, Shiro, Taka, Tani, Taro, Teizo, Tetsu, Tetsuya, Tomi, Toshiro, Uyeda, Yo, Yoshi, Zen.

LATVIAN/LITHUANIAN

Girls Alena, Ane, Antonya, Daila, Magryta, Ona, Zuzanna.

Boys Andris, Imants, Juris, Lauras, Modris, Vilis.

MAORI

Girls Ahorangi, Ahurewa, Aihe, Airini, Akenehi, Akinehi, Amiria, Anahera, Ane, Ani, Anihera, Aniwaniwa, Aperira, Arataki, Areta, Arihana, Aroha, Arorangi, Ataahua, Ata Marama, Atarangi, Atarau, Awatea, Awhina, Ehetere, Ekore, Emere, Erihapeti, Haeata, Hahana, Haki, Hana, Harata, Hariata, Harikoa, Hauku, Haurahi, Heni, Hera, Hihiria, Hikitia, Hikurangi, Hine, Hinengaro, Hira, Hiria, Hokaka, Hoki, Hotoke, Huhana, Huia, Humarie, Hune, Hura, Huria, Huriana, Hurihia, Ihipera, Iriaka, Irihapeti, Iwi, Kahu, Kaku, Kanapa, Kararaina, Karewa, Kataraina, Kea, Kereru, Kerewin, Keri, Kirimei, Koanga, Kopu, Kori, Kowhai, Kuine, Kuku, Kura, Maata, Mahia, Mahuika, Makarena, Makareta, Maku, Mana, Manawa, Manawaroa, Mangu, Mara, Marama, Mareikura, Marie, Marika, Mata, Mei, Mereanna, Miriama, Miromiro, Moana, Moata, Moe, Moerangi, Mokai, Moko, Muka, Nanaia, Nga, Ngahere, Ngahiwi, Ngahuia, Ngahuru, Ngaio, Ngaire, Ngoikore, Nikau, Ohorere, Okeroa, Omaka, Otira, Pani, Pania, Pare, Parirau, Peata, Piki, Pipi, Pounamu, Puna, Pupuhi, Putiputi, Ra, Rahera, Rangi, Rangimarie, Rata, Raukura, Reka, Rere, Riana, Rima, Ripeka, Roimata, Rona, Rongo, Rongopai, Ruhia, Ruiha, Ruihi, Ruihia, Rutu, Tahuri, Taimana, Tamahine, Tangiwai, Tapora, Tarati, Te Atawhai, Te Awatea, Teina, Temepara, Te Paea, Tepora, Te Puna, Terehia, Tia, Tiaki, Tihi, Tui, Tumanako, Turuhira, Uaina, Waimarama, Waipounamu, Waipuna, Weka, Whetu, Whetuaroha, Whetumarama, Whina, Wikitoria, Wini.

Boys Ahi, Akuhata, Amiri, Amoho, Amoka, Amokura, Anaru, Ani, Aperahama, Araketenara, Arama, Arana, Arapata, Arapeta, Arapeti, Arawa, Atonio, Epeha, Eriha, Eruera, Etera, Hahona, Hakaraia, Hami, Hamuera, Hare, Hauora, Hemi, Henare, Heremaia, Herewini, Hoani, Hoera, Hohepa, Hohua, Hona, Hone, Horomona, Huarahi, Huatare, Hura, Huriu, Ihaka, Ihi, Inia, Irirangi, Kaha, Kahika, Kahukura, Kahurangi, Kaka, Kakariki, Kapua, Kapura, Kara, Karo, Kawau, Kerekori, Kereru, Kingi, Kiritowha, Kiwi, Kukuwai, Maaka, Maehe, Maka, Makoa, Manaia, Manu, Marama, Matai, Matiu, Maunga, Mika, Mikaere, Moana, Murihiku, Ngaio, Ngawari, Nui, Nukuhia, Omaka, Onepu, Paora, Paoro, Paraone, Patariki, Petera, Piko, Piripi, Pita, Pouaka, Puke, Puriri, Rakaunui, Rangi, Raniera, Rapata, Rata, Rauiti, Raupo, Rawiri, Rewi, Riki, Rongo, Ropata, Rua, Ruka, Ruru, Taiaha, Takawai, Tamaiti, Tamati, Tame, Tana, Tane, Tane Mahuta, Tangaroa, Tangohia, Tapanui, Tawhaki, Tawhirimatea, Temuera, Tepene, Te Ra, Te Ranginui, Tiare, Timana, Timoti, Tipene, Toa, Topia, Tuaka, Tui, Uenuku, Waiariki, Waihanga, Waitangi, Waitoa, Wata, Werahiko, Whatitiri, Whatu, Whero, Wiremu, Witi.

PERSIAN/IRANIAN

Girls Arezou, Azura, Clorinda, Cyra, Elika, Jasmine, Kira, Kismet, Lilac, Marsena, Nasrin, Parisa, Pashmina, Persia, Persis, Roqia, Roshan, Roxana,

Sadira, Sanaz, Satarah, Shahnaz, Shiraz, Shirin, Simin, Soraya, Souzana, Suri, Vashti, Yalda, Zenda, Zuleika.

Boys Caspar, Cyrus, Darius, Gaspar, Jasper, Javed, Kamal, Kamran, Marsena, Melchior, Pervez, Roshan, Rostam, Sargon, Shah, Shahin, Sohrab, Suran, Tabor, Tallis, Taz, Xerxes, Zircon, Zoroaster.

POLYNESIAN

General

Girls Angarua, Apakura, Aroha, Atanua, Atarapa, Dorit, Elka, Ema, Hapai, Hariata, Hika, Hina, Hina-Uri, Hine, Hinemoa, Hiriwa, Hoku, Hula, Ilisapesi, Ina, Inas, Ira, Jaimia, Kaniva, Kanoa, Kaula, Kaulana, Kearoa, Kini, Kiri, Kiwa, Kohia, Kono, Kura, Laione, Lali, Lani, Latai, Lona, Losa, Mahina, Mahuru, Maili, Makala, Makana, Makani, Marama, Maru, Maweke, Mere, Meri, Moana, Moetuma, Naia, Nanala, Nani, Oliana, Puatara, Ra, Rangi, Rehua, Rewa, Rimu, Ruange, Salote, Samoa, Tahiti, Tai, Taka, Tapairo, Tara, Taranga, Tarita, Tautiti, Tavake, Te Mira, Tonga, Tongatea, Turua, Ulani, Umei, Vana.

Boys Afi, Ahohako, Ahomana, Aikane, Alika, Alipate, Amama, Anaru, Arana, Ariki, Atea, Atiu, Hapu, Hema, Hori, Hotoroa, Ihakara, Ihorangi, Ikale, Irawaru, Jone, Kahil, Kaho, Kahua, Kauariki, Kauri, Keoni, Keretiki, Kupe, Kura, Langi, Lani, Makoa, Manu, Marama, Maru, Matareka, Matu, Maui, Miharo, Milu, Mitiaro, Moana, Moko, Mokoiro, Moroto, Neemia, Ngaru, Nui, Oata, Ora, Oro, Oroiti, Palaki, Palauni, Papa, Patu, Peni, Pipiri, Pomare, Poutini, Ra, Raka, Rakaia, Rangi, Rata, Rehua, Rongo, Ruanaku, Rupe, Saimoni, Taha, Tahu, Tai, Tama, Tane, Tanekaha, Tangaroa, Tawhero, Tawhiri, Te Aroha, Tekea, Tiki, Tongatea, Tu, Tueva, Turi, Tutapu, Utu, Valu, Whetu.

Hawaiian

Girls Aka, Akamai, Akela, Alamea, Alana, Alani, Alaula, Aliikai, Alika, Aloha, Alohi, Anani, Anela, Aolani, Derya, Eleu, Enaki, Ewalani, Gladi, Haimi, Halia, Hanai, Hiwa, Hiwakea, Hoala, Hula, Iniki, Inoki, Iokina, Iolana, Iona, Ipo, Kahili, Kaikala, Kailana, Kailani, Kailmana, Kaimana, Kala, Kalama, Kalani, Kalea, Kalei, Kalena, Kaloni, Kamea, Kanani, Kani, Kanuha, Kapua, Kawena, Keala, Kei, Keilani, Keona, Kiele, Kilia, Kolohe, Kona, Lahela, Laka, Lanikais, Lea, Lei, Leilani, Lilia, Lilo, Lokelani, Loni, Luana, Mahina, Maile, Malana, Malia, Malina, Mana, Meli, Miki, Miliani, Momi, Nalani, Noe, Noelani, Nohea, Okalani, Olena, Palila, Pele, Pualani, Pualena, Puanani, Puna, Roselani, Uilani, Ululani, Wailana, Wanika.

Boys Ailani, Aka, Akamu, Alemana, Amana, Amoka, Anakoni, Analu, Asera, Edega, Edwada, Eleu, Eneki, Etana, Ezera, Havika, Hiwa, Hoku, Kahai, Kahoku, Kai, Kaimana, Kainoa, Kaipo, Kala, Kalani, Kale, Kana, Kanaloa,

Kane, Kanuha, Kapena, Kapono, Kealii, Keanu, Kei, Keiki, Kekipi, Kekoa, Kekona, Keoki, Kimo, Koa, Kona, Laki, Lalama, Liko, Makaha, Makai, Makani, Malo, Mamo, Maui, Meka, Moke, Nahoa, Nainoa, Nalu, Oke, Pakaa, Palani, Pekelo, Phunahele, Tahi.

Samoan

Girls 'Ana, Aveolela, Ema, Folole, Kuini, Manamea, Masina, Sarona, Sina.

Boys Atonio, Eliota, Fale, Fetu, Ioane, Laki, Manu, Matangi, Tua.

Tongan

Girls Amipa, 'Ana, Kalauni, Kaneli, Koula, Lupe, Lupi, Mele, Musika, 'Ofa, Onike, Opeli, Pasifiki, Pepe, Seini, Sela, Soana, Sosefina, Toakase.

Boys Alifeleti, Kulapo, Lopeti, Mosese, Paula, Peni, Piripi, Pita, Semisi, Sione, Tevita, Vali, Viliami.

PORTUGUESE/BRAZILIAN

Girls Almada, Catarina, Cintia, Cristina, Dores, Elena, Elzira, Eufemia, Graça, Jaçana, Madeira, Margarida, Marilia, Noemia, Roseta, Teresinha, Vidonia, Xiomara, Xuxa, Zuza.

Boys Adao, Alexio, Amaro, Carlos, Davi, Duarte, Enrique, Fabio, Gilberto, Guilherme, Heitor, Henrique, Jaco, Jesús, Joaquim, Jorge, Justo, Leonardo, Luciano, Luis, Luiz, Manoel, Marcelo, Marcos, Mateus, Miguel, Moises, Patricio, Paulo, Prospero, Rafael, Renato, Ronaldo, Roque, Rubens, Silvino, Tito, Vasco.

ROMANIAN

Girls Doina, Ileana, Rodica, Sorina, Viorica.

Boys Cornel, Ilie, Ion, Razvan, Sorin.

SANSKRIT/HINDI/SIKH

Girls Ama, Ambar, Ambika, Amrita, Anala, Ananda, Anila, Anisha, Anjali, Anushka, Aruna, Arundhati, Arusha, Asha, Avani, Avara, Bala, Chakra, Chandra, Devi, Devika, Dhani, Dharma, Durga, Ellora, Esha, Gita, Hasika, India, Indira, Ishana, Jarita, Jasvinder, Jaya, Jyoti, Kali, Kalinda, Kalpana, Kalyani, Kama, Kamala, Kamini, Kanti, Kanya, Karma, Kashmira, Kerala, Kerani, Kiran, Kona, Krishna, Kumari, Lakshmi, Lakya, Lali, Lalita, Leela, Madhuri, Mala, Malati, Mandala, Mandara, Mani, Mantra, Matrika, Meena, Meera, Mela, Mohana, Nata, Nila, Nirvana, Nisha, Orissa, Padma, Pameela,

Pandita, Panna, Parvati, Pashmina, Prema, Priya, Purnima, Radha, Rajani, Rani, Rati, Rohana, Rukmini, Sahira, Sameera, Sarala, Sari, Sarisha, Saroja, Shakti, Shakuntala, Shalini, Shanti, Sharmila, Sheela, Shobana, Sita, Sitara, Sujata, Sunita, Surata, Surya, Tara, Tarika, Tula, Uma, Usha, Varuna, Vasanti, Veda, Vidya, Vimala, Vyoma, Yamuna.

Boys Abhijit, Ajay, Ambar, Amrit, Anand, Anil, Arjun, Arun, Ashok, Ashwin, Avatar, Bharat, Bhima, Buddha, Chand, Chandan, Chandra, Damodar, Darshan, Deepak, Dev, Devdan, Dhani, Dhanu, Dharma, Dinesh, Ganesh, Gautama, Gopal, Govinda, Guru, Hari, Hemant, Indra, Isa, Jagdish, Jahan, Jangal, Javan, Jay, Jitender, Johar, Jyotis, Kala, Kami, Karan, Karma, Kiran, Krishna, Kumar, Kumera, Lakshman, Lal, Mahendra, Mahesh, Mani, Mohan, Mohandas, Nanda, Narayan, Narendra, Naresh, Nehru, Prakash, Prasad, Prem, Raj, Rajendra, Rajiv, Rama, Ranjit, Ranjiv, Ravi, Rohan, Sachin, Sanjay, Sanjiv, Sankara, Savan, Seth, Shankar, Sharma, Shashi, Sher, Shiva, Siddartha, Singh, Sirdar, Suman, Suresh, Surya, Swami, Taj, Tara, Taran, Tarun, Uluka, Ushnisha, Vamana, Varuna, Vasudeva, Ved, Vidya, Vijay, Vikram, Vimal, Vishnu, Vyasa.

SCANDINAVIAN

General

Girls Agnethe, Amalia, Anneliese, Annot, Asta, Asther, Astrid, Berit, Birgit, Birgitta, Birgitte, Bodil, Brenda, Brigitta, Dagmar, Dagna, Disa, Eir, Elisabet, Erika, Freya, Fulla, Gerd, Gerda, Gudrun, Gunnhild, Haldana, Hedda, Hedvig, Hedy, Helga, Hjördis, Hulda, Ida, Idona, Inge, Ingrid, Janne, Jannike, Johanna, Kalinn, Karita, Karolina, Katrina, Kelda, Kirby, Kirsten, Klara, Lene, Linnea, Lise, Liv, Marte, Mia, Nissa, Noomi, Nora, Norna, Ola, Quenby, Rakel, Ronalda, Runa, Rut, Saga, Signy, Sigourney, Sigrid, Sigrun, Siri, Sonja, Sonje, Tekla, Thora, Thorberta, Thordis, Ulla, Ulrike, Vaila, Vanja, Veronika, Viktoria, Viveka.

Boys Alvis, Amund, Anders, Arve, Askel, Aslak, Björn, Bo, Bodil, Borg, Brander, Daven, Davin, Dyre, Edvard, Einar, Elvis, Emanuel, Erland, Frans, Frey, Gamel, Garth, Gunnar, Gustav, Hakon, Haldor, Halsten, Halvard, Hamar, Harald, Hendrik, Henrik, Holger, Igor, Ingemar, Inger, Ivar, Jakob, Jan, Jarl, Jensen, Johan, Josef, Karl, Kelsey, Kirk, Kjell, Knut, Konstantin, Kristoffer, Lars, Larson, Leif, Lennart, Ludvig, Magnus, Mikell, Niklaus, Odin, Olaf, Olsen, Ove, Per, Ragnar, Ranulf, Regin, Rikard, Rudolf, Rune, Rurik, Sigurd, Starbuck, Stefan, Stig, Storr, Sven, Thor, Thorald, Torvald, Ulrick, Vali, Valter, Verner, Vidar, Viggo, Viking, Viktor, Vilhelm, Waldemar.

Danish

Girls Agneta, Aleksia, Benedikte, Dorete, Else, Iben, Jonna, Juni, Karen, Kathrina, Kristen, Lene, Magdalone, Malene, Margrethe, Mia, Petrine, Saffi, Sofie, Soren.

Boys Aren, Christer, Diederik, Esbern, Frederik, Gillis, Hagen, Henerik, Henning, Jens, Jesper, Jorgen, Kai, Klaus, Knut, Kristen, Mikkel, Mogens, Morten, Nansen, Niels, Peder, Rosmer, Soren, Steen, Svend, Torben, Valentin.

Icelandic

Girls Artis, Björk, Dalla, Falda, Kristinn, Lilija, Rindill, Sula, Unna, Valdis.

Boys Arni, Eldur, Hinrik, Olafur, Petur, Sindri, Varick, Viking.

Norwegian

Girls Aleksia, Andras, Anitra, Kelsey, Kjersti, Magna, Oktober, Sofia, Solrun, Solveig.

Boys Aksel, Bergen, Bjarne, Eirik, Eivind, Jens, Leiv, Nils, Roald, Stein, Steiner, Svein.

Swedish

Girls Agda, Angelika, Annika, Anouska, Barbro, Britt, Dahlia, Elin, Freja, Greta, Henrika, Juli, Karin, Katarina, Kerstin, Kolina, Kristina, Lova, Lovisa, Mai, Malin, Margit, Marna, Mia, Saga, Sofia, Solvig, Svea.

Boys Adolphus, Alfonso, Christer, Erik, Esbjörn, Fredrik, Goran, Gustaf, Hakan, Isak, Jon, Jorgen, Kristian, Lukas, Mats, Mikael, Nils, Pavel, Staffan, Sten, Torkel, Tre, Ulf, Valentin, Zakarias.

SLAVIC

General

Girls Ajla, Aleksija, Alenka, Ana, Anastasija, Anastazia, Antonetta, Barbica, Bozena, Bronya, Chesna, Danika, Dobrila, Evana, Irena, Iskra, Iva, Ivana, Iveta, Jarka, Jarmila, Jelena, Jovana, Jozefa, Jurisa, Katra, Klara, Lala, Lida, Luba, Lucija, Ludmila, Marika, Mira, Miriana, Monika, Nadia, Neda, Orysia, Rada, Radinka, Radmilla, Rozina, Rusalka, Saba, Suska, Svetlana, Valentina, Velika, Verra, Vesna, Zivka, Zofja, Zora.

Boys Andon, Bogdan, Boris, Casimir, Danijel, Dragan, Franc, Ivan, Ivaylo, Jan, Jaroslav, Jovan, Kristof, Ladislav, Marin, Marko, Mikel, Miroslav, Novak, Pero, Petar, Rudolf, Sasho, Sime, Stanislaus, Stanislav, Tomaz, Upravda, Vekoslav, Vlad, Vladimir, Vladislav, Zbigniew, Ziggy, Zoran.

Czech

Girls Alena, Anastazie, Andela, Anezka, Barbora, Blanka, Dana, Daniela, Dorota, Dusana, Gabriele, Hana, Ivana, Ivanka, Jana, Johana, Judita, Kamila,

Katerina, Katerine, Lida, Marcela, Marjeta, Matylda, Milena, Mirka, Pavla, Raina, Rusalka, Ruzena, Sarka, Svetla, Verushka, Viera, Zofie, Zuzana.

Boys Bedrich, Danek, Dominik, Dusan, Eduard, Jakub, Jan, Jaroslav, Jiri, Josef, Kafka, Kamil, Karel, Kazimir, Kornel, Krystof, Leos, Ludvik, Marek, Miklós, Milan, Milos, Petr, Radek, Radko, Rado, Stepan, Tomas, Václav, Viktor, Vilem, Vladimir, Wenzel.

Polish

Girls Agata, Alicja, Aloyza, Anastazja, Ancela, Aniela, Anusia, Basia, Berta, Blanka, Brygida, Clemenza, Daniela, Danuta, Dorosia, Dulcyna, Edyta, Ewa, Frydryka, Gabriela, Halina, Hania, Helenka, Henryka, Inocenta, Jadwiga, Jakuba, Jana, Janina, Jolanta, Kamila, Karolina, Klaudia, Klementyna, Krystyna, Lidia, Lucya, Martyna, Matylda, Nimfa, Rachela, Raina, Rayna, Renia, Roza, Rula, Salomea, Stefania, Teodora, Ulryka, Valeska, Zofia, Zosia, Zuzanna.

Boys Antoni, Artek, Bartek, Brunon, Casimir, Dobry, Dominik, Donat, Feliks, Filip, Henryk, Jacek, Jakub, Jan, Jeden, Jerzy, Józef, Karol, Kasper, Konrad, Konstantyn, Kornel, Ladislas, Ladislaus, Lech, Ludwik, Lukasz, Marek, Marian, Mariusz, Mateusz, Michal, Pavel, Rafal, Salvator, Stefan, Szymon, Tadcusz, Tomasz, Tytus, Ulryk, Viktor, Walenty, Zbigniew, Ziggy, Ziven.

Russian

Girls Agnessa, Aleksandra, Alexdra, Alla, Anastasia, Anastasiya, Anninka, Annuschka, Anya, Csarina, Darya, Ekaterina, Elisavetta, Evva, Fedora, Feodora, Franka, Galina, Irina, Irisa, Ivanna, Julya, Kaleria, Katerine, Katya, Lara, Larissa, Luba, Magdalina, Mariya, Masha, Matrona, Mischa, Modest, Nadya, Natasha, Nastasia, Nastya, Natalya, Natasha, Nikita, Nina, Nonna, Oksana, Olga, Olien, Raisa, Roksana, Rusalka, Sasha, Savina, Serafima, Sofya, Sonya, Stasya, Svetlana, Talia, Talya, Tamara, Tanya, Tatyana, Tsarina, Ulrika, Ulyana, Valentina, Vanja, Vanka, Varvara, Vera, Yelena, Yeva, Zenovia, Zoia.

Boys Akim, Alexandr, Aleksandr, Alexei, Anatoly, Avel, Boris, Danil, Danya, Demyan, Dmitri, Edvard, Egor, Eriks, Fyodor, Gavril, Georgi, Igor, Ilya, Innokenti, Ivan, Kesar, Kirill, Kliment, Kolya, Konstantin, Kostya, Lavrenti, Leonid, Leonti, Lev, Luka, Maksim, Mikhail, Mischa, Naum, Nika, Nikita, Nikolai, Oleg, Osip, Pavel, Petya, Rurik, Samuil, Sasha, Sasa, Semyon, Sergei, Sevastian, Stanislav, Stefan, Stepan, Timofei, Urvan, Vadim, Vanya, Vasily, Vitali, Vladimir, Yakov, Yefim, Yefrem, Yevgeni, Yona, Yuri, Zakar.

SPANISH

Girls Adella, Adoncia, Agueda, Alameda, Alatea, Aldonza, Alejandra, Aletta, Allegra, Amada, Amalina, Amalita, Amaranta, Amata, Ana, Anabel, Angelita, Anica, Anita, Arabela, Arantxa, Armada, Azucena, Barba, Bautista, Beatriz, Belita, Belize, Benicia, Blanca, Bonita, Brigida, Buena, Calandria, Camila, Caridad, Carilla, Carlota, Carmelita, Carmen, Carmine, Caro, Catalina, Catalonia, Catina, Chiquita, Clarisa, Clarita, Clementina, Concepción, Consuela, Corazón, Dali, Damita, Delfina, Delma, Desirita, Dia, Dolores, Dominga, Dorotea, Duena, Dulcinea, Elbertina, Eldora, Elena, Engracia, Enrica, Esmeralda, Esperanza, Estefania, Estrella, Eufemia, Evita, Fabiola, Felicidad, Felipa, Francisca, Gracia, Graciela, Guadalupe, Havana, Hermosa, Hilaria, Idalia, Imelda, Immaculada, Imperio, Inocencia, Isabella, Isla, Ivelisse, Jacinta, Jimena, Josefina, Juanita, Judita, Julietta, Lana, Leanor, Leticia, Lila, Loida, Lola, Lolita, Lona, Lourdes, Lucia, Lucrecia, Luisa, Luzanne, Madalena, Madra, Manuela, Marcelle, Margarita, Maribel, Marieta, Mariquita, Marta, Mercedes, Natividad, Nazaret, Nimfa, Nina, Nita, Ofelia, Olalla, Ónix, Pacienca, Paloma, Paquita, Pascuala, Paulina, Paz, Pepa, Pepita, Perla, Pia, Pilar, Pina, Primavera, Prisca, Querida, Quirina, Ramona, Raquel, Rebeca, Ria, Rica, Rosa, Rosario, Rosita, Rubi, Santina, Savanna, Segovia, Serafina, Sevilla, Solana, Soledad, Susana, Teodora, Teresita, Trinidad, Tulipan, Valeriana, Ventura, Veracruz, Vina, Violante, Violeta, Vitoria, Xaviera, Ynes, Ynez, Yolandita, Ysabel, Zafira, Zita, Zuela.

Boys Abad, Abran, Adan, Adriano, Agustin, Albino, Alejandro, Alfredo, Alonso, Amado, Anatolio, Andres, Angelino, Anselmo, Antonio, Arnaldo, Arturo, Azul, Basilio, Benito, Bernardo, Calvino, Carlos, Casimiro, Che, Cisco, Claudio, Condor, Constantino, Cortez, Cristo, Cristóbal, Cruz, Demetrio, Desiderio, Diablo, Diego, Domingo, Dorado, Edgardo, Edmundo, Eduardo, Efrain, Eliseo, Eloy, Emilio, Enrique, Ernesto, Estéban, Eugenio, Ezequiel, Fabio, Fabricio, Federico, Feliciano, Felipe, Fernán, Fernando, Fez, Floro, Francilo, Francisco, Fuego, Galeno, Geraldo, Gerardo, Gil, Gilberto, Gomez, Gonzales, Graciano, Gregorio, Guillermo, Hernando, Iago, Ignacio, Inocencio, Jacobo, Jaime, Javier, Jeremias, Jeronimo, Jesús, Joaquin, Jorge, José, Juan, Julio, Junio, Juriel, Leandro, Leonardo, Leoncio, Leopoldo, Lluís, Lorencio, Luciano, Lucio, Macho, Manuel, Marco, Mariano, Mario, Martes, Mateo, Mauricio, Miguel, Montel, Montez, Nacio, Nadal, Narciso, Natal, Nicolas, Oliviero, Oro, Osvaldo, Pablo, Pacifico, Paco, Pancho, Pascual, Patricio, Pedro, Pepe, Pinto, Placido, Prospero, Quirce, Rafael, Ramiro, Ramón, Raúl, Renaldo, Renato, Ricardo, Rico, Rio, Roberto, Roca, Rodolfo, Rodrigo, Rogerio, Roldan, Roque, Salomon, Salvador, Sancho, Santiago, Santos, Silvestre, Tadeo, Teodosio, Terencio, Timoteo, Tito, Tomas, Ulises, Vasco, Vicente, Virgilio, Vittorio, Xavier, Ximen, Ximenes, Yago, Zacarias.

Names by ethnic origin

TIBETAN/SHERPA

Girls Chamba, Choden, Dawa, Dechen, Diki, Dolkar, Dolma, Jetsun, Karma, Kesang, Lhakpa, Lhamu, Lobsang, Nima, Pasang, Pema, Rinzen, Sangmu, Shay, Sonam, Tashi, Tseten, Tshering, Yangchen, Yangzom, Yu.

Boys Chamba, Chewang, Chungda, Dawa, Dhondup, Dorjee, Dzong, Gyalpo, Jigme, Kailash, Kalden, Kan, Karma, Lhakpa, Lhawang, Lobsang, Mingma, Namgyal, Nawang, Nedup, Nima, Norbu, Pasang, Pema, Pemba, Penjor, Phintso, Phurba, Rinzen, Shay, Sonam, Tashi, Tenzing, Tsamcho, Tseten, Tshering, Urgyen, Wangdi, Yeshe, Yu.

TURKISH

Girls Adana, Ajda, Alma, Anka, Ayla, Aylin, Aysel, Cari, Elmas, Ferida, Harika, Havva, Izel, Karli, Magali, Meryem, Nesrin, Nuray, Saril, Tulip.

Boys Abi, Adem, Akar, Artan, Aslan, Aydin, Babar, Cahil, Deniz, Duman, Emre, Hazan, Kamuran, Koray, Krikor, Onan, Osman, Ruslan, Turk, Volkan, Zeki.

FAVOURITE NAMES